. . .

WILLIAM SHAKESPEARE

THE SHAKESPEARE
READER

• • •

WILLIAM SHAKESPEARE

THE SHAKESPEARE
READER

COURAGE
BOOKS

an imprint of
RUNNING PRESS
Philadelphia • London

ZABEL   10.98   4|99

Library of Congress Cataloging-in-Publication Number 96-69247

ISBN 0-7624-0001-3

Cover design by Diane Miljat
Cover illustration: From the Art Collection of the Folger Shakespeare Library
Edited by Tara Ann McFadden
Set in ITC Berkeley Oldstyle

Published by Courage Books, an imprint of
Running Press Book Publishers
125 South Twenty-second Street
Philadelphia, Pennsylvania 19103-4399

. . .

CONTENTS

. . .

A MIDSUMMER-NIGHT'S DREAM

DRAMATIS PERSONÆ

THESEUS, Duke of Athens.

EGEUS, father to Hermia.

LYSANDER, } in love
DEMETRIUS, } with Hermia.

PHILOSTRATE, master of the revels to Theseus.

QUINCE, a carpenter.

SNUG, a joiner.

BOTTOM, a weaver.

FLUTE, a bellows-mender.

SNOUT, a tinker.

STARVELING, a sailor.

HIPPOLYTA, queen of the Amazons, bethrothed to Theseus.

HERMIA, daughter to Egeus, in love with Lysander.

HELENA, in love with Demetrius.

OBERON, king of the fairies.

TITANIA, queen of the fairies.

PUCK, or Robin Goodfellow.

PEASEBLOSSOM, }
COBWEB, }
MOTH, } fairies.
MUSTARDSEED, }

Other fairies attending their King and Queen.

Attendants on Theseus and Hippolyta.

SCENE:
Athens, and a wood near it.

ACT I.

SCENE I. *Athens. The palace of Theseus.*
Enter Theseus, Hippolyta, Philostrate, and Attendants.

THESEUS: Now, fair Hippolyta, our nuptial hour
Draws on apace; four happy days bring in
Another moon: but, O, methinks, how slow
This old moon wanes! she lingers my desires,
Like to a step-dame or a dowager
Long withering out a young man's revenue.
    HIPPOLYTA: Four days will quickly steep themselves in night;
Four nights will quickly dream away the time;
And then the moon, like to a silver bow

New-bent in heaven, shall behold the night
Of our solemnities.
  THESEUS: Go, Philostrate,
Stir up the Athenian youth to merriments;
Awake the pert and nimble spirit of mirth:
Turn melancholy forth to funerals;
The pale companion is not for our pomp. [*Exit Philostrate.*
Hippolyta, I woo'd thee with my sword,
And won thy love, doing thee injuries;
But I will wed thee in another key,
With pomp, with triumph and with revelling.

Enter Egeus, Hermia, Lysander, and Demetrius.

  EGEUS: Happy be Theseus, our renowned duke!
  THESEUS: Thanks, good Egeus: what's the news with thee?
  EGEUS: Full of vexation come I, with complaint
Against my child, my daughter Hermia.
Stand forth, Demetrius. My noble lord,
This man hath my consent to marry her.
Stand forth, Lysander: and, my gracious duke,
This man hath bewitch'd the bosom of my child:
Thou, thou, Lysander, thou hast given her rhymes
And interchanged love-tokens with my child:
Thou hast by moonlight at her window sung
With feigning voice verses of feigning love,
And stolen the impression of her fantasy
With bracelets of thy hair, rings, gawds, conceits,
Knacks, trifles, nosegays, sweetmeats, messengers
Of strong prevailment in unharden'd youth:
With cunning hast thou filch'd my daughter's heart,
Turn'd her obedience, which is due to me,
To stubborn harshness: and, my gracious duke,
Be it so she will not here before your grace
Consent to marry with Demetrius,
I beg the ancient privilege of Athens,

As she is mine, I may dispose of her:
Which shall be either to this gentleman
Or to her death, according to our law
Immediately provided in that case.

THESEUS: What say you, Hermia? be advised, fair maid:
To you your father should be as a god;
One that composed your beauties, yea, and one
To whom you are but as a form in wax
By him imprinted and within his power
To leave the figure or disfigure it.
Demetrius is a worthy gentleman.

HERMIA: So is Lysander.

THESEUS: In himself he is:
But in this kind, wanting your father's voice,
The other must be held the worthier.

HERMIA: I would my father look'd but with my eyes.

THESEUS: Rather your eyes must with his judgement look.

HERMIA: I do entreat your grace to pardon me.
I know not by what power I am made bold,
Nor how it may concern my modesty,
In such a presence here to plead my thoughts;
But I beseech your grace that I may know
The worst that may befall me in this case,
If I refuse to wed Demetrius.

THESEUS: Either to die the death or to abjure
For ever the society of men.
Therefore, fair Hermia, question your desires;
Know of your youth, examine well your blood,
Whether, if you yield not to your father's choice,
You can endure the livery of a nun,
For aye to be in shady cloister mew'd,
To live a barren sister all your life,
Chanting faint hymns to the cold fruitless moon.
Thrice-blessed they that master so their blood,
To undergo such maiden pilgrimage;

But earthlier happy is the rose distill'd,
Than that which withering on the virgin thorn
Grows, lives and dies in single blessedness.
    HERMIA: So will I grow, so live, so die, my lord,
Ere I will yield my virgin patent up
Unto his lordship, whose unwished yoke
My soul consents not to give sovereignty.
    THESEUS: Take time to pause; and, by the next new moon—
The sealing-day betwixt my love and me,
For everlasting bond of fellowship—
Upon that day either prepare to die
For disobedience to your father's will,
Or else to wed Demetrius, as he would;
Or on Diana's altar to protest
For aye austerity and single life.
    DEMETRIUS: Relent, sweet Hermia: and, Lysander, yield,
Thy crazed title to my certain right.
    LYSANDER: You have her father's love, Demetrius;
Let me have Hermia's: do you marry him.
    EGEUS: Scornful Lysander! true, he hath my love,
And what is mine my love shall render him.
And she is mine, and all my right of her
I do estate unto Demetrius.
    LYSANDER: I am, my lord, as well derived as he,
As well possess'd; my love is more than his;
My fortunes every way as fairly rank'd,
If not with vantage, as Demetrius';
And, which is more than all these boasts can be,
I am beloved of beauteous Hermia:
Why should not I then prosecute my right?
Demetrius, I'll avouch it to his head,
Made love to Nedar's daughter, Helena,
And won her soul; and she, sweet lady, dotes,
Devoutly dotes, dotes in idolatry,
Upon this spotted and inconstant man.

THESEUS: I must confess that I have heard so much,
And with Demetrius thought to have spoke thereof;
But, being over-full of self-affairs,
My mind did lose it. But, Demetrius, come;
And come, Egeus; you shall go with me,
I have some private schooling for you both.
For you, fair Hermia, look you arm yourself
To fit your fancies to your father's will;
Or else the law of Athens yields you up—
Which by no means we may extenuate—
To death, or to a vow of single life.
Come, my Hippolyta: what cheer, my love?
Demetrius and Egeus, go along;
I must employ you in some business
Against our nuptial and confer with you
Of something nearly that concerns yourselves.

    EGEUS: With duty and desire we follow you.

                     [*Exeunt all but Lysander and Hermia.*

    LYSANDER: How now, my love! why is your cheek so pale?
How chance the roses there do fade so fast!

    HERMIA: Belike for want of rain, which I could well
Beteem them from the tempest of my eyes.

    LYSANDER: Ay me! for aught that I could ever read,
Could ever hear by tale or history,
The course of true love never did run smooth;
But, either it was different in blood,—

    HERMIA: O cross! too high to be enthrall'd to low.

    LYSANDER: Or else misgraffed in respect of years,—

    HERMIA: O spite! too old to be engaged to young.

    LYSANDER: Or else it stood upon the choice of friends,—

    HERMIA: O hell! to choose love by another's eyes.

    LYSANDER: Or, if there were a sympathy in choice,
War, death, or sickness did lay siege to it,
Making it momentary as a sound,
Swift as a shadow, short as any dream;

Brief as the lightning in the collied night,
That, in a spleen, unfolds both heaven and earth,
And ere a man hath power to say 'Behold!'
The jaws of darkness do devour it up:
So quick bright things come to confusion.

HERMIA: If then true lovers have been ever cross'd,
It stands as an edict in destiny:
Then let us teach our trial patience,
Because it is a customary cross,
As due to love as thoughts and dreams and sighs,
Wishes and tears, poor fancy's followers.

LYSANDER: A good persuasion; therefore, hear me, Hermia.
I have a widow aunt, a dowager
Of great revenue, and she hath no child:
From Athens is her house remote seven leagues;
And she respects me as her only son,
There, gentle Hermia, may I marry thee;
And to that place the sharp Athenian law
Cannot pursue us. If thou lovest me then,
Steal forth thy father's house to-morrow night;
And in the wood, a league without the town,
Where I did meet thee once with Helena,
To do observance to a morn of May,
There will I stay for thee.

HERMIA: My good Lysander!
I swear to thee, by Cupid's strongest bow,
By his best arrow with the golden head,
By the simplicity of Venus' doves,
By that which knitteth souls and prospers loves,
And by that fire which burn'd the Carthage queen,
When the false Troyan under sail was seen,
By all the vows that ever men have broke,
In number more than ever women spoke,
In that same place thou hast appointed me,
To-morrow truly will I meet with thee.

LYSANDER: Keep promise, love. Look, here comes Helena.

Enter Helena.

HERMIA: God speed, fair Helena! whither away?

HELENA: Call you me fair? that fair again unsay.
Demetrius loves your fair: O happy fair!
Your eyes are lode-stars; and your tongue's sweet air
More tuneable than lark to shepherd's ear,
When wheat is green, when hawthorn buds appear.
Sickness is catching: O were favour so,
Yours would I catch, fair Hermia, ere I go;
My ear should catch your voice, my eye your eye,
My tongue should catch your tongue's sweet melody.
Were the world mine, Demetrius being bated,
The rest I' ld give to be to you translated
O, teach me how you look, and with what art
You sway the motion of Demetrius' heart.

HERMIA: I frown upon him, yet he loves me still.

HELENA: O that your frowns would teach my smiles such skill!

HERMIA: I give him curses, yet he gives me love.

HELENA: O that my prayers could such affection move!

HERMIA: The more I hate, the more he follows me.

HELENA: The more I love, the more he hateth me.

HERMIA: His folly, Helena, is no fault of mine.

HELENA: None, but your beauty: would that fault were mine!

HERMIA: Take comfort: he no more shall see my face;
Lysander and myself will fly this place.
Before the time I did Lysander see,
Seem'd Athens as a paradise to me:
O, then, what graces in my love do dwell,
That he hath turn'd a heaven into a hell!

LYSANDER: Helen, to you our minds we will unfold:
To-morrow night, when Phœbe doth behold
Her silver visage in the watery glass,
Decking with liquid pearl the bladed grass,

A time that lovers' flight doth still conceal,
Through Athens' gates we have devised to steal.
   HERMIA: And in the wood, where often you and I
Upon faint primrose-beds were wont to lie,
Emptying our bosoms of their counsel sweet,
There my Lysander and myself shall meet;
And thence from Athens turn away our eyes,
To seek new friends and stranger companies.
Farewell, sweet playfellow; pray thou for us;
And good luck grant thee thy Demetrius!
Keep word, Lysander; we must starve our sight
From lovers' food till morrow deep midnight.
   LYSANDER: I will, my Hermia.   [*Exit Hermia.*
                   Helena, adieu:
As you on him, Demetrius dote on you.   [*Exit.*
   HELENA: How happy some o'er other some can be!
Through Athens I am thought as fair as she.
But what of that? Demetrius thinks not so;
He will not know what all but he do know:
And as he errs, doting on Hermia's eyes,
So I, admiring his qualities:
Things base and vile, holding no quantity,
Love can transpose to form and dignity:
Love looks not with the eyes, but with the mind;
And therefore is wing'd Cupid painted blind:
Nor hath Love's mind of any judgement taste;
Wings and no eyes figure unheedy haste:
And therefore is Love said to be a child,
Because in choice he is so oft beguiled.
As waggish boys in game themselves forswear
So the boy Love is perjured every where:
For ere Demetrius look'd on Hermia's eyne,
He hail'd down oaths that he was only mine;
And when this hail some heat from Hermia felt,
So he dissolved, and showers of oaths did melt.

I will go tell him of fair Hermia's flight:
Then to the wood will he to-morrow night
Pursue her; and for this intelligence
If I have thanks, it is a dear expense:
But herein mean I to enrich my pain,
To have his sight thither and back again.   [*Exit.*

SCENE II. *Athens. Quince's house.*
Enter Quince, Snug, Bottom, Flute, Snout and Starveling.

QUINCE: Is all our company here?

BOTTOM: You were best to call them generally, man by man, according to the script.

QUINCE: Here is the scroll of every man's name, which is thought fit, through all Athens, to play in our interlude before the duke and the duchess, on his wedding-day at night.

BOTTOM: First, good Peter Quince, say what the play treats on, then read the names of the actors, and so grow to a point.

QUINCE: Marry, our play is, The most lamentable comedy, and most cruel death of Pyramus and Thisby.

BOTTOM: A very good piece of work, I assure you, and a merry. Now, good Peter Quince, call forth your actors by the scroll. Masters, spread yourselves.

QUINCE: Answer as I call you. Nick Bottom, the weaver.

BOTTOM: Ready. Name what part I am for, and proceed.

QUINCE: You, Nick Bottom, are set down for Pyramus.

BOTTOM: What is Pyramus? a lover, or a tyrant?

QUINCE: A lover, that kills himself most gallant for love.

BOTTOM: That will ask some tears in the true performing of it: if I do it, let the audience look to their eyes: I will move storms, I will condole in some measure. To the rest: yet my chief humour is for a tyrant: I could play Ercles rarely, or a part to tear a cat in, to make all split.

The raging rocks
And shivering shocks

> Shall break the locks
>   Of prison gates;
> And Phibbus' car
> Shall shine from far
> And make and mar
>   The foolish Fates.

This was lofty! Now name the rest of the players. This is Ercle's vein, a tyrant's vein; a lover is more condoling.

QUINCE: Francis Flute, the bellows-mender.

FLUTE: Here, Peter Quince.

QUINCE: Flute, you must take Thisby on you.

FLUTE: What is Thisby? a wandering knight?

QUINCE: It is the lady that Pyramus must love.

FLUTE: Nay, faith, let me not play a woman; I have a beard coming.

QUINCE: That's all one: you shall play it in a mask. And you may speak as small as you will.

BOTTOM: An I may hide my face, let me play Thisby too, I'll speak in a monstrous little voice, 'Thisne, Thisne;' 'Ah Pyramus, my lover dear! thy Thisby dear, and lady dear!'

QUINCE: No, no; you must play Pyramus; and, Flute, you Thisby.

BOTTOM: Well, proceed.

QUINCE: Robin Starveling, the tailor.

STARVELING: Here, Peter Quince.

QUINCE: Robin Starveling, you must play Thisby's mother. Tom Snout, the tinker.

SNOUT: Here, Peter Quince.

QUINCE: You, Pyramus' father; myself, Thisby's father. Snug, the joiner; you, the lion's part; and, I hope, here is a play fitted.

SNUG: Have you the lion's part written? pray you, if it be, give it me, for I am slow of study.

QUINCE: You may do it extempore, for it is nothing but roaring.

BOTTOM: Let me play the lion too: I will roar, that I will do any man's heart good to hear me; I will roar, that I will make the duke say 'Let him roar again, let him roar again.'

QUINCE: An you should do it too terribly, you would fright the duchess and the ladies, that they would shriek; and that were enough to hang us all.

ALL: That would hang us, every mother's son.

BOTTOM: I grant you, friends, if that you should fright the ladies out of their wits, they would have no more discretion but to hang us: but I will aggravate my voice so that I will roar you as gently as any sucking dove; I will roar you an 'twere any nightingale.

QUINCE: You can play no part but Pyramus; for Pyramus is a sweet-faced man; a proper man, as one shall see in a summer's day; a most lovely gentleman-like man; therefore you must needs play Pyramus.

BOTTOM: Well, I will undertake it. What beard were I best to play it in?

QUINCE: Why, what you will.

BOTTOM: I will discharge it in either your straw-colour beard, your orange-tawny beard, your purple-in-grain beard, or your French-crown-colour beard, your perfect yellow.

QUINCE: Some of your French crowns have no hair at all, and then you will play barefaced. But, masters, here are your parts: and I am to entreat you, request you and desire you, to con them by to-morrow night; and meet me in the palace wood, a mile without the town, by moonlight; there will we rehearse, for if we meet in the city, we shall be dogged with company, and our devices known. In the meantime I will draw a bill of properties, such as our play wants. I pray you, fail me not.

BOTTOM: We will meet; and there we may rehearse most obscenely and courageously. Take pains; be perfect; adieu.

QUINCE: At the duke's oak we meet.

BOTTOM: Enough; hold or cut bow-strings.   [*Exeunt.*

ACT II.

SCENE I. *A wood near Athens.*
Enter, from opposite sides, a Fairy, and Puck.

PUCK: How now, spirit! whither wander you?
FAIRY: Over hill, over dale,
  Through bush, through brier,
  Over park, over pale,
  Through flood, through fire,
I do wander every where,
Swifter than the moon's sphere;
And I serve the fairy queen,
To dew her orbs upon the green.
The cowslips tall her pensioners be:
In their gold coats spots you see;
Those be rubies, fairy favours,
In those freckles live their savours:
I must go seek some dewdrops here
And hang a pearl in every cowslip's ear.
Farewell, thou lob of spirits; I'll be gone:
Our queen and all her elves come here anon.
PUCK: The king doth keep his revels here to-night:
Take heed the queen come not within his sight;
For Oberon is passing fell and wrath,
Because that she as her attendant hath
A lovely boy, stolen from an Indian king;
She never had so sweet a changeling;
And jealous Oberon would have the child
Knight of his train, to trace the forests wild;
But she perforce withholds the loved boy,
Crowns him with flowers and makes him all her joy:
And now they never meet in grove or green,
By fountain clear, or spangled starlight sheen,
But they do square, that all their elves for fear

Creep into acorn-cups and hide them there.

FAIRY: Either I mistake your shape and making quite,
Or else you are that shrewd and knavish sprite
Call'd Robin Goodfellow: are not you he
That frights the maidens of the villagery;
Skim milk, and sometimes labour in the quern
And bootless make the breathless housewife churn;
And sometime make the drink to bear no barm;
Mislead night-wanderers, laughing at their harm?
Those that Hobgoblin call you and sweet Puck,
You do their work, and they shall have good luck:
Are you not he?

PUCK: Thou speak'st aright;
I am that merry wanderer of the night.
I jest to Oberon and make him smile
When I a fat and bean-fed horse beguile,
Neighing in likeness of a filly foal:
And sometime lurk I in a gossip's bowl,
In very likeness of a roasted crab,
And when she drinks, against her lips I bob
And on her wither'd dewlap pour the ale.
The wisest aunt, telling the saddest tale,
Sometime for three-foot stool mistaketh me;
Then slip I from her bum, down topples she,
And 'tailor' cries, and falls into a cough;
And then the whole quire hold their hips and laugh,
And waxen in their mirth and neeze and swear
A merrier hour was never wasted there.
But, room, fairy! here comes Oberon.

FAIRY: And here my mistress. Would that he were gone!

Enter, from one side, Oberon, with his train;
from the other, Titania, with hers.

OBERON: Ill met by moonlight, proud Titania.

TITANIA: What, jealous Oberon! Fairies, skip hence:

I have forsworn his bed and company.

OBERON: Tarry, rash wanton: am not I thy lord?

TITANIA: Then I must be thy lady: but I know
When thou hast stolen away from fairy land,
And in the shape of Corin sat all day,
Playing on pipes of corn and versing love
To amorous Phillida. Why art thou here,
Come from the farthest steppe of India?
But that, forsooth, the bouncing Amazon,
Your buskin'd mistress and your warrior love,
To Theseus must be wedded, and you come
To give their bed joy and prosperity.

OBERON: How canst thou thus for shame, Titania,
Glance at my credit with Hippolyta,
Knowing I know thy love to Theseus?
Didst thou not lead him through the glimmering night
From Perigenia, whom he ravished?
And make him with fair Ægle break his faith,
With Ariadne and Antiopa?

TITANIA: These are the forgeries of jealousy:
And never, since the middle summer's spring,
Met we on hill, in dale, forest or mead,
By paved fountain or by rushy brook,
Or in the beached margent of the sea,
To dance our ringlets to the whistling wind,
But with thy brawls thou hast disturb'd our sport.
Therefore the winds, piping to us in vain,
As in revenge, have suck'd up from the sea,
Contagious fogs; which falling in the land
Have every pelting river made so proud
That they have overborne their continents:
The ox hath therefore stretch'd his yoke in vain,
The ploughman lost his sweat, and the green corn
Hath rotted ere his youth attain'd a beard;
The fold stands empty in the drowned field,

And crows are fatted with the murrion flock;
The nine men's morris is fill'd up with mud,
And the quaint mazes in the wanton green
For lack of tread are undistinguishable:
The human mortals want their winter here;
No night is now with hymn or carol blest:
Therefore the moon, the governess of floods,
Pale in her anger, washes all the air,
That rheumatic diseases do abound:
And through this distemperature we see
The seasons alter: hoary-headed frosts
Fall in the fresh lap of the crimson rose,
And on old Hiems' thin and icy crown
An odorous chaplet of sweet summer buds
Is, as in mockery, set: the spring, the summer,
The childing autumn, angry winter, change
Their wonted liveries, and the mazed world,
By their increase, now knows not which is which:
And this same progeny of evils comes
From our debate, from our dissension;
We are their parents and original.

    OBERON: Do you amend it then; it lies in you:
Why should Titania cross her Oberon?
I do but beg a little changeling boy,
To be my henchman.

    TITANIA: Set your heart at rest;
The fairy land buys not the child of me.
His mother was a votaress of my order,
And, in the spiced Indian air, by night,
Full often hath she gossip'd by my side,
And sat with me on Neptune's yellow sands,
Marking the embarked traders on the flood.
When we have laugh'd to see the sails conceive
And grow big-bellied with the wanton wind;
Which she, with pretty and with swimming gait

Following,—her womb then rich with my young squire,—
Would imitate, and sail upon the land,
To fetch me trifles, and return again,
As from a voyage, rich with merchandise.
But she, being mortal, of that boy did die;
And for her sake do I rear up her boy,
And for her sake I will not part with him.

OBERON: How long within this wood intend you to stay?

TITANIA: Perchance till after Theseus' wedding-day.
If you will patiently dance in our round
And see our moonlight revels, go with us;
If not, shun me, and I will spare your haunts.

OBERON: Give me that boy, and I will go with thee.

TITANIA: Not for thy fairy kingdom. Fairies, away!
We shall chide downright, if I longer stay.

                                    [*Exit Titania with her train.*

OBERON: Well, go thy way: thou shalt not from this grove
Till I torment thee for this injury.
My gentle Puck, come hither. Thou remembrest
Since once I sat upon a promontory,
And heard a mermaid on a dolphin's back
Uttering such dulcet and harmonious breath
That the rude sea grew civil at her song
And certain stars shot madly from their spheres,
To hear the sea-maid's music.

PUCK: I remember.

OBERON: That very time I saw, but thou couldst not,
Flying between the cold moon and the earth,
Cupid all arm'd: a certain aim he took
At a fair vestal throned by the west,
And loosed his love-shaft smartly from his bow,
As it should pierce a hundred thousand hearts;
But I might see young Cupid's fiery shaft
Quench'd in the chaste beams of the watery moon,
And the imperial votaress passed on,

In maiden meditation, fancy-free.
Yet mark'd I where the bolt of Cupid fell:
It fell upon a little western flower,
Before milk-white, now purple with love's wound,
And maidens call it love-in-idleness.
Fetch me that flower; the herb I shew'd thee once:
The juice of it on sleeping eye-lids laid
Will make or man or woman madly dote
Upon the next live creature that it sees.
Fetch me this herb; and be thou here again
Ere the leviathan can swim a league.

    PUCK: I'll put a girdle round about the earth.
In forty minutes.   [*Exit.*

    OBERON: Having once this juice,
I'll watch Titania when she is asleep,
And drop the liquor of it in her eyes.
The next thing then she waking looks upon,
Be it on lion, bear, or wolf, or bull,
On meddling monkey, or on busy ape,
She shall pursue it with the soul of love:
And ere I take this charm from off her sight,
As I can take it with another herb,
I'll make her render up her page to me.
But who comes here? I am invisible;
And I will overhear their conference.

Enter Demetrius, Helena following him.

    DEMETRIUS: I love thee not, therefore pursue me not.
Where is Lysander and fair Hermia?
The one I'll slay, the other slayeth me.
Thou told'st me they were stolen upon this wood;
And here am I, and wode within this wood,
Because I cannot meet my Hermia.
Hence, get thee gone, and follow me no more.

    HELENA: You draw me, you hard-hearted adamant;

But yet you draw not iron, for my heart
Is true as steel: leave you your power to draw,
And I shall have no power to follow you.
    DEMETRIUS: Do I entice you? do I speak you fair?
Or, rather, do I not in plainest truth
Tell you, I do not, nor I cannot love you?
    HELENA: And even for that do I love you the more.
I am your spaniel; and, Demetrius,
The more you beat me, I will fawn on you:
Use me but as your spaniel, spurn me, strike me,
Neglect me, lose me; only give me leave,
Unworthy as I am, to follow you.
What worser place can I beg in your love,—
And yet a place of high respect with me,—
Than to be used as you use your dog?
    DEMETRIUS: Tempt not too much the hatred of my spirit,
For I am sick when I do look on thee.
    HELENA: And I am sick when I look not on you.
    DEMETRIUS: You do impeach your modesty too much,
To leave the city and commit yourself
Into the hands of one that loves you not;
To trust the opportunity of night
And the ill counsel of a desert place
With the rich worth of your virginity.
    HELENA: Your virtue is my privilege; for that
It is not when I do see your face,
Therefore I think I am not in the night;
Nor doth this wood lack worlds of company,
For you in my respect are all the world:
Then how can it be said I am alone,
When all the world is here to look on me?
    DEMETRIUS: I'll run from thee and hide me in the brakes,
And leave thee to the mercy of wild beasts.
    HELENA: The wildest hath not such a heart as you.
Run when you will, the story shall be changed:

Apollo flies, and Daphne holds the chase;
The dove pursues the griffin; the mild hind
Makes speed to catch the tiger; bootless speed,
When cowardice pursues and valour flies.

    DEMETRIUS: I will not stay thy questions; let me go:
Or, if thou follow me, do not believe
But I shall do thee mischief in the wood.

    HELENA: Ay, in the temple, in the town, the field,
You do me mischief. Fie, Demetrius!
Your wrongs do set a scandal on my sex:
We cannot fight for love, as men may do;
We should be woo'd and were not made to woo.   [*Exit Demetrius.*
I'll follow thee and make a heaven of hell,
To die upon the hand I love so well.   [*Exit.*

    OBERON: Fare thee well, nymph: ere he do leave this grove,
Thou shalt fly him and he shall seek thy love.

Re-enter Puck.

Hast thou the flower there? Welcome, wanderer.

    PUCK: Ay, there it is.

    OBERON: I pray thee, give it me.
I know a bank where the wild thyme blows,
Where oxlips and the nodding violet grows,
Quite over-canopied with luscious woodbine,
With sweet musk-roses and with eglantine:
There sleeps Titania sometime of the night,
Lull'd in these flowers with dances and delight;
And there the snake throws her enamell'd skin,
Weed wide enough to wrap a fairy in:
And with the juice of this I'll streak her eyes,
And make her full of hateful fantasies.
Take thou some of it, and seek through this grove:
A sweet Athenian lady is in love
With a disdainful youth: anoint his eyes;
But do it when the next thing he espies

May be the lady: thou shalt know the man
By the Athenian garments he hath on.
Effect it with some care that he may prove
More fond on her than she upon her love:
And look thou meet me ere the first cock crow.

PUCK: Fear not, my lord, you servant shall do so.   [*Exeunt.*

SCENE II. *Another part of the wood.*
Enter Titania, with her train.

TITANIA: Come, now a roundel and a fairy song;
Then, for the third part of a minute, hence;
Some to kill cankers in the musk-rose buds,
Some war with rere-mice for their leathern wings,
To make my small elves coats, and some keep back
The clamorous owl that nightly hoots and wonders
At our quaint spirits. Sing me now asleep;
Then to your offices and let me rest.   .

The Fairies sing.

You spotted snakes with double tongue,
    Thorny hedgehogs, be not seen;
Newts and blind-worms, do no wrong,
    Come not near our fairy queen.
    Philomel, with melody
    Sing in our sweet lullaby;
Lulla, lulla, lullaby, lulla, lulla, lullaby:
        Never harm,
        Nor spell nor charm,
    Come our lovely lady nigh;
    So, good night, with lullaby.
Weaving spiders, come not here;
    Hence, you long-legg'd spinners, hence!
Beetles black, approach not near;
    Worm nor snail, do no offence.

Philomel, with melody, &c.
A FAIRY: Hence, away! now all is well:
    One aloof stand sentinel.

                              [*Exeunt Fairies. Titania sleeps.*

Enter Oberon, and squeezes the flower on Titania's eyelids.

OBERON: What thou seest when thou dost wake,
    Do it for thy true-love take,
    Love and languish for his sake:
    Be it ounce, or cat, or bear,
    Pard, or boar with bristled hair,
    In thy eye that shall appear
    When thou wakest, it is thy dear:
    Wake when some vile thing is near.   [*Exit.*

Enter Lysander and Hermia.

LYSANDER: Fair love, you faint with wandering in the wood;
And to speak troth, I have forgot our way:
We'll rest us, Hermia, if you think it good,
And tarry for the comfort of the day.
HERMIA: Be it so, Lysander: find you out a bed;
For I upon this bank will rest my head.
LYSANDER: One turf shall serve as pillow for us both;
One heart, one bed, two bosoms and one troth.
HERMIA: Nay, good Lysander; for my sake, my dear,
Lie further off yet, do not lie so near.
LYSANDER: O, take the sense, sweet, of my innocence!
Love takes the meaning in love's conference.
I mean, that my heart unto yours is knit
So that but one heart we can make of it;
Two bosoms interchained with an oath;
So then two bosoms and a single troth.
Then by your side no bed-room me deny;
For lying so, Hermia, I do not lie.
HERMIA: Lysander riddles very prettily:

Now much beshrew my manners and my pride,
If Hermia meant to say Lysander lied.
But, gentle friend, for love and courtesy
Lie further off; in human modesty,
Such separation as may well be said
Becomes a virtuous bachelor and a maid,
So far be distant; and, good night, sweet friend:
Thy love ne'er alter till thy sweet life end!

LYSANDER: Amen, amen, to that fair prayer, say I;
And then end life when I end loyalty!
Here is my bed: sleep give thee all his rest!

HERMIA: With half that wish the wisher's eyes be press'd!

[*They sleep.*

Enter Puck.

PUCK: Through the forest have I gone,
But Athenian found I none,
On whose eyes I might approve
This flower's force in stirring love.
Night and silence.—Who is here!
Weeds of Athens he doth wear:
This is he, my master said,
Despised the Athenian maid;
And here the maiden, sleeping sound,
On the dank and dirty ground.
Pretty soul! she durst not lie
Near this lack-love, this kill-courtesy.
Churl, upon thy eyes I throw
All the power this charm doth owe.
When thou wakest, let love forbid
Sleep his seat on thy eyelid:
So awake when I am gone;
For I must now to Oberon.

[*Exit.*

Enter Demetrius and Helena, running.

HELENA: Stay, though thou kill me, sweet Demetrius.

DEMETRIUS: I charge thee, hence, and do not haunt me thus.

HELENA: O, wilt thou darkling leave me? do not so.

DEMETRIUS: Stay, on thy peril: I alone will go.   [*Exit.*

HELENA: O, I am out of breath in this fond chase!

The more my prayer, the lesser is my grace.

Happy is Hermia, whereso'er she lies;

For she hath blessed and attractive eyes.

How came her eyes so bright? Not with salt tears:

If so, my eyes are oftener wash'd than hers.

No, no, I am as ugly as a bear;

For beasts that meet me run away for fear:

Therefore no marvel though Demetrius

Do, as a monster, fly my presence thus.

What wicked and dissembling glass of mine

Made me compare with Hermia's sphery eyne?

But who is here? Lysander! on the ground!

Dead? or asleep? I see no blood, no wound.

Lysander if you live, good sir, awake.

LYSANDER: [*Awakening*] And run through fire I will for thy
     sweet sake.

Transparent Helena! Nature shows art,

That through thy bosom makes me see thy heart.

Where is Demetrius? O, how fit a word

Is that vile name to perish on my sword!

HELENA: Do not say so, Lysander; say not so.

What though he love your Hermia? Lord what though?

Yet Hermia still loves you: then be content.

LYSANDER: Content with Hermia! No; I do repent

The tedious minutes I with her have spent.

Not Hermia but Helena I love;

Who will not change a raven for a dove?

The will of man is by his reason sway'd;

And reason says you are the worthier maid.

Things growing are not ripe until their season:

So I, being young, till now ripe not to reason;
And touching now the point of human skill,
Reason becomes the marshal to my will
And leads me to your eyes, where I o'erlook
Love's stories written in love's richest book.

HELENA: Wherefore was I to this keen mockery born?
When at your hands did I deserve this scorn?
Is 't not enough, is 't not enough, young man,
That I did never, no, nor never can,
Deserve a sweet look from Demetrius' eye,
But you must flout my insufficiency?
Good troth, you do me wrong, good sooth, you do,
In such disdainful manner me to woo.
But fare you well: perforce I must confess
I thought you lord of more true gentleness.
O, that a lady, of one man refused,
Should of another therefore be abused!   [*Exit.*

LYSANDER: She sees not Hermia. Hermia, sleep thou there:
And never mayst thou come Lysander near!
For as a surfeit of the sweetest things
The deepest loathing to the stomach brings,
Or as the heresies that men do leave
Are hated most of those they did deceive,
So thou, my surfeit and my heresy,
Of all be hated, but the most of me!
And, all my powers, address your love and might
To honour Helen and to be her knight!   [*Exit.*

HERMIA: [*Awakening*] Help me, Lysander, help me! do thy best
To pluck this crawling serpent from my breast!
Ay me, for pity! what a dream was here!
Lysander, look how do I quake with fear:
Methought a serpent eat my heart away,
And you sat smiling at his cruel prey.
Lysander! what, removed? Lysander! lord!
What, out of hearing? gone? no sound, no word?

Alack, where are you? speak, an if you hear;
Speak, of all loves! I swoon almost with fear.
No? then I well perceive you are not nigh:
Either death or you I'll find immediately.   [*Exit.*

ACT III.

SCENE I. *The wood. Titania lying asleep.*
Enter Quince, Snug, Bottom, Flute, Snout and Starveling.

BOTTOM: Are we all met?

QUINCE: Pat, pat; and here's a marvellous convenient place for our rehearsal. This green plot shall be our stage, this hawthorn-brake our tiring-house; and we will do it in action as we will do it before the duke.

BOTTOM: Peter Quince,—

QUINCE: What sayest thou, bully Bottom?

BOTTOM: There are things in this comedy of Pyramus and This-by that will never please. First, Pyramus must draw a sword to kill himself; which the ladies cannot abide. How answer you that?

SNOUT: By'r lakin, a parlous fear.

STARVELING: I believe we must leave the killing out, when all is done.

BOTTOM: Not a whit; I have a device to make all well. Write me a prologue; and let the prologue seem to say, we will do no harm with our swords and the Pyramus is not killed indeed; and, for the more better assurance, tell that I Pyramus am not Pyramus, but Bottom the weaver: this will put them out of fear.

QUINCE: Well, we will have such a prologue; and it shall be written in eight and six.

BOTTOM: No, make it two more; let it be written in eight and eight.

SNOUT: Will not the ladies be afeard of the lion?

STARVELING: I fear it, I promise you.

BOTTOM: Masters, you ought to consider with yourselves; to bring in—God shield us!—a lion among ladies is a most dreadful thing; for there is not a more fearful wild-fowl than your lion living; and we ought to look to it.

SNOUT: Therefore another prologue must tell he is not a lion.

BOTTOM: Nay, you must name his name, and half his face must be seen through the lion's neck: and he himself must speak through, saying thus or to the same defect—'Ladies,'—or 'Fair ladies,—I would wish you,'—or 'I would request you,'—or 'I would entreat you,—not to fear, not to tremble: my life for yours. If you think I come hither as a lion, it were pity of my life; no, I am no such thing; I am a man as other men are;' and there indeed let him name his name, and tell them plainly he is Snug the joiner.

QUINCE: Well, it shall be so. But there is two hard things: that is, to bring the moonlight into a chamber; for, you know, Pyramus and Thisby meet by moonlight.

SNOUT: Doth the moon shine that night we play our play?

BOTTOM: A calendar, a calendar! look in the almanac; find out moonshine, find out moonshine.

QUINCE: Yes, it doth shine that night.

BOTTOM: Why, then may you leave a casement of the great chamber window, where we play, open, and the moon may shine in at the casement.

QUINCE: Ay; or else one must come in with a bush or thorns and a lanthorn, and say he comes to disfigure, or to present, the person of Moonshine. Then, there is another thing: we must have a wall in the great chamber; for Pyramus and Thisby, says the story, did talk through the chink of a wall.

SNOUT: You can never bring in a wall. What say you, Bottom?

BOTTOM: Some man or other must present Wall: and let him have some plaster, or some loam, or some rough-cast about him, to signify wall; and let him hold his fingers thus, and through that cranny shall Pyramus and Thisby whisper.

QUINCE: If that may be, then all is well. Come, sit down, every mother's son, and rehearse your parts. Pyramus, you begin; when you have spoken your speech, enter into that brake: and so every one according to his cue.

Enter Puck behind.

PUCK: What hempen home-spuns have we swaggering here,
So near the cradle of the fairy queen?
What, a play toward! I'll be an auditor;
An actor too perhaps, if I see cause.
QUINCE: Speak, Pyramus. Thisby, stand forth.
BOTTOM: Thisby, the flowers of odious savours sweet,—
QUINCE: Odours, odours.
BOTTOM: ———— odours savours sweet:
So hath thy breath, my dearest Thisby dear.
But hark, a voice! stay thou but here awhile,
And by and by I will to thee appear.   [*Exit.*
PUCK: A stranger Pyramus than e'er played here.   [*Exit.*
FLUTE: Must I speak now?
QUINCE: Ay, marry, must you; for you must understand he goes but to see a noise that he heard, and is to come again.
FLUTE: Most radiant Pyramus, most lily-white of hue,
Of colour like the red rose on triumphant brier,
Most briskly juvenal and eke most lovely Jew,
As true as truest horse that yet would never tire.
I'll meet thee, Pyramus, at Ninny's tomb.
QUINCE: 'Ninus' tomb,' man: why you must not speak that yet; that you answer to Pyramus: you speak all your part at once, cues and all. Pyramus enter: your cue is past: it is, 'never tire.'
FLUTE: O,—As true as truest horse; that yet would never tire.

Re-enter Puck, and Bottom with an ass's head.

BOTTOM: If I were fair, Thisby, I were only thine.
QUINCE: O monstrous! O strange! we are haunted. Pray, masters! fly, masters! Help!
                    [*Exeunt Quince, Snug, Flute, Snout, and Starveling.*
PUCK: I'll follow you, I'll lead you about a round,

Through bog, through bush, through brake, through brier:
Sometime a horse I'll be, sometime a hound;
   A hog, a headless bear, sometime a fire:
And neigh, and bark, and grunt, and roar, and burn,
Like horse, hound, hog, bear, fire, at every turn.   [*Exit.*

BOTTOM: Why do they run away? this is a knavery of them to
make me afeard.

Re-enter Snout.

SNOUT: O Bottom, thou art changed! what do I see on thee?

BOTTOM: What do you see? you see an asshead of your own,
do you?   [*Exit Snout.*

Re-enter Quince.

QUINCE: Bless thee, Bottom! bless thee! thou art translated.
      [*Exit.*

BOTTOM: I see their knavery: this is to make an ass of me; to
fright me, if they could. But I will not stir from this place, do what
they can: I will walk up and down here, and I will sing, that they
shall hear I am not afraid.   [*Sings.*

     The ousel cock so black of hue,
        With orange-tawny bill,
     The throstle with his note so true,
        The wren with little quill,—

TITANIA: [*Awakening*] What angel wakes me from my flowery
bed?

BOTTOM: [*Sings*]
     The finch, the sparrow and the lark,
        The plain-song cuckoo gray,
     Whose note full many a man doth mark,
        And dares not answer nay;—

for, indeed, who would set his wit to so foolish a bird? who would
give a bird the lie, though he cry 'cuckoo' never so?

TITANIA: I pray thee, gentle mortal, sing again:
Mine ear is much enamour'd of thy note;

So is mine eye enthralled to thy shape;
And they fair virtue's force perforce doth move me
On the first view to say, to swear, I love thee.

BOTTOM: Methinks, mistress, you should have little reason for that: and yet, to say the truth, reason and love keep little company together now-a-days; the more the pity that some honest neighbours will not make them friends. Nay, I can gleek upon occasion.

TITANIA: Thou art as wise as thou art beautiful.

BOTTOM: Not so, neither: but if I had wit enough to get out of this wood, I have enough to serve mine own turn.

TITANIA: Out of this wood do not desire to go:
Thou shalt remain here, whether thou wilt or no.
I am a spirit of no common rate:
The summer still doth tend upon my state;
And I do love thee: therefore, go with me;
I'll give thee fairies to attend on thee.
And they shall fetch thee jewels from the deep.
And sing while thou on pressed flowers dost sleep:
And I will purge thy mortal grossness so
That thou shalt like an airy spirit go.
Peaseblossom! Cobweb! Moth! and Mustardseed!

Enter Peaseblossom, Cobweb, Moth, and Mustardseed.

PEASEBLOSSOM: Ready.
COBWEB: And I.
MOTH: And I.
MUSTARDSEED: And I.
ALL: Where shall we go?
TITANIA: Be kind and courteous to this gentleman;
Hop in his walks and gambol in his eyes;
Feed him with apricocks and dewberries,
With purple grapes, green figs and mulberries;
The honey-bags steal from the humble-bees,
And for night-tapers crop their waxen thighs

And light them at the fiery glow-worm's eyes,
To have my love to bed and to arise;
And pluck the wings from painted butterflies
To fan the moonbeams from his sleeping eyes:
Nod to him, elves, and do him courtesies.

PEASEBLOSSOM: Hail, mortal!

COBWEB: Hail!

MOTH: Hail!

MUSTARDSEED: Hail!

BOTTOM: I cry your worships mercy, heartily; I beseech your worship's name.

COBWEB: Cobweb.

BOTTOM: I shall desire you of more acquaintance, good Master Cobweb: if I cut my finger, I shall make bold with you. Your name, honest gentleman?

PEASEBLOSSOM: Peaseblossom.

BOTTOM: I pray you, commend me to Mistress Squash, your mother, and to Master Peascod, your father. Good Master Peaseblossom, I shall desire you of more acquaintance too. Your name, I beseech you, sir?

MUSTARDSEED: Mustardseed.

BOTTOM: Good Master Mustardseed, I know your patience well: that same cowardly, giant-like ox-beef hath devoured many a gentleman of your house: I promise you your kindred hath made my eyes water ere now. I desire your more acquaintance, good Master Mustardseed.

TITANIA: Come, wait upon him; lead him to my bower,
The moon methinks looks with a watery eye;
And when she weeps, weeps every little flower.
Lamenting some enforced chastity.
Tie up my love's tongue, bring him silently.   [*Exeunt*.

SCENE II. *Another part of the wood.*
Enter Oberon.

OBERON: I wonder if Titania be awaked;
Then, what it was that next came in her eye,
Which she must dote on in extremity.

Enter Puck.

Here comes my messenger.
                   How now, mad spirit!
What night-rule now about this haunted grove?
PUCK: My mistress with a monster is in love.
Near to her close and consecrated bower,
While she was in her dull and sleeping hour,
A crew of patches, rude mechanicals,
That work for bread upon Athenian stalls,
Were met together to rehearse a play
Intended for great Theseus' nuptial-day.
The shallowest thick-skin of that barren sort,
Who Pyramus presented, in their sport
Forsook his scene and enter'd in a brake:
When I did him at this advantage take,
An ass's nole I fixed on his head:
Anon his Thisbe must be answered,
And forth my mimic comes. When they him spy,
As wild geese that the creeping fowler eye,
Or russet-pated choughs, many in sort,
Rising and cawing at the gun's report,
Sever themselves and madly sweep the sky,
So, at his sight, away his fellows fly;
And, at our stamp, here o'er and o'er one falls;
He murder cries and help from Athens calls.
Their sense thus weak, lost with their fears thus strong,
Made senseless things begin to do them wrong;
For briers and thorns at their apparel snatch;

Some sleeves, some hats, from yielders all things catch.
I led them on in this distracted fear,
And left sweet Pyramus translated there:
When in that moment, so it came to pass,
Titania waked and straightway loved an ass.

OBERON: This falls out better than I could devise.
But hast thou yet latch'd the Athenian's eyes
With the love-juice, as I did bid thee do?

PUCK: I took him sleeping,—that is finish'd too,—
And the Athenian woman by his side;
That, when he waked, of force she must be eyed.

Enter Hermia and Demetrius.

OBERON: Stand close; this is the same Athenian.

PUCK: This is the woman, but not this the man.

DEMETRIUS: O, why rebuke you him that loves you so?
Lay breath so bitter on your bitter foe.

HERMIA: Now I but chide; but I should use thee worse,
For thou, I fear, hast given me cause to curse.
If thou hast slain Lysander in his sleep,
Being o'er shoes in blood, plunge in the deep,
And kill me too.
The sun was not so true unto the day
As he to me: would he have stolen away
From sleeping Hermia? I believe as soon
This whole earth may be bored and that the moon
May through the centre creep and so displease
Her brother's noontide with the Antipodes.
It cannot be but thou hast murder'd him;
So should a murderer look, so dead, so grim.

DEMETRIUS: So should the murder'd look, and so should I,
Pierced through the heart with your stern cruelty:
Yet you, the murderer, look as bright, as clear.
As yonder Venus in her glimmering sphere.

HERMIA: What's this to my Lysander? where is he?

Ah, good Demetrius, wilt thou give him me?

DEMETRIUS: I had rather give his carcass to my hounds.

HERMIA: Out, dog! out, cur! thou drivest me past the bounds
Of maiden's patience. Hast thou slain him, then?
Henceforth be never number'd among men!
O, once tell true, tell true, even for my sake!
Durst thou have look'd upon him being awake,
And hast thou kill'd him sleeping? O brave touch!
Could not a worm, an adder, do so much?
An adder did it; for with doubler tongue
Than thine, thou serpent, never adder stung.

DEMETRIUS: You spend your passion on a misprised mood:
I am not guilty of Lysander's blood;
Nor is he dead, for aught that I can tell.

HERMIA: I pray thee, tell me then that he is well.

DEMETRIUS: An if I could, what should I get therefore?

HERMIA: A privilege never to see me more.
And from thy hated presence part I so;
See me no more, whether he be dead or no.   [*Exit.*

DEMETRIUS: There is no following her in this fierce vein:
Here therefore for a while I will remain.
So sorrow's heaviness doth heavier grow
For debt that bankrupt sleep doth sorrow owe;
Which now in some slight measure it will pay,
If for his tender here I make some stay.

OBERON: What hast thou done? thou hast mistaken quite
And laid the love-juice on some true-love's sight:
Of thy misprision must perforce ensue
Some true love turn'd and not a false turn'd true.

PUCK: Then fate o'er-rules, that, one man holding troth,
A million fail, confounding oath on oath.

OBERON: About the wood go swifter than the wind,
And Helena of Athens look thou find;
All fancy-sick she is and pale of cheer,
With sighs of love, that costs the fresh blood dear:

By some illusion see thou bring her here:
I'll charm his eyes against she do appear.
   PUCK: I go, I go; look how I go,
Swifter than arrow from the Tartar's bow.   [*Exit.*
OBERON: Flower of this purple dye,
        Hit with Cupid's archery,
        Sink in apple of his eye.
        When his love he doth espy,
        Let her shine as gloriously
        As the Venus of the sky.
        When thou wakest, if she be by,
        Beg of her for remedy.

Re-enter Puck.

PUCK: Captain of our fairy band,
        Helena is here at hand;
        And the youth, mistook by me,
        Pleading for a lover's fee.
        Shall we their fond pageant see?
        Lord, what fools these mortals be!
OBERON: Stand aside; the noise they make
        Will cause Demetrius to awake.
PUCK: Then will two at once woo one;
        That must needs be sport alone;
        And those things do best please me
        That befal preposterously.

Enter Lysander and Helena.

  LYSANDER: Why should you think I should woo in scorn?
      Scorn and derision never come in tears:
Look, when I vow, I weep; and vows so born,
      In their nativity all truth appears.
How can these things in me seem scorn to you,
Bearing the badge of faith, to prove them true?
  HELENA: You do advance your cunning more and more.

When truth kills truth, O devilish holy fray!
These vows are Hermia's: will you give her o'er?
    Weigh oath with oath, and you will nothing weigh:
Your vows to her and me, put in two scales,
Will even weigh, and both as light as tales.
    LYSANDER: I had no judgement when to her I swore.
    HELENA: Nor none, in my mind, now you give her o'er.
    Lysander: Demetrius loves her, and he loves not you.
    DEMETRIUS: [*Awaking*] O Helen, goddess, nymph, perfect, divine!
To what, my love, shall I compare thine eye?
Crystal is muddy. O, how ripe in show
Thy lips, those kissing cherries, tempting grow!
That pure congealed white, high Taurus' snow,
Fann'd with the eastern wind, turns to crow
When thou hold'st up thy hand: O, let me kiss
This princess of pure white, this seal of bliss!
    HELENA: O spite! O hell! I see you all are bent
To set against me for your merriment:
If you were civil and knew courtesy,
You would not do me thus much injury.
Can you not hate me, as I know you do,
But you must join in souls to mock me too?
If you were men, as men you are in show,
You would not use a gentle lady so;
To vow and swear and superpraise my parts,
When I am sure you hate me with your hearts.
You both are rivals, and love Hermia;
And now both rivals, to mock Helena:
A trim exploit, a manly enterprise.
To conjure tears up in a poor maid's eyes
With your derision! none of noble sort
Would so offend a virgin and extort
A poor soul's patience, all to make you sport.
    LYSANDER: You are unkind, Demetrius; be not so;
For you love Hermia; this you know I know;

And here, with all good will, with all my heart,
In Hermia's love I yield you up my part;
And yours Helena to me bequeath,
Whom I do love and will do till my death.

HELENA: Never did mockers waste more idle breath.

DEMETRIUS: Lysander, keep thy Hermia; I will none:
If e'er I loved her, all that love is gone.
My heart to her but as guest-wise sojourn'd,
And now to Helen is it home return'd,
There to remain.

LYSANDER: Helen, it is not so.

DEMETRIUS: Disparage not the faith thou dost not know,
Lest, to thy peril, thou aby it dear.
Look, where thy love comes; yonder is thy dear.

Re-enter Hermia.

HERMIA: Dark night, that from the eye his function takes,
The ear more quick of apprehension makes;
Wherein it doth impair the seeing sense,
It pays the hearing double recompense.
Thou art not by mine eye, Lysander, found;
Mine ear, I think it, brought me to thy sound.
But why unkindly didst thou leave me so?

LYSANDER: Why should he stay, whom he doth press to go?

HERMIA: What love could press Lysander from my side?

LYSANDER: Lysander's love, that would not let him bide,
Fair Helena, who more engilds the night
Than all yon fiery oes and eyes of light.
Why seek'st thou me? could not this make thee know,
The hate I bear thee made me leave thee so?

HERMIA: You speak not as you think; it cannot be.

HELENA: Lo, she is one of this confederacy!
Now I perceive they have conjoin'd all three
To fashion this false sport, in spite of me.
Injurious Hermia! most ungrateful maid!

Have you conspired, have you with these contrived
To bait me with this foul derision?
Is all the counsel that we two have shared,
The sisters' vows, the hours that we have spent
When we have chid the hasty-footed time
For parting us,—O, is it all forgot?
All school-days' friendship, childhood innocence?
We, Hermia, like two artificial gods,
Have with our needles created both one flower,
Both on one sampler, sitting on one cushion,
Both warbling of one song, both in one key,
As if our hands, our sides, voices and minds,
Had been incorporate. So we grew together,
Like to a double cherry, seeming parted,
But yet an union in partition;
Two lovely berries moulded on one stem;
So, with two seeming bodies, but one heart;
Two of the first, like coats in heraldry,
Due but to one and crowned with one crest.
And will you rent our ancient love asunder,
To join with men in scorning your poor friend?
It is not friendly, 'tis not maidenly:
Our sex, as well as I, may chide you for it,
Though I alone do feel the injury.

    HERMIA: I am amazed at your passionate words.
I scorn you not: it seems that you scorn me.

    HELENA: Have you not set Lysander, as in scorn,
To follow me and praise my eyes and face?
And made your other love, Demetrius,
Who even but now did spurn me with his foot,
To call me goddess, nymph, divine and rare,
Precious celestial? Wherefore speaks he this
To her he hates? and wherefore doth Lysander
Deny your love, so rich within his soul,
And tender me, forsooth, affection,

But by setting on, by your consent?
What though I be not so in grace as you,
So hung upon with love, so fortunate,
But miserable most, to love unloved?
This you should pity rather than despise.

HERMIA: I understand not what you mean by this.

HELENA: Ay, do persever, counterfeit sad looks,
Make mouths upon me when I turn my back;
Wink each at other; hold the sweet jest up:
This sport, well carried, shall be chronicled.
If you have any pity, grace, or manners,
You would not make me such an argument.
But fare ye well; 'tis partly my own fault;
Which death or absence soon shall remedy.

LYSANDER: Stay, gentle Helena; hear my excuse:
My love, my life, my soul, fair Helena!

HELENA: O excellent!

HERMIA: Sweet, do not scorn her so.

DEMETRIUS: If she cannot entreat, I can compel.

LYSANDER: Thou canst compel no more than she entreat.
Thy threats have no more strength than her weak prayers.
Helen, I love thee; by my life, I do:
I swear by that which I will lose for thee,
To prove him false that says I love thee not.

DEMETRIUS: I say I love thee more than he can do.

LYSANDER: If thou say so, withdraw, and prove it too.

DEMETRIUS: Quick, come!

HERMIA: Lysander, whereto tends all this?

LYSANDER: Away, you Ethiope!

DEMETRIUS: No, no; he'll. . .
Seem to break loose; take on as you would follow,
But yet come not; you are a tame man, go!

LYSANDER: Hang off, thou cat, thou burr! vile thing, let loose.
Or I will shake thee from me like a serpent!

HERMIA: Why are you grown so rude? what change is this?

Sweet love,—

LYSANDER: Thy love! out, tawny Tartar, out!
Out, loathed medicine! hated potion, hence!

HERMIA: Do you not jest?

HELENA: Yes, sooth; and so do you.

LYSANDER: Demetrius, I will keep my word with thee.

DEMETRIUS: I would I had your bond, for I perceive
A weak bond holds you: I'll not trust your word.

LYSANDER: What, should I hurt her, strike her, kill her dead?
Although I hate her, I'll not harm her so.

HERMIA: What, can you do me greater harm than hate!
Hate me! wherefore? O me! what news, my love!
Am not I Hermia? are not you Lysander?
I am as fair now as I was erewhile.
Since night you loved me; yet since night you left me:
Why, then you left me—O, the gods forbid!—
In earnest, shall I say?

LYSANDER: Ay, by my life;
And never did desire to see thee more.
Therefore be out of hope, of question, of doubt;
Be certain, nothing truer; 'tis no jest
That I do hate thee and love Helena.

HERMIA: O me! you juggler! you cankerblossom!
You thief of love! what, have you come by night
And stolen my love's heart from him?

HELENA: Fine, i' faith!
Have you no modesty, no maiden shame,
No touch of bashfulness? What, will you tear
Impatient answers from my gentle tongue?
Fie, fie! you counterfeit, you puppet, you!

HERMIA: Puppet? why so? ay, that way goes the game.
Now I perceive that she hath made compare
Between our statures; she hath urged her height;
And with her personage, her tall personage,
Her height, forsooth, she hath prevail'd with him.

And are you grown so high in his esteem,
Because I am so dwarfish and so low?
How low am I, thou painted Maypole? speak;
How low am I? I am not yet so low
But that my nails can reach unto thine eyes.

HELENA: I pray you, though you mock me, gentlemen,
Let her not hurt me: I was never curst;
I have no gift at all in shrewishness;
I am a right maid for my cowardice:
Let her not strike me. You perhaps may think,
Because she is something lower than myself,
That I can match her.

HERMIA: Lower! hark, again.

HELENA: Good Hermia, do not be so bitter with me.
I evermore did love you, Hermia,
Did ever keep your counsels, never wrong'd you;
Save that, in love unto Demetrius,
I told him of your stealth unto this wood.
He follow'd you; for love I follow'd him;
But he hath chid me hence and threaten'd me
To strike me, spurn me, nay, to kill me too:
And now, so you will let me quiet go,
To Athens will I bear my folly back
And follow you no further: let me go:
You see how simple and how fond I am.

HERMIA: Why, get you gone: who is 't that hinders you?

HELENA: A foolish heart, that I leave here behind.

HERMIA: What, with Lysander?

HELENA: With Demetrius.

LYSANDER: Be not afraid; she shall not harm thee, Helena.

DEMETRIUS: No, sir, she shall not, though you take her part.

HELENA: O, when she's angry, she is keen and shrewd!
She was a vixen when she went to school;
And though she be but little, she is fierce.

HERMIA: 'Little' again! nothing but 'low' and 'little'!

Why will you suffer her to flout me thus?
Let me come to her.
    LYSANDER: Get you gone, you dwarf;
You minimus, of hindering knot-grass made;
You bead, you acorn.
    DEMETRIUS: You art too officious
In her behalf that scorns your services.
Let her alone; speak not of Helena;
Take not her part; for, if thou dost intend
Never so little show of love to her,
Thou shalt aby it.
    LYSANDER: Now she holds me not;
Now follow, if thou darest, to try whose right,
Of thine or mine, is most in Helena.
    DEMETRIUS: Follow! nay, I'll go with thee, cheek by jole.

                                [*Exeunt Lysander and Demetrius.*

    HERMIA: You, mistress, all this coil is 'long of you:
Nay, go not back.
    HELENA: I will not trust you, I,
Nor longer stay in your curst company.
Your hands than mine are quicker for a fray,
My legs are longer, though, to run away.   [*Exit.*
    HERMIA: I am amazed, and know not what to say.   [*Exit.*
    OBERON: This is thy negligence: still thou mistakest,
Or else committ'st thy knaveries wilfully.
    PUCK: Believe me, king of shadows, I mistook.
Did you not tell me I should know the man
By the Athenian garments he had on?
And so far blameless proves my enterprise,
That I have 'nointed an Athenian's eyes;
And so far am I glad it so did sort
As this their jangling I esteem a sport.
    OBERON: Thou see'est these lovers seek a place to fight:
Hie therefore, Robin, overcast the night:
The starry welkin cover thou anon

With drooping fog as black as Acheron,
And lead these testy rivals so astray
As one come not within another's way.
Like to Lysander sometime frame thy tongue,
Then stir Demetrius up with bitter wrong;
And sometime rail thou like Demetrius;
And from each other look thou lead them thus,
Till o'er their brows death-counterfeiting sleep
With leaden legs and batty wings doth creep.
Then crush this herb into Lysander's eye;
Whose liquor hath this virtuous property,
To take from thence all error with his might,
And make his eyeballs roll with wonted sight.
When they next wake, all this derision
Shall seem a dream and fruitless vision,
And back to Athens shall the lovers wend,
With league whose date till death shall never end.
Whiles I in this affair do thee employ,
I'll to my queen and beg her Indian boy;
And then I will her charmed eye release
From monster's view, and all things shall be peace.
        PUCK: My fairy lord, this must be done with haste.
For night's swift dragons cut the clouds full fast,
And yonder shines Aurora's harbinger:
At whose approach, ghosts, wandering here and there,
Troop home to churchyards: damned spirits all,
That in crossways and floods have burial,
Already to their wormy beds are gone;
For fear lest day should look their shames upon,
They wilfully themselves exile from light
And must for aye consort with black-brow'd night.
        OBERON: But we are spirits of another sort:
I with the morning's love have oft made sport,
And, like a forester, the groves my tread,
Even till the eastern gate, all fiery red,

Opening on Neptune with fair blessed beams,
Turns into yellow gold his salt green streams.
But, notwithstanding, haste; make no delay:
We may effect this business yet ere day.   [*Exit.*

PUCK: Up and down, up and down,
     I will lead them up and down:
     I am fear'd in field and town:
     Goblin, lead them up and down.
Here comes one.

Re-enter Lysander.

LYSANDER: Where art thou, proud Demetrius? speak thou now.
PUCK: Here, villain; drawn and ready. Where art thou?
LYSANDER: I will be with thee straight.
PUCK: Follow me, then,
To plainer ground.   [*Exit Lysander, as following the voice.*

Re-enter Demetrius.

DEMETRIUS: Lysander! speak again:
Thou runaway, thou coward, art thou fled?
Speak! In some bush? Where dost thou hide thy head?
    PUCK: Thou coward, art thou bragging to the stars,
Telling the bushes that thou look'st for wars,
And wilt not come? Come, recreant; come, thou child,
I'll whip thee with a rod; he is defiled
That draws a sword on thee.
DEMETRIUS: Yea, art thou there?
PUCK: Follow my voice; we'll try no manhood here.   [*Exeunt.*

Re-enter Lysander.

LYSANDER: He goes before me and still dares me on:
When I come where he calls, then he is gone.
The villain is much lighter-heel'd than I:
I follow'd fast, but faster did he fly;
That fallen am I in dark uneven way,

And here will rest me. [*Lies down.*] Come, thou gentle day!
For if but once thou show me thy grey light.
I'll find Demetrius and revenge this spite.   [*Sleeps.*

Re-enter Puck and Demetrius.

PUCK: Ho, ho, ho! Coward, why comest thou not?
DEMETRIUS: Abide me, if thou darest; for well I wot
Thou runn'st before me, shifting every place,
And darest not stand, nor look me in the face.
Where art thou now?
PUCK: Come hither: I am here.
DEMETRIUS: Nay, then, thou mock'st me. Thou shalt buy this
    dear,
If ever I thy face by daylight see:
Now, go thy way. Faintness constraineth me
To measure out my length on this cold bed.
By day's approach look to be visited.   [*Lies down and sleeps.*

Re-enter Helena.

HELENA: O weary night, O long and tedious night,
    Abate thy hours! Shine comforts from the east,
That I may back to Athens by daylight,
    From these that my poor company detest:
And sleep, that sometimes shuts up sorrow's eye,
Steal me awhile from mine own company.   [*Lies down and sleeps.*
PUCK: Yet but three? Come one more;
        Two of both kinds makes up four.
        Here she comes, curst and sad:
        Cupid is a knavish lad,
        Thus to make poor females mad.

Re-enter Hermia.

HERMIA: Never so weary, never so in woe,
    Bedabbled with the dew and torn with briers,
I can no further crawl, no further go;

My legs can keep no pace with my desires.
Here will I rest me till the break of day.
Heavens shield Lysander, if they mean a fray!

                                [Lies down and sleeps.

PUCK: On the ground
                        Sleep sound;
                        I'll apply
                        To your eye,
                        Gentle lover, remedy.

                      [Squeezing the juice on Lysander's eyes.

                        When thou wakest,
                        Thou takest
                        True delight
                        In the sight
              Of thy former lady's eye:
             And the country proverb known,
             That every man should take his own;
             In your waking shall be shown:
                        Jack shall have Jill;
                        Nought shall go ill;
The man shall have his mare again, and all shall be well. *[Exit.*

ACT IV.

SCENE I. *The same.*

Lysander, Demetrius, Helena, and Hermia lying asleep.
Enter Titania and Bottom; Peaseblossom, Cobweb, Moth,
Mustardseed, and other Fairies attending; Oberon behind unseen.

TITANIA: Come, sit thee down upon this flowery bed,
While I thy amiable cheeks do coy,
And stick musk-roses in thy sleek, smooth head,
And kiss thy fair large ears, my gentle joy.
BOTTOM: Where's Peaseblossom?

PEASEBLOSSOM: Ready.

BOTTOM: Scratch my head, Peaseblossom. Where's Mounsieur Cobweb?

COBWEB: Ready.

BOTTOM: Mounsieur Cobweb, good mounsieur, get you your weapons in your hand, and kill me a red-hipped humble-bee on the top of a thistle; and, good mounsieur, bring me the honey-bag. Do not fret yourself too much in the action, mounsieur; and, good mounsieur, have a care the honey-bag break not; I would be loath to have you overflown with a honey-bag, signior. Where's Mounsieur Mustardseed?

MUSTARDSEED: Ready.

BOTTOM: Give me your neaf, Mounsieur Mustardseed. Pray you, leave your courtesy, good mounsieur.

MUSTARDSEED: What's your will?

BOTTOM: Nothing, good mounsieur, but to help Cavalery Cobweb to scratch. I must to the barber's, monsieur; for methinks I am marvellous hairy about the face; and I am such a tender ass, if my hair do but tickle me, I must scratch.

TITANIA: What, wilt thou hear some music, my sweet love?

BOTTOM: I have a reasonable good ear in music. Let's have the tongs and the bones.

TITANIA: Or say, sweet love, what thou desirest to eat.

BOTTOM: Truly a peck of provender: I could munch your good dry oats. Methinks I have a great desire to a bottle of hay: good hay, sweet hay, hath no fellow.

TITANIA: I have a venturous fairy that shall seek
The squirrel's hoard, and fetch thee new nuts.

BOTTOM: I had rather have a handful or two or dried peas. But, I pray you, let none of your people stir me: I have an exposition of sleep come upon me.

TITANIA: Sleep thou, and I will wind thee in my arms.
Fairies, be gone, and be all ways away.   [Exeunt fairies.
So doth the woodbine the sweet honeysuckle
Gentle entwist; the female ivy so

Enrings the barky fingers of the elm.
O, how I love thee! how I dote on thee!   [*They sleep.*

Enter Puck.

   OBERON: [*Advancing*] Welcome, good Robin.
     See'st thou this sweet sight?
Her dotage now I do begin to pity:
For, meeting her of late behind the wood,
Seeking sweet favours for this hateful fool,
I did upbraid her and fall out with her;
For she his hairy temples then had rounded
With coronet of fresh and fragrant flowers;
And that same dew, which sometime on the buds
Was wont to swell like round and orient pearls,
Stood now within the pretty flowerets' eyes
Like tears that did their own disgrace bewail.
When I had at my pleasure taunted her
And she in mild terms begg'd my patience,
I then did ask of her her changeling child;
Which straight she gave me, and her fairy sent
To bear him to my bower in fairy land.
And now I have the boy, I will undo
This hateful imperfection of her eyes:
And, gentle Puck, take this transformed scalp
From off the head of this Athenian swain;
That, he awaking when the other do,
May all to Athens back again repair
And think no more of this night's accidents
But as the fierce vexation of a dream.
But first I will release the fairy queen.
     Be as thou wast wont to be;
     See as thou wast wont to see:
     Dian's bud o'er Cupid's flower
     Hath such force and blessed power.
Now, my Titania; wake you, my sweet queen.

TITANIA: My Oberon! what visions have I seen!
Methought I was enamour'd of an ass.
    OBERON: There lies your love.
    TITANIA: How came these things to pass?
O, how mine eyes do loathe his visage now!
    OBERON: Silence awhile. Robin, take off this head.
Titania, music call; and strike more dead
Than common sleep of all these five the sense.
    TITANIA: Music, ho! music, such as charmeth sleep!
                                        [*Music, still.*
    PUCK: Now, when thou wakest, with thine own fool's eyes
peep.
    OBERON: Sound, music! Come, my queen take hands with me,
And rock the ground whereon these sleepers be.
Now thou and I are new in amity
And will to-morrow midnight solemnly
Dance in Duke Theseus' house triumphantly
And bless it to all fair prosperity:
There shall the pairs of faithful lovers be
Wedded, with Theseus, all in jollity.
    PUCK: Fairy king, attend, and mark:
              I do hear the morning lark.
    OBERON: Then, my queen, in silence sad,
              Trip we after night's shade:
              We the globe can compass soon,
              Swifter than the wandering moon.
    TITANIA: Come, my lord, and in our flight
              Tell me how it came this night
              That I sleeping here was found
              With these mortals on the ground.   [*Exeunt.*
                                        [*Horns winded within.*

Enter Theseus, Hippolyta, Egeus, and train.

    THESEUS: Go, one of you, find out the forester;
For now our observation is perform'd;

And since we have the vaward of the day,
My love shall hear the music of my hounds.
Uncouple in the western valley; let them go:
Dispatch, I say, and find the forester.   [*Exit an Attendant.*
We will, fair queen, up to the mountain's top
And mark the musical confusion
Of hounds and echo in conjunction.

HIPPOLYTA: I was with Hercules and Cadmus once,
When in a wood of Crete they bay'd the bear
With hounds of Sparta: never did I hear
Such gallant chiding; for, besides the groves,
The skies, the fountains, every region near
Seem'd all one mutual cry: I never heard
So musical a discord, such sweet thunder.

THESEUS: My hounds are bred out of the Spartan kind,
So flew'd, so sanded, and their heads are hung
With ears that sweep away the morning dew;
Crook-knee'd, and dew-lapp'd like Thessalian bulls;
Slow in pursuit, but match'd in mouth like bells,
Each under each. A cry more tuneable
Was never holla'd to, nor cheer'd with horn,
In Crete, in Sparta, nor in Thessaly:
Judge when you hear. But, soft! what nymphs are these?

EGEUS: My lord, this is my daughter here asleep;
And this Lysander; this Demetrius is;
This Helena, old Nedar's Helena:
I wonder of their being here together.

THESEUS: No doubt they rose up early to observe
The rite of May, and, hearing our intent,
Came here in grace of our solemnity.
But speak, Egeus; is not this the day
That Hermia should give answer of her choice?

EGEUS: It is, my lord.

THESEUS: Go, bid the huntsmen wake them with their horns.
                                        [*Horns and shouts within.*

Lysander, Demetrius, Helena, and Hermia wake and start up.

Good morrow, friends. Saint Valentine's is past:
Begin these wood-birds but to couple now?
    LYSANDER: Pardon, my lord.
    THESEUS: I pray you all, stand up.
I know you two are rival enemies:
How comes this gentle concord in the world,
That hatred is so far from jealousy,
To sleep by hate, and fear no enmity?
    LYSANDER: My lord, I shall reply amazedly,
Half sleep, half waking: but as yet, I swear,
I cannot truly say how I came here;
But, as I think,—for truly would I speak,
And now I do bethink me, so it is,—
I came with Hermia hither: our intent
Was to be gone from Athens, where we might,
Without the peril of the Athenian law.
    EGEUS: Enough, enough, my lord; you have enough:
I beg the law, the law, upon his head.
They would have stolen away; they would, Demetrius,
Thereby to have defeated you and me,
You of your wife and me of my consent,
Of my consent that she should be your wife.
    DEMETRIUS: My lord, fair Helen told me of their stealth,
Of this their purpose hither to this wood;
And I in fury hither follow'd them,
Fair Helena in fancy following me.
But, my good lord, I wot not by what power,—
But by some power it is,—my love to Hermia,
Melted as the snow, seems to me now
As the remembrance of an idle gawd
Which in my childhood I did dote upon;
And all the faith, the virtue of my heart,
The object and the pleasure of mine eye,

Is only Helena. To her, my lord,
Was I betroth'd ere I saw Hermia:
But, like in sickness, did I loathe this food:
But, as in health, come to my natural taste,
Now I do wish it, love it, long for it,
And will for evermore be true to it.

THESEUS: Fair lovers, you are fortunately met:
Of this discourse we more will hear anon.
Egeus, I will overbear your will;
For in the temple, by and by, with us
These couples shall eternally be knit:
And, for the morning now is something worn,
Our purposed hunting shall be set aside.
Away with us to Athens; three and three,
We'll hold a feast in great solemnity.
Come, Hippolyta.   [*Exeunt Theseus, Hippolyta, Egeus, and train.*

DEMETRIUS: These things seem small and undistinguishable,
Like far-off mountains turned into clouds.

HERMIA: Methinks I see these things with parted eye,
When every thing seems double.

HELENA: So methinks:
And I have found Demetrius like a jewel,
Mine own, and not mine own.

DEMETRIUS: Are you sure
That we are awake? It seems to me
That yet we sleep, we dream. Do not you think
The duke was here, and bid us follow him?

HERMIA: Yea; and my father.

HELENA: And Hippolyta.

Lysander: And he did bid us follow to the temple.

DEMETRIUS: Why, then, we are away; let's follow him;
And by the way let us recount our dreams.   [*Exeunt.*

BOTTOM: [*Awaking*] When my cue comes, call me, and I will
answer: my next is, 'Most fair Pyramus.' Heigh-ho! Peter Quince!
Flute, the bellows-mender! Snout, the tinker! Starveling! God's

my life, stolen hence, and left me asleep! I have had a most rare vision. I have had a dream, past the wit of man to say what dream it was: man is but an ass, if he go about to expound this dream. Methought I was—there is no man can tell what. Methought I was, —and methought I had,—but man is but a patched fool, if he will offer to say what methought I had. The eye of man hath not heard, the ear of man hath not seen, man's hand is not able to taste, his tongue to conceive, nor his heart to report, what my dream was. I will get Peter Quince to write a ballad of this dream: it shall be called Bottom's Dream, because it hath no bottom; and I will sing it in the latter end of a play, before the duke: peradventure, to make it the more gracious, I shall sing it at her death.

[*Exit.*

SCENE II. *Athens. Quince's house.*
Enter Quince, Flute, Snout, and Starveling.

QUINCE: Have you sent to Bottom's house? is he come home yet?

STARVELING: He cannot be heard of. Out of doubt he is transported.

FLUTE: If he come not, then the play is marred: it goes not forward, doth it?

QUINCE: It is not possible: you have not a man in all Athens able to discharge Pyramus but he.

FLUTE: No, he hath simply the best wit of any handicraft man in Athens.

QUINCE: Yea, and the best person too; and he is a very paramour for a sweet voice.

FLUTE: You must say 'paragon:' a paramour is, God bless us, a thing of naught.

Enter Snug.

SNUG: Masters, the duke is coming from the temple, and there is two or three lords and ladies more married: if our sport had gone forward, we had all been made men.

FLUTE: O sweet bully Bottom! Thus hath he lost sixpence a day during his life; he could not have 'scaped sixpence a day: an the duke had not given him sixpence a day for playing Pyramus, I'll be hanged; he would have deserved it: sixpence a day in Pyramus, or nothing.

Enter Bottom.

BOTTOM: Where are these lads? where are these hearts?

QUINCE: Bottom! O most courageous day! O most happy hour!

BOTTOM: Masters, I am to discourse wonders: but ask me not what; for if I tell you, I am no true Athenian. I will tell you every thing, right as it fell out.

QUINCE: Let us hear, sweet Bottom.

BOTTOM: Not a word of me. All I will tell you is, that the duke hath dined. Get your apparel together, good strings to your beards, new ribbons to your pumps; meet presently at the palace; every man look o'er his part; for the short and the long is, our play is preferred. In any case, let Thisby have clean linen; and let not him that plays the lion pare his nails, for they shall hang out for the lion's claws. And, most dear actors, eat no onions nor garlic, for we are to utter sweet breath; and I do not doubt but to hear them say, it is a sweet comedy. No more words: away! go, away!   [*Exeunt.*

ACT V.

SCENE I. *Athens. The palace of Theseus.*
Enter Theseus, Hippolyta, Philostrate, Lords, and Attendants.

HIPPOLYTA: 'Tis strange, my Theseus, that these lovers speak of.

THESEUS: More strange than true: I never may believe
These antique fables, nor these fairy toys.
Lovers and madmen have such seething brains,
Such shaping fantasies, that apprehend

More than cool reason ever comprehends.
The lunatic, the lover and the poet
Are of imagination all compact:
One sees more devils than vast hell can hold,
That is, the madman: the lover, all as frantic,
Sees Helen's beauty in a brow of Egypt:
The poet's eye, in a fine frenzy rolling,
Doth glance from heaven to earth, from earth to heaven;
And as imagination bodies forth
The forms of things unknown, the poet's pen
Turns them to shapes and gives to airy nothing
A local habitation and a name.
Such tricks hath strong imagination,
That, if it would but apprehend some joy,
It comprehends some bringer of that joy:
Or in the night, imagining some fear,
How easy is a bush supposed a bear!

    HIPPOLYTA: But all the story of the night told over,
And all their minds transfigured so together,
More witnesseth than fancy's images
And grows to something of great constancy;
But, howsoever, strange and admirable.

    THESEUS: Here come the lovers, full of joy and mirth.

Enter Lysander, Demetrius, Hermia, and Helena.

Joy, gentle friends! joy and fresh days of love
Accompany your hearts!

    LYSANDER: More than to us
Wait in your royal walks, your board, your bed!

    THESEUS: Come now; what masques, what dances shall we
        have,
To wear away this long age of three hours
Between our after-supper and bed-time?
Where is our usual manager of mirth?
What revels are in hand? Is there no play,

To ease the anguish of a torturing hour?
Call Philostrate.

   PHILOSTRATE: Here, mighty Theseus.

   THESEUS: Say, what abridgement have you for this evening?
What masque? what music? How shall we beguile
The lazy time, if not with some delight?

   PHILOSTRATE: There is a brief how many sports are ripe:
Make choice of which your highness will see first. [*Giving a paper.*

   THESEUS: [*Reads*] 'The battle with the Centaurs, to be sung
By an Athenian eunuch to the harp.'
We'll none of that: that have I told my love,
In glory of my kinsman Hercules.
[*Reads*] 'The riot of the tipsy Bacchanals,
Tearing the Thracian singer in their rage.'
That is an old device; and it was play'd
When I from Thebes came last a conqueror.
[*Reads*] 'The thrice three Muses mourning for the death
Of Learning, late deceased in beggary.'
That is some satire, keen and critical,
Not sorting with a nuptial ceremony.
[*Reads*] 'A tedious brief scene of young Pyramus
And his love Thisbe; very tragical mirth.'
Merry and tragical! tedious and brief!
   That is, hot ice and wondrous strange snow.
How shall we find the concord of this discord?

   PHILOSTRATE: A play there is, my lord, some ten words long,
Which is as brief as I have known a play;
But by ten words, my lord, it is too long,
Which makes it tedious; for in all the play
There is not one word apt, one player fitted:
And tragical, my noble lord, it is;
For Pyramus therein doth kill himself.
Which, when I saw rehearsed, I must confess,
Made mine eyes water; but more merry tears
The passion of loud laughter never shed.

THESEUS: What are they that do play it?

PHILOSTRATE: Hard-handed men that work in Athens here,
Which never labour'd in their minds till now,
And now have toil'd their unbreathed memories
With this same play, against your nuptial.

THESEUS: And we will hear it.

PHILOSTRATE: No, my noble lord;
It is not for you: I have heard it over,
And it is nothing, nothing in the world;
Unless you can find sport in their intents,
Extremely stretch'd and conn'd with cruel pain,
To do you service.

THESEUS: I will hear that play;
For never anything can be amiss,
When simpleness and duty tender it.
Go, bring them in: and take your places, ladies.   [*Exit Philostrate.*

HIPPOLYTA: I love not to see wretchedness o'er-charged
And duty in his service perishing.

THESEUS: Why, gentle sweet, you shall see no such thing.

HIPPOLYTA: He says they can do nothing in this kind.

THESEUS: The kinder we, to give them thanks for nothing.
Our sport shall be to take what they mistake:
And what poor duty cannot do, noble respect
Takes it in might, not merit.
Where I have come, great clerks have purposed
To greet me with premeditated welcomes;
Where I have seen them shiver and look pale,
Make periods in the midst of sentences,
Throttle their practised accent in their fears
And in conclusion dumbly have broke off,
Not paying me a welcome. Trust me, sweet,
Out of this silence yet I pick'd a welcome;
And in the modesty of fearful duty
I read as much from the rattling tongue
Of saucy and audacious eloquence.

Love, therefore, and tongue-tied simplicity
In least speak most, to my capacity.

Re-enter Philostrate.

> PHILOSTRATE: So please your grace, the Prologue is address'd.
> THESEUS: Let him approach.   [*Flourish of trumpets.*

Enter Quince for the Prologue.

> PROLOGUE: If we offend, it is with our good will,
>   That you should think, we come not to offend,
> But with good will. To show our simple skill,
>   That is the true beginning of our end.
> Consider then we come but in despite.
>   We do not come as minding to content you,
> Our true intent is. All for your delight
>   We are not here. That you should here repent you,
> The actors are at hand and by their show
> You shall know all that you are like to know.
>
> THESEUS: This fellow doth not stand upon points.
>
> LYSANDER: He hath rid his prologue like a rough colt; he knows
> not the stop. A good moral, my lord: it is not enough to speak,
> but to speak true.
>
> HIPPOLYTA: Indeed he hath played on his prologue like a child
> on a recorder; a sound, but not in government.
>
> THESEUS: His speech was like a tangled chain:
> nothing impaired, but all disordered. Who is next?

Enter Pyramus and Thisbe, Wall, Moonshine, and Lion.

> PROLOGUE: Gentles, perchance you wonder at this show;
>   But wonder on, till truth make all things plain.
> This man is Pyramus, if you would know;
>   This beauteous lady Thisby is certain.
> This man, with lime and rough-cast, doth present
>   Wall, that vile Wall which did these lovers sunder;
> And through Wall's chink, poor souls, they are content

To whisper. At the which let no man wonder.
This man, with lanthorn, dog, and bush of thorn,
    Presenteth Moonshine; for, if you will know,
By moonshine did these lovers think no scorn
    To meet at Ninus' tomb, there, there to woo.
This grisly beast, which Lion hight by name,
The trusty Thisby, coming first by night,
Did scare away, or rather did afright;
And, as she fled, her mantle she did fall,
    Which Lion vile with bloody mouth did stain.
Anon comes Pyramus, sweet youth and tall,
    And finds his trusty Thisby's mantle slain;
Whereat, with blade, with bloody blameful blade,
    He bravely broach'd his boiling bloody breast;
And Thisby, tarrying in mulberry shade,
    His dagger drew, and died. For all the rest,
Let Lion, Moonshine, Wall, and lovers twain
At large discourse, while here they do remain.
                    [*Exeunt Prologue, Pyramus, Thisbe, Lion, and Moonshine.*
THESEUS: I wonder if the lion be to speak.
DEMETRIUS: No wonder, my lord; one lion may, when many asses do.
WALL: In this same interlude it doth befall
That I, one Snout by name, present a wall:
And such a wall, as I would have you think,
That had in it a crannied hole or chink,
Through which the lovers, Pyramus and Thisby,
Did whisper often very secretly.
This loam, this rough-cast and this stone doth show
That I am that same wall; the truth is so:
And this the cranny is, right and sinister,
Through which the fearful lovers are to whisper.
    THESEUS: Would you desire lime and hair to speak better?
    DEMETRIUS: It is the wittiest partition that ever I heard discourse, my lord.

Re-enter Pyramus.

THESEUS: Pyramus draws near the wall: silence!
PYRAMUS: O grim-look'd night! O night with hue so black!
    O night, which ever art when day is not!
O night, O night! alack, alack, alack,
    I fear my Thisby's promise is forgot!
And thou, O wall, O sweet, O lovely wall,
    That stand'st between her father's ground and mine!
Thou wall, O wall, O sweet and lovely wall,
    Show me thy chink, to blink through with mine eyne!
                    [*Wall holds up his fingers.*
Thanks, courteous wall: Jove shield thee well for this!
    But what see I? No Thisby do I see.
O wicked wall, through which I see no bliss!
    Curst be thy stones for thus deceiving me.
THESEUS: The wall, methinks, being sensible, should curse again.
PYRAMUS: No, in truth, sir, he should not. 'Deceiving me' is
Thisby's cue: she is to enter now, and I am to spy her through the
wall. You shall see, it will fall pat as I told you. Yonder she comes.

Re-enter Thisbe.

THISBY: O wall, full often hast thou heard my moans,
    For parting my fair Pyramus and me!
My cherry lips have often kiss'd thy stones,
    Thy stones with lime and hair knit up in thee.
PYRAMUS: I see a voice: now will I to the chink,
    To spy an I can hear my Thisby's face. Thisby!
THISBY: My love thou art, my love I think.
PYRAMUS: Think what thou wilt, I am thy lover's grace;
And, like Limander, am I trusty still.
THISBY: And I like Helen, till the Fates me kill.
PYRAMUS: Not Shafalus to Procrus was so true.
THISBY: As Shafalus to Procrus, I to you.
PYRAMUS: O, kiss me through the hole of this vile wall!

THISBY: I kiss the wall's hole, not your lips at all.

PYRAMUS: Wilt thou at Ninny's tomb meet me straightway?

THISBY: 'Tide life, 'tide death, I come without delay.

[Exeunt Pyramus and Thisbe.

WALL: Thus have I, Wall, my part discharged so;

And, being done, thus Wall away doth go.   *[Exit.*

THESEUS: Now is the mural down between the two neighbours.

DEMETRIUS: No remedy, my lord, when walls are so wilful to hear without warning.

HIPPOLYTA: This is the silliest stuff that ever I heard.

THESEUS: The best in this kind are but shadows; and the worst are no worse, if imagination amend them.

HIPPOLYTA: It must be your imagination then, and not theirs.

THESEUS: If we imagine no worse of them than they of themselves, they may pass for excellent men. Here come two noble beasts in, a man and a lion.

Re-enter Lion and Moonshine.

LION: You, ladies, you, whose gentle hearts do fear
     The smallest monstrous mouse that creeps on floor,
May now perchance both quake and tremble here,
     When lion rough in wildest rage doth roar.
Then know that I, one Snug the joiner, am
A lion-fell, nor else no lion's dam;
For, if I should as lion come in strife
Into this place, 'twere pity on my life.

THESEUS: A very gentle beast, and of a good conscience.

DEMETRIUS: The very best at a beast, my lord, that e'er I saw.

LYSANDER: This lion is a very fox for his valour.

THESEUS: True; and a goose for his discretion.

DEMETRIUS: Not so, my lord; for his valour cannot carry his discretion; and the fox carries the goose.

THESEUS: His discretion, I am sure, cannot carry his valour; for the goose carries not the fox. It is well: leave it to his discretion, and let us listen to the moon.

MOONSHINE: This lanthorn doth the horned moon present;—

DEMETRIUS: He should have worn the horns on his head.

THESEUS: He is no crescent, and his horns are invisible within the circumference.

MOONSHINE: This lanthorn doth the horned moon present;
Myself the man i' the moon do seem to be.

THESEUS: This is the greatest error of all the rest: the man should be put into the lanthorn. How is it else the man i' the moon?

DEMETRIUS: He dares not come there for the candle; for, you see, it is already in snuff.

HIPPOLYTA: I am aweary of this moon: would he would change!

THESEUS: It appears, by his small light of discretion, that he is in the wane; but yet, in courtesy, in all reason, we must stay the time.

LYSANDER: Proceed, Moon.

MOONSHINE: All that I have to say, is, to tell you that the lanthorn is the moon; I, the man in the moon; this thorn-bush, my thorn-bush; and this dog, my dog.

DEMETRIUS: Why, all these should be in the lanthorn; for all these are in the moon. But, silence! here comes Thisbe.

Re-enter Thisbe.

THISBY: This is old Ninny's tomb. Where is my love?

LION: [*Roaring*] Oh—   [*Thisbe runs off.*

DEMETRIUS: Well roared, Lion.

THESEUS: Well run, Thisbe.

HIPPOLYTA: Well shone, Moon. Truly, the moon shines with a good grace.   [*The Lion shakes Thisbe's mantle, and exit.*

THESEUS: Well moused, Lion.

LYSANDER: And so the lion vanished.

DEMETRIUS: And then came Pyramus.

Re-enter Pyramus.

PYRAMUS: Sweet Moon, I thank thee for thy sunny beams;
    I thank thee, Moon, for shining now so bright;

For, by thy gracious, golden, glittering gleams,
    I trust to take of truest Thisby sight.
        But stay, O spite!
        But mark, poor knight,
    What dreadful dole is here!
        Eyes, do you see?
        How can it be?
    O dainty duck! O dear!
        Thy mantle good,
        What, stain'd with blood!
    Approach, ye Furies fell!
        O Fates, come, come,
        Cut thread and thrum;
    Quail, crush, conclude, and quell!

THESEUS: This passion, and the death of a dear friend, would go near to make a man look sad.

HIPPOLYTA: Beshrew my heart, but I pity the man.

PYRAMUS: O wherefore, Nature, didst thou lions frame?
    Since lion vile hath here deflower'd my dear:
Which is—no, no—which was the fairest dame
    That lived, that loved, that liked, that look'd with cheer.
        Come, tears, confound;
        Out, sword, and wound
    The pap of Pyramus;
        Ay, that left pap,
        Where heart doth hop: [*Stabs himself.*
Thus die I, thus, thus, thus.
        Now am I dead,
        Now am I fled;
    My soul is in the sky:
        Tongue, lose thy light;
        Moon, take thy flight: [*Exit Moonshine.*
    Now die, die, die, die, die.   [*Dies.*

DEMETRIUS: No die, but an ace, for him; for he is but one.

LYSANDER: Less than an ace, man; for he is dead; he is nothing.

THESEUS: With the help of a surgeon he might yet recover, and prove an ass.

HIPPOLYTA: How chance Moonshine is gone before Thisbe comes back and finds her lover?

THESEUS: She will find him by starlight. Here she comes; and her passion ends the play.

Re-enter Thisbe.

HIPPOLYTA: Methinks she should not use a long one for such a Pyramus: I hope she will be brief.

DEMETRIUS: A mote will turn the balance, which Pyramus, which Thisbe, is the better; he for a man, God warrant us; she for a woman, God bless us.

LYSANDER: She hath spied him already with those sweet eyes.

DEMETRIUS: And thus she means, videlicet:—

THISBE: Asleep, my love?
    What, dead, my dove?
O Pyramus, arise?
    Speak, speak. Quite dumb?
    Dead, dead? A tomb
Must cover thy sweet eyes.
    These lily lips.
    This cherry nose,
These yellow cowslip cheeks,
    Are gone, are gone:
    Lovers, make moan:
His eyes were green as leeks.
    O Sisters Three,
    Come, come to me,
With hands as pale as milk;
    Lay them in gore,
    Since you have shore
With shears his thread of silk.
    Tongue, not a word:
    Come, trusty sword;

Come, blade, my breast imbrue: [*Stabs herself.*
    And, farewell, friends;
    Thus Thisby ends:
Adieu, adieu, adieu.   [*Dies.*

THESEUS: Moonshine and Lion are left to bury the dead.

DEMETRIUS: Ay, and Wall too.

BOTTOM: [*Starting up*] No, I assure you; the wall is down that parted their fathers. Will it please you to see the epilogue, or to hear a Bergomask dance between two of our company?

THESEUS: No epilogue, I pray you; for your play needs no excuse. Never excuse; for when the players are all dead, there need none to be blamed. Marry, if he that writ it had played Pyramus and hanged himself in Thisbe's garter, it would have been a fine tragedy: and so it is, truly; and very notably discharged. But, come, your Bergomask; let your epilogue alone.   [*A dance.*
The iron tongue of midnight hath told twelve;
Lovers, to bed; 'tis almost fairy time.
I fear we shall out-sleep the coming morn
As much as we this night have overwatch'd.
This palpable-gross play hath well beguiled
The heavy gait of night. Sweet friends, to bed.
A fortnight hold we this solemnity,
In nightly revels and new jollity.   [*Exeunt.*

Enter Puck.

PUCK: Now the hungry lion roars,
    And the wolf behowls the moon;
Whilst the heavy ploughman snores,
    All with weary task fordone.
Now the wasted brands do glow,
    Whilst the screech-owl, screeching loud,
Puts the wretch that lies in woe
    In remembrance of a shroud.
Now it is the time of night
    That the graves all gaping wide,

Every one lets forth his sprite,
    In the church-way paths to glide:
And we fairies, that do run
    By the triple Hecate's team,
From the presence of the sun,
    Following darkness like a dream,
Now are frolic: not a mouse
Shall disturb this hallow'd house:
I am sent with broom before,
To sweep the dust behind the door.

Enter Oberon and Titania with their train.

OBERON: Through the house give glimmering light,
    By the dead and drowsy fire:
Every elf and fairy sprite
    Hop as light as bird from brier;
And this ditty, after me,
Sing, and dance it trippingly.
TITANIA: First, rehearse your song by rote,
    To each word a warbling note:
Hand in hand, with fairy grace,
Will we sing, and bless this place.   *[Song and dance.*
OBERON: Now, until the break of day,
    Through this house each fairy stray.
To the best bride-bed will we,
    Which by us shall blessed be;
And the issue there create
    Ever shall be fortunate.
So shall all the couples three
    Ever true in loving be;
And the blots of Nature's hand
    Shall not in their issue stand;
Never mole, hare lip, nor scar,
    Nor mark prodigious, such as are
Despised in nativity.

Shall upon their children be.
    With this field-dew consecrate,
Every fairy take his gait;
And each several chamber bless,
Through this palace, with sweet peace;
And the owner of it blest
Ever shall in safety rest.
Trip away; make no stay;
Meet me all by break of day.

                           [Exeunt Oberon, Titania, and train.

PUCK: If we shadows have offended,
Think but this, and all is mended,
That you have but slumber'd here
While these visions did appear.
And this weak and idle theme,
No more yielding but a dream,
Gentles, do not reprehend:
If you pardon, we will mend:
And, as I am an honest Puck,
If we have unearned luck
Now to 'scape the serpent's tongue,
We will make amends ere long;
Else the Puck a liar call:
So, good night unto you all.
Give me your hands, if we be friends,
And Robin shall restore amends.   *[Exit.*

• • •

MUCH ADO ABOUT NOTHING

DRAMATIS PERSONÆ

DON PEDRO, prince of Arragon.
DON JOHN, his bastard brother.
CLAUDIO, a young lord of
    Florence.
BENEDICK, a young lord of
    Padua.
LEONATO, governor of Messina.
ANTONIO, his brother.
BALTHASAR, attendant of Don
    Pedro.
CONRADE, ⎫ followers of
BORACHIO, ⎭ Don John.
FRIAR FRANCIS.

DOGBERRY, a constable.
VERGES, a headborough.
A Sexton.
A Boy.
HERO, daughter to Leonato.
BEATRICE, niece to Leonato.
MARGARET, ⎫ gentlewomen
URSULA,   ⎭ attending on Hero.
Messengers, Watch, Atten-
    dants, &c.

SCENE:
Messina.

ACT I.

SCENE I. *Before Leonato's house.*
Enter Leonato, Hero, and Beatrice, with a Messenger.

LEONATO: I learn in this letter that Don Peter of Arragon comes this night to Messina.

MESSENGER: He is very near by this: he was not three leagues off when I left him.

LEONATO: How many gentlemen have you lost in this action?

MESSENGER: But few of any sort, and none of name.

LEONATO: A victory is twice itself when the achiever brings home full numbers. I find here that Don Peter hath bestowed much honour on a young Florentine called Claudio.

MESSENGER: Much deserved on his part and equally remembered by Don Pedro; he hath borne himself beyond the promise of his age, doing, in the figure of a lamb, the feats of a lion: he hath indeed better bettered expectation than you must expect of me to tell you how.

LEONATO: He hath an uncle here in Messina will be very much glad of it.

MESSENGER: I have already delivered him letters, and there appears much joy in him; even so much that joy could not show itself modest enough without a badge of bitterness.

LEONATO: Did he break out into tears?

MESSENGER: In great measure.

LEONATO: A kind overflow of kindness: there are no faces truer than those that are so washed. How much better is it to weep at joy than to joy at weeping!

BEATRICE: I pray you, is Signior Mountanto returned from the wars or no?

MESSENGER: I know none of that name, lady: there was none such in the army of any sort.

LEONATO: What is he that you ask for, niece?

HERO: My cousin means Signior Benedick of Padua.

MESSENGER: O, he's returned; and as pleasant as ever he was.

BEATRICE: He set up his bills here in Messina and challenged Cupid at the flight; and my uncle's fool, reading the challenge, subscribed for Cupid, and challenged him at the bird-bolt. I pray you, how many hath he killed and eaten in these wars? But how many hath he killed? for indeed I promised to eat all of his killing.

LEONATO: Faith, niece, you tax Signior Benedick too much; but he'll be meet with you, I doubt it not.

MESSENGER: He hath done good service, lady, in these wars.

BEATRICE: You had musty victual, and he hath holp to eat it: he is a very valiant trencherman; he hath an excellent stomach.

MESSENGER: And a good soldier too, lady.

BEATRICE: And a good soldier to a lady: but what is he to a lord?

MESSENGER: A lord to a lord, a man to a man; stuffed with all honourable virtues.

BEATRICE: It is so, indeed; he is no less than a stuffed man: but for the stuffing,—well, we are all mortal.

LEONATO: You must not, sir, mistake my niece. There is a kind of merry war betwixt Signior Benedick and her: they never meet but there's a skirmish of wit between them.

BEATRICE: Alas! he gets nothing by that. In our last conflict four of his five wits went halting off, and now is the whole man governed with one: so that if he have wit enough to keep himself warm, let him bear it for a difference between himself and his horse; for it is all the wealth that he hath left, to be known a reasonable creature. Who is his companion now? He hath every month a new sworn brother.

MESSENGER: Is't possible?

BEATRICE: Very easily possible: he wears his faith but as the fashion of his hat; it ever changes with the next block.

MESSENGER: I see, lady, the gentleman is not in your books.

BEATRICE: No; an he were, I would burn my study. But, I pray you, who is his companion? Is there no young squarer now that will make a voyage with him to the devil?

MESSENGER: He is most in the company of the right noble Claudio.

BEATRICE: O Lord, he will hang upon him like a disease: he is sooner caught than the pestilence, and the taker runs presently mad. God help the noble Claudio! if he have caught the Benedick, it will cost him a thousand pound ere a' be cured.

MESSENGER: I will hold friends with you, lady.

BEATRICE: Do, good friend.

LEONATO: You will never run mad, niece.

BEATRICE: No, not till a hot January.

MESSENGER: Don Pedro is approached.

Enter Don Pedro, Don John, Claudio, Benedick, and Balthasar.

DON PEDRO: Good Signior Leonato, you are come to meet your trouble: the fashion of the world is to avoid cost, and you encounter it.

LEONATO: Never came trouble to my house in the likeness of your grace: for trouble being gone, comfort should remain; but when you depart from me, sorrow abides and happiness takes his leave.

DON PEDRO: You embrace your charge too willingly. I think this is your daughter.

LEONATO: Her mother hath many times told me so.

BENEDICK: Were you in doubt, sir, that you asked her?

LEONATO: Signior Benedick, no; for then were you a child.

DON PEDRO: You have it full, Benedick: we may guess by this what you are, being a man. Truly, the lady fathers herself. Be happy, lady; for you are like an honourable father.

BENEDICK: If Signior Leonato be her father, she would not have his head on her shoulders for all Messina, as like him as she is.

BEATRICE: I wonder that you will still be talking, Signior Benedick: nobody marks you.

BENEDICK: What, my dear Lady Disdain! are you yet living?

BEATRICE: Is it possible disdain should die while she hath such meet food to feed it as Signior Benedick? Courtesy itself must convert to disdain, if you come in her presence.

BENEDICK: Then is courtesy a turncoat. But it is certain I am loved of all ladies, only you excepted: and I would I could find in my heart that I had not a hard heart; for, truly, I love none.

BEATRICE: A dear happiness to women: they would else have been troubled with a pernicious suitor. I thank God and my cold blood, I am of your humour for that: I had rather hear my dog bark at a crow than a man swear he loves me.

BENEDICK: God keep your ladyship still in that mind! so some gentleman or other shall 'scape a predestinate scratched face.

BEATRICE: Scratching could not make it worse, an 'twere such a face as yours were.

BENEDICK: Well, you are a rare parrot-teacher.

BEATRICE: A bird of my tongue is better than a beast of yours.

BENEDICK: I would my horse had the speed of your tongue, and so good a continuer. But keep your way, i' God's name; I have done.

BEATRICE: You always end with a jade's trick: I know you of old.

DON PEDRO: That is the sum of all, Leonato. Signior Claudio and Signior Benedick, my dear friend Leonato hath invited you all. I tell him we shall stay here at the least a month; and he heartily prays some occasion may detain us longer. I dare swear he is no hypocrite, but prays from his heart.

LEONATO: If you swear, my lord, you shall not be forsworn. [*To Don John*] Let me bid you welcome, my lord: being reconciled to the prince your brother, I owe you all duty.

DON JOHN: I thank you: I am not of many words, but I thank you.

LEONATO: Please it your grace lead on?

DON PEDRO: Your hand, Leonato; we will go together.

[*Exeunt all except Benedick and Claudio.*

CLAUDIO: Benedick, didst thou note the daughter of Signior Leonato?

BENEDICK: I noted her not; but I looked on her.

CLAUDIO: Is she not a modest young lady?

BENEDICK: Do you question me, as an honest man should do, for my simple true judgement; or would you have me speak after my custom, as being a professed tyrant to their sex?

CLAUDIO: No; I pray thee speak in sober judgement.

BENEDICK: Why, i' faith, methinks she's too low for a high praise, too brown for a fair praise and too little for a great praise: only this commendation I can afford her, that were she other than she is, she were unhandsome; and being no other but as she is, I do not like her.

CLAUDIO: Thou thinkest I am in sport: I pray thee tell me truly how thou likest her.

BENEDICK: Would you buy her, that you inquire after her?

CLAUDIO: Can the world buy such a jewel?

BENEDICK: Yea, and a case to put it into. But speak you this with a sad brow? or do you play the flouting Jack, to tell us Cupid is a good hare-finder and Vulcan a rare carpenter? Come, in what key shall a man take you, to go in the song?

CLAUDIO: In mine eye she is the sweetest lady that ever I looked on.

BENEDICK: I can see yet without spectacles and I see no such matter: there's her cousin, an she were not possessed with a fury, exceeds her as much in beauty as the first of May doth the last of December. But I hope you have no intent to turn husband, have you?

CLAUDIO: I would scarce trust myself, though I had sworn the contrary, if Hero would be my wife.

BENEDICK: Is't come to this? In faith, hath not the world one man but he will wear his cap with suspicion? Shall I never see a bachelor of threescore again? Go to, i' faith; an thou wilt needs thrust thy neck into a yoke, wear the print of it and sigh away Sundays. Look; Don Pedro is returned to seek you.

Re-enter Don Pedro.

DON PEDRO: What secret hath held you here, that you followed not to Leonato's?

BENEDICK: I would your grace would constrain me to tell.

DON PEDRO: I charge thee on thy allegiance.

BENEDICK: You hear, Count Claudio: I can be secret as a dumb man; I would have you think so; but, on my allegiance, mark you this, on my allegiance. He is in love. With who? now that is your grace's part. Mark how short his answer is;—With Hero, Leonato's short daughter.

CLAUDIO: If this were so, so were it uttered.

BENEDICK: Like the old tale, my lord: It is not so, nor 'twas not so, but indeed, God forbid it should be so,

CLAUDIO: If my passion change not shortly, God forbid it should be otherwise.

DON PEDRO: Amen, if you love her; for the lady is very well worthy.

CLAUDIO: You speak this to fetch me in, my lord.

DON PEDRO: By my troth, I speak my thought.

CLAUDIO: And, in faith, my lord, I spoke mine.

BENEDICK: And, by my two faiths and troths, my lord, I spoke mine.

CLAUDIO: That I love her, I feel.

DON PEDRO: That she is worthy, I know.

BENEDICK: That I neither feel how she should be loved nor

know how she should be worthy, is the opinion that fire cannot melt out of me: I will die in it at the stake.

DON PEDRO: Thou wast ever an obstinate heretic in the despite of beauty.

CLAUDIO: And never could maintain his part but in the force of his will.

BENEDICK: That a woman conceived me, I thank her; that she brought me up, I likewise give her most humble thanks: but that I will have a recheat winded in my forehead, or hang my bugle in an invisible baldrick, all women shall pardon me. Because I will not do them the wrong to mistrust any, I will do myself the right to trust none; and the fine is, for the which I may go the finer, I will live a bachelor.

DON PEDRO: I shall see thee, ere I die, look pale with love.

BENEDICK: With anger, with sickness, or with hunger, my lord, not with love: prove that ever I lose more blood with love than I will get again with drinking, pick out mine eye with a ballad-maker's pen and hang me up at the door of a brother-house for the sign of blind Cupid.

DON PEDRO: Well, if ever thou dost fall from this faith, thou wilt prove a notable argument.

BENEDICK: If I do, hang me in a bottle like a cat and shoot at me; and he that hits me, let him be clapped on the shoulder, and called Adam.

DON PEDRO: Well, as time shall try:
'In time the savage bull doth bear the yoke.'

BENEDICK: The savage bull may; but if ever the sensible Benedick bear it, pluck off the bull's horns and set them in my forehead: and let me be vilely painted, and in such great letters as they write 'Here is a good horse to hire,' let them signify under my sign 'Here you may see Benedick the married man.'

CLAUDIO: If this should ever happen, thou wouldst be horn-mad.

DON PEDRO: Nay, if Cupid have not spent all his quiver in Venice, thou wilt quake for this shortly.

BENEDICK: I look for an earthquake too, then.

DON PEDRO: Well, you will temporize with the hours. In the meantime, good Signior Benedick, repair to Leonato's: commend me to him and tell him I will not fail him at supper; for indeed he hath made great preparation.

BENEDICK: I have almost matter enough in me for such an embassage; and so I commit you—

CLAUDIO: To the tuition of God: From my house, if I had it,—

DON PEDRO: The sixth of July: Your loving friend, Benedick.

BENEDICK: Nay, mock not, mock not. The body of your discourse is sometime guarded with fragments, and the guards are but slightly basted on neither: ere you flout old ends any further, examine your conscience: and so I leave you.   [Exit.

CLAUDIO: My liege, your highness now may do me good.

DON PEDRO: My love is thine to teach: teach it but how,
And thou shalt see how apt it is to learn
Any hard lesson that may do thee good.

CLAUDIO: Hath Leonato any son, my lord?

DON PEDRO: No child but Hero; she's his only heir.
Dost thou affect her, Claudio?

CLAUDIO: O, my lord,
When you went onward on this ended action,
I look'd upon her with a soldier's eye,
That liked, but had a rougher task in hand
Than to drive liking to the name of love:
But now I am return'd and that war-thoughts
Have left their places vacant, in their rooms
Come thronging soft and delicate desires,
All prompting me how fair young Hero is,
Saying, I liked her ere I went to wars.

DON PEDRO: Thou wilt be like a lover presently
And tire the hearer with a book of words.
If thou dost love fair Hero, cherish it,
And I will break with her and with her father
And thou shalt have her. Was't not to this end

That thou began'st to twist so fine a story?

CLAUDIO: How sweetly you do minister to love,
That know love's grief by his complexion!
But lest my liking might too sudden seem,
I would have salved it with a longer treatise.

DON PEDRO: What need the bridge much broader than the
    flood?
The fairest grant is the necessity.
Look, what will serve is fit; 'tis once, thou lovest,
And I will fit thee with the remedy.
I know we shall have revelling to-night:
I will assume thy part in some disguise
And tell fair Hero I am Claudio,
And in her bosom I'll unclasp my heart
And take her hearing prisoner with the force
And strong encounter of my amorous tale;
Then after to her father will I break;
And the conclusion is, she shall be thine.
In practice let us put it presently.   [Exeunt.

SCENE II. *A room in Leonato's house.*
Enter Leonato and Antonio, meeting.

LEONATO: How now, brother! Where is my cousin, your son?
hath he provided this music?

ANTONIO: He is very busy about it. But, brother, I can tell you
strange news that you yet dreamt not of.

LEONATO: Are they good?

ANTONIO: As the event stamps them: but they have a good
cover; they show well outward. The prince and Count Claudio,
walking in a thick-pleached alley in mine orchard, were thus much
overheard by a man of mine: the prince discovered to Claudio that
he loved my niece your daughter and meant to acknowledge it this
night in a dance; and if he found her accordant, he meant to take
the present time by the top and instantly break with you of it.

LEONATO: Hath the fellow any wit that told you this?

ANTONIO: A good sharp fellow: I will send for him; and question him yourself.

LEONATO: No, no; we will hold it as a dream till it appear itself; but I will acquaint my daughter withal, that she may be the better prepared for an answer, if peradventure this be true. Go you and tell her of it. [*Enter attendants.*] Cousins, you know what you have to do. O, I cry you mercy, friend; go you with me, and I will use your skill. Good cousin, have a care this busy time.   [*Exeunt.*

SCENE III. *The same.*
Enter Don John and Conrade.

CONRADE: What the good-year, my lord! why are you thus out of measure sad?

DON JOHN: There is no measure in the occasion that breeds; therefore the sadness is without limit.

CONRADE: You should hear reason.

DON JOHN: And when I have heard it, what blessing brings it?

CONRADE: If not a present remedy, at least a patient sufferance.

DON JOHN: I wonder that thou, being, as thou sayest thou art, born under Saturn, goest about to apply a moral medicine to a mortifying mischief. I cannot hide what I am: I must be sad when I have cause and smile at no man's jests, eat when I have stomach and wait for no man's leisure, sleep when I am drowsy and tend on no man's business, laugh when I am merry and claw no man in his humour.

CONRADE: Yea, but you must not make the full show of this till you may do it without controlment. You have of late stood out against your brother, and he hath ta'en you newly into his grace; where it is impossible you should take true root but by the fair weather that you make yourself: it is needful that you frame the season for your own harvest.

DON JOHN: I had rather be a canker in a hedge than a rose in his grace, and it better fits my flood to be disdained of all than to fashion a carriage to rob love from any: in this, though I cannot be said to be a flattering honest man, it must not be denied but I am a plain-dealing villain. I am trusted with a muzzle and enfranchised with a clog; therefore I have decreed not to sing in my cage. If I had my mouth, I would bite; if I had my liberty, I would do my liking: in the meantime let me be that I am and seek not to alter me.

CONRADE: Can you make no use of your discontent?

DON JOHN: I make all use of it, for I use it only. Who comes here?

Enter Borachio.

What news, Borachio?

BORACHIO: I came yonder from a great supper: the prince your brother is royally entertained by Leonato; and I can give you intelligence of an intended marriage.

DON JOHN: Will it serve for any model to build mischief on? What is he for a fool that betroths himself to unquietness?

BORACHIO: Marry, it is your brother's right hand.

DON JOHN: Who? the most exquisite Claudio?

BORACHIO: Even he.

DON JOHN: A proper squire! And who, and who? which way looks he?

BORACHIO: Marry on Hero, the daughter and heir of Leonato.

DON JOHN: A very forward March-chick! How came you to this?

BORACHIO: Being entertained for a perfumer, as I was smoking a musty room, comes me the prince and Claudio, hand in hand, in sad conference: I whipt me behind the arras; and there heard it agreed upon that the prince should woo Hero for himself, and having obtained her, give her to Count Claudio.

DON JOHN: Come, come, let us thither; this may prove food to my displeasure. That young start-up hath all the glory of my overthrow: if I can cross him any way, I bless myself every way. You are both sure, and will assist me?

CONRADE: To the death, my lord.

DON JOHN: Let us to the great supper: their cheer is the greater that I am subdued. Would the cook were of my mind! Shall we go prove what's to be done?

BORACHIO: We'll wait upon your lordship. [*Exeunt.*

ACT II.

SCENE I. *A hall in Leonato's house.*
Enter Leonato, Antonio, Hero, Beatrice, and others.

LEONATO: Was not Count John here at supper?

ANTONIO: I saw him not.

BEATRICE: How tartly that gentleman looks! I never can see him but I am heart-burned an hour after.

HERO: He is of a very melancholy disposition.

BEATRICE: He were an excellent man that were made just in the midway between him and Benedick: the one is too like an image and says nothing, and the other too like my lady's eldest son, evermore tattling.

LEONATO: Then half Signior Benedick's tongue in Count John's mouth, and half Count John's melancholy in Signior Benedick's face,—

BEATRICE: With a good leg and a good foot, uncle, and money enough in his purse, such a man would win any woman in the world, if a' could get her good-will.

LEONATO: By my troth, niece, thou wilt never get thee a husband, if thou be so shrewd of thy tongue.

ANTONIO: In faith, she's too curst.

BEATRICE: Too curst is more than curst: I shall lessen God's sending that way; for it is said, 'God sends a curst cow short horns;' but to a cow too curst he sends none.

LEONATO: So, by being too curst, God will send you no horns.

BEATRICE: Just, if he send me no husband; for the which blessing I am at him upon my knees every morning and evening. Lord,

I could not endure a husband with a beard on his face: I had rather lie in the woollen.

LEONATO: You may light on a husband that hath no beard.

BEATRICE: What should I do with him? dress him in my apparel and make him my waiting-gentlewoman? He that hath a beard is more than a youth, and he that hath no beard is less than a man: and he that is more than a youth is not for me, and he that is less than a man, I am not for him: therefore I will even take sixpence in earnest of the bear-ward, and lead his apes into hell.

LEONATO: Well, then, go you into hell?

BEATRICE: No, but to the gate; and there will the devil meet me, like an old cuckold, with horns on his head, and say 'Get you to heaven, for Beatrice, get you to heaven; here's no place for you maids:' so deliver I up my apes, and away to Saint Peter for the heavens; he shows me where the bachelors sit, and there live we as merry as the day is long.

ANTONIO: [*To Hero*] Well, niece, I trust you will be ruled by your father.

BEATRICE: Yes, faith; it is my cousin's duty to make curtsy and say, 'Father, as it please you.' But yet for all that, cousin, let him be a handsome fellow, or else make another curtsy and say, 'Father, as it please me.'

LEONATO: Well, niece, I hope to see you one day fitted with a husband.

BEATRICE: Not till God make men of some other metal than earth. Would it not grieve a woman to be overmastered with a piece of valiant dust? to make an account of her life to a clod of wayward marl? No, uncle, I'll none: Adam's sons are my brethren; and, truly, I hold it a sin to match in my kindred.

LEONATO: Daughter, remember what I told you: if the prince do solicit you in that kind, you know your answer.

BEATRICE: The fault will be in the music, cousin, if you be not wooed in good time: if the prince be too important, tell him there is measure in every thing and so dance out the answer. For, hear me, Hero: wooing, wedding, and repenting, is as a Scotch jig, a

measure, and a cinque pace: the first suit is hot and hasty, like a
Scotch jig, and full as fantastical; the wedding, mannerly-modest,
as a measure, full of state and ancientry; and then comes repentance and, with his bad legs, falls into the cinque pace faster and
faster, till he sink into his grave.

LEONATO: Cousin, you apprehend passing shrewdly.

BEATRICE: I have a good eye, uncle; I can see a church by daylight.

LEONATO: The revellers are entering, brother: make good room.
                                                [*All put on their masks.*

*Enter Don Pedro, Claudio, Benedick, Balthasar, Don John, Borachio,
Margaret, Ursula, and others, masked.*

DON PEDRO: Lady, will you walk about with your friend?

HERO: So you walk softly and look sweetly and say nothing, I
am yours for the walk; and especially when I walk away.

DON PEDRO: With me in your company?

HERO: I may say so, when I please.

DON PEDRO: And when please you to say so?

HERO: When I like your favour; for God defend the lute should
be like the case!

DON PEDRO: My visor is Philemon's roof; within the house is
Jove.

HERO: Why, then, your visor should be thatched.

DON PEDRO: Speak low, if you speak love.   [*Drawing her aside.*

BALTHASAR: Well, I would you did like me.

MARGARET: So would not I, for your own sake; for I have many
ill qualities.

BALTHASAR: Which is one?

MARGARET: I say my prayers aloud.

BALTHASAR: I love you the better: the hearers may cry, Amen.

MARGARET: God match me with a good dancer!

BALTHASAR: Amen.

MARGARET: And God keep him out of my sight when the dance
is done! Answer, clerk.

BALTHASAR: No more words: the clerk is answered.

URSULA: I know you well enough; you are Signior Antonio.

ANTONIO: At a word, I am not.

URSULA: I know you by the waggling of your head.

ANTONIO: To tell you true, I counterfeit him.

URSULA: You could never do him so ill-well, unless you were the very man. Here's his dry hand up and down: you are he, you are he.

ANTONIO: At a word, I am not.

URSULA: Come, come, do you think I do not know you by your excellent wit? can virtue hide itself? Go to, mum, you are he: graces will appear, and there's an end.

BEATRICE: Will you not tell me who told you so?

BENEDICK: No, you shall pardon me.

BEATRICE: Nor will you tell me who you are?

BENEDICK: Not now.

BEATRICE: That I was disdainful, and that I had my good wit out of the 'Hundred Merry Tales:'—well, this was Signior Bene-dick that said so.

BENEDICK: What's he?

BEATRICE: I am sure you know him well enough.

BENEDICK: Not I, believe me.

BEATRICE: Did he never make you laugh?

BENEDICK: I pray you, what is he?

BEATRICE: Why, he is the prince's jester; a very dull fool; only his gift is in devising impossible slanders: none but libertines delight in him; and the commendation is not in his wit, but in his villany; for he both pleases men and angers them, and then they laugh at him and beat him. I am sure he is in the fleet: I would he had boarded me.

BENEDICK: When I know the gentleman, I'll tell him what you say.

BEATRICE: Do, do: he'll but break a comparison or two on me; which, peradventure not marked or not laughed at, strikes him into melancholy; and then there's a partridge wing saved, for the fool will eat no supper that night. [*Music.*] We must follow the leaders.

BENEDICK: In every good thing.

BEATRICE: Nay, if they lead to any ill, I will leave them at the next turning.   [*Dance. Then exeunt all except Don John, Borachio, and Claudio.*

DON JOHN: Sure my brother is amorous on Hero and hath withdrawn her father to break with him about it. The ladies follow her and but one visor remains.

BORACHIO: And that is Claudio: I know him by his bearing.

DON JOHN: Are not you Signior Benedick?

CLAUDIO: You know me well; I am he.

DON JOHN: Signior, you are very near my brother in his love: he is enamoured on Hero; I pray you, dissuade him from her: she is no equal for his birth: you may do the part of an honest man in it.

CLAUDIO: How know you he loves her?

DON JOHN: I heard him swear his affection.

BORACHIO: So did I too; and he swore he would marry her to-night.

DON JOHN: Come, let us to the banquet.

   [*Exeunt Don John and Borachio.*

CLAUDIO: Thus answer I in name of Benedick,
But hear these ill news with the ears of Claudio.
'Tis certain so; the prince wooes for himself.
Friendship is constant in all other things
Save in the office and affairs of love:
Therefore all hearts in love use their own tongues;
Let every eye negotiate for itself
And trust no agent; for beauty is a witch
Against whose charms faith melteth into blood.
This is an accident of hourly proof,
Which I mistrusted not. Farewell, therefore, Hero!

Re-enter Benedick.

BENEDICK: Count Claudio?

CLAUDIO: Yea, the same.

BENEDICK: Come, will you go with me?

CLAUDIO: Whither?

BENEDICK: Even to the next willow, about your own business, county. What fashion will you wear the garland of? about your neck, like an usurer's chain? or under your arm, like a lieutenant's scarf? You must wear it one way, for the prince hath got your Hero.

CLAUDIO: I wish him joy of her.

BENEDICK: Why, that's spoken like an honest drovier! so they sell bullocks. But did you think the prince would have served you thus?

CLAUDIO: I pray you, leave me.

BENEDICK: Ho! now you strike like the blind man: 'twas the boy that stole your meat, and you'll beat the post.

CLAUDIO: If it will not be, I'll leave you.   [*Exit.*

BENEDICK: Alas, poor hurt fowl! now will he creep into sedges. But that my Lady Beatrice should know me, and not know me! The prince's fool! Ha? It may be I go under that title because I am merry. Yea, but so I am apt to do myself wrong; I am not so reputed: it is the base, though bitter, disposition of Beatrice that puts the world into her person, and so gives me out. Well, I'll be revenged as I may.

Re-enter Don Pedro.

DON PEDRO: Now, signior, where's the count? did you see him?

BENEDICK: Troth, my lord, I have played the part of Lady Fame. I found him here as melancholy as a lodge in a warren: I told him, and I think I told him true, that your grace had got the good will of this young lady; and I offered him my company to a willow-tree, either to make him a garland, as being forsaken, or to bind him up a rod, as being worthy to be whipped.

DON PEDRO: To be whipped! What's his fault?

BENEDICK: The flat transgression of a school-boy, who, being overjoyed with finding a birds' nest, shows it his companion, and he steals it.

DON PEDRO: Wilt thou make a trust a transgression? The transgression is in the stealer.

BENEDICK: Yet it had not been amiss the rod had been made, and the garland too; for the garland he might have worn himself, and the rod he might have bestowed on you, who, as I take it, have stolen his birds' nest.

DON PEDRO: I will but teach them to sing, and restore them to the owner.

BENEDICK: If their singing answer your saying, by my faith, you say honestly.

DON PEDRO: The Lady Beatrice hath a quarrel to you: the gentleman that danced with her told her she is much wronged by you.

BENEDICK: O, she misused me past the endurance of a block! an oak but with one green leaf on it would have answered her; my very visor began to assume life and scold with her. She told me, not thinking I had been myself, that I was the prince's jester, that I was duller than a great thaw; huddling jest upon jest with such impossible conveyance upon me that I stood like a man at a mark, with a whole army shooting at me. She speaks poniards, and every word stabs: if her breath were as terrible as her terminations, there were no living near her; she would infect to the north star. I would not marry her, though she were endowed with all that Adam had left him before he transgressed: she would have made Hercules have turned spit, yea, and have cleft his club to make the fire too. Come, talk not of her: you shall find her the infernal Ate in good apparel. I would to God some scholar would conjure her; for certainly, while she is here, a man may live as quiet in hell as in a sanctuary; and people sin upon purpose, because they would go thither; so, indeed, all disquiet, horror and perturbation follows her.

DON PEDRO: Look, here she comes.

Re-enter Claudio, Beatrice, Hero, and Leonato.

BENEDICK: Will your grace command me any service to the world's end? I will go on the slightest errand now to the

Antipodes that you can devise to send me on; I will fetch you a toothpicker now from the furthest inch of Asia, bring you the length of Prester John's foot, fetch you a hair off the great Cham's beard, do you any embassage to the Pigmies, rather than hold three words' conference with this harpy. You have no employment for me?

DON PEDRO: None, but to desire your good company.

BENEDICK: O God, sir, here's a dish I love not: I cannot endure my Lady Tongue.　　　　　　　　　　　　　　　　　　[Exit.

DON PEDRO: Come, lady, come; you have lost the heart of Signior Benedick.

BEATRICE: Indeed, my lord, he lent it me awhile; and I gave him use for it, a double heart for his single one: marry, once before he won it of me with false dice, therefore your grace may well say I have lost it.

DON PEDRO: You have put him down, lady, you have put him down.

BEATRICE: So I would not he should do me, my lord, lest I should prove the mother of fools. I have brought Count Claudio, whom you sent me to seek.

DON PEDRO: Why, how now, count! wherefore are you sad?

CLAUDIO: Not sad, my lord.

DON PEDRO: How then? sick?

CLAUDIO: Neither, my lord.

BEATRICE: The count is neither sad, nor sick, nor merry, nor well; but civil count, civil as an orange, and something of that jealous complexion.

DON PEDRO: I' faith, lady, I think your blazon to be true; though, I'll be sworn, if he be so, his conceit is false. Here, Claudio, I have wooed in thy name, and fair Hero is won: I have broke with her father, and his good will obtained: name the day of marriage, and God give thee joy!

LEONATO: Count, take of me my daughter, and with her my fortunes: his grace hath made the match, and all grace say Amen to it.

BEATRICE: Speak, count, 'tis your cue.

CLAUDIO: Silence is the perfectest herald of joy: I were but little happy, if I could say how much. Lady, as you are mine, I am yours: I give away myself for you and dote upon the exchange.

BEATRICE: Speak, cousin; or, if you cannot, stop his mouth with a kiss, and let not him speak neither.

DON PEDRO: In faith, lady, you have a merry heart.

BEATRICE: Yea, my lord; I thank it, poor fool, it keeps on the windy side of care. My cousin tells him in his ear that he is in her heart.

CLAUDIO: And so she doth, cousin.

BEATRICE: Good Lord, for alliance! Thus goes every one to the world but I, and I am sunburnt; I may sit in a corner and cry heigh-ho for a husband!

DON PEDRO: Lady Beatrice, I will get you one.

BEATRICE: I would rather have one of your father's getting. Hath your grace ne'er a brother like you? Your father got excellent husbands, if a maid could come by them.

DON PEDRO: Will you have me, lady?

BEATRICE: No, my lord, unless I might have another for working-days: your grace is too costly to wear every day. But, I beseech your grace, pardon me: I was born to speak all mirth and no matter.

DON PEDRO: Your silence most offends me, and to be merry best becomes you; for, out of question, you were born in a merry hour.

BEATRICE: No, sure, my lord, my mother cried; but then there was a star danced, and under that was I born. Cousins, God give you joy!

LEONATO: Niece, will you look to those things I told you of?

BEATRICE: I cry you mercy, uncle. By your grace's pardon. [*Exit.*

DON PEDRO: By my troth, a pleasant-spirited lady.

LEONATO: There's little of the melancholy element in her, my lord: she is never sad but when she sleeps, and not ever sad then; for I have heard my daughter say, she hath often dreamed of unhappiness and waked herself with laughing.

Don Pedro: She cannot endure to hear tell of a husband.

Leonato: O, by no means: she mocks all her wooers out of suit.

Don Pedro: She were an excellent wife for Benedick.

Leonato: O lord, my lord, if they were but a week married, they would talk themselves mad.

Don Pedro: County Claudio, when mean you to go to church?

Claudio: To-morrow, my lord, time goes on crutches till love have all his rites.

Leonato: Not till Monday, my dear son, which is hence a just seven-night; and a time too brief, too, to have all things answer my mind.

Don Pedro: Come, you shake the head at so long a breathing: but, I warrant thee, Claudio, the time shall not go dully by us. I will in the interim undertake one of Hercules' labours; which is, to bring Signior Benedick and the Lady Beatrice into a mountain of affection the one with the other. I would fain have it a match, and I doubt not but to fashion it, if you three will but minister such assistance as I shall give you direction.

Leonato: My lord, I am for you, through it cost me ten nights' watchings.

Claudio: And I, my lord.

Don Pedro: And you too, gentle Hero?

Hero: I will do any modest office, my lord, to help my cousin to a good husband.

Don Pedro: And Benedick is not the unhopefullest husband that I know. Thus far can I praise him; he is of a noble strain, of approved valor and confirmed honesty. I will teach you how to humour your cousin, that she shall fall in love with Benedick; and I, with your two helps, will so practise on Benedick, that, in despite of his quick wit and his queasy stomach, he shall fall in love with Beatrice. If we can do this, Cupid is no longer an archer: his glory shall be ours, for we are the only love-gods. Go in with me, and I will tell you my drift.   [*Exeunt*.

SCENE II. *The same.*
Enter Don John and Borachio.

DON JOHN: It is so; the Count Claudio shall marry the daughter of Leonato.

BORACHIO: Yea, my lord; but I can cross it.

DON JOHN: Any bar, any cross, any impediment will be medicinable to me: I am sick in displeasure to him, and whatsoever comes athwart his affection ranges evenly with mine. How canst thou cross this marriage?

BORACHIO: Not honestly, my lord; but so covertly that no dishonesty shall appear in me.

DON JOHN: Show me briefly how.

BORACHIO: I think I told your lordship a year since, how much I am in the favour of Margaret, the waiting gentlewoman to Hero.

DON JOHN: I remember.

BORACHIO: I can, at any unseasonable instant of the night, appoint her to look out at her lady's chamber-window.

DON JOHN: What life is in that, to be the death of this marriage?

BORACHIO: The poison of that lies in you to temper. Go you to the prince your brother; spare not to tell him that he hath wronged his honour in marrying the renowned Claudio—whose estimation do you mightily hold up—to a contaminated stale, such a one as Hero.

DON JOHN: What proof shall I make of that?

BORACHIO: Proof enough to misuse the prince, to vex Claudio, to undo Hero and kill Leonato. Look you for any other issue?

DON JOHN: Only to despite them, I will endeavour any thing.

BORACHIO: Go, then; find me a meet hour to draw Don Pedro and the Count Claudio alone: tell them that you know that Hero loves me; intend a kind of zeal both to the prince and Claudio, as,—in love of your brother's honour, who hath made this match, and his friend's reputation, who is thus like to be cozened with the semblance of a maid,—that you have discovered thus. They will scarcely believe this without trial: offer them instances; which shall bear no less likelihood than to see me at her chamber-window, hear me call Margaret Hero, hear Margaret term me Claudio; and bring them to see this the very night before the intended wedding,—for in the meantime I will so fashion the matter that Hero shall be absent,—and there shall appear such seeming truth of Hero's disloyalty that jealousy shall be called assurance and all the preparation overthrown.

DON JOHN: Grow this to what adverse issue it can, I will put it in practice. Be cunning in the working this, and thy fee is a thousand ducats.

BORACHIO: Be you constant in the accusation, and my cunning shall not shame me.

DON JOHN: I will presently go learn their day of marriage.

[*Exeunt.*

SCENE III. *Leonato's orchard.*
Enter Benedick.

BENEDICK: Boy!

Enter Boy.

BOY: Signior?

BENEDICK: In my chamber-window lies a book: bring it hither to me in the orchard.

Boy: I am here already, sir.

BENEDICK: I know that: but I would have thee hence, and here again. [*Exit Boy.*] I do much wonder that one man, seeing how much another man is a fool when he dedicates his behaviours to love, will, after he hath laughed at such shallow follies in others, become the argument of his own scorn by falling in love: and such a man is Claudio. I have known when there was no music with him but the drum and the fife; and now had he rather hear the tabor and the pipe: I have known when he would have walked ten mile a-foot to see a good armour; and now will he lie ten nights awake, carving the fashion of a new doublet. He was

wont to speak plain and to the purpose, like an honest man and a
soldier; and now is he turned orthography; his words are a very
fantastical banquet, just so many strange dishes. May I be so converted and see with these eyes? I cannot tell; I think not: I will not
be sworn but love may transform me to an oyster; but I'll take my
oath on it, till he have made an oyster of me, he shall never make
me such a fool. One woman is fair, yet I am well; another is wise,
yet I am well; another virtuous, yet I am well; but till all graces be
in one woman, one woman shall not come in my grace. Rich she
shall be, that's certain; wise, or I'll none: virtuous, or I'll never
cheapen her; fair, or I'll never look on her; mild, or come not near
me; noble, or not I for an angel; of good discourse, an excellent
musician, and her hair shall be of what colour it please God. Ha!
the prince and Monsieur Love! I will hide me in the arbour.

                                                    [*Withdraws.*

Enter Don Pedro, Claudio, and Leonato.

DON PEDRO: Come, shall we hear this music?
CLAUDIO: Yea, my good lord. How still the evening is,
As hush'd on purpose to grace harmony!
DON PEDRO: See you where Benedick hath hid himself?
CLAUDIO: O, very well, my lord: the music ended,
We'll fit the kid-fox with a pennyworth.

Enter Balthasar with Music.

DON PEDRO: Come, Balthasar, we'll hear that song again.
BALTHASAR: O, good my lord, tax not so bad a voice
To slander music any more than once.
DON PEDRO: It is the witness still of excellency
To put a strange face on his own perfection.
I pray thee, sing, and let me woo no more.
BALTHASAR: Because you talk of wooing, I will sing;
Since many a wooer doth commence his suit
To her he thinks not worthy, yet he wooes,
Yet will he swear he loves.

DON PEDRO: Now, pray thee, come;
Or, if thou wilt hold longer argument,
Do it in notes.

BALTHASAR: Note this before my notes;
There's not a note of mine that's worth the noting.

DON PEDRO: Why, these are very crotchets that he speaks;
Notes, notes, forsooth, and nothing.   [*Air.*

BENEDICK: Now, divine sir! now is his soul ravished! Is it not strange that sheeps' guts should hale souls out of men's bodies? Well, a horn for my money, when all's done.

THE SONG.

BALTHASAR: Sigh no more, ladies, sigh no more,
       Men were deceivers ever,
     One foot in sea and one on shore,
       To one thing constant never:
   Then sigh not so, but let them go,
       And be you blithe and bonny,
   Converting all your sounds of woe
       Into Hey nonny, nonny.
   Sing no more ditties, sing no moe,
       Of dumps so dull and heavy:
   The fraud of men was ever so,
       Since summer first was leavy:
       Then sigh not so, &c.

DON PEDRO: By my troth, a good song.

BALTHASAR: And an ill singer, my lord.

DON PEDRO: Ha, no, no, faith; thou singest well enough for a shift.

BENEDICK: An he had been a dog that should have howled thus, they would have hanged him; and I pray God his bad voice bode no mischief. I had as lief have heard the night-raven, come what plague could have come after it.

DON PEDRO: Yea, marry, dost thou hear, Balthasar? I pray thee, get us some excellent music; for to-morrow night we would have it at the Lady Hero's chamber-window.

BALTHASAR: The best I can, my lord.

DON PEDRO: Do so; farewell.   [*Exit Balthasar.* Come hither, Leonato. What was it you told me of to-day, that your niece Beatrice was in love with Signior Benedick?

CLAUDIO: O, ay; stalk on, stalk on; the fowl sits. I did never think that lady would have loved any man.

LEONATO: No, nor I neither; but most wonderful that she should so dote on Signior Benedick, whom she hath in all outward behaviours seemed ever to abhor.

BENEDICK: Is't possible? Sits the wind in that corner?

LEONATO: By my troth, my lord, I cannot tell what to think of it but that she loves him, with an enraged affection; it is past the infinite of thought.

DON PEDRO: May be she doth but counterfeit.

CLAUDIO: Faith, like enough.

LEONATO: O God, counterfeit! There was never counterfeit of passion came so near the life of passion as she discovers it.

DON PEDRO: Why, what effects of passion shows she?

CLAUDIO: Bait the hook well; this fish will bite.

LEONATO: What effects, my lord? She will sit you, you heard my daughter tell you how.

CLAUDIO: She did, indeed.

DON PEDRO: How, how, I pray you? you amaze me: I would have thought her spirit had been invincible against all assaults of affection.

LEONATO: I would have sworn it had, my lord; especially against Benedick.

BENEDICK: I should think this is a gull, but that the white-bearded fellow speaks it: knavery cannot, sure, hide himself in such reverence.

CLAUDIO: He hath ta'en the infection: hold it up.

DON PEDRO: Hath she made her affection known to Benedick?

LEONATO: No; and swears she never will: that's her torment.

CLAUDIO: 'Tis true, indeed; so your daughter says: 'Shall I,' says she, 'that have so oft encountered him with scorn, write to him that I love him?'

LEONATO: This says she now when she is beginning to write to him; for she'll be up twenty times a night, and there will she sit in her smock till she have writ a sheet of paper: my daughter tells us all.

CLAUDIO: Now you talk of a sheet of paper, I remember a pretty jest your daughter told us of.

LEONATO: O, when she had writ it and was reading it over, she found Benedick and Beatrice between the sheet?

CLAUDIO: That.

LEONATO: O, she tore the letter into a thousand halfpence; railed at herself, that she should be so immodest to write to one that she knew would flout her: 'I measure him,' says she, 'by my own spirit; for I should flout him, if he writ to me; yea, though I love him, I should.'

CLAUDIO: Then down upon her knees she falls, weeps, sobs, beats her heart, tears her hair, prays, curses; 'O sweet Benedick! God give me patience!'

LEONATO: She doth indeed; my daughter says so: and the ecstasy hath so much overborne her that my daughter is sometime afeard she will do a desperate outrage to herself: it is very true.

DON PEDRO: It were good that Benedick knew of it by some other, if she will not discover it.

CLAUDIO: To what end? He would make but a sport of it and torment the poor lady worse.

DON PEDRO: An he should, it were an alms to hang him. She's an excellent sweet lady; and, out of all suspicion, she is virtuous.

CLAUDIO: And she is exceeding wise.

DON PEDRO: In every thing but in loving Benedick.

LEONATO: O, my lord, wisdom and blood combating in so tender a body, we have ten proofs to one that blood hath the victory. I am sorry for her, as I have just cause, being her uncle and her guardian.

DON PEDRO: I would she had bestowed this dotage on me: I would have daffed all other respects and made her half myself. I pray you, tell Benedick of it, and hear what a' will say.

LEONATO: Were it good, think you?

CLAUDIO: Hero thinks surely she will die; for she says she will die, if he love her not, and she will die, ere she make her love known, and she will die, if he woo her, rather than she will bate one breath of her accustomed crossness.

DON PEDRO: She doth well: if she should make tender of her love, 'tis very possible he'll scorn it; for the man, as you know all, hath a contemptible spirit.

CLAUDIO: He is a very proper man.

DON PEDRO: He hath indeed a good outward happiness.

CLAUDIO: Before God! and, in my mind, very wise.

DON PEDRO: He doth indeed show some sparks that are like wit.

CLAUDIO: And I take him to be valiant.

DON PEDRO: As Hector, I assure you: and in the managing of quarrels you may say he is wise; for either he avoids them with great discretion, or undertakes them with a most Christian-like fear.

LEONATO: If he do fear God, a' must necessarily keep peace: if he break the peace, he ought to enter into a quarrel with fear and trembling.

DON PEDRO: And so will he do; for the man doth fear God, howsoever it seems not in him by some large jests he will make. Well, I am sorry for your niece. Shall we go seek Benedick, and tell him of her love?

CLAUDIO: Never tell him, my lord: let her wear it out with good counsel.

LEONATO: Nay, that's impossible: she may wear her heart out first.

DON PEDRO: Well, we will hear further of it by your daughter: let it cool the while. I love Benedick well; and I could wish he would modestly examine himself, to see how much he is unworthy so good a lady.

LEONATO: My lord, will you walk? dinner is ready.

CLAUDIO: If he do not dote on her upon this, I will never trust my expectation.

DON PEDRO: Let there be the same net spread for her; and that must your daughter and her gentlewoman carry. The sport will be, when they hold one an opinion of another's dotage, and no such matter: that's the scene that I would see, which will be merely a dumb-show. Let us send her to call him in to dinner.

                     [*Exeunt Don Pedro, Claudio, and Leonato.*

BENEDICK: [*Coming forward*] This can be no trick: the conference was sadly borne. They have the truth of this from Hero. They seem to pity the lady: it seems her affections have their full bent. Love me! why, it must be requited. I hear how I am censured: they say I will bear myself proudly, if I perceive the love come from her: they say too that she will rather die than give any sign of affection. I did never think to marry: I must not seem proud: happy are they that hear their detractions and can put them to mending. They say the lady is fair: 'tis a truth, I can bear them witness; and virtuous; 'tis so, I cannot reprove it; and wise, but for loving me; by my troth, it is no addition to her wit, nor no great argument of her folly, for I will be horribly in love with her. I may chance have some odd quirks and remnants of wit broken on me, because I have railed so long against marriage: but doth not the appetite alter? a man loves the meat in his youth that he cannot endure in his age. Shall quips and sentences and these paper bullets of the brain awe a man from the career of his humour? No, the world must be peopled. When I said I would die a bachelor, I did not think I should live till I were married. Here comes Beatrice. By this day! she's a fair lady: I do spy some marks of love in her.

Enter Beatrice.

BEATRICE: Against my will I am sent to bid you come in to dinner.

BENEDICK: Fair Beatrice, I thank you for your pains.

BEATRICE: I took no more pains for those thanks than you take pains to thank me: if it had been painful, I would not have come.

BENEDICK: You take pleasure then in the message?

BEATRICE: Yea, just so much as you may take upon a knife's point and choke a daw withal. You have no stomach, signior: fare you well.   [*Exit.*

BENEDICK: Ha! 'Against my will I am sent to bid you come in to dinner;' there's a double meaning in that. 'I took no more pains for those thanks than you took pains to thank me;' that's as much as to say, Any pains that I take for you is as easy as thanks. If I do not take pity of her, I am a villain; if I do not love her, I am a Jew. I will go get her picture.   [*Exit.*

ACT III.

SCENE I. *Leonato's garden.*
Enter Hero, Margaret, and Ursula.

HERO: Good Margaret, run thee to the parlour;
There shalt thou find my cousin Beatrice
Proposing with the prince and Claudio:
Whisper her ear and tell her, I and Ursula
Walk in the orchard and our whole discourse
Is all of her; say that thou overheard'st us;
And bid her steal into the pleached bower,
Where honeysuckles, ripen'd by the sun,
Forbid the sun to enter, like favorites,
Make proud by princes, that advance their pride
Against that power that bred it: there will she hide her,
To listen our purpose. This is thy office;
Bear thee well in it and leave us alone.

MARGARET: I'll make her come, I warrant you, presently.   [*Exit.*

HERO: Now, Ursula, when Beatrice doth come,
As we do trace this alley up and down,
Our talk must only be of Benedick.
When I do name him, let it be thy part

To praise him more than ever man did merit:
My talk to thee must be how Benedick
Is sick in love with Beatrice. Of this matter
Is little Cupid's crafty arrow made,
That only wounds by hearsay.

Enter Beatrice, behind.

                              Now begin;
For lock where Beatrice, like a lapwing, runs
Close by the ground, to hear our conference.
   URSULA: The pleasant'st angling is to see the fish
Cut with her golden oars the silver stream,
And greedily devour the treacherous bait:
So angle we for Beatrice; who even now
Is couched in the woodbine coverture.
Fear you not my part of the dialogue.
   HERO: Then go we near her, that her ear lose nothing
Of the false sweet bait that we lay for it.   [*Approaching the bower.*
No, truly, Ursula, she is too disdainful;
I know her spirits are as coy and wild
As haggerds of the rock.
   URSULA: But are you sure
That Benedick loves Beatrice so entirely?
   HERO: So says the prince and my new-trothed lord.
   URSULA: And did they bid you tell her of it, madam?
   HERO: They did entreat me to acquaint her of it;
But I persuaded them, if they loved Benedick,
To wish him wrestle with affection,
And never to let Beatrice know of it.
   URSULA: Why did you so? Doth not the gentleman
Deserve as full as fortunate a bed
As ever Beatrice shall couch upon?
   HERO: O god of love! I know he doth deserve
As much as may be yielded to a man:
But nature never framed a woman's heart

Of prouder stuff than that of Beatrice;
Disdain and scorn ride sparkling in her eyes,
Misprising what they look on, and her wit
Values itself so highly that to her
All matter else seems weak: she cannot love,
Nor take no shape nor project of affection,
She is so self-endeared.

    URSULA: Sure. I think so;
And therefore certainly it were not good
She knew his love, lest she make sport at it.

    HERO: Why, you speak truth. I never yet saw man,
How wise, how noble, young, how rarely featured,
But she would spell him backward: if fair-faced,
She would swear the gentleman should be her sister;
If black, why, Nature, drawing of an antique,
Made a foul blot; if tall, a lance ill-headed;
If low, an agate very vilely cut;
If speaking, why, a vane blown with all winds;
If silent, why, a block moved with none.
So turns she every man the wrong side out
And never gives to truth and virtue that
Which simpleness and merit purchaseth.

    URSULA: Sure, sure, such carping is not commendable.

    HERO: No, not to be so odd and from all fashions
As Beatrice is, cannot be commendable:
But who dare tell her so? If I should speak,
She would mock me into air: O, she would laugh me
Out of myself, press me to death with wit.
Therefore let Benedick, like cover'd fire,
Consume away in sighs, waste inwardly:
It were a better death than die with mocks,
Which is as bad as die with tickling.

    URSULA: Yet tell her of it: hear what she will say.

    HERO: No; rather I will go to Benedick
And counsel him to fight against his passion.

And, truly, I'll devise some honest slanders
To stain my cousin with: one doth not know
How much an ill word may empoison liking.

    URSULA: O, do not do your cousin such a wrong,
She can not be so much without true judgement—
Having so swift and excellent a wit
As she is prized to have—as to refuse
So rare a gentleman as Signior Benedick.

    HERO: He is the only man of Italy,
Always excepted my dear Claudio.

    URSULA: I pray you, be not angry with me, madam,
Speaking my fancy: Signior Benedick,
For shape, for bearing, argument and valour
Goes foremost in report through Italy.

    HERO: Indeed, he hath an excellent good name.

    URSULA: His excellence did earn it, ere he had it.
When are you married, madam?

    HERO: Why, every day, to-morrow. Come, go in:
I'll show thee some attires, and have thy counsel
Which is the best to furnish me to-morrow.

    URSULA: She's limed, I warrant you: we have caught her, madam.

    HERO: If it proves so, then loving goes by haps:
Some Cupid kills with arrows, some with traps.

                         [*Exeunt Hero and Ursula.*

    BEATRICE: [*Coming forward*] What fire is in mine ears? Can this
        be true?
Stand I condemn'd for pride and scorn so much?
Contempt, farewell! and maiden pride, adieu!
    No glory lives behind the back of such.
And, Benedick, love on; I will requite thee,
    Taming my wild heart to thy loving hand:
If thou dost love, my kindness shall incite thee
    To bind our loves up in a holy band;
For others say thou dost deserve, and I
Believe it better than reportingly.   [*Exit.*

SCENE II. *A room in Leonato's house.*
Enter Don Pedro, Claudio, Benedick, and Leonato.

DON PEDRO: I do but stay till your marriage be consummate, and then go I toward Arragon.

CLAUDIO: I'll bring you thither, my lord, if you'll vouchsafe me.

DON PEDRO: Nay, that would be as great a soil in the new gloss of your marriage as to show a child his new coat and forbid him to wear it. I will only be bold with Benedick for his company; for, from the crown of his head to the sole of his foot, he is all mirth: he hath twice or thrice cut Cupid's bow-string and the little hangman dare not shoot at him; he hath a heart as sound as a bell and his tongue is the clapper, for what his heart thinks his tongue speaks.

BENEDICK: Gallants, I am not as I have been.

LEONATO: So say I: methinks you are sadder.

CLAUDIO: I hope he be in love.

DON PEDRO: Hang him, truant! there's no true drop of blood in him, to be truly touched with love: if he be sad, he wants money.

BENEDICK: I have the toothache.

DON PEDRO: Draw it.

BENEDICK: Hang it!

CLAUDIO: You must hang it first, and draw it afterwards.

DON PEDRO: What! sigh for the toothache?

LEONATO: Where is but a humour or a worm.

BENEDICK: Well, every one can master a grief but he that has it.

CLAUDIO: Yet say I, he is in love.

DON PEDRO: There is no appearance of fancy in him, unless it be a fancy that he hath to strange disguises; as, to be a Dutchman to-day, a Frenchman to-morrow, or in the shape of two countries at once, as, a German from the waist downward, all slops, and a Spaniard from the hip upward, no doublet. Unless he have a fancy to this foolery, as it appears he hath, he is no fool for fancy, as you would have it appear he is.

CLAUDIO: If he be not in love with some woman, there is no

believing old signs: a' brushes his hat o' mornings; what should that bode?

DON PEDRO: Hath any man seen him at the barber's?

CLAUDIO: No, but the barber's man hath been seen with him, and the old ornament of his cheek hath already stuffed tennis-balls.

LEONATO: Indeed, he looks younger than he did, by the loss of a beard.

DON PEDRO: Nay, a' rubs himself with civet: can you smell him out by that?

CLAUDIO: That's as much as to say, the sweet youth's in love.

DON PEDRO: The greatest note of it is his melancholy.

CLAUDIO: And when was he wont to wash his face?

DON PEDRO: Yea, or to paint himself? for the which, I hear what they say of him.

CLAUDIO: Nay, but his jesting spirit; which is now crept into a lute-string and now governed by stops.

DON PEDRO: Indeed, that tells a heavy tale for him: conclude, conclude he is in love.

CLAUDIO: Nay, but I know who loves him.

DON PEDRO: That would I know too: I warrant one that knows him not.

CLAUDIO: Yes, and his ill conditions; and, in despite of all, dies for him.

DON PEDRO: She shall be buried with her face upwards.

BENEDICK: Yet is this no charm for the toothache. Old signior, walk aside with me: I have studied eight or nine wise words to speak to you, which these hobby-horses must not hear.

                              [*Exeunt Benedick and Leonato.*

DON PEDRO: For my life, to break with him about Beatrice.

CLAUDIO: 'Tis even so. Hero and Margaret have by this played their parts with Beatrice; and then the two bears will not bite one another when they meet.

Enter Don John.

DON JOHN: My lord and brother, God save you!

DON PEDRO: Good den, brother.

DON JOHN: If your leisure served, I would speak with you.

DON PEDRO: In private?

DON JOHN: If it please you: yet Count Claudio may hear; for what I would speak of concerns him.

DON PEDRO: What's the matter?

DON JOHN: [*To Claudio*] Means your lordship to be married to-morrow?

DON PEDRO: You know he does.

DON JOHN: I know not that, when he knows what I know.

CLAUDIO: If there be any impediment, I pray you discover it.

DON JOHN: You may think I love you not: let that appear hereafter, and aim better at me by that I now will manifest. For my brother, I think he holds you well, and in dearness of heart hath holp to effect your ensuing marriage,—surely suit ill spent and labour ill bestowed.

DON PEDRO: Why, what's the matter?

DON JOHN: I came hither to tell you; and, circumstances shortened, for she has been too long a talking of, the lady is disloyal.

CLAUDIO: Who, Hero?

DON JOHN: Even she; Leonato's Hero, your Hero, every man's Hero.

CLAUDIO: Disloyal?

DON JOHN: The word is too good to paint out her wickedness; I could say she were worse: think you of a worse title, and I will fit her to it. Wonder not till further warrant: go but with me tonight, you shall see her chamber-window entered, even the night before her wedding-day: if you love her then, to-morrow wed her; but it would better fit your honour change your mind.

CLAUDIO: May this be so?

DON PEDRO: I will not think it.

DON JOHN: If you dare not trust that you see, confess not that you know: if you will follow me, I will show you enough; and when you have seen more and heard more, proceed accordingly.

CLAUDIO: If I see any thing to-night why I should not marry her to-morrow, in the congregation, where I should wed, here will I shame her.

DON PEDRO: And, as I wooed for thee to obtain her, I will join with thee to disgrace her.

DON JOHN: I will disparage her no farther till you are my witness: bear it coldly but till midnight, and let the issue show itself.

DON PEDRO: O day untowardly turned!

CLAUDIO: O mischief strangely thwarting!

DON JOHN: O plague right well prevented! so will you say when you have seen the sequel.   [*Exeunt.*

SCENE III. *A street.*
Enter Dogberry and Verges with the Watch.

DOGBERRY: Are you good men and true?

VERGES: Yea, or else it were pity but they should suffer salvation, body and soul.

DOGBERRY: Nay, that were a punishment too good for them, if they should have any allegiance in them, being chosen for the prince's watch.

VERGES: Well, give them their charge, neighbour Dogberry.

DOGBERRY: First, who think you are the most desartless man to be constable?

FIRST WATCH: Hugh Otecake, sir, or George Seacole; for they can write and read.

DOGBERRY: Come hither, neighbour Seacole, God hath blessed you with a good name: to be a well-favoured man is the gift of fortune: but to write and read comes by nature.

SECOND WATCH: Both which, master constable,—

DOGBERRY: You have: I knew it would be your answer. Well, for your favour, sir, why give God thanks, and make no boast of it; and for your writing and reading, let that appear when there is no need of such vanity. You are thought here to be the most senseless and fit man for the constable of the watch; therefore bear you the lantern. This is your charge: you shall comprehend all vagrom men; you are to bid any man stand, in the prince's name.

SECOND WATCH: How if a' will not stand?

DOGBERRY: Why, then, take no note of him, but let him go; and presently call the rest of the watch together and thank God you are rid of a knave.

VERGES: If he will not stand when he is bidden, he is none of the prince's subjects.

DOGBERRY: True, and they are to meddle with none but the prince's subjects. You shall also make no noise in the streets; for for the watch to babble and to talk is most tolerable and not to be endured.

WATCH: We will rather sleep than talk; we know what belongs to a watch.

DOGBERRY: Why, you speak like an ancient and most quiet watchman; for I cannot see how sleeping should offend: only, have a care that your bills be not stolen. Well, you are to call at all the ale-houses, and bid those that are drunk get them to bed.

WATCH: How if they will not?

DOGBERRY: Why, then, let them alone till they are sober: if they make you not then the better answer, you may say they are not the men you took them for.

WATCH: Well, sir.

DOGBERRY: If you meet a thief, you may suspect him, by virtue of your office, to be no true man: and, for such kind of men, the less you meddle or make with them, why, the more is for your honesty.

WATCH: If we know him to be a thief, shall we not lay hands on him?

DOGBERRY: Truly, by your office, you may; but I think they that touch pitch will be defiled: the most peaceable way for you, if you do take a thief, is to let him show himself what he is and steal out of your company.

VERGES: You have been always called a merciful man, partner.

DOGBERRY: Truly, I would not hang a dog by my will, much more a man who hath any honesty in him.

VERGES: If you hear a child cry in the night, you must call to the nurse and bid her still it.

WATCH: How if the nurse be asleep and will not hear us?

DOGBERRY: Why, then, depart in peace, and let the child wake her with crying; for the ewe that will not hear her lamb when it baes will never answer a calf when he bleats.

VERGES: 'Tis very true.

DOGBERRY: This is the end of the charge:—you, constable, are to present the prince's own person: if you meet the prince in the night, you may stay him.

VERGES: Nay, by'r lady, that I think a' cannot.

DOGBERRY: Five shillings to one on't, with any man that knows the statutes, he may stay him: marry, not without the prince be willing; for, indeed, the watch ought to offend no man; and it is an offence to stay a man against his will.

VERGES: By'r lady, I think it be so.

DOGBERRY: Ha, ah, ha! Well, masters, good night: an there by any matter of weight chances, call up me: keep your fellows' counsels and your own; and good night. Come, neighbour.

WATCH: Well, masters, we hear our charge: let us go sit here upon the church-bench till two, and then all to bed.

DOGBERRY: One word more, honest neighbours. I pray you, watch about Signior Leonato's door; for the wedding being there to-morrow, there is a great coil to-night. Adieu: be vigilant, I beseech you.   [*Exeunt Dogberry and Verges.*

Enter Borachio and Conrade.

BORACHIO: What, Conrade!

Watch: [*Aside*] Peace! stir not.

BORACHIO: Conrade, I say!

CONRADE: Here, man; I am at thy elbow.

BORACHIO: Mass, and my elbow itched; I thought there would a scab follow.

CONRADE: I will owe thee an answer for that: and now forward with thy tale.

BORACHIO: Stand thee close, then, under this pent-house, for it drizzles rain; and I will, like a true drunkard, utter all to thee.

WATCH: [*Aside*] Some treason, masters: yet stand close.

BORACHIO: Therefore know I have earned of Don John a thousand ducats.

CONRADE: Is it possible that any villany should be so dear?

BORACHIO: Thou shouldst rather ask if it were possible any villany should be so rich; for when rich villains have need of poor ones, poor ones may make what price they will.

CONRADE: I wonder at it.

BORACHIO: That shows thou art unconfirmed. Thou knowest that the fashion of a doublet or a hat, or a cloak, is nothing to a man.

CONRADE: Yes, it is apparel.

BORACHIO: I mean, the fashion.

CONRADE: Yes, the fashion is the fashion.

BORACHIO: Tush! I may as well say the fool's the fool. But seest thou not what a deformed thief this fashion is?

WATCH: [*Aside*] I know that Deformed; a' has been a vile thief this seven year; a' goes up and down like a gentleman: I remember his name.

BORACHIO: Didst thou not hear somebody?

CONRADE: No; 'twas the vane on the house.

BORACHIO: Seest thou not, I say, what a deformed thief this fashion is? how giddily a' turns about all the hot bloods between fourteen and five-and-thirty? sometimes fashioning them like Pharaoh's soldiers in the reechy painting, sometime like god Bel's priests in the old church-window, sometime like the shaven Hercules in the smirched worm-eaten tapestry, where his codpiece seems as massy as his club?

CONRADE: All this I see; and I see that the fashion wears out more apparel than the man. But art not thou thyself giddy with the fashion too, that thou hast shifted out of thy tale into telling me of the fashion?

BORACHIO: Not so, neither: but know that I have to-night

wooed Margaret, the Lady Hero's gentlewoman, by the name of Hero: she leans me out at her mistress' chamber-window, bids me a thousand times good night,—I tell this tale vilely:—I should first tell thee how the prince, Claudio and my master, planted and possessed by my master Don John, saw afar off in the orchard this amiable encounter.

CONRADE: And thought they Margaret was Hero?

BORACHIO: Two of them did, the prince and Claudio; but the devil my master knew she was Margaret; and partly by his oaths, which first possessed them, partly by the dark night, which did deceive them, but chiefly by my villany, which did confirm any slander that Don John had made, away went Claudio enraged; swore he would meet her, as he was appointed, next morning at the temple, and there, before the whole congregation, shame her with what he saw o'er night and send her home again without a husband.

FIRST WATCH: We charge you, in the prince's name, stand!

SECOND WATCH: Call up the right master constable. We have here recovered the most dangerous piece of lechery that ever was known in the commonwealth.

FIRST WATCH: And one Deformed is one of them: I know him; a' wears a lock.

CONRADE: Masters, masters,—

SECOND WATCH: You'll be made bring Deformed forth, I warrant you.

CONRADE: Masters,—

FIRST WATCH: Never speak: we charge you let us obey you to go with us.

BORACHIO: We are like to prove a goodly commodity, being taken up of these men's bills.

CONRADE: A commodity in question, I warrant you. Come, we'll obey you.   [*Exeunt.*

SCENE IV. *Hero's apartment.*
Enter Hero, Margaret, and Ursula.

HERO: Good Ursula, wake my cousin Beatrice and desire her
to rise.

URSULA: I will, lady.

HERO: And bid her come hither.

URSULA: Well.   [*Exit.*

MARGARET: Troth, I think your other rabato were better.

HERO: No, pray thee, good Meg, I'll wear this.

MARGARET: By my troth, 's not so good; and I warrant your
cousin will say so.

HERO: My cousin's a fool, and thou art another: I'll wear none
but this.

MARGARET: I like the new tire within excellently, if the hair
were a thought browner; and your gown's a most rare fashion, i'
faith. I saw the Duchess of Milan's gown that they praise so.

HERO: O, that exceeds, they say.

MARGARET: By my troth, 's but a night-gown in respect of
yours: cloth o' gold, and cuts, and laced with silver, set with
pearls, down sleeves, side sleeves, and skirts, round underborne
with a bluish tinsel: but for a fine, quaint, graceful and excellent
fashion, yours is worth ten on't.

HERO: God give me joy to wear it! for my heart is exceedingly heavy.

MARGARET: 'Twill be heavier soon by the weight of a man.

HERO: Fie upon thee! art not ashamed?

MARGARET: Of what, lady? of speaking honourably? Is not
marriage honourable in a beggar? Is not your lord honourable
without marriage? I think you would have me say, 'saving your
reverence, a husband:' an bad thinking do not wrest true speaking, I'll offend nobody: is there any harm in 'the heavier for a
husband'? None, I think, an it be the right husband and the right
wife: otherwise 'tis light, and not heavy: ask my Lady Beatrice
else; here she comes.

Enter Beatrice.

HERO: Good morrow, coz.

BEATRICE: Good morrow, sweet Hero.

HERO: Why, how now? do you speak in the sick tune?

BEATRICE: I am out of all other tune, methinks.

MARGARET: Clap 's into 'Light o' love;' that goes without a burden: do you sing, and I'll dance it.

BEATRICE: Ye light o' love, with your heels! then, if your husband have stables enough, you'll see he shall lack no barns.

MARGARET: O illegitimate construction! I scorn that with my
heels.

BEATRICE: 'Tis almost five o'clock, cousin; 'tis time you were
ready. By my troth, I am exceeding ill: heigh-ho!

MARGARET: For a hawk, a horse, or a husband?

BEATRICE: For the letter that begins them all. H.

MARGARET: Well, an you be not turned Turk, there's no more
sailing by the star.

BEATRICE: What means the fool, trow?

MARGARET: Nothing I; but God send every one their heart's
desire!

HERO: These gloves the count sent me; they are an excellent perfume.

BEATRICE: I am stuffed, cousin; I cannot smell.

MARGARET: A maid, and stuffed! there's goodly catching of
cold.

BEATRICE: O, God help me! God help me! how long have you
professed apprehension?

MARGARET: Ever since you left it. Doth not my wit become
me rarely?

BEATRICE: It is not seen enough, you should wear it in your
cap. By my troth, I am sick.

MARGARET: Get you some of this distilled Carduus Benedictus,
and lay it to your heart: it is the only thing for a qualm.

HERO: There thou prickest her with a thistle.

BEATRICE: Benedictus! why Benedictus: you have some moral in this Benedictus.

MARGARET: Moral! no, by my troth, I have no moral meaning; I meant, plain holy-thistle. You may think perchance that I think you are in love: nay, by'r lady, I am not such a fool to think what I list, nor I list not to think what I can, nor indeed I cannot think, if I would think my heart out of thinking, that you are in love or that you will be in love or that you can be in love. Yet Benedick was such another, and now is he become a man: he swore he would never marry, and yet now, in despite of his heart, he eats his meat without grudging: and how you may be converted I know not, but methinks you look with your eyes as other women do.

BEATRICE: What pace is this that thy tongue keeps?

MARGARET: Not a false gallop.

Re-enter Ursula.

URSULA: Madam, withdraw: the prince, the count, Signior Benedick, Don John, and all the gallants of the town, are come to fetch you to church.

HERO: Help to dress me, good coz, good Meg, good Ursula.

[*Exeunt.*

SCENE V. *Another room in Leonato's house.*
Enter Leonato, with Dogberry and Verges.

LEONATO: What would you with me, honest neighbour?

DOGBERRY: Marry, sir, I would have some confidence with you that decerns you nearly.

LEONATO: Brief, I pray you; for you see it is a busy time with me.

DOGBERRY: Marry, this it is, sir.

VERGES: Yes, in truth it is, sir.

LEONATO: What is it, my good friends?

DOGBERRY: Goodman Verges, sir, speaks a little off the matter: an old man, sir, and his wits are not so blunt as, God help, I would desire they were; but, in faith, honest as the skin between his brows.

VERGES: Yes, I thank God I am as honest as any man living that
is an old man and no honester than I.

DOGBERRY: Comparisons are odorous: palabras, neighbour Verges.

LEONATO: Neighbours, you are tedious.

DOGBERRY: It pleases your worship to say so, but we are the poor
duke's officers; but truly, for mine own part, if I were as tedious as a
king, I could find it in my heart to bestow it all of your worship.

LEONATO: All thy tediousness on me, ah?

DOGBERRY: Yea, an 'twere a thousand pound more than 'tis; for I
hear as good exclamation on your worship as of any man in the
city; and though I be but a poor man, I am glad to hear it.

VERGES: And so am I.

LEONATO: I would fain know what you have to say.

VERGES: Marry, sir, our watch to-night, excepting your worship's
presence, ha' ta'en a couple of as arrant knaves as any in Messina.

DOGBERRY: A good old man, sir; he will be talking: as they say,
When the age is in, the wit is out: God help us! it is a world to
see. Well said, i' faith, neighbour Verges: well, God's a good man;
an two men ride of a horse, one must ride behind. An honest
soul, i' faith, sir; by my troth he is, as ever broke bread; but God is
to be worshipped; all men are not alike; alas, good neighbour!

LEONATO: Indeed, neighbour, he comes too short of you.

DOGBERRY: Gifts that God gives.

LEONATO: I must leave you.

DOGBERRY: One word, sir: our watch, sir, have indeed compre-
hended two aspicious persons, and we would have them this
morning examined before your worship.

LEONATO: Take their examination yourself and bring it me; I
am now in great haste, as it may appear unto you.

DOGBERRY: It shall be suffigance.

LEONATO: Drink some wine ere you go: fare you well.

Enter a Messenger.

MESSENGER: My lord, they stay for you to give your daughter to
her husband.

LEONATO: I 'll wait upon them: I am ready.

[*Exeunt Leonato and Messenger.*

DOGBERRY: Go, good partner, go, get you to Francis Seacole; bid him bring his pen and inkhorn to the gaol: we are now to examination these men.

VERGES: And we must do it wisely.

DOGBERRY: We will spare for no wit, I warrant you; here's that shall drive some of them to a noncome: only get the learned writer to set down their excommunication and meet me at the gaol.   [*Exeunt.*

ACT IV.

SCENE I. *A church.*

Enter Don Pedro, Don John, Leonato, Friar Francis, Claudio, Benedick, Hero, Beatrice, and attendants.

LEONATO: Come, Friar Francis, be brief; only to the plain form of marriage, and you shall recount their particular duties afterwards.

FRIAR: You come hither, my lord, to marry this lady.

CLAUDIO: No.

LEONATO: To be married to her: friar, you come to marry her.

FRIAR: Lady, you come hither to be married to this count.

HERO: I do.

FRIAR: If either of you know any inward impediment why you should not be conjoined, I charge you, on your souls, to utter it.

CLAUDIO: Know you any, Hero?

HERO: None, my lord.

FRIAR: Know you any, count?

LEONATO: I dare make his answer, none.

CLAUDIO: O, what men dare do! what men may do! what men daily do, not knowing what they do!

BENEDICK: How now! interjections? Why, then, some be of laughing, as, ah, ha, he!

CLAUDIO: Stand thee by, friar. Father, by your leave:
Will you with free and unconstrained soul
Give me this maid, your daughter?

    LEONATO: As freely, son, as God did give her me.

    CLAUDIO: And what have I to give you back, whose worth
May counterpoise this rich and precious gift?

    DON PEDRO: Nothing, unless you render her again.

    CLAUDIO: Sweet prince, you learn me noble thankfulness.
There, Leonato, take her back again:
Give not this rotten orange to your friend;
She's but the sign and semblance of her honour.
Behold how like a maid she blushes here!
O, what authority and show of truth
Can cunning sin cover itself withal!
Comes not that blood as modest evidence
To witness simple virtue? Would you not swear,
All you that see her, that she were a maid,
By these exterior shows? But she is none:
She knows the heat of luxurious bed;
Her blush is guiltiness, not modesty.

    LEONATO: What do you mean, my lord?

    CLAUDIO: Not to be married,
Not to knit my soul to an approved wanton.

    LEONATO: Dear my lord, if you, in your own proof,
Have vanquish'd the resistance of her youth,
And made defeat of her virginity,—

    CLAUDIO: I know what you would say: if I have known her,
You will say she did embrace me as a husband,
And so extenuate the 'forehand sin:
No, Leonato,
I never tempted her with word too large;
But, as a brother to his sister, show'd
Bashful sincerity and comely love.

    HERO: And seem'd I ever otherwise to you?

    CLAUDIO: Out on thee! Seeming! I will write against it:

You seem to me as Dian in her orb,
As chaste as is the bud ere it be blown;
But you are more intemperate in your blood
Than Venus, or those pamper'd animals
That rage in savage sensuality.

    HERO: Is my lord well, that he doth speak so wide?

    LEONATO: Sweet prince, why speak not you?

    DON PEDRO: What should I speak?
I stand dishonour'd, that have gone about
To link my dear friend to a common stale.

    LEONATO: Are these things spoken, or do I but dream?

    DON JOHN: Sir, they are spoken, and these things are true.

    BENEDICK: This looks not like a nuptial.

    HERO: True! O God!

    CLAUDIO: Leonato, stand I here?
Is this the prince? is this the prince's brother?
Is this face Hero's? are our eyes our own?

    LEONATO: All this is so: but what of this, my lord?

    CLAUDIO: Let me but move one question to your daughter;
And, by that fatherly and kindly power
That you have in her, bid her answer truly.

    LEONATO: I charge thee do so, as thou art my child.

    HERO: O, God defend me! how am I beset!
What kind of catechising call you this?

    CLAUDIO: To make you answer truly to your name.

    HERO: Is it not Hero? Who can blot that name
With any just reproach?

    CLAUDIO: Marry, that can Hero;
Hero itself can blot out Hero's virtue.
What man was he talk'd with you yesternight
Out at your window betwixt twelve and one?
Now, if you are a maid, answer to this.

    HERO: I talk'd with no man at that hour, my lord.

    DON PEDRO: Why, then are you no maiden. Leonato,
I am sorry you must hear: upon mine honour,

Myself, my brother and this grieved count
Did see her, hear her, at that hour last night
Talk with a ruffian at her chamber-window;
Who hath indeed, most like a liberal villain,
Confess'd the vile encounters they have had
A thousand times in secret.

    DON JOHN: Fie, fie! they are not to be named, my lord,
Not to be spoke of;
There is not chastity enough in language
Without offence to utter them. Thus, pretty lady,
I am sorry for thy much misgovernment.

    CLAUDIO: O Hero, what a Hero hadst thou been,
If half thy outward graces had been placed
About thy thoughts and counsels of thy heart!
But fare thee well, most foul, most fair! farewell,
Thou pure impiety and impious purity! For thee I'll lock up all
the gates of love.
And on my eyelids shall conjecture hang,
To turn all beauty into thoughts of harm,
And never shall it more be gracious.

    LEONATO: Hath no man's dagger here a point for me?

                                         [*Hero swoons.*

    BEATRICE: Why, how now, cousin! wherefore sink you down?

    DON JOHN: Come, let us go. These things, come thus to light,
Smother her spirits up. [*Exeunt Don Pedro, Don John, and Claudio.*

    BENEDICK: How doth the lady?

    BEATRICE: Dead, I think. Help, uncle!
Hero! why, Hero! Uncle! Signior Benedick! Friar!

    LEONATO: O Fate! take not away thy heavy hand.
Death is the fairest cover for her shame
That may be wish'd for.

    BEATRICE: How now, cousin Hero!

    FRIAR: Have comfort, lady.

    LEONATO: Dost thou look up?

    FRIAR: Yea, wherefore should she not?

LEONATO: Wherefore! Why, doth not every earthly thing
Cry shame upon her? Could she here deny
The story that is printed in her blood?
Do not live, Hero; do not ope thine eyes:
For, did I think thou wouldst not quickly die,
Thought I thy spirits were stronger then thy shames.
Myself would, on the rearward of reproaches,
Strike at thy life. Grieved I, I had but one?
Chid I for that at frugal nature's frame?
O, one too much by thee! Why had I one?
Why ever wast thou lovely in my eyes?
Why had I not with charitable hand
Took up a beggar's issue at my gates,
Who smirched thus and mired with infamy,
I might have said 'No part of it is mine;
This shame derives itself from unknown loins'?
But mine and mine I loved and mine I praised
And mine that I was proud on, mine so much
That I myself was to myself not mine.
Valuing of her,—why, she, O, she is fallen
Into a pit of ink, that the wide sea
Hath drops too few to wash her clean again
And salt too little which may season give
To her foul-tainted flesh!
BENEDICK: Sir, sir, be patient.
For my part, I am so attired in wonder,
I know not what to say.
BEATRICE: O, on my soul, my cousin is belied!
BENEDICK: Lady, were you her bedfellow last night?
BEATRICE: No, truly not; although, until last night,
I have this twelvemonth been her bedfellow.
LEONATO: Confirm'd, confirm'd! O, that is stronger made
Which was before barr'd up with ribs of iron!
Would the two princes lie, and Claudio lie,
Who loved her so, that, speaking of her foulness,

Wash'd it with tears? Hence from her! let her die.

    FRIAR: Hear me a little; for I have only been
Silent so long and given way unto
This course of fortune. . . .
By noting of the lady I have mark'd
A thousand blushing apparitions
To start into her face, a thousand innocent shames
In angel whiteness beat away those blushes;
And in her eye there hath appear'd a fire,
To burn the errors that these princes hold
Against her maiden truth. Call me a fool;
Trust not my reading nor my observations,
Which with experimental seal doth warrant
The tenour of my book: trust not my age,
My reference, calling, nor divinity,
If this sweet lady lie not guiltless here
Under some biting error.

    LEONATO: Friar, it cannot be.
Thou seest that all the grace that she hath left
Is that she will not add to her damnation
A sin of perjury; she not denies it:
Why seek'st thou then to cover with excuse
That which appears in proper nakedness?

    FRIAR: Lady, what man is he you are accused of?

    HERO: They know that do accuse me: I know none:
If I know more of any man alive
Than that which maiden modesty doth warrant,
Let all my sins lack mercy! O my father,
Prove you that any man with me conversed
At hours unmeet, or that I yesternight
Maintain'd the change of words with any creature,
Refuse me, hate me, torture me to death!

    FRIAR: There is some strange misprision in the princes.

    BENEDICK: Two of them have the very bent of honour;
And if their wisdoms be misled in this,

The practice of it lives in John the bastard,
Whose spirits toil in frame of villanies.

LEONATO: I know not. If they speak but truth of her,
These hands shall tear her; if they wrong her honour,
The proudest of them shall well hear of it.
Time hath not yet so dried this blood of mine,
Nor age so eat up my invention,
Nor fortune made such havoc by my means,
Nor my bad life reft me so much of friends,
But they shall find, awaked in such a kind,
Both strength of limb and policy of mind,
Ability in means and choice of friends,
To quit me of them throughly.

FRIAR: Pause awhile,
And let my counsel sway you in this case.
Your daughter here the princes left for dead
Let her awhile be secretly kept in,
And publish it that she is dead indeed;
Maintain a mourning ostentation
And on your family's old monument
Hang mournful epitaphs and do all rites
That appertain unto a burial.

LEONATO: What shall become of this? what will this do?

FRIAR: Marry, this well carried shall on her behalf
Change slander to remorse; that is some good:
But not for that dream I on this strange course,
But on this travail look for greater birth.
She dying, as it must be so maintain'd,
Upon the instant that she was accused,
Shall be lamented, pitied and excused
Of every hearer: for it so falls out
That what we have we prize not to the worth
Whiles we enjoy it, but being lack'd and lost,
Why, then we rack the value, then we find
The virtue that possession would not show us

While it was ours. So will it fare with Claudio:
When he shall hear she died upon his words,
The idea of her life shall sweetly creep
Into his study of imagination,
And every lovely organ of her life
Shall come apparell'd in more precious habit,
More moving-delicate and full of life,
Into the eye and prospect of his soul,
Than when she lived indeed; then shall he mourn,
If ever love had interest in his liver,
And wish he had not so accused her,
No, though he thought his accusation true.
Let this be so, and doubt not but success
Will fashion the event in better shape
Than I can lay it down in likelihood.
But if all aim but this be levell'd false,
The supposition of the lady's death
Will quench the wonder of her infamy:
And if it sort not well, you may conceal her,
As best befits her wounded reputation,
In some reclusive and religious life,
Out of all eyes, tongues, minds and injuries.
BENEDICK: Signior Leonato, let the friar advise you:
And though you know my inwardness and love
Is very much unto the prince and Claudio,
Yet, by mine honour, I will deal in this
As secretly and justly as your soul
Should with your body.
LEONATO: Being that I flow in grief,
The smallest twine may lead me.
FRIAR: 'Tis well consented: presently away;
For to strange sores strangely they strain the cure.
Come, lady, die to live: this wedding-day
Perhaps is but prolong'd: have patience and endure.
                    [*Exeunt all but Benedick and Beatrice.*

BENEDICK: Lady Beatrice, have you wept all this while?

BEATRICE: Yea, and I will weep a while longer.

BENEDICK: I will not desire that.

BEATRICE: You have no reason; I do it freely.

BENEDICK: Surely I do believe your fair cousin is wronged.

BEATRICE: Ah, how much might the man deserve of me that would right her!

BENEDICK: Is there any way to show such friendship?

BEATRICE: A very even way, but no such friend.

BENEDICK: May a man do it?

BEATRICE: It is a man's office, but not yours.

BENEDICK: I do love nothing in the world so well as you: is not that strange?

BEATRICE: As strange as the thing I know not. It were as possible for me to say I loved nothing so well as you: but believe me not; and yet I lie not; I confess nothing, nor I deny nothing. I am sorry for my cousin.

BENEDICK: By my sword, Beatrice, thou lovest me.

BEATRICE: Do not swear, and eat it.

BENEDICK: I will swear by it that you love me; and I will make him eat it that says I love not you.

BEATRICE: Will you not eat your word?

BENEDICK: With no sauce that can be devised to it. I protest I love thee.

BEATRICE: Why, then, God forgive me!

BENEDICK: What offence, sweet Beatrice?

BEATRICE: You have stayed me in a happy hour: I was about to protest I loved you.

BENEDICK: And do it with all thy heart.

BEATRICE: I love you with so much of my heart that none is left to protest.

BENEDICK: Come, bid me do any thing for thee.

BEATRICE: Kill Claudio.

BENEDICK: Ha! not for the wide world.

BEATRICE: You kill me to deny it. Farewell.

BENEDICK: Tarry, sweet Beatrice.

BEATRICE: I am gone, though I am here: there is no love in you: nay, I pray you, let me go.

BENEDICK: Beatrice,—

BEATRICE: In faith, I will go.

BENEDICK: We 'll be friends first.

BEATRICE: You dare easier be friends with me than fight with mine enemy.

BENEDICK: Is Claudio thine enemy?

BEATRICE: Is he not approved in the height a villain, that hath slandered, scorned, dishonoured my kinswoman? O that I were a man! What, bear her in hand until they come to take hands; and then, with public accusation, uncovered slander, unmitigated rancour,—O God, that I were a man! I would eat his heart in the market-place.

BENEDICK: Hear me, Beatrice,—

BEATRICE: Talk with a man out at a window! A proper saying!

BENEDICK: Nay, but, Beatrice,—

BEATRICE: Sweet Hero! She is wronged, she is slandered, she is undone.

BENEDICK: Beat—

BEATRICE: Princes and counties! Surely, a princely testimony, a goodly count, Count Comfect; a sweet gallant, surely! O that I were a man for his sake! or that I had any friend would be a man for my sake! But manhood is melted into courtesies, valour into compliment, and men are only turned into tongue, and trim ones too: he is now as valiant as Hercules that only tells a lie and swears it. I cannot be a man with wishing, therefore I will die a woman with grieving.

BENEDICK: Tarry, good Beatrice. By this hand, I love thee.

BEATRICE: Use it for my love some other way than swearing by it.

BENEDICK: Think you in your soul the Count Claudio hath wronged Hero?

BEATRICE: Yea, as sure as I have a thought or a soul.

BENEDICK: Enough, I am engaged; I will challenge him. I will kiss your hand, and so I leave you. By this hand, Claudio shall render me a dear account. As you hear of me, so think of me. Go, comfort your cousin: I must say she is dead: and so, farewell.

[*Exeunt.*

SCENE II. *A prison.*

Enter Dogberry, Verges, and Sexton, in gowns; and the Watch, with Conrade and Borachio.

DOGBERRY: Is our whole dissembly appeared?

VERGES: O, a stool and a cushion for the sexton.

SEXTON: Which be the malefactors?

DOGBERRY: Marry, that am I and my partner.

VERGES: Nay, that's certain; we have the exhibition to examine.

SEXTON: But which are the offenders that are to be examined? let them come before master constable.

DOGBERRY: Yea, marry, let them come before me. What is your name, friend?

BORACHIO: Borachio.

DOGBERRY: Pray, write down, Borachio. Yours, sirrah?

CONRADE: I am a gentleman, sir, and my name is Conrade.

DOGBERRY: Write down, master gentleman Conrade. Masters, do you serve God?

CONRADE:
BORACHIO: } Yea, sir, we hope.

DOGBERRY: Write down, that they hope they serve God: and write God first; for God defend but God should go before such villains! Masters, it is proved already that you are little better than false knaves; and it will go near to be thought so shortly. How answer you for yourselves.

CONRADE: Marry, sir, we say we are none.

DOGBERRY: A marvellous witty fellow, I assure you; but I will go about with him. Come you hither, sirrah; a word in your ear: sir, I say to you, it is thought you are false knaves.

BORACHIO: Sir, I say to you we are none.

DOGBERRY: Well, stand aside. 'Fore God, they are both in a tale. Have you writ down, that they are none?

SEXTON: Master constable, you go not the way to examine: you must call forth the watch that are their accusers.

DOGBERRY: Yea, marry, that's the eftest way. Let the watch come forth. Masters, I charge you, in the prince's name, accuse these men.

FIRST WATCH: This man said, sir, that Don John, the prince's brother, was a villain.

DOGBERRY: Write down Prince John a villain. Why, this is flat perjury, to call a prince's brother villain.

BORACHIO: Master constable,—

DOGBERRY: Pray thee, fellow, peace: I do not like thy look, I promise thee.

SEXTON: What heard you him say else?

SECOND WATCH: Marry, that he had received a thousand ducats of Don John for accusing the Lady Hero wrongfully.

DOGBERRY: Flat burglary as ever was committed.

VERGES: Yea, by mass, that it is.

SEXTON: What else, fellow?

FIRST WATCH: And that Count Claudio did mean, upon his words, to disgrace Hero before the whole assembly, and not marry her.

DOGBERRY: O villain! thou wilt be condemned into everlasting redemption for this.

SEXTON: What else?

WATCH: This is all.

SEXTON: And this is more, masters, than you can deny. Prince John is this morning secretly stolen away; Hero was in this manner accused, in this very manner refused, and upon the grief of this suddenly died. Master constable, let these men be bound, and brought to Leonato's: I will go before and show him their examination.

DOGBERRY: Come, let them be opinioned.

VERGES: Let them be in the hands—

CONRADE: Off, coxcomb!

DOGBERRY: God's my life, where's the sexton? let him write down the prince's officer coxcomb. Come, bind them. Thou naughty varlet!

CONRADE: Away! you are an ass, you are an ass.

DOGBERRY: Dost thou not suspect my place? dost thou not suspect my years? O that he were here to write me down an ass! But, masters, remember that I am an ass; though it be not written down, yet forget not that I am an ass. No, thou villain, thou art full of piety, as shall be proved upon thee by good witness. I am a wise fellow, and, which is more, an officer, and which is more, a householder, and, which is more, as pretty a piece of flesh as any is in Messina, and one that knows the law, go to; and a rich fellow enough, go to; and a fellow that hath had losses, and one that hath two gowns and every thing handsome about him. Bring him away. O that I had been writ down an ass!   [*Exeunt.*

ACT V.

SCENE I. *Before Leonato's house.*
Enter Leonato and Antonio.

ANTONIO: If you go on thus, you will kill yourself;
And 'tis not wisdom thus to second grief
Against yourself.

LEONATO: I pray thee, cease thy counsel,
Which falls into mine ears as profitless
As water in a sieve: give not me counsel;
Nor let no comforter delight mine ear
But such a one whose wrongs do suit with mine.
Bring me a father that so loved his child,
Whose joy of her is overwhelm'd like mine,
And bid him speak of patience;
Measure his woe the length and breadth of mine
And let it answer every strain for strain,

As thus for thus and such a grief for such,
In every lineament, branch, shape, and form:
If such a one will smile and stroke his beard,
Bid sorrow wag, cry 'hem!' when he should groan,
Patch grief with proverbs, make misfortune drunk
With candle-wasters; bring him yet to me,
And I of him will gather patience.
But there is no such man: for, brother, men
Can counsel and speak comfort to that grief
Which they themselves not feel; but, tasting it,
Their counsel turns to passion, which before
Would give preceptial medicine to rage,
Fetter strong madness in a silken thread,
Charm ache with air and agony with words:
No, no; 'tis all men's office to speak patience
To those that wring under the load of sorrow,
But no man's virtue nor sufficiency
To be so moral when he shall endure
The like himself. Therefore give me no counsel:
My griefs cry louder than advertisement.

     ANTONIO: Therein do men from children nothing differ.

     LEONATO: I pray thee, peace. I will be flesh and blood;
For there was never yet philosopher
That could endure the toothache patiently,
However they have writ the style of gods
And made a push at chance and sufferance.

     ANTONIO: Yet bend not all the harm upon yourself;
Make those that do offend you suffer too.

     LEONATO: There thou speak'st reason: nay, I will do so.
My soul doth tell me Hero is belied;
And that shall Claudio know; so shall the prince
And all of them that thus dishonour her.

     ANTONIO: Here comes the prince and Claudio hastily.

Enter Don Pedro and Claudio.

DON PEDRO: Good den, good den.

CLAUDIO: Good day to both of you.

LEONATO: Hear you, my lords,—

DON PEDRO: We have some haste, Leonato.

LEONATO: Some haste, my lord! well, fare you well, my lord:
Are you so hasty now? well, all is one.

DON PEDRO: Nay, do not quarrel with us, good old man.

ANTONIO: If he could right himself with quarrelling,
Some of us would lie low.

CLAUDIO: Who wrongs him?

LEONATO: Marry, thou dost wrong me; thou dissembler, thou:—
Nay, never lay thy hand upon thy sword:
I fear thee not.

CLAUDIO: Marry, beshrew my hand,
If it should give your age such cause of fear:
In faith, my hand meant nothing to my sword.

LEONATO: Tush, tush, man; never fleer and jest at me:
I speak not like a dotard nor a fool,
As under privilege of age to brag
What I have done being young, or what would do
Were I not old. Know, Claudio, to thy head,
Thou hast so wrong'd mine innocent child and me
That I am forced to lay my reverence by
And, with grey hairs and bruise of many days,
Do challenge thee to trial of a man.
I say thou hast belied mine innocent child;
Thy slander hath gone through and through her heart.
And she lies buried with her ancestors;
O, in a tomb where never scandal slept,
Save this of hers, framed by thy villany!

CLAUDIO: My villany?

LEONATO: Thine, Claudio; thine, I say.

DON PEDRO: You say not right, old man.

LEONATO: My lord, my lord,
I'll prove it on his body, if he dare,

Despite his nice fence and his active practice,
His May of youth and bloom of lustihood.
   CLAUDIO: Away! I will not have to do with you.
   LEONATO: Canst thou so daff me? Thou hast kill'd my child:
If thou kill'st me, boy, thou shalt kill a man.
   ANTONIO: He shall kill two of us, and men indeed:
But that's no matter; let him kill one first;
Win me and wear me; let him answer me.
Come, follow me, boy; come, sir boy, come, follow me:
Sir boy, I'll whip you from your foining fence;
Nay, as I am a gentleman, I will.
LEONATO: Brother,—
   ANTONIO: Content yourself. God knows I loved my niece;
And she is dead, slander'd to death by villains,
That dare as well answer a man indeed
As I dare take a serpent by the tongue:
Boys, apes, braggarts, Jacks, milksops!
   LEONATO: Brother Anthony,—
   ANTONIO: Hold you content. What, man! I know them, yea,
And what they weigh, even to the utmost scruple,—
Scrambling, out-facing, fashion-monging boys,
That lie and cog and flout, deprave and slander,
Go anticly, show outward hideousness,
And speak off half a dozen dangerous words,
How they might hurt their enemies, if they durst;
And this is all.
   LEONATO: But, brother Anthony,—
   ANTONIO: Come, 'tis no matter:
Do not you meddle; let me deal in this.
   DON PEDRO: Gentlemen both, we will not wake your patience.
My heart is sorry for your daughter's death:
But, on my honour, she was charged with nothing
But what was true and very full of proof.
   LEONATO: My lord, my lord,—
   DON PEDRO: I will not hear you.

LEONATO: No? Come, brother; away! I will be heard.

ANTONIO: And shall, or some of us will smart for it.

　　　　　　　　　　　　　[*Exeunt Leonato and Antonio.*

DON PEDRO: See, see; here comes the man we went to seek.

Enter Benedick.

CLAUDIO: Now, signior, what news?

BENEDICK: Good day, my lord.

DON PEDRO: Welcome, signior: you are almost come to part almost a fray.

CLAUDIO: We had like to have had our two noses snapped off with two old men without teeth.

DON PEDRO: Leonato and his brother. What thinkest thou? Had we fought, I doubt we should have been too young for them.

BENEDICK: In a false quarrel there is no true valour. I came to seek you both.

CLAUDIO: We have been up and down to seek thee; for we are high-proof melancholy and would fain have it beaten away. Wilt thou use thy wit?

BENEDICK: It is in my scabbard: shall I draw it?

DON PEDRO: Dost thou wear thy wit by thy side?

CLAUDIO: Never any did so, though very many have been beside their wit. I will bid thee draw, as we do the minstrels; draw, to pleasure us.

DON PEDRO: As I am an honest man, he looks pale. Art thou sick, or angry?

CLAUDIO: What, courage, man! What though care killed a cat, thou hast mettle enough in thee to kill care.

BENEDICK: Sir, I shall meet your wit in the career, an you charge it against me. I pray you choose another subject.

CLAUDIO: Nay, then, give him another staff: this last was broke cross.

DON PEDRO: By this light, he changes more and more: I think he be angry indeed.

CLAUDIO: If he be, he knows how to turn his girdle.

BENEDICK: Shall I speak a word in your ear?

CLAUDIO: God bless me from a challenge!

BENEDICK: [*Aside to Claudio*] You are a villain; I jest not: I will make it good how you dare, with what you dare, and when you dare. Do me right, or I will protest your cowardice. You have killed a sweet lady, and her death shall fall heavy on you. Let me hear from you.

CLAUDIO: Well, I will meet you, so I may have good cheer.

DON PEDRO: What, a feast, a feast?

CLAUDIO: I' faith, I thank him; he hath bid me to a calf's head and a capon; the which if I do not carve most curiously, say my knife's naught. Shall I not find a woodcock too?

BENEDICK: Sir, your wit ambles well; it goes easily.

DON PEDRO: I'll tell thee how Beatrice praised thy wit the other day. I said, thou hadst a fine wit: 'True,' said she, 'a fine little one.' 'No,' said I, 'a great wit:' 'Right,' says she, 'a great gross one.' 'Nay,' said I, 'a good wit;' 'Just,' said she, 'it hurts nobody.' 'Nay,' said I, 'the gentleman is wise;' 'Certain,' said she, 'a wise gentleman.' 'Nay,' said I, 'he hath the tongues:' 'That I believe,' said she, 'for he swore a thing to me on Monday night, which he forswore on Tuesday morning; there's a double tongue; there's two tongues.' Thus did she, an hour, together, trans-shape thy particular virtues: yet at last she concluded with a sigh, thou wast the properest man in Italy.

CLAUDIO: For the which she wept heartily and said she cared not.

DON PEDRO: Yea, that she did; but yet, for all that, an if she did not hate him deadly, she would love him dearly: the old man's daughter told us all.

CLAUDIO: all, all; and, moreover, God saw him when he was hid in the garden.

DON PEDRO: But when shall we set the savage bull's horns on the sensible Benedick's head?

Claudio : Yea, and text underneath, 'Here dwells Benedick the married man'?

BENEDICK: Fare you well, boy: you know my mind. I will leave you now to your gossip-like humour: you break jests as braggards do their blades, which, God be thanked, hurt not. My lord, for your many courtesies I thank you: I must discontinue your company: your brother the bastard is fled from Messina: you have among you killed a sweet and innocent lady. For my Lord Lackbeard thee, he and I shall meet: and, till then, peace be with him.

[*Exit.*

DON PEDRO: He is in earnest.

CLAUDIO: In most profound earnest; and, I'll warrant you, for the love of Beatrice.

DON PEDRO: And hath challenged thee.

CLAUDIO: Most sincerely.

DON PEDRO: What a pretty thing man is when he goes in his doublet and hose and leaves off his wit.

CLAUDIO: He is then a giant to an ape; but then is an ape a doctor to such a man.

DON PEDRO: But, soft you, let me be: pluck up, my heart, and be sad. Did he not say, my brother was fled?

Enter Dogberry, Verges, and the Watch, with Conrade and Borachio.

DOGBERRY: Come you, sir: if justice cannot tame you, she shall ne'er weigh more reasons in her balance: nay, an you be a cursing hypocrite once, you must be looked to.

DON PEDRO: How now? two of my brother's men bound! Borachio one!

CLAUDIO: Hearken after their offence, my lord.

DON PEDRO: Officers, what offence have these men done?

DOGBERRY: Marry, sir, they have committed false report; moreover, they have spoken untruths; secondarily, they are slanders; sixth and lastly, they have belied a lady; thirdly, they have verified unjust things; and, to conclude, they are lying knaves.

DON PEDRO: First, I ask thee what they have done; thirdly, I ask thee what's their offence; sixth and lastly, why they are committed; and to conclude, what you lay to their charge.

CLAUDIO: Rightly reasoned, and in his own division; and, by my troth, there's one meaning well suited.

DON PEDRO: Who have you offended, masters, that you are thus bound to your answer? this learned constable is too cunning to be understood: what's your offence?

BORACHIO: Sweet prince, let me go no farther to mine answer: do you hear me, and let this count kill me. I have deceived even your very eyes: what your wisdoms could not discover, these shallow fools have brought to light; who in the night overheard me confessing to this man how Don John your brother incensed me to slander the Lady Hero, how you were brought into the orchard and saw me court Margaret in Hero's garments, how you disgraced her, when you should marry her: my villany they have upon record; which I had rather seal with my death than repeat over to my shame. The lady is dead upon mine and my master's false accusation; and, briefly, I desire nothing but the reward of a villain.

DON PEDRO: Runs not this speech like iron through your blood?

CLAUDIO: I have drunk poison whiles he utter'd it.

DON PEDRO: But did my brother set thee on to this?

BORACHIO: Yea, and paid me richly for the practice of it.

DON PEDRO: He is composed and framed of treachery:
And fled he is upon this villany.

CLAUDIO: Sweet Hero! now thy image doth appear
In the rare semblance that I loved it first.

DOGBERRY: Come, bring away the plaintiffs: by this time our sexton hath reformed Signior Leonato of the matter: and, masters, do not forget to specify, when time and place shall serve, that I am an ass.

VERGES: Here, here comes master Signior Leonato, and the sexton too.

Re-enter Leonato and Antonio, with the Sexton.

LEONATO: Which is the villain? let me see his eyes,
That, when I note another man like him,
I may avoid him: which of these is he?

BORACHIO: If you would know your wronger, look on me.

LEONATO: Art thou the slave that with thy breath hast killed
Mine innocent child?

BORACHIO: Yea, even I alone.

LEONATO: No, not so, villain; thou beliest thyself:
Here stand a pair of honourable men;
A third is fled, that had a hand in it.
I thank you, princes, for my daughter's death:
Record it with your high and worthy deeds:
'Twas bravely done, if you bethink you of it.

CLAUDIO: I know not how to pray your patience;
Yet I must speak. Choose your revenge yourself;
Impose me to what penance your invention
Can lay upon my sin: yet sinn'd I not
But in mistaking.

DON PEDRO: By my soul, nor I:
And yet, to satisfy this good old man,
I would bend under any heavy weight
That he'll enjoin me to.

LEONATO: I cannot bid you bid my daughter live;
That were impossible: but, I pray you both,
Possess the people in Messina here
How innocent she died; and if your love
Can labour aught in sad invention,
Hang her an epitaph upon her tomb
And sing it to her bones, sing it to-night:
To-morrow morning come you to my house,
And since you could not be my son-in-law,
Be yet my nephew: my brother hath a daughter,
Almost the copy of my child that's dead,
And she alone is heir to both of us:
Give her the right you should have given her cousin,
And so dies my revenge.

CLAUDIO: O noble sir,
Your over-kindness doth wring tears from me!

I do embrace your offer; and dispose
For henceforth of poor Claudio.

LEONATO: To-morrow then I will expect your coming;
To-night I take my leave. This naughty man
Shall face to face be brought to Margaret,
Who I believe was pack'd in all this wrong,
Hired to it by your brother.

BORACHIO: No, by my soul, she was not,
Nor knew not what she did when she spoke to me,
But always hath been just and virtuous
In any thing that I do know by her.

DOGBERRY: Moreover, sir, which indeed is not under white and black, this plaintiff here, the offender, did call me ass: I beseech you, let it be remembered in his punishment. And also, the watch heard them talk of one Deformed: they say he wears a key in his ear and a lock hanging by it, and borrows money in God's name, the which he hath used so long and never paid that now men grow hard-hearted and will lend nothing for God's sake: pray you, examine him upon that point.

LEONATO: I thank thee for thy care and honest pains.

DOGBERRY: Your worship speaks like a most thankful and reverend youth; and I praise God for you.

LEONATO: There's for thy pains.

DOGBERRY: God save the foundation!

LEONATO: Go, I discharge thee of thy prisoner, and I thank thee.

DOGBERRY: I leave an arrant knave with your worship; which I beseech your worship to correct yourself, for the example of others. God keep your worship! I wish your worship well; God restore you to health! I humbly give you leave to depart; and if a merry meeting may be wished, God prohibit it! Come, neighbour.

                          [*Exeunt Dogberry and Verges.*

LEONATO: Until to-morrow morning, lords, farewell.

ANTONIO: Farewell, my lords: we look for you to-morrow.

DON PEDRO: We will not fail.

CLAUDIO: To-night I'll mourn with Hero.
LEONATO: [*To the Watch*] Bring you these fellows on. We 'll talk
     with Margaret,
How her acquaintance grew with this lewd fellow.

                                             [*Exeunt, severally.*

SCENE II. *Leonato's garden.*
Enter Benedick and Margaret, meeting.

BENEDICK: Pray thee, sweet Mistress Margaret, deserve well at
my hands by helping me to the speech of Beatrice.

MARGARET: Will you then write me a sonnet in praise of
my beauty?

BENEDICK: In so high a style, Margaret, that no man living shall
come over it; for, in most comely truth, thou deservest it.

MARGARET: To have no man come over me! why, shall I always
keep below stairs?

BENEDICK: Thy wit is as quick as the grey-hound's mouth;
it catches.

MARGARET: And yours as blunt as the fencer's foils, which hit,
but hurt not.

BENEDICK: A most manly wit, Margaret; it will not hurt a
woman: and so, I pray thee, call Beatrice: I give thee the bucklers.

MARGARET: Give us the swords; we have bucklers of our own.

BENEDICK: If you use them, Margaret, you must put in the
pikes with a vice; and they are dangerous weapons for maids.

MARGARET: Well, I will call Beatrice to you, who I think hath
legs.

BENEDICK: And therefore will come.   [*Exit Margaret.*
     [*Sings*]   The god of love,
                              That sits above,
                         And knows me, and knows me,
                              How pitiful I deserve,—
I mean in singing; but in loving, Leander the good swimmer,
Troilus the first employer of pandars, and a whole bookful of

these quondam carpet-mongers, whose names yet run smoothly in the even road of a blank verse, why, they were never so truly turned over and over as my poor self in love. Marry, I cannot show it in rhyme; I have tried: I can find out no rhyme to 'lady' but 'baby,' an innocent rhyme; for 'scorn,' 'horn,' a hard rhyme; for 'school,' 'fool,' a babbling rhyme; very ominous endings: no, I was not born under a rhyming planet, nor I cannot woo in festival terms.

Enter Beatrice.

Sweet Beatrice, wouldst thou come when I called thee?

BEATRICE: Yea, signior, and depart when you bid me.

BENEDICK: O, stay but till then!

BEATRICE: 'Then' is spoken; fare you well now; and yet, ere I go, let me go with that I came; which is, with knowing what hath passed between you and Claudio.

BENEDICK: Only foul words; and thereupon I will kiss thee.

BEATRICE: Foul words is but foul wind, and foul wind is but foul breath, and foul breath is noisome; therefore I will depart unkissed.

BENEDICK: Thou hast frighted the word out of his right sense, so forcible is thy wit. But I must tell thee plainly, Claudio undergoes my challenge; and either I must shortly hear from him, or I will subscribe him a coward. And, I pray thee now, tell me for which of my bad parts didst thou first fall in love with me?

BEATRICE: For them all together; which maintained so politic a state of evil that they will not admit any good part to intermingle with them. But for which of my good parts did you first suffer love for me?

BENEDICK: Suffer love! a good epithet! I do suffer love indeed, for I love thee against my will.

BEATRICE: In spite of your heart, I think; alas, poor heart! If you spite it for my sake, I will spite it for yours; for I will never love that which my friend hates.

BENEDICK: Thou and I are too wise to woo peaceably.

BEATRICE: It appears not in this confession: there's not one wise man among twenty that will praise himself.

BENEDICK: An old, an old instance, Beatrice, that lived in the time of good neighbours. If a man do not erect in this age his own tomb ere he dies, he shall live no longer in monument than the bell rings and the widow weeps.

BEATRICE: And how long is that, think you?

BENEDICK: Question: why, an hour in clamour and a quarter in rheum: therefore is it most expedient for the wise, if Don Worm, his conscience, find no impediment to the contrary, to be the trumpet of his own virtues, as I am to myself. So much for praising myself, who, I myself will bear witness, is praiseworthy: and now tell me, how doth your cousin?

BEATRICE: Very ill.

BENEDICK: And how do you?

BEATRICE: Very ill too.

BENEDICK: Serve God, love me and mend. There will I leave you too, for here comes one in haste.

Enter Ursula.

URSULA: Madam, you must come to your uncle. Yonder's old coil at home: it is proved my Lady Hero hath been falsely accused, the prince and Claudio mightily abused; and Don John is the author of all, who is fled and gone. Will you come presently?

BEATRICE: Will you go hear this news, signior?

BENEDICK: I will live in thy heart, die in thy lap and be buried in thy eyes; and moreover I will go with thee to thy uncle's.

[*Exeunt.*

SCENE III. *A church.*
Enter Don Pedro, Claudio, and three or four with tapers.

CLAUDIO: Is this the monument of Leonato?

A LORD: It is, my lord.

CLAUDIO: [*Reading out of a scroll*]

Done to death by slanderous tongues
   Was the Hero that here lies:
Death, in guerdon of her wrongs,
   Gives her fame which never dies.
So the life that died with shame
Lives in death with glorious fame.
Hang thou there upon the tomb,
Praising her when I am dumb.
Now, music, sound, and sing your solemn hymn.

SONG.

   Pardon, goddess of the night,
Those that slew thy virgin knight;
   For the which, with songs of woe,
Round about her tomb they go.
   Midnight, assist our moan;
   Help us to sigh and groan,
      Heavily, heavily:
   Graves, yawn and yield your dead,
   Till death be uttered,
      Heavily, heavily.

CLAUDIO: Now, unto thy bones good night!
   Yearly will I do this rite.
DON PEDRO: Good morrow, masters; put your torches out:
The wolves have prey'd; and look, the gentle day,
Before the wheels of Phœbus, round about
Dapples the drowsy east with spots of grey.
Thanks to you all, and leave us: fare you well.
CLAUDIO: Good morrow, masters: each his several way.
DON PEDRO: Come, let us hence, and put on other weeds;
And then to Leonato's we will go.
CLAUDIO: And Hymen now with luckier issue speed 's
Than this for whom we render'd up this woe.   [*Exeunt.*

SCENE IV. *A room in Leonato's house.*
Enter Leonato, Antonio, Benedick, Beatrice, Margaret, Ursula,
Friar Francis, and Hero.

FRIAR: Did I not tell you she was innocent?

LEONATO: So are the prince and Claudio, who accused her
Upon the error that you heard debated:
But Margaret was in some fault for this,
Although against her will, as it appears
In the true course of all the question.

ANTONIO: Well, I am glad that all things sort so well.

BENEDICK: And so am I, being else by faith enforced
To call young Claudio to a reckoning for it.

LEONATO: Well, daughter, and you gentlewomen all,
Withdraw into a chamber by yourselves,
And when I send for you, come hither mask'd.   [*Exeunt Ladies.*
The prince and Claudio promised by this hour
To visit me. You know your office, brother:
You must be father to your brother's daughter,
And give her to young Claudio.

ANTONIO: Which I will do with confirm'd countenance.

BENEDICK: Friar, I must entreat your pains, I think.

FRIAR: To do what, signior?

BENEDICK: To bind me, or undo me; one of them.
Signior Leonato, truth it is, good signior,
Your niece regards me with an eye of favour.

LEONATO: That eye my daughter lent her: 'tis most true.

BENEDICK: And I do with an eye of love requite her.

LEONATO: The sight whereof I think you had from me,
From Claudio and the prince: but what's your will?

BENEDICK: Your answer, sir, is enigmatical:
But, for my will, my will is your good will
May stand with ours, this day to be conjoin'd
In the state of honourable marriage:
In which, good friar, I shall desire your help.

LEONATO: My heart is with your liking.

FRIAR: And my help,
Here comes the prince and Claudio.

Enter Don Pedro and Claudio, and two or three others.

DON PEDRO: Good morrow to this fair assembly.

LEONATO: Good morrow, prince; good morrow, Claudio;
We here attend you. Are you yet determined
To-day to marry with my brother's daughter?

CLAUDIO: I 'll hold my mind, were she an Ethiope.

LEONATO: Call her forth, brother; here's the friar ready.

                                         [Exit Antonio.

DON PEDRO: Good morrow, Benedick. Why, what's the matter.
That you have such a February face,
So full of frost, of storm and cloudiness?

CLAUDIO: I think he thinks upon the savage bull.
Tush, fear not, man; we 'll tip thy horns with gold
And all Europa shall rejoice at thee,
As once Europa did at lusty Jove,
When he would play the noble beast in love.

BENEDICK: Bull Jove, sir, had an amiable low;
And some such strange bull leap'd your father's cow,
And got a calf in that same noble feat
Much like to you, for you have just his bleat.

CLAUDIO: For this I owe you: here comes other reckonings.

Re-enter Antonio, with the Ladies masked.

Which is the lady I must seize upon?

ANTONIO: This same is she, and I do give you her.

CLAUDIO: Why, then she's mine. Sweet, let me see your face.

LEONATO: No, that you shall not, till you take her hand
Before this friar and swear to marry her.

CLAUDIO: Give me your hand: before this holy friar,
I am your husband, if you like of me.

HERO: And when I lived, I was your other wife: *[Unmasking.*

And when you loved, you were my other husband.

CLAUDIO: Another Hero!

HERO: Nothing certainer:

One Hero died defiled, but I do live,

And surely as I live, I am a maid.

DON PEDRO: The former Hero! Hero that is dead!

LEONATO: She died, my lord, but whiles her slander lived.

FRIAR: All this amazement can I qualify;

When after that the holy rites are ended,

I 'll tell you largely of fair Hero's death:

Meantime let wonder seem familiar,

And to the chapel let us presently.

BENEDICK: Soft and fair, friar. Which is Beatrice?

BEATRICE: [*Unmasking*] I answer to that name. What is your
will?

BENEDICK: Do not you love me?

BEATRICE: Why, no; no more than reason.

BENEDICK: Why, then your uncle and the prince and Claudio

Have been deceived; they swore you did.

BEATRICE: Do not you love me?

BENEDICK: Troth, no; no more than reason.

BEATRICE: Why, then my cousin Margaret and Ursula

Are much deceived; for they did swear you did.

BENEDICK: They swore that you were almost sick for me.

BEATRICE: They swore that you were well-nigh dead for me.

BENEDICK: 'Tis no such matter. Then you do not love me?

BEATRICE: No, truly, but in friendly recompense.

LEONATO: Come, cousin, I am sure you love the gentleman.

CLAUDIO: And I 'll be sworn upon't that he loves her;

For here's a paper written in his hand,

A halting sonnet of his own pure brain,

Fashion'd to Beatrice.

HERO: And here's another

Writ in my cousin's hand, stolen from her pocket,

Containing her affection unto Benedick.

BENEDICK: A miracle! here's our own hands against our hearts. Come, I will have thee; but, by this light, I take thee for pity.

BEATRICE: I would not deny you; but, by this good day, I yield upon great persuasion; and partly to save your life, for I was told you were in a consumption.

BENEDICK: Peace! I will stop your mouth.   [*Kissing her.*

DON PEDRO: How dost thou, Benedick, the married man?

BENEDICK: I'll tell thee what, prince; a college of wit-crackers cannot flout me out of my humour. Dost thou think I care for a satire or an epigram? No: if a man will be beaten with brains, a' shall wear nothing handsome about him. In brief, since I do purpose to marry, I will think nothing to any purpose that the world can say against it; and therefore never flout at me for what I have said against it; for man is a giddy thing, and this is my conclusion. For thy part, Claudio, I did think to have beaten thee; but in that thou art like to be my kinsman, live unbruised and love my cousin.

CLAUDIO: I had well hoped thou wouldst have denied Beatrice, that I might have cudgelled thee out of thy single life, to make thee a double-dealer; which, out of question, thou wilt be, if my cousin do not look exceeding narrowly to thee.

BENEDICK: Come, come, we are friends: let's have a dance ere we are married, that we may lighten our own hearts and our wives' heels.

LEONATO: We'll have dancing afterward.

BENEDICK: First, of my word; therefore play, music. Prince, thou art sad; get thee a wife, get thee a wife: there is no staff more reverend than one tipped with horn.

Enter a Messenger.

MESSENGER: My lord, your brother John is ta'en in flight,
And brought with armed men back to Messina.

BENEDICK: Think not on him till to-morrow:
I'll devise thee brave punishments for him.
Strike up, pipers.

                                                            [*Dance.*
                                                            [*Exeunt.*

. . .

ROMEO AND JULIET

DRAMATIS PERSONÆ

ESCALUS, prince of Verona.

PARIS, a young nobleman, kinsman to the prince.

MONTAGUE,⎱ heads of two
CAPULET, ⎰ houses at variance
with each other.

An old man, cousin to Capulet.

ROMEO, son to Montague.

MERCUTIO, kinsman to the
prince, and friend to
Romeo.

BENVOLIO, nephew to Mon-
tague, and friend to Romeo.

TYBALT, nephew to Lady
Capulet.

FRIAR LAURENCE,⎱ Franciscans.
FRIAR JOHN, ⎰

BALTHASAR, servant to Romeo.

SAMPSON,⎱ servants to Capulet.
GREGORY,⎰

PETER, servant to Juliet's nurse.

ABRAHAM, servant to Montague.

An Apothecary.

Three Musicians.

Page to Paris; another Page; an
Officer.

LADY MONTAGUE, wife to
Montague.

LADY CAPULET, wife to Capulet.

JULIET, daughter to Capulet.

Nurse to Juliet.

Citizens of Verona; several
Men and Women, relations
to both houses; Maskers,
Guards, Watchmen, and
Attendants.

Chorus.

SCENE:
Verona: Mantua.

PROLOGUE.

Two households, both alike in dignity,
  In fair Verona, where we lay our scene,
From ancient grudge break to new mutiny,
  Where civil blood makes civil hands unclean.
From forth the fatal loins of these two foes
  A pair of star-cross'd lovers take their life;
Whose misadventured piteous overthrows
  Do with their death bury their parents' strife.

The fearful passage of their death-mark'd love,
   And the continuance of their parents' rage,
Which, but their children's end, nought could remove,
   Is now the two hours' traffic of our stage;
The which if you with patient ears attend,
What here shall miss, our toil shall strive to mend.

ACT I.

SCENE I. *Verona. A public place.*
Enter Sampson and Gregory, of the house of Capulet,
armed with swords and bucklers.

SAMPSON: Gregory, o' my word, we'll not carry coals.

GREGORY: No, for then we should be colliers.

SAMPSON: I mean, an we be in choler, we'll draw.

GREGORY: Ay, while you live, draw your neck out o' the collar.

SAMPSON: I strike quickly, being moved.

GREGORY: But thou art not quickly moved to strike.

SAMPSON: A dog of the house of Montague moves me.

GREGORY: To move is to stir; and to be valiant is to stand: therefore, if thou art moved, thou runn'st away.

SAMPSON: A dog of that house shall move me to stand: I will take the wall of any man or maid of Montague's.

GREGORY: That shows thee a weak slave; for the weakest goes to the wall.

SAMPSON: True; and therefore women, being the weaker vessels, are ever thrust to the wall: therefore I will push Montague's men from the wall, and thrust his maids to the wall.

GREGORY: The quarrel is between our masters and us their men.

SAMPSON: 'Tis all one, I will show myself a tyrant: when I have fought with the men, I will be cruel with the maids, and cut off their heads.

GREGORY: The heads of the maids?

SAMPSON: Ay, the heads of the maids, or their maidenheads: take it in what sense thou wilt.

GREGORY: They must take it in sense that feel it.

SAMPSON: Me they shall feel while I am able to stand: and 'tis known I am a pretty piece of flesh.

GREGORY: 'Tis well thou art not fish; if thou hadst, thou hadst been poor John. Draw thy tool; here comes two of the house of the Montagues.

SAMPSON: My naked weapon is out: quarrel, I will back thee.

GREGORY: How! turn thy back and run?

SAMPSON: Fear me not.

GREGORY: No, marry; I fear thee!

SAMPSON: Let us take the law of our sides; let them begin.

GREGORY: I will frown as I pass by, and let them take it as they list.

SAMPSON: Nay, as they dare. I will bite my thumb at them; which is a disgrace to them, if they bear it.

Enter Abraham and Balthasar.

ABRAHAM: Do you bite your thumb at us, sir?

SAMPSON: I do bite my thumb, sir.

ABRAHAM: Do you bite your thumb at us, sir?

SAMPSON: [*Aside to Gregory.*] Is the law of our side, if I say ay?

GREGORY: No.

SAMPSON: No, sir. I do not bite my thumb at you, sir, but I bite my thumb, sir.

GREGORY: Do you quarrel, sir?

ABRAHAM: Quarrel, sir! no, sir.

SAMPSON: If you do, sir, I am for you: I serve as good a man as you.

ABRAHAM: No better.

SAMPSON: Well, sir.

GREGORY: Say 'better:' here comes one of my master's kinsmen.

SAMPSON: Yes, better, sir.

ABRAHAM: You lie.

SAMPSON: Draw, if you be men. Gregory, remember thy swashing blow. *[They fight.*

Enter Benvolio.

BENVOLIO: Part, fools!
Put up your swords; you know not what you do.
[Beats down their swords.

Enter Tybalt.

TYBALT: What, art thou drawn among these heartless hinds?
Turn thee, Benvolio, look upon thy death.
BENVOLIO: I do but keep the peace: put up thy sword,
Or manage it to part these men with me.
TYBALT: What, drawn, and talk of peace! I hate the word,
As I hate hell, all Montagues, and thee:
Have to thee, coward! *[They fight.*

Enter several of both houses, who join the fray:
then enter Citizens, with clubs.

FIRST CITIZEN: Clubs, bills, and partisans! strike! beat them down!
Down with the Capulets! down with the Montagues!

Enter Capulet in his gown, and Lady Capulet.

CAPULET: What noise is this? Give me my long sword, ho!
LADY CAPULET: A crutch, a crutch! why call you for a sword?
CAPULET: My sword, I say! Old Montague is come,
And flourishes his blade in spite of me.

Enter Montague and Lady Montague.

MONTAGUE: Thou villain Capulet,—Hold me not, let me go.
LADY MONTAGUE: Thou shalt not stir a foot to seek a foe.

Enter Prince, with Attendants.

PRINCE: Rebellious subjects, enemies to peace,

Profaners of this neighbour-stained steel,—
Will they not hear? What, ho! you men you beasts,
That quench the fire of your pernicious rage
With purple fountains issuing from your veins,
On pain of torture, from those bloody hands
Throw your mistemper'd weapons to the ground,
And hear the sentence of your moved prince,
Three civil brawls, bred of an airy word,
By thee, old Capulet, and Montague,
Have thrice disturb'd the quiet of our streets,
And made Verona's ancient citizens
Cast by their grave beseeming ornaments,
To wield old partisans, in hands as old,
Canker'd with peace, to part your canker'd hate:
If ever you disturb our streets again,
Your lives shall pay the forfeit of the peace.
For this time, all the rest depart away:
You, Capulet, shall go along with me:
And, Montague, come you this afternoon,
To know our further pleasure in this case,
To old Free-town, our common judgement-place.
Once more, on pain of death, all men depart.
          [*Exeunt all but Montague, Lady Montague, and Benvolio.*
     MONTAGUE: Who set this ancient quarrel new abroach?
Speak, nephew, were you by when it began?
     BENVOLIO: Here were the servants of your adversary,
And yours, close fighting ere I did approach:
I drew to part them: in the instant came
The fiery Tybalt, with his sword prepared,
Which, as he breathed defiance to my ears,
He swung about his head and cut the winds,
Who nothing hurt withal hiss'd him in scorn:
While we were interchanging thrusts and blows,
Came more and more and fought on part and part,
Till the prince came, who parted either part.

LADY MONTAGUE: O, where is Romeo? saw you him to-day?
Right glad I am he was not at this fray.
BENVOLIO: Madam, an hour before the worshipp'd sun
Peer'd forth the golden window of the east,
A troubled mind drave me to walk abroad;
Where, underneath the grove of sycamore
That westward rooteth from the city's side,
So early walking did I see your son:
Towards him I made, but he was ware of me
And stole into the covert of the wood:
I, measuring his affections by my own,
That most are busied when they 're most alone,
Pursued my honour not pursuing his,
And gladly shunn'd who gladly fled from me.
MONTAGUE: Many a morning hath he there been seen,
With tears augmenting the fresh morning's dew,
Adding to clouds more clouds with his deep sighs;
But all so soon as the all-cheering sun
Should in the furthest east begin to draw
The shady curtains from Aurora's bed,
Away from light steals home my heavy son,
And private in his chamber pens himself,
Shuts up his windows, locks fair daylight out
And makes himself an artificial night:
Black and portentous must this humour prove,
Unless good counsel may the cause remove.
BENVOLIO: My noble uncle, do you know the cause?
MONTAGUE: I neither know it nor can learn of him.
BENVOLIO: Have you importuned him by any means?
MONTAGUE: Both by myself and many other friends:
But he, his own affections' counsellor,
Is to himself—I will not say how true—
But to himself so secret and so close,
So far from sounding and discovery,
As is the bud bit with an envious worm,

Ere he can spread his sweet leaves to the air,
Or dedicate his beauty to the sun.
Could we but learn from whence his sorrows grow,
We would as willingly give cure as know.

Enter Romeo.

BENVOLIO: See, where he comes: so please you, step aside;
I'll know his grievance, or be much denied.
MONTAGUE: I would thou wert so happy by thy stay,
To hear true shrift. Come, madam, let's away.

                                           [Exeunt Montague and Lady.

BENVOLIO: Good morrow, cousin.
ROMEO: Is the day so young?
BENVOLIO: But new struck nine.
ROMEO: Ay me! sad hours seem long,
Was that my father that went hence so fast?
BENVOLIO: It was. What sadness lengthens Romeo's hours?
ROMEO: Not having that, which, having, makes them short.
BENVOLIO: In love?
ROMEO: Out—
BENVOLIO: Of love?
ROMEO: Out of her favour, where I am in love.
BENVOLIO: Alas, that love, so gentle in his view,
Should be so tyrannous and rough in proof!
ROMEO: Alas, that love, whose view is muffled still,
Should, without eyes, see pathways to his will!
Where shall we dine? O me! What fray was here?
Yet, tell me not, for I have heard it all.
Here's much to do with hate, but more with love.
Why, then, O brawling love! O loving hate!
O any thing, of nothing first create!
O heavy lightness! serious vanity!
Mis-shapen chaos of well-seeming forms!
Feather of lead, bright smoke, cold fire, sick health!
Still-waking sleep, that is not what it is!

This love feel I, that feel no love in this.
Dost thou not laugh?

BENVOLIO: No, coz, I rather weep.

ROMEO: Good heart, at what?

BENVOLIO: At thy good heart's oppression.

ROMEO: Why, such is love's transgression.
Griefs of mine own lie heavy in my breast,
Which thou wilt propagate, to have it prest
With more of thine: this love that thou hast shown
Doth add more grief to too much of mine own.
Love is a smoke raised with the fume of sighs;
Being purged, a fire sparkling in lovers' eyes;
Being vex'd, a sea nourish'd with lovers' tears:
What is it else? a madness most discreet,
A choking gall and a preserving sweet.
Farewell, my coz.

BENVOLIO: Soft! I will go along;
An if you leave me so, you do me wrong.

ROMEO: Tut, I have lost myself; I am not here;
This is not Romeo, he's some other where.

BENVOLIO: Tell me in sadness, who is that you love.

ROMEO: What, shall I groan and tell thee?

BENVOLIO: Groan! why, no:
But sadly tell me who.

ROMEO: Bid a sick man in sadness make his will:
Ah, word ill urged to one that is so ill!
In sadness, cousin, I do love a woman.

BENVOLIO: I aim'd so near, when I supposed you loved.

ROMEO: A right good mark-man! And she's fair I love.

BENVOLIO: A right fair mark, fair coz, is soonest hit.

ROMEO: Well, in that hit you miss: she'll not be hit
With Cupid's arrow; she hath Dian's wit;
And, in strong proof of chastity well arm'd,
From love's weak childish bow she lives unharm'd.
She will not stay the siege of loving terms,

Nor bide the encounter of assailing eyes,
Nor ope her lap to saint-seducing gold:
O, she is rich in beauty, only poor,
That when she dies with beauty dies her store.

BENVOLIO: Then she hath sworn that she will still live chaste?

ROMEO: She hath, and in that sparing makes huge waste,
For beauty starved with her severity
Cuts beauty off from all posterity.
She is too fair, too wise, wisely too fair,
To merit bliss by making me despair:
She hath forsworn to love, and in that vow
Do I live dead that live to tell it now.

BENVOLIO: Be ruled by me, forget to think of her.

ROMEO: O, teach me how I should forget to think.

BENVOLIO: By giving liberty unto thine eyes;
Examine other beauties.

ROMEO: 'Tis the way
To call hers exquisite, in question more:
These happy masks that kiss fair ladies' brows
Being black puts us in mind they hide the fair;
He that is strucken blind cannot forget
The precious treasure of his eyesight lost:
Show me a mistress that is passing fair,
What doth her beauty serve, but as a note
Where I may read who pass'd that passing fair?
Farewell: thou canst not teach me to forget.

BENVOLIO: I'll pay that doctrine, or else die in debt.   [*Exeunt.*

SCENE II. *A street.*
Enter Capulet, Paris, and Servant.

CAPULET: But Montague is bound as well as I,
In penalty alike; and 'tis not hard, I think,
For men so old as we to keep the peace.

PARIS: Of honourable reckoning are you both;

And pity 'tis you lived at odds so long.
But now, my lord, what say you to my suit?
    CAPULET: But saying o'er what I have said before:
My child is yet a stranger in the world;
She hath not seen the change of fourteen years;
Let two more summers wither in their pride,
Ere we may think her ripe to be a bride.
    PARIS: Younger than she are happy mothers made.
    CAPULET: And too soon marr'd are those so early made.
The earth hath swallow'd all my hopes but she,
She is the hopeful lady of my earth:
But woo her, gentle Paris, get her heart,
My will to her consent is but a part;
An she agree, within her scope of choice,
Lies my consent and fair according voice.
This night I hold an old accustom'd feast,
Whereto I have invited many a guest,
Such as I love; and you, among the store,
One more, most welcome, makes my number more.
At my poor house look to behold this night
Earth-treading stars that make dark heaven light:
Such comfort as do lusty young men feel
When well-apparell'd April on the heel
Of limping winter treads, even such delight
Among fresh female buds shall you this night
Inherit at my house; hear all, all see,
And like her most whose merit most shall be:
Which on more view, of many mine being one
May stand in number, though in reckoning none.
Come, go with me.   [*To Servant, giving a paper.*
   Go, sirrah, trudge about
Through fair Verona; find those persons out
Whose names are written there, and to them say,
My house and welcome on their pleasure stay.
                           [*Exeunt Capulet and Paris.*

SERVANT: Find them out whose names are written here! It is written, that the shoemaker should meddle with his yard, and the tailor with his last, the fisher with his pencil, and the painter with his nets; but I am sent to find those persons whose names are here writ, and can never find what names the writing person hath here writ. I must to the learned.—In good time.

Enter Benvolio and Romeo.

BENVOLIO: Tut, man, one fire burns out another's burning.
One pain is lessen'd by another's anguish;
Turn giddy, and be holp by backward turning;
One desperate grief cures with another's languish:
Take thou some new infection to thy eye,
And the rank poison of the old will die.
ROMEO: Your plaintain-leaf is excellent for that.
BENVOLIO: For what, I pray thee?
ROMEO: For your broken shin.
BENVOLIO: Why, Romeo, art thou mad?
ROMEO: Not mad, but bound more than a madman is;
Shut up in prison, kept without my food,
Whipp'd and tormented and—God-den, good fellow.
SERVANT: God gi' god-den. I pray, sir, can you read?
ROMEO: Ay, mine own fortune in my misery.
SERVANT: Perhaps you have learned it without book: but, I pray, can you read any thing you see?
ROMEO: Ay, if I know the letters and the language.
SERVANT: Ye say honestly: rest you merry!
ROMEO: Stay, fellow; I can read.   [*Reads.*
'Signior Martino and his wife and daughters; County Anselme and his beauteous sisters; the lady widow of Vitruvio; Signior Placentio and his lovely nieces; Mercutio and his brother Valentine; mine uncle Capulet, his wife, and daughters; my fair niece Rosaline; Livia; Signior Valentio and his cousin Tybalt; Lucio and the lively Helena.'
A fair assembly: whither should they come?

SERVANT: Up.

ROMEO: Whither?

SERVANT: To supper; to our house.

ROMEO: Whose house?

SERVANT: My master's.

ROMEO: Indeed, I should have asked you that before.

SERVANT: Now I'll tell you without asking: my master is the great rich Capulet; and if you be not of the house of Montagues, I pray, come and crush a cup of wine. Rest you merry!   [*Exit.*

BENVOLIO: At this same ancient feast of Capulet's
Sups the fair Rosaline whom thou so lovest,
With all the admired beauties of Verona:
Go thither; and, with unattainted eye,
Compare her face with some that I shall show,
And I will make thee think thy swan a crow.

ROMEO: When the devout religion of mine eye
Maintains such falsehood, then turn tears to fires;
And these, who often drown'd could never die,
Transparent heretics, be burnt for liars!
One fairer than my love! the all-seeing sun
Ne'er saw her match since first the world begun.

BENVOLIO: Tut, you saw her fair, none else being by,
Herself poised with herself in either eye:
But in that crystal scales let there be weigh'd
Your lady's love against some other maid
That I will show you shining at this feast,
And she shall scant show well that now shows best.

ROMEO: I'll go along, no such sight to be shown,
But to rejoice in splendour of mine own.   [*Exeunt.*

SCENE III. *A room in Capulet's house.*
Enter Lady Capulet and Nurse.

LADY CAPULET: Nurse, where 's my daughter? call her forth to me.

NURSE: Now, by my maidenhead, at twelve year old.
I bade her come. What, lamb! what, lady-bird!
God forbid! Where's this girl? What, Juliet!

Enter Juliet.

JULIET: How now! who calls?
NURSE: Your mother.
JULIET: Madam, I am here.
What is your will?
LADY CAPULET: This is the matter:—Nurse, give leave awhile,
We must talk in secret:—nurse, come back again;
I have remember'd me, thou 's hear our counsel.
Thou know' st my daughter's of a pretty age.
NURSE: Faith, I can tell her age unto an hour.
LADY CAPULET: She's not fourteen.
NURSE: I'll lay fourteen of my teeth,—
And yet, to my teen be it spoken, I have but four,—
She is not fourteen. How long is it now
To Lammas-tide?
LADY CAPULET: A fortnight and odd days.
NURSE: Even or odd, of all days in the year,
Come Lammas-eve at night shall she be fourteen.
Susan and she—God rest all Christian souls!—
Were of an age: well, Susan is with God;
She was too good for me; but, as I said,
On Lammas-eve at night shall she be fourteen;
That shall she, marry; I remember it well.
'Tis since the earthquake now eleven years;
And she was wean'd,—I never shall forget it,—
Of all the days of the year, upon that day:
For I had then laid wormwood to my dug,
Sitting in the sun under the dove-house wall;
My lord and you were then at Mantua:—
Nay, I do bear a brain:—but, as I said,
When it did taste the wormwood on the nipple

Of my dug and felt it bitter, pretty fool,
To see it tetchy and fall out with the dug!
'Shake' quoth the dove-house: 'twas no need, I trow,
To bid me trudge:
And since that time it is eleven years;
For then she could stand alone; nay, by the rood,
She could have run and waddled all about;
For even the day before, she broke her brow:
And then my husband—God be with his soul!
A' was a merry man—took up the child:
'Yea,' quoth he, 'dost thou fall upon thy face?
Thou wilt fall backward when thou hast more wit;
Wilt thou not, Jule?' and, by my holidame,
The pretty wretch left crying and said, 'Ay.'
To see, now, how a jest shall come about!
I warrant, an I should live a thousand years,
I never should forget it: 'Wilt thou not, Jule?' quoth he;
And, pretty fool, it stinted and said 'Ay.'
    LADY CAPULET: Enough of this; I pray thee, hold thy peace.
    NURSE: Yes, madam, yet I cannot choose but laugh,
To think it should leave crying and say 'Ay.'
And yet, I warrant, it had upon its brow
A bump as big as a young cockerel's stone;
A parlous knock; and it cried bitterly:
'Yea,' quoth my husband, 'fall'st upon thy face?
Thou wilt fall backward when thou comest to age;
Wilt thou not, Jule?' it stinted and said 'Ay.'
    JULIET: And stint thou too, I pray thee, nurse, say I.
    NURSE: Peace, I have done. God mark thee to his grace!
Thou wast the prettiest babe that e'er I nursed:
An I might live to see thee married once,
I have my wish.
    LADY CAPULET: Marry, that 'marry' is the very theme
I came to talk of. Tell me, daughter Juliet,
How stands your disposition to be married?

JULIET: It is an honour that I dream not of.

NURSE: An honour! were not I thine only nurse,
I would say thou hadst suck'd wisdom from thy teat.

LADY CAPULET: Well, think of marriage new; younger than you,
Here in Verona, ladies of esteem,
Are made already mothers: by my count,
I was your mother much upon these years
That you are now a maid. Thus then in brief:
The valiant Paris seeks you for his love.

NURSE: A man, young lady! lady, such a man
As all the world—why, he's a man of wax.

LADY CAPULET: Verona's summer hath not such a flower.

NURSE: Nay, he's a flower; in faith, a very flower.

LADY CAPULET: What say you? can you love the gentleman?
This night you shall behold him at our feast;
Read o'er the volume of young Paris' face
And find delight writ there with beauty's pen;
Examine every married lineament
And see how one another lends content,
And what obscured in this fair volume lies
Find written in the margent of his eyes.
This precious book of love, this unbound lover,
To beautify him, only lacks a cover:
The fish lives in the sea, and 'tis much pride
For fair without the fair within to hide:
That book in many's eyes doth share the glory,
That in gold clasps locks in the golden story;
So shall you share all that he doth possess,
By having him, making yourself no less.

NURSE: No less! nay, bigger; women grow by men.

LADY CAPULET: Speak briefly, can you like of Paris' love?

JULIET: I'll look to like, if looking liking move:
But no more deep will I endart mine eye
Than your consent gives strength to make it fly.

Enter a Servant.

SERVANT: Madam, the guests are come, supper served up, you
called, my young lady asked for, the nurse cursed in the pantry,
and every thing in extremity. I must hence to wait; I beseech you,
follow straight.

LADY CAPULET: We follow thee.   [*Exit Servant.*
    Juliet, the county stays.

NURSE: Go, girl, seek happy nights to happy days.   [*Exeunt.*

SCENE IV. *A street.*

Enter Romeo, Mercutio, Benvolio, with five or six Maskers,
Torch-bearers, and others.

ROMEO: What, shall this speech be spoke for our excuse?
Or shall we on without apology?

BENVOLIO: The date is out of such prolixity:
We'll have no Cupid hoodwink'd with a scarf,
Bearing a Tartar's painted bow of lath,
Scaring the ladies like a crow-keeper;
Nor no without-book prologue, faintly spoke
After the prompter, for our entrance:
But let them measure us by what they will;
We'll measure them a measure, and be gone.

ROMEO: Give me a torch: I am not for this ambling;
Being but heavy, I will bear the light.

MERCUTIO: Nay, gentle Romeo, we must have you dance.

ROMEO: Not I, believe me: you have dancing shoes
With nimble soles: I have a soul of lead
So stakes me to the ground I cannot move.

MERCUTIO: You are a lover; borrow Cupid's wings,
And soar with them above a common bound.

ROMEO: I am too sore enpierced with his shaft
To soar with his light feathers, and so bound,
I cannot bound a pitch above dull woe:

Under love's heavy burden do I sink.

MERCUTIO: And, to sink it in, should you burden love;
Too great oppression for a tender thing.

ROMEO: Is love a tender thing? it is too rough,
Too rude, too boisterous, and it pricks like thorn.

MERCUTIO: If love be rough with you, be rough with love;
Prick love for pricking, and you beat love down.
Give me a case to put my visage in:
A visor for a visor! what care I
What curious eye doth quote deformities?
Here are the beetle brows shall blush for me.

BENVOLIO: Come, knock and enter; and no sooner in,
But every man betake him to his legs.

ROMEO: A torch for me: let wantons light of heart
Tickle the senseless rushes with their heels,
For I am proverb'd with a grandsire phrase;
I'll be a candle-holder, and look on.
The game was ne'er so fair, and I am done.

MERCUTIO: Tut, dun 's the mouse, the constable's own word:
If thou art dun, we'll draw thee from the mire
Of this sir-reverence love, wherein thou stick'st
Up to the ears. Come, we burn daylight, ho!

ROMEO: Nay, that 's not so.

MERCUTIO: I mean, sir, in delay
We waste our lights in vain, like lamps by day.
Take our good meaning, for our judgement sits
Five times in that ere once in our five wits.

ROMEO: And we mean well in going to this mask;
But 'tis no wit to go.

MERCUTIO: Why, may one ask?

ROMEO: I dream'd a dream to-night.

MERCUTIO: And so did I.

ROMEO: Well, what was yours?

MERCUTIO: That dreamers often lie.

ROMEO: In bed asleep, while they do dream things true.

MERCUTIO: O, then, I see Queen Mab hath been with you.
She is the fairies' midwife, and she comes
In shape no bigger than an agate-stone
On the fore-finger of an alderman,
Drawn with a team of little atomies
Athwart men's noses as they lie asleep;
Her waggon-spokes made of long spinners' legs,
The cover of the wings of grasshoppers,
The traces of the smallest spider's web,
The collars of the moonshine's watery beams,
Her whip of cricket's bone, the lash of film,
Her waggoner a small grey-coated gnat,
Not half so big as a round little worm
Prick'd from the lazy finger of a maid;
Her chariot is an empty hazel-nut
Made by the joiner squirrel or old grub,
Time out o' mind the fairies' coachmakers.
And in this state she gallops night by night
Through lovers' brains, and then they dream of love;
O'er courtiers' knees, that dream on court'sies straight,
O'er lawyers' fingers, who straight dream on fees,
O'er ladies' lips, who straight on kisses dream,
Which oft the angry Mab with blisters plagues,
Because their breaths with sweetmeats tainted are:
Sometime she gallops o'er a courtier's nose,
And then dreams he of smelling out a suit;
And sometime comes she with a tithe-pig's tail
Tickling a parson's nose as a' lies asleep,
Then dreams he of another benefice:
Sometime she driveth o'er a soldier's neck,
And then dreams he of cutting foreign throats,
Of breaches, ambuscadoes, Spanish blades,
Of healths five-fathom deep; and then anon
Drums in his ear, at which he starts and wakes,
And being thus frighted, swears a prayer or two

And sleeps again. This is that very Mab
That plats the manes of horses in the night,
And bakes the elf-locks in foul sluttish hairs,
Which once untangled much misfortune bodes:
This is the hag, when maids lie on their backs,
That presses them and learns them first to bear,
Making them women of good carriage:
This is she—

    ROMEO: Peace, peace, Mercutio, peace!
Thou talk'st of nothing.

    MERCUTIO: True, I talk of dreams,
Which are the children of an idle brain,
Begot of nothing but vain fantasy,
Which is as thin of substance as the air
And more inconstant than the wind, who wooes
Even now the frozen bosom of the north,
And, being anger'd, puffs away from thence,
Turning his face to the dew-dropping south.

    BENVOLIO: This wind, you talk of, blows us from ourselves;
Supper is done, and we shall come too late.

    ROMEO: I fear, too early: for my mind misgives
Some consequence yet hanging in the stars
Shall bitterly begin his fearful date
With this night's revels and expires the term
Of a despised life closed in my breast
By some vile forfeit of untimely death.
But He, that hath the steerage of my course,
Direct my sail! On, lusty gentlemen.

    BENVOLIO: Strike, drum.   *[Exeunt.*

SCENE V. *A hall in Capulet's house.*
Musicians waiting. Enter Servingmen, with napkins.

FIRST SERVINGMAN: Where's Potpan, that he helps not to take away? He shift a trencher? he scrape a trencher!

SECOND SERVINGMAN: When good manners shall lie all in one or two men's hands and they unwashed too, 'tis a foul thing.

FIRST SERVINGMAN: Away with the joint-stools, remove the court-cupboard, look to the plate. Good thou, save me a piece of marchpane; and, as thou lovest me, let the porter let in Susan Grindstone and Nell. Antony, and Potpan!

SECOND SERVINGMAN: Ay, boy, ready.

FIRST SERVINGMAN: You are looked for and called for, asked for and sought for, in the great chamber.

SECOND SERVINGMAN: We cannot be here and there too. Cheerly, boys; be brisk awhile, and the longer liver take all.

Enter Capulet, with Juliet and others of his house,
meeting with Guests and Maskers.

CAPULET: Welcome, gentlemen! ladies that have their toes
Unplagued with corns will have a bout with you.
Ah ha, my mistress! which of you all
Will now deny to dance? she that makes dainty,
She, I'll swear, hath corns; am I come near ye now?
Welcome, gentlemen! I have seen the day
That I have worn a visor and could tell
A whispering tale in a fair lady's ear,
Such as would please: 'tis gone, 'tis gone, 'tis gone:
You are welcome, gentlemen! Come, musicians, play.
A hall, a hall! give room! and foot it, girls.
                    [*Music plays, and they dance.*
More light, you knaves; and turn the tables up,
And quench the fire, the room is grown too hot.
Ah, sirrah, this unlook'd-for sport comes well.
Nay, sit, nay, sit, good cousin Capulet;
For you and I are past our dancing days:
How long is 't now since last yourself and I
Were in a mask?

SECOND CAPULET: By 'r lady, thirty years.

CAPULET: What, man! 'tis not so much, 'tis not so much:

'Tis since the nuptial of Lucentio,
Come pentecost as quickly as it will,
Some five and twenty years; and then we mask'd.

SECOND CAPULET: 'Tis more, 'tis more: his son is elder, sir;
His son is thirty.

CAPULET: Will you tell me that?
His son was but a ward two years ago.

ROMEO: [*To a Servingman*] What lady is that, which doth en-
    rich the hand
Of yonder knight?

SERVINGMAN: I know not, sir.

ROMEO: O, she doth teach the torches to burn bright!
It seems she hangs upon the cheek of night
Like a rich jewel in an Ethiope's ear;
Beauty too rich for use, for earth too dear!
So shows a snowy dove trooping with crows,
As yonder lady o'er her fellows shows.
The measure done I'll watch her place of stand,
And, touching hers, make blessed my rude hand.
Did my heart love till now? forswear it, sight!
For I ne'er saw true beauty till this night.

TYBALT: This, by his voice, should be Montague.
Fetch me my rapier, boy. What dares the slave
Come hither, cover'd with an antic face,
To fleer and scorn at our solemnity?
Now, by the stock and honour of my kin,
To strike him dead I hold it not a sin.

CAPULET: Why, how now, kinsman! wherefore storm you so?

TYBALT: Uncle, this is a Montague, our foe,
A villain that is hither come in spite,
To scorn at our solemnity this night.

CAPULET: Young Romeo is it?

TYBALT: 'Tis he, that villain Romeo.

CAPULET: Content thee, gentle coz, let him alone;
He bears him like a portly gentleman;

And, to say truth, Verona brags of him
To be a virtuous and well goven'd youth:
I would not for the wealth of all the town
Here in my house do him disparagement:
Therefore be patient, take no note of him:
It is my will, the which if thou respect,
Show a fair presence and put off these frowns,
An ill-beseeming semblance for a feast.
    TYBALT: It fits, when such a villain is a guest:
I 'll not endure him.
    CAPULET: He shall be endured:
What, goodman, boy! I say, he shall: go to;
Am I the master here, or you? go to.
You 'll not endure him! God shall mend my soul!
You 'll make a mutiny among my guests!
You will set cock-a-hoop! you 'll be the man!
    TYBALT: Why, uncle, 'tis a shame.
    CAPULET: Go to, go to;
You are a saucy boy: is 't so, indeed?
This trick may chance to scathe you, I know what:
You must contrary me! marry 'tis time.
Well said, my hearts! You are a princox; go:
Be quiet, or—More light, more light! For shame!
I 'll make you quiet. What, cheerly, my hearts!
    TYBALT: Patience perforce with wilful choler meeting
Makes my flesh tremble in their different greeting.
I will withdraw: but this intrusion shall
Now seeming sweet convert to bitter gall.   [*Exit.*
    ROMEO: [*To Juliet*] If I profane with my unworthiest hand
        This holy shrine, the gentle fine is this:
My lips, two blushing pilgrims, ready stand
        To smooth that rough touch with a tender kiss.
    JULIET: Good pilgrim, you do wrong your hand too much,
        Which mannerly devotion shows in this;
For saints have hands that pilgrims' hands do touch,

And palm to palm is holy palmers' kiss.

ROMEO: Have not saints lips, and holy palmers too?

JULIET: Ay, pilgrim, lips that they must use in prayer.

ROMEO: O, then, dear saint, let lips do what hands do;
They pray, grant thou, lest faith turn to despair.

JULIET: Saints do not move, though grant for prayers' sake.

ROMEO: Then move not while my prayer's effect I take.
Thus from my lips, by yours, my sin is purged.

JULIET: Then have my lips the sin that they have took.

ROMEO: Sin from my lips? O trespass sweetly urged!
Give me my sin again.

JULIET: You kiss by the book.

NURSE: Madam, your mother craves a word with you.

ROMEO: What is her mother?

NURSE: Marry, bachelor,
Her mother is the lady of the house,
And a good lady, and a wise and virtuous:
I nursed her daughter, that you talk'd withal;
I tell you, he that can lay hold of her
Shall have the chinks.

ROMEO: Is she a Capulet?
O dear account! my life is my foe's debt.

BENVOLIO: Away, be gone; the sport is at the best.

ROMEO: Ay, so I fear; the more is my unrest.

CAPULET: Nay, gentlemen, prepare not to be gone;
We have a trifling foolish banquet towards.
Is it e'en so? why, then, I thank you all;
I thank you, honest gentlemen; good night.
More torches here! Come on then, let's to bed.
Ah, sirrah, by my fay, it waxes late:
I'll to my rest.   [*Exeunt all but Juliet and Nurse.*

JULIET: Come hither, nurse. What is yond gentleman?

NURSE: The son and heir of old Tiberio.

JULIET: What's he that now is going out of door?

NURSE: Marry, that, I think, be young Petrucio.

JULIET: What's he that follows there, that would not dance?

NURSE: I know not.

JULIET: Go, ask his name: if he be married,
My grave is like to be my wedding bed.

NURSE: His name is Romeo, and a Montague;
The only son of your great enemy.

JULIET: My only love sprung from my only hate!
Too early seen unknown, and known too late!
Prodigious birth of love it is to me,
That I must love a loathed enemy.

NURSE: What 's this? what 's this?

JULIET: A rhyme I learn'd even now
Of one I danced withal.   [*One calls within* 'Juliet.'

NURSE: Anon, anon!
Come, let's away; the strangers all are gone.   [*Exeunt.*

ACT II.

PROLOGUE.

Enter Chorus.

CHORUS: Now old desire doth in his death-bed lie.
    And young affection gapes to be his heir:
That fair for which love groan'd for and would die,
    With tender Juliet match'd, is now not fair.
Now Romeo is beloved and loves again,
    Alike bewitched by the charm of looks,
But to his foe supposed he must complain,
    And she steal love's sweet bait from fearful hooks:
Being held a foe, he may not have access
    To breathe such vows as lovers use to swear;
And she as much in love, her means much less
    To meet her new-beloved any where:
But passion lends them power, time means, to meet,
Tempering extremities with extreme sweet.   [*Exit.*

SCENE I. *A lane by the wall of Capulet's orchard.*
Enter Romeo.

ROMEO: Can I go forward when my heart is here?
Turn back, dull earth, and find thy centre out.
          [*He climbs the wall, and leaps down within it.*

Enter Benvolio and Mercutio.

BENVOLIO: Romeo! my cousin Romeo!
MERCUTIO: He is wise;
And, on my life, hath stol'n him home to bed.
BENVOLIO: He ran this way, and leap'd this orchard wall:
Call, good Mercutio.
MERCUTIO: Nay, I' ll conjure too.
Romeo! humours! madman! passion! lover!
Appear thou in the likeness of a sigh:
Speak but one rhyme, and I am satisfied;
Cry but 'Ay me' pronounce but 'love' and 'dove;'
Speak to my gossip Venus one fair word,
One nick-name for her purblind son and heir,
Young Adam Cupid, he that shot so trim,
When King Cophetua loved the beggar-maid!
He heareth not, he stirreth not, he moveth not;
The ape is dead, and I must conjure him.
I conjure thee by Rosaline's bright eyes,
By her high forehead and her scarlet lip,
By her fine foot, straight leg and quivering thigh
And the demesnes that there adjacent lie,
That in thy likeness thou appear to us!
BENVOLIO: An if he hear thee, thou wilt anger him.
MERCUTIO: This cannot anger him: 'twould anger him
To raise a spirit in his mistress' circle
Of some strange nature, letting it there stand
Till she had laid it and conjured it down;
That were some spite: my invocation

Is fair and honest, and in his mistress' name
I conjure only but to raise up him.
   BENVOLIO: Come, he hath hid himself among these trees,
To be consorted with the humorous night:
Blind is his love and best befits the dark.
   MERCUTIO: If love be blind, love cannot hit the mark.
Now will he sit under a medlar tree,
And wish his mistress were that kind of fruit
As maids call medlars, when they laugh alone.
O, Romeo, that she were, O, that she were
An open et cætera, thou a poperin pear!
Romeo, good night: I 'll to my truckle-bed;
This field-bed is too cold for me to sleep:
Come, shall we go?
   BENVOLIO: Go, then; for 'tis in vain
To seek him here that means not to be found.   [*Exeunt.*

SCENE II. *Capulet's orchard.*
Enter Romeo.

   ROMEO: He jests at scars that never felt a wound.
                [*Juliet appears above at a window.*
But, soft! what light through yonder window breaks?
It is the east, and Juliet is the sun.
Arise, fair sun, and kill the envious moon,
Who is already sick and pale with grief,
That thou her maid art far more fair than she:
Be not her maid, since she is envious;
Her vestal livery is but sick and green
And none but fools do wear it; cast it off.
It is my lady, O, it is my love!
O, that she knew she were!
She speaks, yet she says nothing: what of that?
Her eye discourses; I will answer it.
I am too bold, 'tis not to me she speaks:

Two of the fairest stars in all the heaven,
Having some business, do entreat her eyes
To twinkle in their spheres till they return.
What if her eyes were there, they in her head?
The brightness of her cheek would shame those stars,
As daylight doth a lamp; her eyes in heaven
Would through the airy region stream so bright
That birds would sing and think it were not night.
See, how she leans her cheek upon her hand!
O, that I were a glove upon that hand,
That I might touch that cheek!

   JULIET: Ay me!
   ROMEO: She speaks:
O, speak again, bright angel! for thou art
As glorious to this night, being o'er my head,
As is a winged messenger of heaven
Unto the white-upturned wondering eyes
Of mortals that fall back to gaze on him
When he bestrides the lazy-pacing clouds
And sails upon the bosom of the air.

   JULIET: O Romeo, Romeo! wherefore art thou Romeo?
Deny thy father and refuse thy name;
Or, if thou wilt not, be but sworn my love,
And I 'll no longer be a Capulet.

   ROMEO: [*Aside*] Shall I hear more, or shall I speak at this?

   JULIET: 'Tis but thy name that is my enemy;
Thou art thyself, though not a Montague.
What 's Montague? it is nor hand, nor foot,
Nor arm, nor face, nor any other part
Belonging to a man. O, be some other name!
What 's in a name? that which we call a rose
By any other name would smell as sweet;
So Romeo would, were he not Romeo call'd,
Retain thy dear perfection which he owes
Without that title. Romeo, doff thy name,

And for that name which is no part of thee
Take all myself.

    ROMEO: I take thee at thy word:
Call me but love, and I 'll be new baptized;
Henceforth I never will be Romeo.

    JULIET: What man art thou that thus bescreen'd in night
So stumblest on my counsel?

    ROMEO: By a name
I know not how to tell thee who I am:
My name, dear saint, is hateful to myself,
Because it is an enemy to thee;
Had I it written, I would tear the word.

    JULIET: My ears have not yet drunk a hundred words
Of that tongue's utterance, yet I know the sound:
Art thou not Romeo and a Montague?

    ROMEO: Neither, fair saint, if either thee dislike.

    JULIET: How camest thou hither, tell me, and wherefore?
The orchard walls are high and hard to climb,
And the place death, considering who thou art,
If any of my kinsmen find thee here.

    ROMEO: With love's light wings did I o'erperch these walls;
For stony limits cannot hold love out,
And what love can do that dares love attempt;
Therefore thy kinsmen are no let to me.

    JULIET: If they do see thee, they will murder thee.

    ROMEO: Alack, there lies more peril in thine eye
Than twenty of their swords: look thou but sweet,
And I am proof against their enmity.

    JULIET: I would not for the world they saw thee here.

    ROMEO: I have night's cloak to hide me from their sight;
And thou but love me, let them find me here:
My life were better ended by their hate,
Than death prorogued, wanting of thy love.

    JULIET: By whose direction found'st thou out this place?

    ROMEO: By love, who first did prompt me to inquire;

He lent me counsel and I lent him eyes.
I am no pilot; yet, wert thou as far
As that vast shore wash'd with the farthest sea,
I would adventure for such merchandise.
    JULIET: Thou know'st the mask of night is on my face,
Else would a maiden blush bepaint my cheek
For that which thou hast heard me speak to-night.
Fain would I dwell on form, fain, fain deny
What I have spoke: but farewell compliment!
Dost thou love me? I know thou wilt say 'Ay,'
And I will take thy word: yet, if thou swear'st,
Thou mayst prove false; at lovers' perjuries,
They say, Jove laughs. O gentle Romeo,
If thou dost love, pronounce it faithfully:
Of if thou think'st I am too quickly won,
I 'll frown and be perverse and say thee nay,
So thou wilt woo; but else, not for the world.
In truth, fair Montague, I am too fond,
And therefore thou mayst think my 'haviour light:
But trust me, gentleman, I 'll prove more true
Than those that have more cunning to be strange.
I should have been more strange, I must confess,
But that thou overheard'st, ere I was ware,
My true love's passion: therefore pardon me
And not impute this yielding to light love,
Which the dark night hath so discovered.
    ROMEO: Lady, by yonder blessed moon I swear
That tips with silver all these fruit-tree tops—
    JULIET: O, swear not by the moon, the inconstant moon,
That monthly changes in her circled orb,
Lest that thy love prove likewise variable.
    ROMEO: What shall I swear by?
    JULIET: Do not swear at all;
Or, if thou wilt, swear by thy gracious self,
Which is the god of my idolatry,

And I 'll believe thee.

ROMEO: If my heart's dear love—

JULIET: Well, do not swear: although I joy in thee,
I have no joy of this contract to-night:
It is too rash, too unadvised, too sudden;
Too like the lightning, which doth cease to be
Ere one can say 'It lightens.' Sweet, good night!
This bud of love, by summer's ripening breath,
May prove a beauteous flower when next we meet.
Good night, good night! as sweet repose and rest
Come to thy heart as that within my breast!

ROMEO: O, wilt thou leave me so unsatisfied?

JULIET: What satisfaction canst thou have to-night?

ROMEO: The exchange of thy love's faithful vow for mine.

JULIET: I gave thee mine before thou didst request it:
And yet I would it were to give again.

ROMEO: Wouldst thou withdraw it? for what purpose, love?

JULIET: But to be frank, and give it thee again.
And yet I wish but for the thing I have:
My bounty is as boundless as the sea,
My love as deep; the more I give thee,
The more I have, for both are infinite.   [*Nurse calls within.*
I hear some noise within; dear love, adieu!
Anon, good nurse! Sweet Montague, be true.
Stay but a little, I will come again.   [*Exit, above.*

ROMEO: O blessed, blessed night! I am afeard,
Being in night, all this is but a dream,
Too flattering-sweet to be substantial.

Re-enter Juliet, above.

JULIET: Three words, dear Romeo, and good night indeed.
If that thy bent of love be honourable,
Thy purpose marriage, send me word tomorrow,
By one that I'll procure to come to thee,
Where and what time thou wilt perform the rite;

And all my fortunes at thy foot I'll lay
And follow thee my lord throughout the world.
    NURSE: [*Within*] Madam!
    JULIET: I come, anon.—But if thou mean'st not well,
I do beseech thee—
    NURSE: [*Within*] Madam!
    JULIET: By and by, I come:—
To cease thy suit, and leave me to my grief:
To-morrow will I send.
    ROMEO: So thrive my soul—
    JULIET: A thousand times good night!   [*Exit, above.*
    ROMEO: A thousand times the worse, to want thy light.
Love goes toward love, as schoolboys from their books,
But love from love, toward school with heavy looks.   [*Retiring.*

Re-enter Juliet, above.

    JULIET: Hist! Romeo, hist! O, for a falconer's voice,
To lure this tassel-gentle back again!
Bondage is hoarse, and may not speak aloud;
Else would I tear the cave where Echo lies,
And make her airy tongue more hoarse than mine,
With repetition of my Romeo's name.
    ROMEO: It is my soul that calls upon my name:
How silver-sweet sound lovers' tongues by night,
Like softest music to attending ears!
    JULIET: Romeo!
    ROMEO: My dear?
    JULIET: At what o'clock to-morrow
Shall I send to thee?
    ROMEO: At the hour of nine.
    JULIET: I will not fail: 'tis twenty years till then.
I have forgot why I did call thee back.
    ROMEO: Let me stand here till thou remember it.
    JULIET: I shall forget, to have thee still stand there,
Remembering how I love thy company.

ROMEO: And I'll still stay, to have thee still forget,
Forgetting any other home but this.

JULIET: 'Tis almost morning; I would have thee gone:
And yet no further than a wanton's bird;
Who lets it hop a little from her hand,
Like a poor prisoner in his twisted gyves,
And with a silk thread plucks it back again,
So loving-jealous of his liberty.

ROMEO: I would I were thy bird.

JULIET: Sweet, so would I:
Yet I should kill thee with much cherishing.
Good night, good night! parting is such sweet sorrow,
That I shall say good night till it be morrow.   [*Exit above.*

ROMEO: Sleep dwell upon thine eyes, peace in thy breast!
Would I were sleep and peace, so sweet to rest!
Hence will I to my ghostly father's cell.
His help to crave, and my dear hap to tell.   [*Exit.*

SCENE III. *Friar Laurence's cell.*
Enter Friar Laurence, with a basket.

FRIAR LAURENCE: The grey-eyed morn smiles on the frowning
          night,
Chequering the eastern clouds with streaks of light,
And flecked darkness like a drunkard reels
From forth day's path and Titan's fiery wheels:
Now, ere the sun advance his burning eye,
The day to cheer and night's dank dew to dry,
I must up-fill this osier cage of ours
With baleful weeds and precious-juiced flowers.
The earth that 's nature's mother is her tomb;
What is her burying grave that is her womb,
And from her womb children of divers kind
We sucking on her natural bosom find,
Many for many virtues excellent,

None but for some and yet all different.
O, mickle is the powerful grace that lies
In herbs, plants, stones, and their true qualities:
For nought so vile that on the earth doth live
But to the earth some special good doth give,
Nor aught so good but strain'd from that fair use
Revolts from true birth, stumbling on abuse:
Virtue itself turns vice, being misapplied;
And vice sometimes by action dignified.
Within the infant rind of this small flower
Poison hath residence and medicine power:
For this, being smelt, with that part cheers each part;
Being tasted, slays all senses with the heart.
Two such opposed kings encamp them still
In man as well as herbs, grace and rude will;
And where the worser is predominant,
Full soon the canker death eats up that plant.

Enter Romeo.

ROMEO: Good morrow, father.
FRIAR LAURENCE: Benedicite!
What early tongue so sweet saluteth me?
Young son, it argues a distemper'd head
So soon to bid good morrow to thy bed:
Care keeps his watch in every old man's eye,
And where care lodges, sleep will never lie;
But where unbruised youth with unstuff'd brain
Doth couch his limbs, there golden sleep doth reign:
Therefore thy earliness doth me assure
Thou art up-roused by some distemperature;
Or, if not so, then here I hit it right,
Our Romeo hath not been in bed to-night.
ROMEO: That last is true; the sweeter rest was mine.
FRIAR LAURENCE: God pardon sin! wast thou with Rosaline?
ROMEO: With Rosaline, my ghostly father? no;

I have forgot that name, and that name's woe.

 Friar Laurence: That 's my good son: but where
hast thou been, then?

 Romeo: I'll tell thee, ere thou ask it me again.
I have been feasting with mine enemy,
Where on a sudden one hath wounded me,
That 's by me wounded: both our remedies
Within thy help and holy physic lies:
I bear no hatred, blessed man, for, lo,
My intercession likewise steads my foe.

 Friar Laurence: Be plain, good son, and homely in thy drift;
Riddling confession finds but riddling shrift.

 Romeo: Then plainly know my heart's dear love is set
On the fair daughter of rich Capulet:
As mine on hers, so hers is set on mine;
And all combined, save what thou must combine
By holy marriage: when and where and how
We met, we woo'd and made exchange of vow,
I 'll tell thee as we pass; but this I pray,
That thou consent to marry us to-day.

 Friar Laurence: Holy Saint Francis, what a change is here!
Is Rosaline, whom thou didst love so dear,
So soon forsaken? young men's love then lies
Not truly in their hearts, but in their eyes.
Jesu Maria, what a deal of brine
Hath wash'd thy sallow cheeks for Rosaline!
How much salt water thrown away in waste,
To season love, that of it doth not taste!
The sun not yet thy sighs from heaven clears,
Thy old groans ring yet in my ancient ears;
Lo, here upon thy cheek the stain doth sit
Of an old tear that is not wash'd off yet:
If e'er thou wast thyself and these woes thine,
Thou and these woes were all for Rosaline:
And thou art changed? pronounce this sentence then,

Women may fall, when there's no strength in men.

ROMEO: Thou chid'st me oft for loving Rosaline.

FRIAR LAURENCE: For doting, not for loving, pupil mine.

ROMEO: And bad'st me bury love.

FRIAR LAURENCE: Not in a grave,
To lay one in, another out to have.

ROMEO: I pray thee, chide not: she whom I love now
Doth grace for grace and love for love allow;
The other did not so.

FRIAR LAURENCE: O, she knew well
Thy love did not read by rote and could not spell.
But come, young waverer, come, go with me,
In one respect I 'll thy assistant be;
For this alliance may so happy prove,
To turn your households' rancour to pure love.

ROMEO: O, let us hence; I stand on sudden haste.

FRIAR LAURENCE: Wisely and slow; they stumble that run fast.

                                                    [*Exeunt.*

Scene IV. *A street.*
Enter Benvolio and Mercutio.

MERCUTIO: Where the devil should this Romeo be?
Came he not home to-night?

BENVOLIO: Not to his father's; I spoke with his man.

MERCUTIO: Ah, that same pale hard-hearted wench, that Rosa-
          line,
Torments him so, that he will sure run mad.

BENVOLIO: Tybalt, the kinsman of old Capulet,
Hath sent a letter to his father's house.

MERCUTIO: A challenge, on my life.

BENVOLIO: Romeo will answer it.

MERCUTIO: Any man that can write may answer a letter.

BENVOLIO: Nay, he will answer the letter's master, how he dares,
being dared.

MERCUTIO: Alas, poor Romeo! he is already dead; stabbed with a white wench's black eye; shot thorough the ear with a love-song; the very pin of his heart cleft with the blind bow-boy's butt-shaft: and is he a man to encounter Tybalt?

BENVOLIO: Tybalt, the kinsman of old Capulet,
Hath sent a letter to his father's house.

MERCUTIO: A challenge, on my life.

BENVOLIO: Romeo will answer it.

MERCUTIO: Any man that can write may answer a letter.

BENVOLIO: Nay, he will answer the letter's master, how he dares, being dared.

MERCUTIO: Alas, poor Romeo! he is already dead; stabbed with a white wench's black eye; shot thorough the ear with a love-song; the very pin of his heart cleft with the blind bow-boy's butt-shaft: and is he a man to encounter Tybalt?

BENVOLIO: Why, what is Tybalt?

MERCUTIO: More than prince of cats, I can tell you. O, he is the courageous captain of complements. He fights as you sing prick-song, keeps time, distance, and proportion; rest me his minim rest, one, two, and the third in your bosom: the very butcher of a silk button, a duellist, a duellist; a gentleman of the very first house, of the first and second cause: ah, the immortal passado! the punto reverso! the hai!

BENVOLIO: The what?

MERCUTIO: The pox of such antic, lisping, affecting fantasti-coes; these new tuners of accents! 'By Jesu, a very good blade! a very tall man! a very good whore!' Why, is not this a lamentable thing, grandsire, that we should be thus afflicted with these strange flies, these fashion-mongers, these perdona-mi's, who stand so much on the new form, that they cannot sit at ease on the old bench? O, their bones, their bones!

Enter Romeo.

BENVOLIO: Here comes Romeo, here comes Romeo.

MERCUTIO: Without his roe, like a dried herring: O flesh, flesh, how art thou fishified! Now is he for the numbers that Petrarch flowed in: Laura to his lady was but a kitchen-wench; marry, she had a better love to berhyme her; Dido a dowdy; Cleopatra a gipsy; Helen and Hero hildings and harlots; Thisbe a grey eye or so, but not to the purpose. Signior Romeo, bon jour! there's a French salutation to your French slop. You gave us the counterfeit fairly last night.

ROMEO: Good morrow to you both. What counterfeit did I give you?

MERCUTIO: The slip, sir, the slip; can you not conceive?

ROMEO: Pardon, good Mercutio, my business was great; and in such a case as mine a man may strain courtesy.

MERCUTIO: That 's as much as to say, such a case as yours constrain a man to bow in the hams.

ROMEO: Meaning, to court'sy.

MERCUTIO: Thou hast most kindly hit it.

ROMEO: A most courteous exposition.

MERCUTIO: Nay, I am the very pink of courtesy.

ROMEO: Pink for flower.

MERCUTIO: Right.

ROMEO: Why, then is my pump well flowered.

MERCUTIO: Well said: follow me this jest now till thou hast worn out thy pump, that when the single sole of it is worn, the jest may remain after the wearing sole singular.

ROMEO: O single-soled jest, solely singular for the singleness!

MERCUTIO: Come between us, good Benvolio; my wits faint.

ROMEO: Switch and spurs, switch and spurs; or I 'll cry a match.

MERCUTIO: Nay, if thy wits run the wild-goose chase, I have done, for thou hast more of the wild-goose in one of thy wits than, I am sure, I have in my whole five: was I with you there for the goose?

ROMEO: Thou wast never with me for any thing when thou wast not there for the goose.

MERCUTIO: I will bite thee by the ear for that jest.

ROMEO: Nay, good goose, bite not.

MERCUTIO: Thy wit is a very bitter sweeting; it is a most sharp sauce.

ROMEO: And is it not well served in to a sweet goose?

MERCUTIO: O, here 's a wit of cheveril, that stretches from an inch narrow to an ell broad!

ROMEO: I stretch it out for that word 'broad;' which added to the goose, proves thee far and wide a broad goose.

MERCUTIO: Why, is not this better now than groaning for love? now art thou sociable, now art thou Romeo; now art thou what thou art, by art as well as by nature: for this drivelling love is like a great natural, that runs lolling up and down to hide his bauble in a hole.

BENVOLIO: Stop there, stop there.

MERCUTIO: Thou desirest me to stop in my tale against the hair.

BENVOLIO: Thou wouldst else have made thy tale large.

MERCUTIO: O, thou art deceived; I would have made it short: for I was come to the whole depth of my tale; and meant, indeed, to occupy the argument no longer.

ROMEO: Here 's goodly gear!

Enter Nurse and Peter.

MERCUTIO: A sail, a sail!

BENVOLIO: Two, two; a shirt and a smock.

NURSE: Peter!

PETER: Anon!

NURSE: My fan, Peter.

MERCUTIO: Good Peter, to hide her face; for her fan's the fairer face.

NURSE: God ye good morrow, gentlemen.

MERCUTIO: God ye good den, fair gentlewoman.

NURSE: Is it good den?

MERCUTIO: 'Tis no less, I 'll tell you, for the bawdy hand of the dial is now upon the prick of noon.

NURSE: Out upon you! what a man are you!

ROMEO: One, gentlewoman, that God hath made for himself to mar.

NURSE: By my troth, it is well said: 'for himself to mar,' quoth a'?
Gentlemen, can any of you tell where I may find the young Romeo?

ROMEO: I can tell you; but young Romeo will be older when
you have found him than he was when you sought him: I am the
youngest of that name, for fault of a worse.

NURSE: You say well.

MERCUTIO: Yea, is the worst well? very well took, i' faith; wisely, wisely.

NURSE: If you be he, sir, I desire some confidence with you.

BENVOLIO: She will indite him to some supper.

MERCUTIO: A bawd, a bawd, a bawd! So ho!

ROMEO: What hast thou found?

MERCUTIO: No hare, sir; unless a hare, sir, in a lenten pie, that
is something stale and hoar ere it be spent.   [Sings.

> An old hare hoar,
> And an old hare hoar,
> Is very good meat in lent:
> But a hare that is hoar
> Is too much for a score,
> When it hoars ere it be spent.

Romeo, will you come to your father's? we 'll to dinner, thither.

ROMEO: I will follow you.

MERCUTIO: Farewell, ancient lady; farewell, [singing] 'lady, lady,
lady.'   [Exeunt Mercutio and Benvolio.

NURSE: Marry, farewell! I pray you, sir, what saucy merchant
was this, that was so full of his ropery?

ROMEO: A gentleman, nurse, that loves to hear himself talk,
and will speak more in a minute than he will stand to in a month.

NURSE: An a' speak any thing against me, I 'll take him down,
and a' were lustier than he is, and twenty such Jacks; and if I cannot, I 'll find those that shall. Scurvy knave! I am none of his
flirt-gills; I am none of his skains-mates. And thou must stand by
too, and suffer every knave to use me at his pleasure?

PETER: I saw no man use you at his pleasure; if I had, my
weapon should quickly have been out, I warrant you: I dare draw

as soon as another man, if I see ocasion in a good quarrel, and the law on my side.

NURSE: Now, afore God, I am so vexed, that every part about me quivers. Scurvy knave! Pray you, sir, a word: and as I told you, my young lady bade me inquire you out; what she bade me say, I will keep to myself: but first let me tell ye, if ye should lead her into a fool's paradise, as they say, it were a very gross kind of behaviour, as they say: for the gentlewoman is young; and, there-fore, if you should deal double with her, truly it were an ill thing to be offered to any gentlewoman, and very weak dealing.

ROMEO: Nurse, commend me to thy lady and mistress. I pro-test unto thee—

NURSE: Good heart, and, i' faith, I will tell her as much: Lord, Lord, she will be a joyful woman.

ROMEO: What wilt thou tell her, nurse? thou dost not mark me.

NURSE: I will tell her, sir, that you do protest; which, as I take it, is a gentlemanlike offer.

ROMEO: Bid her devise
Some means to come to shrift this afternoon;
And there she shall at Friar Laurence' cell
Be shrived and married. Here is for thy pains.

NURSE: No, truly, sir; not a penny.

ROMEO: Go to; I say you shall.

NURSE: This afternoon, sir? well, she shall be there.

ROMEO: And stay, good nurse, behind the abbey wall:
Within this hour my man shall be with thee,
And bring thee cords made like a tackled stair;
Which to the high top-gallant of my joy
Must be my convoy in the secret night.
Farewell; be trusty, and I'll quit thy pains:
Farewell; commend me to thy mistress.

NURSE: Now God in heaven bless thee!
    Hark, you, sir.

ROMEO: What say'st thou, my dear nurse?

NURSE: Is your man secret? Did you ne'er hear say,

Two may keep counsel, putting one away?

NURSE: Well, sir; my mistress is the sweetest lady—Lord, Lord! when 'twas a little prating thing:—O, there is a nobleman in town, one Paris, that would fain lay knife aboard; but she, good soul, had as lief see a toad, a very toad, as see him. I anger her sometimes and tell her that Paris is the properer man; but, I'll warrant you, when I say so, she looks as pale as any clout in the versal world. Doth not rosemary and Romeo begin both with a letter?

ROMEO: Ay, nurse! what of that? both with an R.

NURSE: Ah, mocker? that's the dog's name; R is for the—No; I know it begins with some other letter:—and she hath the prettiest sententious of it, of you and rosemary, that it would do you good to hear it.

ROMEO: Commend me to thy lady.

NURSE: Ay, a thousand times.   [*Exit Romeo.* Peter!

PETER: Anon!

NURSE: Peter, take my fan, and go before, and apace.   [*Exeunt.*

SCENE V. *Capulet's orchard.*
Enter Juliet.

JULIET: The clock struck nine when I did send the nurse;
In half an hour she promised to return.
Perchance she cannot meet him: that's not so.
O, she is lame! love's heralds should be thoughts,
Which ten times faster glide than the sun's beams,
Driving back shadows over louring hills:
Therefore do nimble-pinion'd doves draw love,
And therefore hath the wind-swift Cupid wings.
Now is the sun upon the highmost hill
Of this day's journey, and from nine till twelve
Is three long hours, yet she is not come.
Had she affections and warm youthful blood,

She would be as swift in motion as a ball;
My words would bandy her to my sweet love,
And his for me:
But old folks, many feign as they were dead;
Unwieldy, slow, heavy and pale as lead.
O God, she comes!

Enter Nurse and Peter.

                O honey nurse, what news?
Hast thou met with him? Send thy man away.

NURSE: Peter, stay at the gate.   [*Exit Peter.*

JULIET: Now, good sweet nurse,—O Lord, why look'st thou sad?
Though the news be sad, yet tell them merrily;
If good, thou shamest the music of sweet news
By playing it to me with so sour a face.

NURSE: I am a-weary, give me leave awhile:
Fie, how my bones ache! what a jaunt have I had!

JULIET: I would thou hadst my bones, and I thy news.
Nay, come, I pray thee, speak; good, good nurse, speak.

NURSE: Jesu, what haste? can you not stay awhile?
Do you not see that I am out of breath?

JULIET: How art thou out of breath, when thou hast breath
To say to me that thou art out of breath?
The excuse that thou dost make in this delay
Is longer than the tale thou dost excuse.
Is thy news good, or bad? answer to that;
Say either, and I'll stay the circumstance:
Let me be satisfied, is 't good or bad?

NURSE: Well, you have made a simple choice; you know not
how to choose a man: Romeo! no, not he; though his face be better than any man's, yet his leg excels all men's; and for a hand, and
a foot, and a body, though they be not to be talked on, yet they are
past compare: he is not the flower of courtesy, but I 'll warrant
him, as gentle as a lamb. Go thy ways, wench; serve God. What,
have you dined at home?

JULIET: No, no: but all this did I know before.
What says he of our marriage? what of that?

NURSE: Lord, how my head aches! what a head have I!
It beats me as it would fall in twenty pieces.
My back o' t' other side,—O, my back, my back!
Beshrew your heart for sending me about,
To catch my death with jaunting up and down!

JULIET: I' faith, I am sorry that thou art not well.
Sweet, sweet, sweet nurse, tell me, what says my love?

NURSE: Your love says, like an honest gentleman, and a courteous, and a kind, and a handsome, and, I warrant, a virtuous,
—Where is your mother?

JULIET: Where is my mother! why, she is within;
Where should she be? How oddly thou repliest!
'Your love say, like an honest gentleman,
Where is your mother?'

NURSE: O God's lady dear!
Are you so hot? marry, come up, I trow;
Is this the poultice for my aching bones?
Henceforward do your messages yourself.

JULIET: Here 's such a coil! come, what says Romeo?

NURSE: Have you got leave to go to shrift to-day?

JULIET: I have.

NURSE: Then hie you hence to Friar Laurence' cell;
There stays a husband to make you a wife:
Now comes the wanton blood up in your cheeks,
They'll be in scarlet straight at any news.
Hie you to church; I must another way,
To fetch a ladder, by the which your love
Must climb a bird's nest soon when it is dark:
I am the drudge and toil in your delight,
But you shall bear the burden soon at night.
Go; I 'll to dinner; hie you to the cell.

JULIET: Hie to high fortune! Honest nurse, farewell.   [*Exeunt.*

SCENE VI. *Friar Laurence's cell.*
Enter Friar Laurence and Romeo.

FRIAR LAURENCE: So smile the heavens, upon this unholy act,
That after hours with sorrow chide us not!
ROMEO: Amen, amen! but come what sorrow can,
It cannot countervail the exchange of joy
That one short minute gives me in her sight:
Do thou but close our hands with holy words,
Then love-devouring death do what he dare;
It is enough I may but call her mine.
FRIAR LAURENCE: These violent delights have violent ends
And in their triumph die, like fire and powder,
Which as they kiss consume: the sweetest honey
Is loathsome in his own deliciousness
And in the taste confounds the appetite:
Therefore love moderately; long love doth so;
Too swift arrives as tardy as too slow.

Enter Juliet.

Here comes the lady: O, so light a foot
Will ne'er wear out the everlasting flint:
A lover may bestride the gossamer
That idles in the wanton summer air,
And yet not fall; so light is vanity.
JULIET: Good even to my ghostly confessor.
FRIAR LAURENCE: Romeo shall thank thee, daughter, for us
both.
JULIET: As much to him, else is his thanks too much.
ROMEO: Ah, Juliet, if the measure of thy joy
Be heap'd like mine and that thy skill be more
To blazon it, then sweeten with thy breath
This neighbour air, and let rich music's tongue
Unfold the imagined happiness that both
Receive in either by this dear encounter.

JULIET: Conceit, more rich in matter than in words,
Brags of his substance, not of ornament:
They are but beggars that can count their worth;
But my true love is grown to such excess
I cannot sum up sum half my wealth.

FRIAR LAURENCE: Come, come with me, and we will make
    short work;
For, by your leaves, you shall not stay alone
Till holy church incorporate two in one.   [*Exeunt.*

ACT III.

SCENE I. *A public place.*
Enter Mercutio, Benvolio, Page, and Servants.

BENVOLIO: I pray thee, good Mercutio, let's retire:
The day is hot, the Capulets abroad,
And, if we meet, we shall not escape a brawl:
For now, these hot days, is the mad blood stirring.

MERCUTIO: Thou art like one of those fellows that when he enters the confines of a tavern claps me his sword upon the table and says 'God send me no need of thee!' and by the operation of the second cup draws it on the drawer, when indeed there is no need.

BENVOLIO: Am I like such a fellow?

MERCUTIO: Come, come, thou art as hot a Jack in thy mood as any in Italy, and as soon moved to be moody, and as soon moody to be moved.

BENVOLIO: And what to?

MERCUTIO: Nay, an there were two such, we should have none shortly, for one would kill the other. Thou! why, thou wilt quarrel with a man that hath a hair more, or a hair less, in his beard than thou hast: thou wilt quarrel with a man for cracking nuts, having no other reason but because thou hast hazel eyes: what eye but such an eye would spy out such a quarrel? Thy head is as full of quarrels as an egg is full of meat, and yet thy head hath been beaten as addle as an egg for quarrelling: thou hast quarrelled with a man for coughing in the street, because he hath wakened thy dog that hath lain asleep in the sun: didst thou not fall out with a tailor for wearing his new doublet before Easter? with another, for tying his new shoes with old riband? and yet thou wilt tutor me from quarrelling!

BENVOLIO: An I were so apt to quarrel as thou art, any man should buy the fee-simple of my life for an hour and a quarter.

MERCUTIO: The fee-simple! O simple!

BENVOLIO: By my head, here come the Capulets.

MERCUTIO: By my heel, I care not.

Enter Tybalt and others.

TYBALT: Follow me close, for I will speak to them.
Gentlemen, good den: a word with one of you.

MERCUTIO: And but one word with one of us? couple it with something; make it a word and a blow.

TYBALT: You shall find me apt enough to that, sir, an you will give me occasion.

MERCUTIO: Could you not take some occasion without giving?

TYBALT: Mercutio, thou consort'st with Romeo,—

MERCUTIO: Consort! what, dost thou make us minstrels? an thou make minstrels of us, look to hear nothing but discords: here 's my fiddlestick; here's that shall make you dance. 'Zounds, consort!

BENVOLIO: We talk here in the public haunt of men:
Either withdraw unto some private place,
And reason coldly of your grievances,
Or else depart; here all eyes gaze on us.

MERCUTIO: Men's eyes were made to look, and let them gaze;
I will not budge for no man's pleasure, I.

Enter Romeo.

TYBALT: Well, peace be with you, sir: here comes my man.

MERCUTIO: But I 'll be hang'd, sir, if he wear your livery:
Marry, go before the field, he 'll be your follower;
Your worship in that sense may call him 'man.'
    TYBALT: Romeo, the hate I bear thee can afford
No better term than this,—thou art a villain.
    ROMEO: Tybalt, the reason that I have to love thee
Doth much excuse the appertaining rage
To such a greeting: villain am I none;
Therefore farewell; I see thou know'st me not.
    TYBALT: Boy, this shall not excuse the injuries
That thou hast done me; therefore turn and draw.
    ROMEO: I do protest, I never injured thee,
But love thee better than thou canst devise,
Till thou shalt know the reason of my love:
And so, good Capulet,—which name I tender
As dearly as my own,—be satisfied.
    MERCUTIO: O calm, dishonourable, vile submission!
Alla stoccata carries it away.   [*Draws.*
Tybalt, you rat-catcher, will you walk?
    TYBALT: What wouldst thou have with me?
    MERCUTIO: Good king of cats, nothing but one of your nine
lives; that I mean to make bold withal, and, as you shall use me
hereafter, dry-beat the rest of the eight. Will you pluck your
sword out of his pilcher by the ears? make haste, lest mine be
about your ears ere it be out.
    TYBALT: I am for you.   [*Drawing.*
    ROMEO: Gentle Mercutio, put thy rapier up.
    MERCUTIO: Come, sir, your passado.   [*They fight.*
    ROMEO: Draw, Benvolio; beat down their weapons.
Gentlemen, for shame, forbear this outrage!
Tybalt, Mercutio, the prince expressly hath
Forbidden bandying in Verona streets:
Hold, Tybalt! good Mercutio!
                    [*Tybalt under Romeo's arm stabs Mercutio,
                    and flies with his followers.*

MERCUTIO: I am hurt.
A plague o' both your houses! I am sped.
Is he gone, and hath nothing?
    BENVOLIO: What, art thou hurt?
    MERCUTIO: Ay, ay, a scratch, a scratch; marry, 'tis enough.
Where is my page? Go, villain, fetch a surgeon.   [*Exit Page.*
    ROMEO: Courage, man; the hurt cannot be much.
    MERCUTIO: No, 'tis not so deep as a well, nor so wide as a
church-door; but 'tis enough, 'twill serve: ask me for to-morrow,
and you shall find me a grave man. I am peppered, I warrant, for
this world. A plague o' both your houses! 'Zounds, a dog, a rat, a
mouse, a cat, to scratch a man to death! a braggart, a rogue, a vil-
lain, that fights by the book of arithmetic! Why the devil came
you between us? I was hurt under your arm.
    ROMEO: I thought all for the best.
    MERCUTIO: Help me into some house, Benvolio,
Or I shall faint. A plague o' both your houses!
They have made worms' meat of me: I have it,
And soundly too: your houses!   [*Exeunt Mercutio and Benvolio.*
    ROMEO: This gentlemen, the prince's near ally,
My very friend, hath got his mortal hurt
In my behalf; my reputation stain'd
With Tybalt's slander,—Tybalt, that an hour
Hath been my kinsman! O sweet Juliet,
Thy beauty hath made me effeminate
And in my temper soften'd valour's steel!

Re-enter Benvolio.

    BENVOLIO: O Romeo, Romeo, brave Mercutio's dead!
That gallant spirit hath aspired the clouds,
Which too untimely here did scorn the earth.
    ROMEO: This day's black fate on more days doth depend;
This but begins the woe others must end.
    BENVOLIO: Here comes the furious Tybalt back again.
    ROMEO: Alive, in triumph! and Mercutio slain!

Away to heaven, respective lenity,
And fire-eyed fury be my conduct now!

Re-enter Tybalt.

Now, Tybalt, take the villain back again,
That late thou gavest me; for Mercutio's soul
Is but a little way above our heads,
Staying for thine to keep him company:
Either thou, or I, or both, must go with him.

TYBALT: Thou, wretched boy, that didst consort him here,
Shalt with him hence.

ROMEO: This shall determine that.

                                        [*They fight; Tybalt falls.*

BENVOLIO: Romeo, away, be gone!
The citizens are up, and Tybalt slain.
Stand not amazed: the prince will doom thee death,
If thou art taken: hence, be gone, away!

ROMEO: O, I am fortune's fool!

BENVOLIO: Why dost thou stay?

                                        [*Exit Romeo.*

Enter Citizens, &c.

FIRST CITIZEN: Which way ran he that kill'd Mercutio?
Tybalt, that murderer, which way ran he?

BENVOLIO: There lies that Tybalt.

FIRST CITIZEN: Up, sir, go with me;
I charge thee in the prince's name, obey.

*Enter Prince, attended; Montague, Capulet
their Wives, and others.*

PRINCE: Where are the vile beginners of this fray?

BENVOLIO: O noble prince, I can discover all
The unlucky manage of this fatal brawl:
There lies the man, slain by young Romeo,
That slew thy kinsman, brave Mercutio.

LADY CAPULET: Tybalt, my cousin! O my brother's child!
O prince! O cousin! husband! O, the blood is spilt
Of my dear kinsman! Prince, as thou art true,
For blood of ours, shed blood of Montague.
O cousin, cousin!
    PRINCE: Benvolio, who began this bloody fray?
    BENVOLIO: Tybalt, here slain, whom Romeo's hand did slay;
Romeo that spoke him fair, bade him bethink
How nice the quarrel was, and urged withal
Your high displeasure: all this uttered
With gentle breath, calm look, knees humbly bow'd,
Could not truce with the unruly spleen
Of Tybalt deaf to peace, but that he tilts
With piercing steel at bold Mercutio's breast,
Who, all as hot, turns deadly point to point,
And, with a martial scorn, with one hand beats
Cold death aside, and with the other sends
It back to Tybalt, whose dexterity
Retorts it: Romeo he cries aloud,
'Hold, friends! friends, part!' and, swifter than his tongue,
His agile arm beats down their fatal points,
And 'twixt them rushes; underneath whose arm
An envious thrust from Tybalt hit the life
Of stout Mercutio, and then Tybalt fled;
But by and by comes back to Romeo,
Who had but newly entertain'd revenge,
And to 't they go like lightning, for, ere I
Could draw to part them, was stout Tybalt slain,
And, as he fell, did Romeo turn and fly.
This is the truth, or let Benvolio die.
    LADY CAPULET: He is a kinsman to the Montague;
Affection makes him false; he speaks not true:
Some twenty of them fought in this black strife,
And all those twenty could but kill one life.
I beg for justice, which thou, prince, must give;

Romeo slew Tybalt, Romeo must not live.

    PRINCE: Romeo slew him, he slew Mercutio;
Who now the price of his dear blood doth owe?

    MONTAGUE: Not Romeo, prince, he was Mercutio's friend;
His fault concludes but what the law should end,
The life of Tybalt.

    PRINCE: And for that offence
Immediately we do exile him hence:
I have an interest in your hate's proceeding,
My blood for your rude brawls doth lie a-bleeding;
But I 'll amerce you with so strong a fine
That you shall all repent the loss of mine:
I will be deaf to pleading and excuses;
Nor tears nor prayers shall purchase out abuses;
Therefore use none: let Romeo hence in haste,
Else, when he 's found, that hour is his last.
Bear hence this body, and attend our will:
Mercy but murders, pardoning those that kill.   [*Exeunt.*

SCENE II. *Capulet's orchard.*
Enter Juliet.

    JULIET: Gallop apace, you fiery-footed steeds,
Towards Phoebus' lodging: such a waggoner
As Phaethon would whip you to the west,
And bring in cloudy night immediately.
Spread thy close curtain, love-performing night,
That runaways' eyes may wink, and Romeo
Leap to these arms, untalk'd of and unseen.
Lovers can see to do their amorous rites
By their own beauties; or, if love be blind,
It best agrees with night. Come, civil night,
Thou sober-suited matron, all in black,
And learn me how to lose a winning match,
Play'd for a pair of stainless maidenhoods:

Hood my unmann'd blood, bating in my cheeks,
With thy black mantle; till strange love, grown bold,
Think true love acted simple modesty.
Come, night; come, Romeo; come, thou day in night;
For thou wilt lie upon the wings of night
Whiter than new snow on a raven's back.
Come, gentle night, come, loving, black-brow'd night,
Give me my Romeo; and, when he shall die,
Take him and cut him out in little stars,
And he will make the face of heaven so fine
That all the world will be in love with night
And pay no worship to the garish sun.
O, I have bought the mansion of a love,
But not possess'd it, and, though I am sold,
Not yet enjoy'd: so tedious is this day
As is the night before some festival
To an impatient child that hath new robes
And may not wear them. O, here comes my nurse,
And she brings news; and every tongue that speaks
But Romeo's name speaks heavenly eloquence.

Enter Nurse, with cords.

Now, nurse, what news? What hast thou there? the cords
That Romeo did thee fetch?
    NURSE: Ay, ay, the cords.   [*Throws them down.*
    JULIET: Ay me! what news? why dost thou wring thy hands?
    NURSE: Ah, well-a-day! he 's dead, he 's dead, he 's dead!
We are undone, lady, we are undone!
Alack the day! he 's gone, he 's kill'd, he 's dead!
    JULIET: Can heaven be so envious?
    NURSE: Romeo can,
Though heaven cannot: O Romeo, Romeo!
Who ever would have thought it? Romeo!
    JULIET: What devil art thou, that dost torment me thus?
This torture should be roar'd in dismal hell.

Hath Romeo slain himself? say thou but 'I,'
And that bare vowel 'I' shall poison more
Than the death-darting eye of cockatrice:
I am not I, if there be such an I;
Or those eyes shut, that make thee answer 'I.'
If he be slain, say 'I'; or if not, no:
Brief sounds determine of my weal or woe

    NURSE: I saw the wound, I saw it with mine eyes,—
God save the mark!—here on his manly breast:
A piteous corse, a bloody piteous corse;
Pale, pale as ashes, all bedaub'd in blood,
All in gore-blood; I swounded at the sight.

    JULIET: O, break, my heart! poor bankrupt, break at once!
To prison, eyes, ne'er look on liberty!
Vile earth, to earth resign; end motion here;
And thou and Romeo press one heavy bier!

    NURSE: O Tybalt, Tybalt, the best friend I had!
O courteous Tybalt! honest gentleman!
That ever I should live to see thee dead!

    JULIET: What storm is this that blows so contrary?
Is Romeo slaughter'd, and is Tybalt dead?
My dear-loved cousin, and my dearer lord?
Then, dreadful trumpet, sound the general doom!
For who is living if those two are gone?

    NURSE: Tybalt is gone, and Romeo banished;
Romeo that kill'd him, he is banished.

    JULIET: O God! did Romeo's hand shed Tybalt's blood?

    NURSE: It did, it did; alas the day, it did!

    JULIET: O serpent heart, hid with a flowering face!
Did ever dragon keep so fair a cave?
Beautiful tyrant! fiend angelical!
Dove-feather'd raven! wolvish-ravening lamb!
Despised substance of divinest show!
Just opposite to what thou justly seem'st,
A damned saint, an honourable villain!

O nature, what hadst thou to do in hell,
When thou didst bower the spirit of fiend
In mortal paradise of such sweet flesh?
Was ever book containing such vile matter
So fairly bound? O, that deceit should dwell
In such a gorgeous palace!

NURSE: There 's no trust,
No faith, no honesty in men; all perjured,
All forsworn, all naught, all dissemblers.
Ah, where's my man? give me some aqua vitæ:
These griefs, these woes, these sorrows make me old.
Shame come to Romeo!

JULIET: Blister'd be thy tongue
For such a wish! he was not born to shame:
Upon his brow shame is ashamed to sit;
For 'tis a throne where honour may be crown'd
Sole monarch of the universal earth.
O, what a beast was I to chide at him!

NURSE: Will you speak well of him that kill'd your cousin?

JULIET: Shall I speak ill of him that is my husband?
Ah, poor my lord, what tongue shall smooth thy name,
When I, thy three-hours wife, have mangled it?
But, wherefore, villain, didst thou kill my cousin?
That villain cousin would have kill'd my husband:
Back, foolish tears, back to your native spring;
Your tributary drops belong to woe,
Which you, mistaking, offer up to joy.
My husband lives, that Tybalt would have slain;
And Tybalt's dead, that would have slain my husband:
All this is comfort; wherefore weep I then?
Some word there was, worser than Tybalt's death,
That murder'd me: I would forget it fain;
But, O, it presses to my memory,
Like damned guilty deeds to sinners' minds:
'Tybalt is dead, and Romeo—banished;'

That 'banished,' that one word 'banished,'
Hath slain ten thousand Tybalts. Tybalt's death
Was woe enough, if it had ended there:
Or, if sour woe delights in fellowship
And needly will be rank'd with other griefs,
Why follow'd not, when she said 'Tybalt's dead,'
Thy father, or thy mother, nay, or both,
Which modern lamentation might have moved?
But with a rearward following Tybalt's death,
'Romeo is banished,' to speak that word,
Is father, mother, Tybalt, Romeo, Juliet,
All slain, all dead. 'Romeo is banished!'
There is no end, no limit, measure, bound,
In that word's death; no words can that woe sound.
Where is my father, and my mother, nurse?

NURSE: Weeping and wailing over Tybalt's corse:
Will you go to them? I will bring you thither.

JULIET: Wash they his wounds with tears; mine shall be spent,
When theirs are dry, for Romeo's banishment.
Take up those cords: poor ropes, you are beguiled,
Both you and I; for Romeo is exiled:
He made you for a highway to my bed;
But I, a maid, die maiden-widowed.
Come, cords, come nurse; I'll to my wedding-bed;
And death, not Romeo take my maidenhead!

NURSE: Hie to your chamber: I'll find Romeo
To comfort you: I wot well where he is.
Hark ye, your Romeo will be here at night:
I 'll to him; he is hid at Laurence' cell.

JULIET: O, find him! give this ring to my true knight,
And bid him come to take his last farewell.　　　　　　[*Exeunt.*

SCENE III. *Friar Laurence's cell.*
Enter Friar Laurence.

FRIAR LAURENCE: Romeo, come forth; come forth, thou fearful
    man:
Affliction is enamour'd of thy parts,
And thou art wedded to calamity.

Enter Romeo.

ROMEO: Father, what news! what is the prince's doom?
What sorrow craves acquaintance at my hand,
That I yet know not?
FRIAR LAURENCE: Too familiar
Is my dear son with such sour company:
I bring thee tidings of the prince's doom.
    ROMEO: What less than dooms-day is the prince's doom?
    FRIAR LAURENCE: A gentler judgement vanish'd from his lips,
Not body's death, but body's banishment.
    ROMEO: Ha, banishment! be merciful, say 'death;'
For exile hath more terror in his look,
Much more than death: do not say 'banishment.'
    FRIAR LAURENCE: Hence from Verona art thou banished:
Be patient, for the world is broad and wide.
    ROMEO: There is no world without Verona walls,
But purgatory, torture, hell itself.
Hence-banished is banish'd from the world,
And world's exile is death: then banished,
Is death mis-term'd: calling death banishment,
Thou cutt'st my head off with a golden axe,
And smilest upon the stroke that murders me.
    FRIAR LAURENCE: O deadly sin! O rude unthankfulness!
Thy fault our law calls death; but the kind prince,
Taking my part, hath rush'd aside the law,
And turn'd that black word death to banishment:
This is dear mercy, and thou seest it not.

ROMEO: 'Tis torture, and not mercy: heaven is here,
Where Juliet lives; and every cat and dog
And little mouse, every unworthy thing,
Live here in heaven and may look on her;
But Romeo may not: more validity,
More honourable state, more courtship lives
In carrion-flies than Romeo: they may seize
On the white wonder of dear Juliet's hand
And steal immortal blessing from her lips,
Who, even in pure and vestal modesty,
Still blush, as thinking their own kisses sin;
But Romeo may not; he is banished:
Flies may do this, but I from this must fly:
They are free men, but I am banished
And say'st thou yet that exile is not death?
Hadst thou no poison mix'd, no sharp-ground knife,
No sudden mean of death, though ne'er so mean,
But 'banished' to kill me?—'banished'?
O friar, the damned use that word in hell;
Howlings attend it; how hast thou the heart,
Being a divine, a ghostly confessor,
A sin-absolver, and my friend profess'd,
To mangle me with that word 'banished'?

    FRIAR LAURENCE: Thou fond mad man, hear me but speak
    a word.

    ROMEO: O, thou wilt speak again of banishment.

    FRIAR LAURENCE: I 'll give thee armour to keep off that word;
Adversity's sweet milk, philosophy,
To comfort thee, though thou art banished.

    ROMEO: Yet 'banished'? Hang up philosophy!
Unless philosophy can make a Juliet,
Displant a town, reverse a prince's doom,
It helps not, it prevails not: talk no more.

    FRIAR LAURENCE: O, then I see that mad men have no ears,
    ROMEO: How should they, when that wise men have no eyes?

FRIAR LAURENCE: Let me dispute with thee of thy estate.

ROMEO: Thou canst not speak of that thou dost not feel:
Wert thou as young as I, Juliet thy love,
An hour but married, Tybalt murdered,
Doting like me and like me banished,
Then mightst thou speak, then mightst thou tear thy hair,
And fall upon the ground, as I do now.
Taking the measure of an unmade grave.   [Knocking within.

FRIAR LAURENCE: Arise; one knocks; good Romeo, hide thyself.

ROMEO: Not I; unless the breath of heartsick groans,
Mist-like, infold me from the search of eyes.   [Knocking.

FRIAR LAURENCE: Hark, how they knock! Who's there? Romeo,
    arise:
Thou wilt be taken. Stay awhile! Stand up;   [Knocking.
Run to my study. By and by! God's will,
What simpleness is this! I come, I come!   [Knocking.
Who knocks so hard? whence come you? what's your will?

NURSE: [Within] Let me come in, and you shall know my errand;
I come from Lady Juliet.

FRIAR LAURENCE: Welcome, then.

Enter Nurse.

NURSE: O holy friar, O, tell me, holy friar,
Where is my lady's lord, where's Romeo?

FRIAR LAURENCE: There on the ground, with his own tears
    made drunk.

NURSE: O, he is even in my mistress's case,
Just in her case! O woful sympathy!
Piteous predicament! Even so lies she,
Blubbering and weeping, weeping and blubbering.
Stand up, stand up; stand, an you be a man;
For Juliet's sake, for her sake, rise and stand;
Why should you fall into so deep an O?

ROMEO: Nurse!

NURSE: Ah sir! ah sir! Well, death 's the end of all.

ROMEO: Spakest thou of Juliet? how is it with her?
Doth she not think me an old murderer,
Now I have stain'd the childhood of our joy
With blood removed but little from her own?
Where is she? and how doth she? and what says
My conceal'd lady to our cancell'd love?

NURSE: O, she says nothing, sir, but weeps and weeps;
And Tybalt calls; and then on Romeo cries,
And then down falls again.

ROMEO: As if that name,
Shot from the deadly level of a gun,
Did murder her; as the name's cursed hand
Murder'd her kinsman. O, tell me, friar, tell me,
In what vile part of this anatomy
Doth my name lodge? tell me, that I may sack
The hateful mansion.   [*Drawing his sword.*

FRIAR LAURENCE: Hold thy desperate hand:
Art thou a man? thy form cries out thou art:
Thy tears are womanish; thy wild acts denote
The unreasonable fury of a beast:
Unseemly woman in a seeming man!
Or ill-beseeming beast in seeming both!
Thou hast amazed me; by my holy order,
I thought thy disposition better temper'd.
Hast thou slain Tybalt? wilt thou slay thyself?
And slay thy lady too that lives in thee,
By doing damned hate upon thyself?
Why rail'st thou on thy birth, the heaven, and earth?
Since birth, and heaven, and earth, all three do meet
In thee at once; which thou at once wouldst lose.
Fie, fie, thou shamest thy shape, thy love, thy wit;
Which like a usurer, abound'st in all,
And usest none in that true use indeed
Which should bedeck thy shape, thy love, thy wit:
Thy noble shape is but a form of wax,

Digressing from the valour of a man;
Thy dear love sworn but hollow perjury,
Killing that love which thou hast vow'd to cherish;
Thy wit, that ornament to shape and love,
Mis-shapen in the conduct of them both,
Like powder in a skilless soldier's flask,
Is set a-fire by thine own ignorance,
And thou dismember'd with thine own defence.
What, rouse thee, man! thy Juliet is alive,
For whose dear sake thou wast but lately dead;
There art thou happy: Tybalt would kill thee,
But thou slew'st Tybalt; there art thou happy too;
The law that threaten'd death becomes thy friend
And turns it to exile; there art thou happy:
A pack of blessings lights upon thy back;
Happiness courts thee in her best array;
But, like a misbehaved and sullen wench,
Thou pout'st upon thy fortune and thy love:
Take heed, take heed, for such die miserable.
Go, get thee to thy love, as was decreed,
Ascend her chamber, hence and comfort her:
But look thou stay not the watch be set,
For then thou canst not pass to Mantua;
Where thou shalt live, till we can find a time
To blaze your marriage, reconcile your friends,
Beg pardon of the prince, and call thee back
With twenty hundred thousand times more joy
Than thou went'st forth in lamentation.
Go before, nurse: commend me to thy lady;
And bid her hasten all the house to bed,
Which heavy sorrow makes them apt unto:
Romeo is coming.
    NURSE: O Lord, I could have stay'd here all the night
To hear good counsel: O, what learning is!
My lord, I 'll tell my lady you will come.

ROMEO: Do so, and bid my sweet prepare to chide.

NURSE: Here, sir, a ring she bid me give you, sir:
Hie you, make haste, for it grows very late.   [*Exit.*

ROMEO: How well my comfort is revived by this!

FRIAR LAURENCE: Go hence; good night; and here stands all
    your state:
Either be gone before the watch be set,
Or by the break of day disguised from hence:
Sojourn in Mantua; I 'll find out your man,
And he shall signify from time to time
Every good hap to you that chances here:
Give me thy hand; 'tis late: farewell; good night.

ROMEO: But that a joy past joy calls out on me,
It were grief, so brief to part with thee:
Farewell.   [*Exeunt.*

SCENE IV. *A room in Capulet's house.*
Enter Capulet, Lady Capulet, and Paris.

CAPULET: Things have fall'n out, sir, so unluckily,
That we have had no time to move our daughter:
Look you, she loved her kinsman Tybalt dearly,
And so did I:—Well, we were born to die.
'Tis very late, she 'll not come down to-night:
I promise you, but for your company,
I would have been a-bed an hour ago.

PARIS: These times of woe afford no time to woo.
Madam, good night; commend me to your daughter.

LADY CAPULET: I will, and know her mind early to-morrow;
To-night she is mew'd up to her heaviness.

CAPULET: Sir Paris, I will make a desperate tender
Of my child's love: I think she will be ruled
In all respects by me; nay, more, I doubt it not.
Wife, go you to her ere you go to bed;
Acquaint her here of my son Paris' love;

And bid her, mark you me, on Wednesday next—
But, soft! what day is this?
    PARIS: Monday, my lord.
    CAPULET: Monday! ha, ha! Well, Wednesday is too soon,
O' Thursday let it be: o' Thursday, tell her,
She shall be married to this noble earl.
Will you be ready? do you like this haste?
We'll keep no great ado,—a friend or two;
For, hark you, Tybalt being slain so late,
It may be thought we held him carelessly,
Being our kinsman, if we revel much:
Therefore we 'll have some half a dozen friends,
And there an end. But what say you to Thursday?
    PARIS: My lord, I would that Thursday were to-morrow.
    CAPULET: Well, get you gone: o' Thursday be it, then.
Go you to Juliet ere you go to bed,
Prepare her, wife, against this wedding-day.
Farewell, my lord. Light to my chamber, ho!
Afore me! it is so very late,
That we may call it early by and by.
Good night.   [*Exeunt.*

SCENE V. *Capulet's orchard.*
Enter Romeo and Juliet above, at the window.

    JULIET: Wilt thou be gone? it is not yet near day:
It was the nightingale, and not the lark,
That pierced the fearful hollow of thine ear;
Nightly she sings on yond pomegranate-tree:
Believe me, love, it was the nightingale.
    ROMEO: It was the lark, the herald of the morn
No nightingale; look, love, what envious streaks
Do lace the severing clouds in yonder east:
Night's candles are burnt out, and jocund day
Stands tiptoe on the misty mountain tops.

I must be gone and live, or stay and die.

JULIET: Yond light is not day-light, I know it, I:
It is some meteor that the sun exhales,
To be to thee this night a torch-bearer,
And light thee on thy way to Mantua:
Therefore stay yet: thou need'st not to be gone.

ROMEO: Let me be ta'en, let me be put to death;
I am content, so thou wilt have it so.
I'll say yon grey is not the morning's eye,
'Tis but the pale reflex of Cynthia's brow;
Nor that is not the lark, whose notes do beat
The vaulty heaven so high above our heads:
I have more care to stay than will to go:
Come, death, and welcome! Juliet wills it so.
How is 't, my soul? let 's talk; it is not day.

JULIET: It is, it is: hie hence, be gone, away!
It is the lark that sings so out of tune,
Straining harsh discords and unpleasing sharps.
Some say the lark makes sweet division;
This doth not so, for she divideth us:
Some say the lark and loathed toad change eyes:
O, now I would they had changed voices too!
Since arm from arm that voice doth us affray,
Hunting thee hence with hunt's-up to the day.
O, now be gone; more light and light it grows.

ROMEO: More light and light; more dark and dark our woes!

Enter Nurse, to the chamber.

NURSE: Madam!

JULIET: Nurse?

NURSE: Your lady mother is coming to your chamber:
The day is broke; be wary, look about.   [*Exit.*

JULIET: Then, window, let day in, and let life out.

ROMEO: Farewell, farewell! one kiss, and I 'll descend.
                                        [*He goeth down.*

JULIET: Art thou gone so? love, lord, ay, husband, friend!
I must hear from thee every day in the hour,
For in a minute there are many days:
O, by this count I shall be much in years
Ere I again behold my Romeo!
    ROMEO: Farewell!
I will omit no opportunity
That may convey my greetings, love, to thee.
    JULIET: O think'st thou we shall ever meet again?
    ROMEO: I doubt it not; and all these woes shall serve
For sweet discourses in our time to come.
    JULIET: O God, I have an ill-divining soul!
Methinks I see thee, now thou art below,
As one dead in the bottom of a tomb;
Either my eyesight fails, or thou look'st pale.
    ROMEO: And trust me, love, in my eye so do you:
Dry sorrow drinks our blood. Adieu, adieu!   [*Exit.*
    JULIET: O fortune, fortune! all men call thee fickle:
If thou art fickle, what dost thou with him
That is renown'd for faith? Be fickle, fortune;
For then, I hope, thou wilt not keep him long,
But send him back.
    LADY CAPULET: [*Within*] Ho, daughter! are you up?
    JULIET: Who is 't that calls? is it my lady mother?
Is she not down so late, or up so early?
What unaccustom'd cause procures her hither?

Enter Lady Capulet.

    LADY CAPULET: Why, how now, Juliet!
    JULIET: Madam, I am not well.
    LADY CAPULET: Evermore weeping for your cousin's death?
What, wilt thou wash him from his grave with tears?
An if thou couldst, thou couldst not make him live;
Therefore, have done: some grief shows much of love;
But much of grief shows still some want of wit.

JULIET: Yet let me weep for such a feeling loss.

LADY CAPULET: So shall you feel the loss, but not the friend
Which you weep for.

JULIET: Feeling so the loss,
I cannot choose but ever weep the friend.

LADY CAPULET: Well, girl, thou weep'st not so much for his
    death,
As that the villain lives which slaughter'd him.

JULIET: What villain, madam?

LADY CAPULET: That same villain, Romeo.

JULIET: [*Aside*] Villain and he be many miles asunder.—
God pardon him! I do, with all my heart;
And yet no man like he doth grieve my heart.

LADY CAPULET: That is, because the traitor murderer lives.

JULIET: Ay, madam, from the reach of these my hands:
Would none but I might venge my cousin's death!

LADY CAPULET: We will have vengeance for it, fear thou not:
Then weep no more. I 'll send to one in Mantua,
Where that same banish'd runagate doth live,
Shall give him such an unaccustom'd dram,
That he shall soon keep Tybalt company:
And then, I hope, thou wilt be satisfied.

JULIET: Indeed, I never shall be satisfied
With Romeo, till I behold him—dead—
Is my poor heart so for a kinsman vex'd:
Madam, if you could find out but a man
To bear a poison, I would temper it;
That Romeo should, upon receipt thereof,
Soon sleep in quiet. O, how my heart abhors
To hear him named, and cannot come to him,
To wreak the love I bore my cousin
Upon his body that hath slaughter'd him!

LADY CAPULET: Find thou the means, and I'll find such a man.
But now I 'll tell thee joyful tidings, girl.

JULIET: And joy comes well in such a needy time:

What are they, I beseech your ladyship?

LADY CAPULET: Well, well, thou hast a careful father, child;
One who, to put thee from thy heaviness,
Hath sorted out a sudden day of joy,
That thou expect'st not nor I look'd not for.

JULIET: Madam, in happy time, what day is that?

LADY CAPULET: Marry, my child, early next Thursday morn,
The gallant, young and noble gentleman,
The County Paris, at Saint Peter's Church,
Shall happily make thee there a joyful bride.

JULIET: Now, by Saint Peter's Church and Peter too,
He shall not make me there a joyful bride.
I wonder at his haste; that I must wed
Ere he, that should be husband, comes to woo.
I pray you, tell my lord and father, madam,
I will not marry yet; and, when I do, I swear,
It shall be Romeo, whom you know I hate,
Rather than Paris. These are news indeed!

LADY CAPULET: Here comes your father; tell him so yourself,
And see how he will take it at your hands.

Enter Capulet and Nurse.

CAPULET: When the sun sets, the air doth drizzle dew;
But for the sunset of my brother's son
It rains downright.
How now! a conduit, girl? what, still in tears?
Evermore showering? In one little body
Thou counterfeit'st a bark, a sea, a wind;
For still thy eyes, which I may call the sea,
Do ebb and flow with tears; the bark thy body is,
Sailing in this salt flood; the winds, thy sighs;
Who, raging with thy tears, and they with them,
Without a sudden calm, will overset
Thy tempest-tossed body. How now, wife!
Have you deliver'd to her our decree?

LADY CAPULET: Ay, sir; but she will none, she gives you thanks.
I would the fool were married to her grave!

CAPULET: Soft! take me with you, take me with you, wife.
How! will she none? doth she not give us thanks?
Is she not proud? doth she not count her blest,
Unworthy as she is, that we have wrought
So worthy a gentleman to be her bridegroom?

JULIET: Not proud, you have; but thankful, that you have:
Proud can I never be of what I hate;
But thankful even for hate, that is meant love.

CAPULET: How now, how now, chop-logic! What is this!
'Proud,' and 'I thank you,' and 'I thank you not;'
And yet 'not proud:' mistress minion, you,
Thank me no thankings, nor proud me no prouds,
But fettle your fine joints 'gainst Thursday next,
To go with Paris to Saint Peter's Church,
Or I will drag thee on a hurdle thither.
Out, you green-sickness carrion! out, you baggage!
You tallow-face!

LADY CAPULET: Fie, fie! what, are you mad?

JULIET: Good father, I beseech you on my knees,
Hear me with patience but to speak a word.

CAPULET: Hang thee, young baggage! disobedient wretch!
I tell thee what: get thee to church o' Thursday,
Or never after look me in the face:
Speak not, reply not, do not answer me;
My fingers itch. Wife, we scarce thought us blest
That God had lent us but this only child;
But now I see this one is one too much,
And that we have a curse in having her:
Out on her, hilding!

NURSE: God in heaven bless her!
You are to blame, my lord, to rate her so.

CAPULET: And why, my lady wisdom? hold your tongue,
Good prudence; smatter with your gossips, go.

NURSE: I speak no treason.

CAPULET: O, God ye god-den.

NURSE: May not one speak?

CAPULET: Peace, you mumbling fool!
Utter your gravity o'er a gossip's bowl;
For here we need it not.

LADY CAPULET: You are too hot.

CAPULET: God's bread! it makes me mad:
Day, night, hour, tide, time, work, play,
Alone, in company, still my care hath been
To have her match'd: and having now provided
A gentleman of noble parentage,
Of fair demesnes, youthful, and nobly train'd,
Stuff'd, as they say, with honourable parts,
Proportion'd as one's thought would wish a man;
And then to have a wretched puling fool,
A whining mammet, in her fortune's tender,
To answer 'I 'll not wed; I cannot love,
I am too young! I pray you, pardon me.'
But, an you will not wed, I 'll pardon you:
Graze where you will, you shall not house with me:
Look to 't, think on 't, I do not use to jest.
Thursday is near; lay hand on heart, advise:
An you be mine, I 'll give you to my friend;
An you be not, hang, beg, starve, die in the streets,
For, by my soul, I 'll ne'er acknowledge thee,
Nor what is mine shall never do thee good:
Trust to 't, bethink you; I'll not be forsworn.   [*Exit.*

JULIET: Is there no pity sitting in the clouds,
That sees into the bottom of my grief?
O, sweet my mother, cast me not away!
Delay this marriage for a month, a week;
Or, if you do not, make the bridal bed
In that dim monument where Tybalt lies.

LADY CAPULET: Talk not to me, for I'll not speak a word:

Do as thou wilt, for I have done with thee.   [*Exit.*

    JULIET: O God!—O nurse, how shall this be prevented?
My husband is on earth, my faith in heaven;
How shall that faith return again to earth,
Unless that husband send it me from heaven
By leaving earth? comfort me, counsel me.
Alack, alack, that heaven should practise stratagems
Upon so soft a subject as myself!
What say'st thou? hast thou not a word of joy?
Some comfort, nurse,

    NURSE: Faith, here it is.
Romeo is banish'd; and all the world to nothing,
That he dares ne'er come back to challenge you;
Or, if he do, it needs must be by stealth.
Then, since the case so stands as now it doth,
I think it best you married with the county.
O, he's a lovely gentleman!
Romeo's a dishclout to him: an eagle, madam,
Hath not so green, so quick, so fair an eye
As Paris hath. Beshrew my very heart,
I think you are happy in this second match,
For it excels your first: or if it did not,
Your first is dead; or 'twere as good he were,
As living here and you no use of him.

    JULIET: Speakest thou from thy heart?

    NURSE: And from my soul too;
Or else beshrew them both.

    JULIET: Amen!

    NURSE: What?

    JULIET: Well, thou hast comforted me marvelous much.
Go in; and tell my lady I am gone,
Having displeased my father, to Laurence' cell,
To make confession and to be absolved.

    NURSE: Marry, I will; and this is wisely done.   [*Exit.*

    JULIET: Ancient damnation! O most wicked fiend!

Is it more sin to wish me thus forsworn,
Or to dispraise my lord with that same tongue
Which she hath praised him with above compare
So many thousand times? Go, counsellor:
Thou and my bosom henceforth shall be twain.
I'll to the friar, to know his remedy:
If all else fail, myself have power to die.   [*Exit.*

ACT IV.

SCENE I. *Friar Laurence's cell.*
Enter Friar Laurence and Paris.

FRIAR LAURENCE: On Thursday, sir? the time is very short.
PARIS: My father Capulet will have it so;
And I am nothing slow to slack his haste.
FRIAR LAURENCE: You say you do not know the lady's mind:
Uneven is the course, I like it not.
PARIS: Immoderately she weeps for Tybalt's death,
And therefore have I little talk'd of love;
For Venus smiles not in a house of tears.
Now, sir, her father counts it dangerous
That she doth give her sorrow so much sway,
And in his wisdom hastes our marriage,
To stop the inundation of her tears;
Which, too much minded by herself alone,
May be put from her by society:
Now do you know the reason of this haste.
FRIAR LAURENCE: [*Aside*] I would I knew not why it should be
     slow'd.
Look, sir, here comes the lady towards my cell.

Enter Juliet.

PARIS: Happily met, my lady and my wife!

JULIET: That may be, sir, when I may be a wife.

PARIS: That may be must be, love, on Thursday next.

JULIET: What must be shall be.

FRIAR LAURENCE: That's a certain text.

PARIS: Come you to make confession to this father?

JULIET: To answer that, I should confess to you.

PARIS: Do not deny to him that you love me.

JULIET: I will confess to you that I love him.

PARIS: So will ye, I am sure, that you love me.

JULIET: If I do so, it will be of more price,
Being spoke behind your back, than to your face.

PARIS: Poor soul, thy face is much abused with tears.

JULIET: The tears have got small victory by that;
For it was bad enough before their spite.

PARIS: Thou wrongs't it, more than tears, with that report.

Juliet: That is no slander, sir, which is a truth;
And what I spake, I spake it to my face.

PARIS: Thy face is mine, and thou hast slander'd it.

JULIET: It may be so, for it is not mine own.
Are you at leisure, holy father, now;
Or shall I come to you at evening mass?

FRIAR LAURENCE: My leisure serves me, pensive daughter, now.
My lord, we must entreat the time alone.

PARIS: God shield I should disturb devotion!
Juliet, on Thursday early will I rouse ye:
Till then, adieu; and keep this holy kiss.   [*Exit.*

JULIET: O, shut the door! and when thou hast done so,
Come weep with me; past hope, past cure, past help!

FRIAR LAURENCE: Ah, Juliet, I already know thy grief;
It strains me past the compass of my wits:
I hear thou must, and nothing may prorogue it,
On Thursday next be married to this county.

JULIET: Tell me not, friar, that thou hear'st of this,
Unless thou tell me how I may prevent it:

If, in thy wisdom, thou canst give no help,
Do thou but call my resolution wise,
And with this knife I 'll help it presently.
God join'd my heart and Romeo's, thou our hands;
And ere this hand, by thee to Romeo seal'd,
Shall be the label to another deed,
Or my true heart with treacherous revolt
Turn to another, this shall slay them both:
Therefore, out of thy long-experienced time,
Give me some present counsel, or, behold,
'Twixt my extremes and me this bloody knife
Shall play the umpire, arbitrating that
Which the commission of thy years and art
Could to no issue of true honour bring.
Be not so long to speak; I long to die,
If what thou speak'st speak not of remedy.

 FRIAR LAURENCE: Hold, daughter: I do spy a kind of hope,
Which craves as desperate an execution
As that is desperate which we would prevent.
If, rather than to marry County Paris,
Thou hast the strength of will to slay thyself,
Then is it likely thou wilt undertake
A thing like death to chide away this shame,
That copest with death himself to scape from it;
And, if thou darest, I 'll give thee remedy.

 JULIET: O, bid me leap, rather than marry Paris,
From off the battlements of yonder tower;
Or walk in thievish ways; or bid me lurk
Where serpents are; chain me with roaring bears;
Or shut me nightly in a charnel-house,
O'er-cover'd quite with dead men's rattling bones,
With reeky shanks and yellow chapless-skulls;
Or bid me go into a new-made grave
And hide me with a dead man in his shroud;
Things that, to hear them told, have made me tremble;

And I will do it without fear or doubt,
To live an unstain'd wife to my sweet love.

    FRIAR LAURENCE: Hold, then; go home, be merry, give consent
To marry Paris: Wednesday is to-morrow;
To-morrow night look that thou lie alone;
Let not thy nurse lie with thee in thy chamber:
Take thou this vial, being then in bed,
And this distilled liquor drink thou off;
When presently through all thy veins shall run
A cold and drowsy humour, for no pulse
Shall keep his native progress, but surcease:
No warmth, no breath, shall testify thou livest;
The roses in thy lips and cheeks shall fade
To paly ashes, thy eyes' windows fall,
Like death, when he shuts up the day of life;
Each part, deprived of supple government,
Shall, stiff and stark and cold, appear like death:
And in this borrow'd likeness of shrunk death
Thou shalt continue two and forty hours,
And then awake as from a pleasant sleep.
Now, when the bridegroom in the morning comes
To rouse thee from thy bed, there art thou dead:
Then, as the manner of our country is,
In thy best robes uncover'd on the bier
Thou shalt be borne to that same ancient vault
Where all the kindred of the Capulets lie.
In the mean time, against thou shalt awake,
Shall Romeo by my letters know our drift,
And hither shall he come: and he and I
Will watch thy waking, and that very night
Shall Romeo bear thee hence to Mantua.
And this shall free thee from this present shame;
If no inconstant toy, nor womanish fear,
Abate thy valour in the acting it.

    JULIET: Give me, give me! O, tell not me of fear!

FRIAR LAURENCE: Hold; get you gone, be strong and prosperous
In this resolve: I 'll send a friar with speed
To Mantua, with my letters to thy lord.

JULIET: Love give me strength! and strength shall help afford.
Farewell, dear father!   [*Exeunt.*

SCENE II. *Hall in Capulet's house.*
Enter Capulet, Lady Capulet, Nurse, and two Servingmen.

CAPULET: So many guests invite as here are writ.
                                        [*Exit First Servant.*
Sirrah, go hire me twenty cunning cooks.

SECOND SERVANT: You shall have none ill, sir; for
I 'll try if they can lick their fingers.

CAPULET: How canst thou try them so?

SECOND SERVANT: Marry, sir, 'tis an ill cook that cannot lick his
own fingers: therefore he that cannot lick his fingers goes not
with me.

CAPULET: Go, be gone.   [*Exit Second Servant.*
We shall be much unfurnish'd for this time.
What, is my daughter gone to Friar Laurence?

NURSE: Ay, forsooth.

CAPULET: Well, he may chance to do some good on her:
A peevish self-will'd harlotry it is.

NURSE: See where she comes from shrift with merry look.

Enter Juliet.

CAPULET: How now, my headstrong! where have you been
      gadding?

JULIET: Where I have learn'd me to repent the sin
Of disobedient opposition
To you and your behests, and am enjoin'd
By holy Laurence to fall prostrate here,
And beg your pardon: pardon, I beseech you!
Henceforward I am ever ruled by you.

CAPULET: Send for the county; go tell him of this:
I'll have this knot knit up to-morrow morning.

JULIET: I met the youthful lord at Laurence' cell;
And gave him what becomed love I might,
Not stepping o'er the bounds of modesty.

CAPULET: Why, I am glad on 't; this is well: stand up:
This is as 't should be. Let me see the county;
Ay, marry, go, I say, and fetch him hither.
Now, afore God! this reverend holy friar,
All our whole city is much bound to him.

JULIET: Nurse, will you go with me into my closet,
To help me sort such needful ornaments
As you think fit to furnish me to-morrow?

LADY CAPULET: No, not till Thursday; there is time enough.

CAPULET: Good nurse, go with her: we 'll to church to-morrow.
                                    [*Exeunt Juliet and Nurse.*

LADY CAPULET: We shall be short in our provision:
'Tis now near night.

CAPULET: Tush, I will stir about,
And all things shall be well, I warrant thee, wife:
Go thou to Juliet, help to deck up her;
I 'll not to bed to-night; let me alone;
I 'll play the housewife for this once. What, ho!
They are all forth. Well, I will walk myself
To County Paris, to prepare him up
Against to-morrow: my heart is wondrous light,
Since this same wayward girl is so reclaim'd.

SCENE III. *Juliet's chamber.*
Enter Juliet and Nurse.

JULIET: Ay, those attires are best; but, gentle nurse,
I pray thee, leave me to myself to-night;
For I have need of many orisons
To move the heavens to smile upon my state.

Which, well thou know'st, is cross and full of sin.

Enter Lady Capulet

LADY CAPULET: What, are you busy, ho? need you my help?
JULIET: No, madam; we have cull'd such necessaries
As are behoveful for our state to-morrow:
So please you, let me now be left alone,
And let the nurse this night sit up with you;
For, I am sure, you have your hands full all,
In this so sudden business.
LADY CAPULET: Good night:
Get thee to bed, and rest; for thou hast need.

                              [*Exeunt Lady Capulet and Nurse.*
JULIET: Farewell! God knows when we shall meet again.
I have a faint cold fear thrills through my veins,
That almost freezes up the heat of life:
I 'll call them back again to comfort me:
Nurse! What should she do here?
My dismal scene I needs must act alone.
Come, vial.
What if this mixture do not work at all?
Shall I be married then to-morrow morning?
No, no: this shall forbid it: lie thou there.

                              [*Laying down her dagger.*
What if it be a poison, which the friar
Subtly hath minister'd to have me dead,
Lest in this marriage he should be dishonour'd,
Because he married me before to Romeo?
I fear it is: and yet, methinks, I should not,
For he hath still been tried a holy man.
How if, when I am laid into the tomb,
I wake before the time that Romeo
Come to redeem me? there 's a fearful point!
Shall I not, then, be stifled in the vault,
To whose foul mouth no healthsome air breathes in,

And there die strangled ere my Romeo comes?
Or, if I live, is it not very like,
The horrible conceit of death and night,
Together with the terror of the place,—
As in a vault, an ancient receptacle,
Where, for these many hundred years, the bones
Of all my buried ancestors are pack'd:
Where bloody Tybalt, yet but green in earth,
Lies festering in his shroud; where, as they say,
At some hours in the night spirits resort;—
Alack, alack, is it not like that I,
So early waking, what with loathsome smells,
And shrieks like mandrakes' torn out of the earth,
That living mortals, hearing them, run mad:—
O, if I wake, shall I not be distraught,
Environed with all these hideous fears?
And madly play with my forefathers' joints?
And pluck the mangled Tybalt from his shroud?
And, in this rage, with some great kinsman's bone,
As with a club, dash out my desperate brains?
O, look! methinks I see my cousin's ghost
Seeking out Romeo, that did spit his body
Upon a rapier's point: stay, Tybalt, stay!
Romeo, I come! this do I drink to thee.

                [*She falls upon her bed, within the curtains.*

SCENE IV. *Hall in Capulet's house.*
Enter Lady Capulet and Nurse.

LADY CAPULET: Hold, take these keys, and fetch more spices,
    nurse.
NURSE: They call for dates and quinces in the pastry.

Enter Capulet.

CAPULET: Come, stir, stir, stir! the second cock hath crow'd,

The curfew-bell hath rung, 'tis three o'clock:
Look to the baked meats, good Angelica:
Spare not for cost.

  NURSE: Go, you cot-quean, go,
Get you to bed; faith, you 'll be sick to-morrow
For this night's watching.

  CAPULET: No, not a whit: what! I have watch'd ere now
All night for lesser cause, and ne'er been sick.

  LADY CAPULET: Ay, you have been a mouse-hunt in your time;
But I will watch you from such watching now.

         [*Exeunt Lady Capulet and Nurse.*

  CAPULET: A jealous-hood, a jealous-hood!

Enter three or four Servingmen, with spits, logs, and baskets.

              Now, fellow,
What's there?

  FIRST SERVANT: Things for the cook, sir; but I know not what.

  CAPULET: Make haste, make haste.   [*Exit First Servant*
Sirrah, fetch drier logs:
Call Peter, he will show thee where they are.

  SECOND SERVANT: I have a head, sir, that will find out logs,
And never trouble Peter for the matter.   [*Exit.*

  CAPULET: Mass, and well said; a merry whoreson, ha!
Thou shalt be logger-head. Good faith, 'tis day:
The county will be here with music straight,
For so he said he would: I hear him near. [*Music within.*
Nurse! Wife! What, ho! What, nurse, I say!

Re-enter Nurse.

Go waken Juliet, go and trim her up;
I 'll go and chat with Paris: hie, make haste,
Make haste; the bridegroom he is come already:
Make haste, I say.   [*Exeunt.*

SCENE V. *Juliet's chamber.*
Enter Nurse.

NURSE: Mistress! what, mistress! Juliet! fast, I warrant her, she:
Why, lamb! why, lady! fie, you slug-a-bed!
Why, love, I say! madam! sweet-heart! why, bride!
What, not a word? you take your pennyworths now;
Sleep for a week; for the next night, I warrant,
The County Paris hath set up his rest,
That you shall rest but little. God forgive me,
Marry, and amen, how sound is she asleep!
I must needs wake her. Madam, madam, madam!
Ay, let the county take you in your bed:
He'll fright you up, i' faith. Will it not be?   [*Undraws the curtains.*
What, dress'd! and in your clothes! and down again!
I must needs wake you: Lady! lady! lady!
Alas, alas! Help, help! my lady's dead!
O, well-a-day, that ever I was born!
Some aqua vitæ, ho! My lord! my lady!

Enter Lady Capulet.

LADY CAPULET: What noise is here?
NURSE: O lamentable day!
LADY CAPULET: What is the matter?
NURSE: Look, look! O heavy day!
LADY CAPULET: O me, O me! My child, my only life,
Revive, look up, or I will die with thee!
Help, help! Call help.

Enter Capulet.

CAPULET: For shame, bring Juliet forth; her lord is come,
NURSE: She 's dead, deceased, she 's dead; alack the day!
LADY CAPULET: Alack the day, she 's dead, she 's dead, she 's dead!
CAPULET: Ha! let me see her: out, alas! she 's cold;
Her blood is settled, and her joints are stiff;

Life and these lips have long been separated:
Death lies on her like an untimely frost
Upon the sweetest flower of all the field.

    NURSE: O lamentable day!
    LADY CAPULET: O woful time!
    CAPULET: Death, that hath ta'en her hence to make me wail,
Ties up my tongue, and will not let me speak.

Enter Friar Laurence and Paris, with Musicians.

    FRIAR LAURENCE: Come, is the bride ready to go to church?
    CAPULET: Ready to go, but never to return.
O son! the night before thy wedding-day
Hath Death lain with thy wife. There she lies,
Flower as she was, deflowered by him.
Death is my son-in-law, Death is my heir;
My daughter he hath wedded: I will die,
And leave him all; life, living, all is Death's.

    PARIS: Have I thought long to see this morning's face,
And doth it give me such a sight as this?

    LADY CAPULET: Accursed, unhappy, wretched, hateful day!
Most miserable hour that e'er time saw
In lasting labour of his pilgrimage!
But one, poor one, one poor and loving child,
But one thing to rejoice and solace in,
And cruel death hath catch'd it from my sight!

    NURSE: O woe! O woful, woful, woful day!
Most lamentable day, most woful day,
That ever, ever, I did yet behold!
O day! O day! O day! O hateful day!
Never was seen so black a day as this:
O woful day, O woful day!

    PARIS: Beguiled, divorced, wronged, spited, slain!
Most detestable death, by thee beguiled,
By cruel cruel thee quite overthrown!
O love! O life! not life, but love in death!

CAPULET: Despised, distressed, hated, martyr'd, kill'd!
Uncomfortable time, why camest thou now
To murder, murder our solemnity?
O child! O child! my soul, and not my child!
Dead art thou! Alack! my child is dead;
And with my child my joys are buried.

FRIAR LAURENCE: Peace, ho, for shame! confusion's cure lives not
In these confusions. Heaven and yourself
Had part in this fair maid; now heaven hath all,
And all the better is it for the maid:
Your part in her you could not keep from death,
But heaven keeps his part in eternal life.
The most you sought was her promotion;
For 'twas your heaven she should be advanced:
And weep ye now, seeing she is advanced
Above the clouds, as high as heaven itself?
O, in this love, you love your child so ill,
That you run mad, seeing that she is well:
She 's not well married that lives married long;
But she 's best married that dies married young.
Dry up your tears, and stick your rosemary
On this fair corse; and, as the custom is,
In all her best array bear her to church:
For though fond nature bids us all lament,
Yet nature's tears are reason's merriment.

CAPULET: All things that we ordained festival,
Turn from their office to black funeral;
Our instruments to melancholy bells,
Our wedding cheer to a sad burial feast,
Our solemn hymns to sullen dirges change,
Our bridal flowers serve for a buried corse,
And all things change them to the contrary.

FRIAR LAURENCE: Sir, go you in; and, madam, go with him;
And go, Sir Paris; every one prepare
To follow this fair corse unto her grave:

The heavens do lour upon you for some ill;
Move them no more by crossing their high will.

                [Exeunt Capulet, Lady Capulet, Paris, and Friar.

FIRST MUSICIAN: Faith, we may put up our pipes, and be gone.

NURSE: Honest good fellows, ah, put up, put up;
For, well you know, this is a pitiful case.   *[Exit.*

FIRST MUSICIAN: Ay, by my troth, the case may be amended.

Enter Peter.

PETER: Musicians, O, musicians, 'Heart's ease, Heart's ease:' O, an you will have me live, play 'Heart's ease,'

FIRST MUSICIAN: Why 'Heart's ease'?

PETER: O, musicians, because my heart itself plays 'My heart is full of woe:' O, play me some merry dump, to comfort me.

FIRST MUSICIAN: Not a dump we; 'tis no time to play now.

PETER: You will not, then?

FIRST MUSICIAN: No.

PETER: I will then give it you soundly.

FIRST MUSICIAN: What will you give us?

PETER: No money, on my faith, but the gleek; I will give you the minstrel.

FIRST MUSICIAN: Then will I give you the serving-creature.

PETER: Then will I lay the serving-creature's dagger on your pate. I will carry no crotchets: I 'll re you, I 'll fa you; do you note me?

FIRST MUSICIAN: An you re us and fa us, you note us.

SECOND MUSICIAN: Pray you, put up your dagger, and put out your wit.

PETER: Then have at you with my wit! I will dry-beat you with an iron wit, and put up my iron dagger. Answer me like men:

'When gripping grief the heart doth wound,
    And doleful dumps the mind oppress,
Then music with her silver sound'—

why 'silver sound'? why 'music with her silver sound'? What say you, Simon Catling?

FIRST MUSICIAN: Marry, sir, because silver hath a sweet sound.

PETER: Pretty! what say you, Hugh Rebeck?

SECOND MUSICIAN: I say 'silver sound,' because musicians sound for silver.

PETER: Pretty too! What say you, James Soundpost?

THIRD MUSICIAN: Faith, I know not what to say.

PETER: O, I cry you mercy; you are the singer; I will say for you. It is 'music with her silver sound,' because musicians have no gold for sounding:

'Then music with her silver sound
    With speedy help doth lend redress.'   [*Exit.*

FIRST MUSICIAN: What a pestilent knave is this same!

SECOND MUSICIAN: Hang him, Jack! Come, we 'll in here; tarry for the mourners, and stay dinner.   [*Exeunt.*

ACT V.

SCENE I. *Mantua. A street.*
Enter Romeo.

ROMEO: If I may trust the flattering truth of sleep,
My dreams presage some joyful news at hand:
My bosom's lord sits lightly in his throne;
And all this day an unaccustom'd spirit
Lifts me above the ground with cheerful thoughts.
I dreamt my lady came and found me dead—
Strange dream, that gives a dead man leave to think!—
And breathed such life with kisses in my lips,
That I revived, and was an emperor.
Ah me! how sweet is love itself possess'd,
When but love's shadows are so rich in joy!

Enter Balthasar, booted.

News from Verona!—How now, Balthasar!
Dost thou not bring me letters from the friar?

How doth my lady? Is my father well?
How fares my Juliet? that I ask again;
For nothing can be ill, if she be well.
 BALTHASAR: Then she is well, and nothing can be ill:
Her body sleeps in Capels' monument,
And her immortal part with angels lives.
I saw her laid low in her kindred's vault,
And presently took post to tell it you:
O, pardon me for bringing these ill news,
Since you did leave it for my office, sir.
 ROMEO: Is it even so? then I defy you, stars!
Thou know'st my lodging: get me ink and paper,
And hire post-horses; I will hence to-night.
 BALTHASAR: I do beseech you, sir, have patience:
Your looks are pale and wild, and do import
Some misadventure.
 ROMEO: Tush, thou art deceived:
Leave me, and do the thing I bid thee do.
Hast thou no letters to me from the friar?
 BALTHASAR: No, my good lord.
 ROMEO: No matter: get thee gone,
And hire those horses; I 'll be with thee straight [*Exit Balthasar.*
Well, Juliet, I will lie with thee to-night.
Let 's see for means: O mischief, thou art swift
To enter in the thoughts of desperate men!
I do remember an apothecary,—
And hereabouts he dwells,—which late I noted
In tatter'd weeds, with overwhelming brows,
Culling of simples; meagre were his looks,
Sharp misery had worn him to the bones:
And in his needy shop a tortoise hung,
An alligator stuff'd, and other skins
Of ill-shaped fishes; and about his shelves
A beggarly account of empty boxes,
Green earthen pots, bladders and musty seeds,

Remnants of packthread and old cakes of roses,
Were thinly scatter'd, to make up a show.
Noting this penury, to myself I said
'An if a man did need a poison now,
Whose sale is present death in Mantua,
Here lives a caitiff wretch would sell it him.'
O, this same thought did but forerun my need;
And this same needy man must sell it me.
As I remember, this should be the house.
Being holiday, the beggar's shop is shut.
What, ho! apothecary!

Enter Apothecary.

APOTHECARY: Who calls so loud?
ROMEO: Come hither, man. I see that thou art poor:
Hold, there is forty ducats: let me have
A dram of poison, such soon-speeding gear
As will disperse itself through all the veins
That the life-weary taker may fall dead
And that the trunk may be discharged of breath
As violently as hasty powder fired
Doth hurry from the fatal cannon's womb.
APOTHECARY: Such mortal drugs I have; but Mantua's law
Is death to any he that utters them.
ROMEO: Art thou so bare and full of wretchedness,
And fear'st to die? famine is in thy cheeks,
Need and oppression starveth in thine eyes,
Contempt and beggary hangs upon thy back;
The world is not thy friend nor the world's law;
The world affords no law to make thee rich;
Then be not poor, but break it, and take this.
APOTHECARY: My poverty, but not my will, consents.
ROMEO: I pay thy poverty, and not thy will.
APOTHECARY: Put this in any liquid thing you will,
And drink it off; and, if you had the strength

Of twenty men, it would dispatch you straight.

　　ROMEO: There 's thy gold, worse poison to men's souls,
Doing more murders in this loathsome world,
Than these poor compounds that thou mayst not sell.
I sell thee poison; thou hast sold me none.
Farewell: buy food, and get thyself in flesh.
Come, cordial and not poison, go with me
To Juliet's grave; for there must I use thee.　　　　　　　　　[*Exeunt.*

SCENE II. Friar Laurence's cell.
Enter Friar John.

　　FRIAR JOHN: Holy Franciscan friar! brother, ho!

Enter Friar Laurence.

　　FRIAR LAURENCE: This same should be the voice of Friar John.
Welcome from Mantua: what says Romeo?
Or, if his mind be writ, give me his letter.

　　FRIAR JOHN: Going to find a bare-foot brother out,
One of our order, to associate me,
Here in this city visiting the sick,
And finding him, the searchers of the town,
Suspecting that we both were in a house
Where the infectious pestilence did reign,
Seal'd up the doors, and would not let us forth;
So that my speed to Mantua there was stay'd.

　　FRIAR LAURENCE: Who bare my letter, then, to Romeo?

　　FRIAR JOHN: I could not send it,—here it is again,—
Nor get a messenger to bring it thee,
So fearful were they of infection.

　　FRIAR LAURENCE: Unhappy fortune! by my brotherhood,
The letter was not nice but full of charge
Of dear import, and the neglecting it
May do much danger. Friar John, go hence;
Get me an iron crow, and bring it straight

Unto my cell.

    FRIAR JOHN: Brother, I'll go and bring it thee.   [*Exit.*

    FRIAR LAURENCE: Now must I to the monument alone;

Within this three hours will fair Juliet wake:

She will beshrew me much that Romeo

Hath had no notice of these accidents;

But I will write again to Mantua,

And keep her at my cell till Romeo come;

Poor living corse, closed in a dead man's tomb!   [*Exit.*

SCENE III. *A churchyard; in it a tomb*
belonging to the Capulets.Enter Paris, and his Page
bearing flowers and a torch.

PARIS: Give me thy torch, boy: hence, and stand aloof:

Yet put it out, for I would not be seen.

Under yond yew-trees lay thee all along,

Holding thine ear close to the hollow ground;

So shall no foot upon the churchyard tread,

Being loose, unfirm, with digging up of graves,

But thou shalt hear it; whistle then to me,

As signal that thou hear'st something approach.

Give me those flowers. Do as I bid thee, go.

    PAGE: [*Aside*] I am almost afraid to stand alone

Here in the churchyard; yet I will adventure.   [*Retires.*

    PARIS: Sweet flower, with flowers thy bridal bed I strew,—

    O woe! thy canopy is dust and stones;—

Which with sweet water nightly I will dew,

    Or, wanting that, with tears distill'd by moans:

The obsequies that I for thee will keep

Nightly shall be to strew thy grave and weep.   [*The Page whistles.*

The boy gives warning something doth approach.

What cursed foot wanders this way to-night,

To cross my obsequies and true love's rite?

What, with a torch! muffle me, night, awhile.   [*Retires.*

Enter Romeo and Balthasar, with a torch, mattock, &c.

ROMEO: Give me that mattock and the wrenching iron.
Hold, take this letter: early in the morning
See thou deliver it to my lord and father.
Give me the light: upon thy life, I charge thee,
Whate'er thou hear'st or seeest, stand all aloof,
And do not interrupt me in my course.
Why I descend into this bed of death,
Is partly to behold my lady's face;
But chiefly to take thence from her dead finger
A precious ring, a ring that I must use
In dear employment: therefore hence, be gone:
But if thou, jealous, dost return to pry
In what I further shall intend to do,
By heaven, I will tear thee joint by joint
And strew this hungry churchyard with thy limbs:
The time and my intents are savage-wild,
More fierce and more inexorable far
Than empty tigers or the roaring sea.
     BALTHASAR: I will be gone, sir, and not trouble you.
     ROMEO: So shalt thou show me friendship.
     Take thou that:
Live, and be prosperous: and farewell, good fellow.
     BALTHASAR: [*Aside*] For all this same, I 'll hide me hereabout:
His looks I fear, and his intents I doubt.   [*Retires.*
     ROMEO: Thou detestable maw, thou womb of death,
Gorged with the dearest morsel of the earth,
Thus I enforce thy rotten jaws to open,
And, in despite, I 'll cram thee with more food!   [*Opens the tomb.*
     PARIS: This is that banish'd haughty Montague,
That murder'd my love's cousin, with which grief,
It is supposed, the fair creature died;
And here is come to do some villanous shame
To the dead bodies: I will apprehend him.   [*Comes forward.*

Stop thy unhallow'd toil, vile Montague!
Can vengeance be pursued further than death?
Condemned villain, I do apprehend thee:
Obey, and go with me; for thou must die.

ROMEO: I must indeed; and therefore came I hither.
Good gentle youth, tempt not a desperate man;
Fly hence, and leave me: think upon these gone;
Let them affright thee. I beseech thee, youth,
Put not another sin upon my head,
By urging me to fury: O, be gone!
By heaven, I love thee better than myself;
For I come hither arm'd against myself:
Stay not, be gone; live, and hereafter say,
A madman's mercy bade thee run away.

PARIS: I do defy thy conjurations,
And apprehend thee for a felon here.

ROMEO: Wilt thou provoke me? then have at thee, boy!

[*They fight.*

PAGE: O Lord, they fight! I will go call the watch.   [*Exit.*

PARIS: O, I am slain! [*Falls.*] If thou be merciful,
Open the tomb, lay me with Juliet.   [*Dies.*

ROMEO: In faith, I will. Let me peruse this face.
Mercutio's kinsman, noble County Paris!
What said my man, when my betossed soul
Did not attend him as we rode? I think
He told me Paris should have married Juliet:
Said he not so? or did I dream it so?
Or am I mad, hearing him talk of Juliet,
To think it was so? O, give me thy hand,
One writ with me in sour misfortune's book!
I'll bury thee in a triumphant grave;
A grave? O, no! a lantern, slaughter'd youth,
For here lies Juliet, and her beauty makes
This vault a feasting presence full of light.
Death, lie thou there, by a dead man interr'd.

[Laying Paris in the tomb.

How oft when men are at the point of death
Have they been merry! which their keepers call
A lightning before death: O, how may I
Call this a lightning? O my love! my wife!
Death, that hath suck'd the honey of thy breath,
Hath no power yet upon thy beauty:
Thou art not conquer'd; beauty's ensign yet
Is crimson in thy lips and in thy cheeks,
And death's pale flag is not advanced there.
Tybalt, liest thou there in thy bloody sheet?
O, what more favour can I do to thee,
Than with that hand that cut thy youth in twain
To sunder his that was thine enemy?
Forgive me, cousin! Ah, dear Juliet,
Why art thou yet so fair? shall I believe
That unsubstantial death is amorous,
And that the lean abhorred monster keeps
Thee here in dark to be his paramour?
For fear of that, I still will stay with thee;
And never from this palace of dim night
Depart again: here, here will I remain
With worms that are thy chamber-maids; O, here
Will I set up my everlasting rest,
And shake the yoke of inauspicious stars
From this world-wearied flesh. Eyes, look your last!
Arms, take your last embrace! and, lips, O you
The doors of breath, seal with a righteous kiss
A dateless bargain to engrossing death!
Come, bitter conduct, come, unsavoury guide!
Thou desperate pilot, now at once run on
The dashing rocks thy sea-sick weary bark!
Here's to my love! [*Drinks.*] O true apothecary!
Thy drugs are quick. Thus with a kiss I die.   [*Dies.*

Enter, at the other end of the churchyard.
Friar Laurence, with a lantern, crow, and spade.

FRIAR LAURENCE: Saint Francis be my speed! how oft to-night
Have my old feet stumbled at graves! Who's there?

BALTHASAR: Here 's one a friend, and one that knows you well.

FRIAR LAURENCE: Bliss be upon you! Tell me, good my friend,
What torch is yond, that vainly lends his light
To grubs and eyeless skulls? as I discern,
It burneth in the Capels' monument.

BALTHASAR: It doth so, holy sir; and there's my master,
One that you love.

FRIAR LAURENCE: Who is it?

BALTHASAR: Romeo.

FRIAR LAURENCE: How long hath he been there?

BALTHASAR: Full half an hour.

FRIAR LAURENCE: Go with me to the vault.

BALTHASAR: I dare not, sir:
My master knows but I am gone hence;
And fearfully did menace me with death,
If I did stay to look on his intents.

FRIAR LAURENCE: Stay, then; I'll go alone. Fear comes upon me:
O, much I fear some ill unlucky thing.

BALTHASAR: As I did sleep under this yew-tree here,
I dreamt my master and another fought,
And that my master slew him.

FRIAR LAURENCE: Romeo!   [*Advances.*
Alack, alack, what blood is this, which stains
The stony entrance of this sepulchre?
What mean these masterless and gory swords
To lie discolour'd by this place of peace?   [*Enters the tomb.*
Romeo! O, pale! Who else? what, Paris too?
And steep'd in blood? Ah, what an unkind hour
Is guilty of this lamentable chance!
The lady stirs.   [*Juliet wakes.*

JULIET: O comfortable friar! where is my lord?
I do remember well where I should be,
And there I am. Where is my Romeo?   [*Noise within.*

    FRIAR LAURENCE: I hear some noise. Lady, come from that nest
Of death, contagion, and unnatural sleep:
A greater power than we can contradict
Hath thwarted our intents. Come, come away,
Thy husband in thy bosom there lies dead;
And Paris too. Come, I'll dispose of thee
Among a sisterhood of holy nuns:
Stay not to question, for the watch is coming;
Come, go, good Juliet [*Noise again*], I dare no longer stay.

    JULIET: Go, get thee hence, for I will not away.
                                        [*Exit Friar Laurence.*

What's here? a cup, closed in my true love's hand?
Poison, I see, hath been his timeless end:
O churl! drunk all, and left no friendly drop
To help me after? I will kiss thy lips;
Haply some poison yet doth hang on them,
To make me die with a restorative.   [*Kisses him.*
Thy lips are warm.

    FIRST WATCH: [*Within*] Lead, boy: which way?

    JULIET: Yea, noise? then I 'll be brief. O happy dagger!
                                        [*Snatching Romeo's dagger.*
This is thy sheath [*Stabs herself*]; there rust, and let me die.
                                        [*Falls on Romeo's body, and dies.*

Enter Watch, with the Page of Paris.

    PAGE: This is the place; there, where the torch doth burn.

    FIRST WATCH: The ground is bloody; search about the church-
        yard:
Go, some of you, whoe'er you find attach.
Pitiful sight! here lies the county slain;
And Juliet bleeding, warm, and newly dead,
Who here hath lain these two days buried.

Go, tell the prince: run to the Capulets:
Raise up the Montagues: some others search:
We see the ground whereon these woes do lie;
But the true ground of all these piteous woes
We cannot without circumstance descry.

Re-enter some of the Watch, with Balthasar.

SECOND WATCH: Here's Romeo's man; we found him in the
churchyard.
FIRST WATCH: Hold him in safety, till the prince come hither.

Re-enter others of the Watch, with Friar Laurence.

THIRD WATCH: Here is a friar, that trembles, sighs, and weeps:
We took this mattock and this spade from him,
As he was coming from this churchyard side.
FIRST WATCH: A great suspicion: stay the friar too.

Enter the Prince and Attendants.

PRINCE: What misadventure is so early up,
That calls our person from our morning's rest?

Enter Capulet, Lady Capulet, and others.

CAPULET: What should it be, that they so shriek abroad?
LADY CAPULET: The people in the street cry Romeo,
Some Juliet, and some Paris; and all run.
With open outcry, toward our monument.
PRINCE: What fear is this which startles in our ears?
FIRST WATCH: Sovereign, here lies the County Paris slain;
And Romeo dead; and Juliet, dead before,
Warm and new kill'd.
PRINCE: Search, seek, and know how this foul murder comes.
FIRST WATCH: Here is a friar, and slaughtered Romeo's man;
With instruments upon them, fit to open
These dead men's tombs.
CAPULET: O heavens! O wife, look how our daughter bleeds!

This dagger hath mista'en,—for, lo, his house
Is empty on the back of Montague,—
And it mis-sheathed in my daughter's bosom!
    LADY CAPULET: O me! this sight of death is as a bell,
That warns my old age to a sepulchre.

Enter Montague and others.

    PRINCE: Come, Montague; for thou art early up,
To see thy son and heir more early down.
    MONTAGUE: Alas, my liege, my wife is dead to-night;
Grief of my son's exile hath stopp'd her breath:
What further woe conspires against mine age?
    PRINCE: Look, and thou shalt see.
    MONTAGUE: O thou untaught! what manners is in this,
To press before thy father to a grave?
    PRINCE: Seal up the mouth of outrage for a while,
Till we can clear these ambiguities,
And know their spring, their head, their true descent;
And then will I be general of your woes,
And lead you even to death: meantime forbear,
And let mischance be slave to patience.
Bring forth the parties of suspicion.
    FRIAR LAURENCE: I am the greatest, able to do least,
Yet most suspected, as the time and place
Doth make against me, of this direful murder:
And here I stand, both to impeach and purge
Myself condemned and myself excused.
    PRINCE: Then say at once what thou dost know in this.
    FRIAR LAURENCE: I will be brief, for my short date of breath
Is not so long as is a tedious tale.
Romeo, there dead, was husband to that Juliet;
And she, there dead, that Romeo's faithful wife:
I married them; and their stol'n marriage-day
Was Tybalt's dooms-day, whose untimely death
Banish'd the new-made bridegroom from this city,

For whom, and not for Tybalt, Juliet pined.
You, to remove the siege of grief from her,
Betroth'd and would have married her perforce
To County Paris: then comes she to me,
And, with wild looks, bid me devise some mean
To rid her from this second marriage,
Or in my cell there would she kill herself.
Then gave I her, so tutor'd by my art,
A sleeping potion; which so took effect
As I intended, for it wrought on her
The form of death: meantime I writ to Romeo,
That he should hither come as this dire night,
To help to take her from her borrow'd grave,
Being the time the potion's force should cease.
But he which bore my letter, Friar John,
Was stay'd by accident, and yesternight
Return'd my letter back. Then all alone
At the prefixed hour of her waking,
Came I to take her from her kindred's vault;
Meaning to keep her closely at my cell,
Till I conveniently could send to Romeo:
But when I came, some minute ere the time
Of her awaking, here untimely lay
The noble Paris and true Romeo dead.
She wakes; and I entreated her come forth,
And bear this work of heaven with patience;
But then a noise did scare me from the tomb;
And she, too desperate, would not go with me,
But, as it seems, did violence on herself.
All this I know; and to the marriage
Her nurse is privy: and, if aught in this
Miscarried by my fault, let my old life
Be sacrificed, some hour before his time,
Unto the rigour of severest law.

    PRINCE: We still have known thee for a holy man.

Where's Romeo's man? what can he say in this?
BALTHASAR: I brought my master news of Juliet's death;
And then in post he came from Mantua
To this same place, to this same monument.
This letter he early bid me give his father,
And threaten'd me with death, going in the vault,
If I departed not and left him there.
PRINCE: Give me the letter; I will look on it.
Where is the county's page, that raised the watch?
Sirrah, what made your master in this place?
PAGE: He came with flowers to strew his lady's grave;
And bid me stand aloof, and so I did:
Anon comes one with light to ope the tomb;
And by and by my master drew on him;
And then I ran away to call the watch.
PRINCE: This letter doth make good the friar's words,
Their course of love, the tidings of her death:
And here he writes that he did buy a poison
Of a poor 'pothecary, and therewithal
Came to this vault to die, and lie with Juliet.
Where be these enemies? Capulet! Montague!
See, what a scourge is laid upon your hate,
That heaven finds means to kill your joys with love.
And I for winking at your discords too
Have lost a brace of kinsmen: all are punish'd.
CAPULET: O brother Montague, give me thy hand:
This is my daughter's jointure, for no more
Can I demand.
MONTAGUE: But I can give thee more:
For I will raise her statue in pure gold;
That while Verona by that name is known,
There shall no figure at such rate be set
As that of true and faithful Juliet.
CAPULET: As rich shall Romeo's by his lady's lie;
Poor sacrifices of our enmity!

PRINCE: A glooming peace this morning with it brings;
The sun, for sorrow, will not show his head:
Go hence, to have more talk of these sad things;
Some shall be pardon'd, and some punished:
For never was a story of more woe
Than this of Juliet and her Romeo.   [*Exeunt.*

. . .

OTHELLO

THE MOOR OF VENICE

DRAMATIS PERSONÆ

DUKE OF VENICE.
BRABANTIO, a senator.
Other Senators.
GRATIANO, brother of Brabantio.
LODOVICO, kinsman to
    Brabantio.
OTHELLO, a noble Moor in the
    service of the Venetian
    state.
CASSIO, his lieutenant.
IAGO, his ancient.
RODERIGO, a Venetian gentle-
    man.
MONTANO, Othello's prede-

cessor in the government
    of Cyprus.
CLOWN, servant to Othello.
DESDEMONA, daughter to
    Brabantio and wife
    to Othello.
EMILIA, wife to Iago.
BIANCA, mistress to Cassio.
Sailor, Messenger, Herald,
    Officers, Gentlemen, Musi-
    cians, and Attendants.

SCENE:
Venice: a Sea-port in Cyprus.

ACT I.

SCENE I. *Venice. A street.*
Enter Roderigo and Iago.

RODERIGO: Tush! never tell me; I take it much unkindly
That thou, Iago, who hast had my purse
As if the strings were thine, shouldst know of this.

IAGO: 'Sblood, but you will not hear me:
If ever I did dream of such a matter,
Abhor me.

RODERIGO: Thou told'st me thou didst hold him in thy hate.

IAGO: Despise me, if I do not. Three great ones of the city,
In personal suit to make me his lieutenant,
Off-capp'd to him: and, by the faith of man,
I know my price, I am worth no worse a place:
But he, as loving his own pride and purposes,

Evades them, with a bombast circumstance
Horribly stuff'd with epithets of war;
And, in conclusion,
Nonsuits my mediators; for, 'Certes,' says he,
'I have already chose my officer.'
And what was he?
Forsooth, a great arithmetician,
One Michael Cassio, a Florentine,
A fellow almost damn'd in a fair wife;
That never set a squadron in the field,
Nor the division of a battle knows
More than a spinster; unless the bookish theorie,
Wherein the toged consuls can propose
As masterly as he: more prattle, without practice,
Is all his soldiership. But he, sir, had the election:
And I, of whom his eyes had seen the proof
At Rhodes, at Cyprus and on other grounds
Christian and heathen, must be be-lee'd and calm'd
By debitor and creditor: this counter-caster,
He, in good time, must his lieutenant be,
And I—God bless the mark!—his Moorship's ancient.
    RODERIGO: By heaven, I rather would have been his hangman.
    IAGO: Why, there's no remedy; 'tis the curse of service,
Preferment goes by letter and affection,
And not by old gradation, where each second
Stood heir to the first. Now, sir, be judge yourself,
Whether I in any just term am affined
To love the Moor.
    RODERIGO: I would not follow him then.
    IAGO: O, sir, content you;
I follow him to serve my turn upon him:
We cannot all be masters, nor all masters
Cannot be truly follow'd. You shall mark
Many a duteous and knee-crooking knave,
That, doting on his own obsequious bondage,

Wears out his time, much like his master's ass,
For nought but provender, and when he's old, cashier'd:
Whip me such honest knaves. Others there are
Who, trimm'd in forms and visages of duty,
Keep yet their hearts attending on themselves,
And, throwing but shows of service on their lords,
Do well thrive by them and when they have lined their coats
Do themselves homage: these fellows have some soul;
And such a one do I profess myself. For, sir,
It is as sure as you are Roderigo,
Were I the Moor, I would not be Iago:
In following him, I follow but myself;
Heaven is my judge, not I for love and duty,
But seeming so, for my peculiar end:
For when my outward action doth demonstrate
The native act and figure of my heart
In compliment extern, 'tis not long after
But I will wear my heart upon my sleeve
For daws to peck at: I am not what I am.

   RODERIGO: What a full fortune does the thicklips owe,
If he can carry 't thus!

   IAGO: Call up her father,
Rouse him: make after him, poison his delight,
Proclaim him in the streets; incense her kinsmen,
And, though he in a fertile climate dwell,
Plague him with flies: though that his joy be joy,
Yet throw such changes of vexation on 't,
As it may lose some colour.

   RODERIGO: Here is her father's house; I 'll call aloud.

   IAGO: Do, with like timorous accent and dire yell
As when, by night and negligence, the fire
Is spied in populous cities.

   RODERIGO: What, ho, Brabantio! Signior Brabantio, ho!

   IAGO: Awake! what, ho, Brabantio! thieves! thieves! thieves!
Look to your house, your daughter and your bags!

Thieves! thieves!

Brabantio appears above, at a window.

BRABANTIO: What is the reason of this terrible summons?
What is the matter there?

RODERIGO: Signior, is all your family within?

IAGO: Are your doors lock'd?

BRABANTIO: Why, wherefore ask you this?

IAGO: 'Zounds, sir, you're robb'd; for shame, put on your gown;
Your heart is burst, you have lost half your soul;
Even now, now, very now, an old black ram
Is tupping your white ewe. Arise, arise;
Awake the snorting citizens with the bell,
Or else the devil will make a grandsire of you:
Arise, I say.

BRABANTIO: What, have you lost your wits?

RODERIGO: Most reverend signior, do you know my voice?

BRABANTIO: Not I: what are you?

RODERIGO: My name is Roderigo.

BRABANTIO: The worser welcome:
I have charged thee not to haunt about my doors:
In honest plainness thou hast heard me say
My daughter is not for thee; and now, in madness,
Being full of supper and distempering draughts,
Upon malicious bravery, dost thou come
To start my quiet.

RODERIGO: Sir, sir, sir,—

BRABANTIO: But thou must needs be sure
My spirit and my place have in them power
To make this bitter to thee.

RODERIGO: Patience, good sir.

BRABANTIO: What tell'st thou me of robbing? this is Venice;
My house is not a grange.

RODERIGO: Most grave Brabantio,
In simple and pure soul I come to you.

IAGO: 'Zounds, sir, you are one of those that will not serve
God, if the devil bid you. Because we come to do you service and
you think we are ruffians, you 'll have your daughter covered with
a Barbary horse; you 'll have your nephews neigh to you; you 'll
have coursers for cousins and gennets for germans.

BRABANTIO: What profane wretch art thou?

IAGO: I am one, sir, that comes to tell you your daughter and
the Moor are now making the beast with two backs.

BRABANTIO: Thou art a villain.

IAGO: You are—a senator.

BRABANTIO: This thou shalt answer; I know thee, Roderigo.

RODERIGO: Sir, I will answer any thing. But, I beseech you,
If 't be your pleasure and most wise consent,
As partly I find it is, that your fair daughter,
At this odd-even and dull watch o' the night,
Transported, with no worse nor better guard
But with a knave of common hire, a gondolier,
To the gross clasps of a lascivious Moor,—
If this be known to you and your allowance,
We then have done you bold and saucy wrongs;
But if you know not this, my manners tell me
We have your wrong rebuke. Do not believe
That, from the sense of all civility,
I thus would play and trifle with your reverence:
Your daughter, if you have not given her leave,
I say again, hath made a gross revolt;
Tying her duty, beauty, wit and fortunes
In an extravagant and wheeling stranger
Of here and every where. Straight satisfy yourself:
If she be in her chamber or your house,
Let loose on me the justice of the state
For thus deluding you.

BRABANTIO: Strike on the tinder, ho!
Give me a taper! call up all my people!
This accident is not unlike my dream:

Belief of it oppresses me already.
Light, I say! light!   [*Exit above.*

IAGO: Farewell; for I must leave you:
It seems not meet, nor wholesome to my place,
To be produced—as, if I stay, I shall—
Against the Moor: for, I do know, the state,
However this may gall him with some check,
Cannot with safety cast him, for he 's embark'd
With such loud reason to the Cyprus wars,
Which even now stand in act, that, for their souls,
Another of his fathom they have none,
To lead their business: in which regard,
Though I do hate him as I do hell-pains,
Yet, for necessity of present life,
I must show out a flag and sign of love,
Which is indeed but sign. That you shall surely find him,
Lead to the Sagittary the raised search;
And there will I be with him. So, farewell.   [*Exit.*

Enter, below, Brabantio, and Servants with torches.

BRABANTIO: It is too true an evil: gone she is;
And what 's to come of my despised time
Is nought but bitterness. Now, Roderigo,
Where didst thou see her? O unhappy girl!
With the Moor, say'st thou? Who would be a father!
How didst thou know 'twas she? O, she deceives me
Past thought! What said she to you? Get more tapers:
Raise all my kindred. Are they married, think you?

RODERIGO: Truly, I think they are.

BRABANTIO: O heaven! How got she out? O treason of the blood!
Fathers, from hence trust not your daughters' minds
By what you see them act. Is there not charms
By which the property of youth and maidhood
May be abused? Have you not read, Roderigo,
Of some such thing?

RODERIGO: Yes, sir, I have indeed.

BRABANTIO: Call up my brother. O, would you had had her!
Some one way, some another. Do you know
Where we may apprehend her and the Moor?

RODERIGO: I think I can discover him, if you please
To get good guard and go along with me.

BRABANTIO: Pray you, lead on. At every house I 'll call;
I may command at most. Get weapons, ho!
And raise some special officers of night.
On, good Roderigo: I 'll deserve your pains.   [*Exeunt.*

SCENE II. *Another street.*
Enter Othello, Iago, and Attendants with torches.

IAGO: Though in the trade of war I have slain men,
Yet do I hold it very stuff o' the conscience
To do no contrived murder: I lack iniquity
Sometimes to do me service: nine or ten times
I had thought to have yerk'd him here under the ribs.

OTHELLO: 'Tis better as it is.

IAGO: Nay, but he prated,
And spoke such scurvy and provoking terms
Against your honour
That, with the little godliness I have,
I did full hard forbear him. But, I pray you, sir,
Are you fast married? Be assured of this,
That the magnifico is much beloved,
And hath in his effect voice potential
As double as the duke's: he will divorce you;
Or put upon you what restraint and grievance
The law, with all his might to enforce it on,
Will give him cable.

OTHELLO: Let him do his spite;
My services which I have done the signiory
Shall out-tongue his complaints. 'Tis yet to know,—

Which, when I know that boasting is an honour,
I shall promulgate—I fetch my life and being
From men of royal siege, and my demerits
May speak unbonneted to as proud a fortune
As this that I have reach'd: for know, Iago,
But that I love the gentle Desdemona,
I would not my unhoused free condition
Put into circumscription and confine
For the sea's worth. But, look! what lights come yond?

IAGO: Those are the raised father and his friends:
You were best go in.

OTHELLO: Not I; I must be found:
My parts, my title and my perfect soul
Shall manifest me rightly. Is it they?

IAGO: By Janus, I think no.

Enter Cassio, and certain Officers with torches.

OTHELLO: The servants of the duke, and my lieutenant.
The goodness of the night upon you, friends!
What is the news?

CASSIO: The duke does greet you, general,
And he requires your haste-post-haste appearance,
Even on the instant.

OTHELLO: What is the matter, think you?

CASSIO: Something from Cyprus, as I may divine:
It is a business of some heat: the galleys
Have sent a dozen sequent messengers
This very night at one another's heels,
And many of the consuls raised and met,
Are at the duke's already: you have been hotly call'd for;
When, being not at your lodging to be found,
The senate hath sent about three several quests
To search you out.

OTHELLO: 'Tis well I am found by you.
I will but spend a word here in the house,

And go with you.   [*Exit.*
    CASSIO: Ancient, what makes he here?
    IAGO: 'Faith, he to-night hath boarded a land carack:
If it prove lawful prize, he 's made for ever.
    CASSIO: I do not understand.
    IAGO: He 's married.
    CASSIO: To who?

Re-enter Othello.

    IAGO: Marry, to—Come, captain, will you go?
    OTHELLO: Have with you.
    CASSIO: Here comes another troop to seek for you.
    IAGO: It is Brabantio. General, be advised;
He comes to bad intent.

Enter Brabantio, Roderigo, and Officers with torches and weapons.

    OTHELLO: Holla! stand there!
    RODERIGO: Signior, it is the Moor.
    BRABANTIO: Down with him, thief!
                           [*They draw on both sides.*
    IAGO: You, Roderigo! come, sir, I am for you.
    OTHELLO: Keep up your bright swords, for the dew will rust
    them.
Good signior, you shall more command with years
Than with your weapons.
    BRABANTIO: O thou foul thief, where hast thou stow'd my
    daughter?
Damn'd as thou art, thou hast enchanted her;
For I 'll refer me to all things of sense,
If she in chains of magic were not bound,
Whether a maid so tender, fair and happy,
So opposite to marriage that she shunn'd
The wealthy curled darlings of our nation,
Would ever have, to incur a general mock,
Run from her guardage to the sooty bosom

Of such a thing as thou, to fear, not to delight.
Judge me the world, if 'tis not gross in sense
That thou hast practised on her with foul charms,
Abused her delicate youth with drugs or minerals
That weaken motion: I 'll have 't disputed on;
'Tis probable and palpable to thinking.
I therefore apprehend and do attach thee
For an abuser of the world, a practiser
Of arts inhibited and out of warrant.
Lay hold upon him: if he do resist,
Subdue him at his peril.

OTHELLO: Hold your hands,
Both you of my inclining, and the rest:
Were it my cue to fight, I should have known it
Without a prompter. Where will you that I go
To answer this your charge?

BRABANTIO: To prison, till fit time
Of law and course of direct session
Call thee to answer.

OTHELLO: What if I do obey?
How may the duke be therewith satisfied,
Whose messengers are here about my side,
Upon some present business of the state
To bring me to him?

FIRST OFFICER: 'Tis true, most worthy signior;
The duke 's in council, and your noble self,
I am sure, is sent for.

BRABANTIO: How! the duke in council!
In this time of the night! Bring him away:
Mine 's not an idle cause: the duke himself,
Or any of my brothers of the state,
Cannot but feel this wrong as 'twere their own;
For if such actions may have passage free,
Bond-slaves and pagans shall our statesmen be.   [*Exeunt.*

SCENE III. *A council-chamber.*
The Duke and Senators sitting at a table; Officers attending.

DUKE: There is no composition in these news
That gives them credit.

FIRST SENATOR: Indeed, they are disproportion'd;
My letters say a hundred and seven galleys.

DUKE: And mine, a hundred and forty.

SECOND SENATOR: And mine, two hundred:
But though they jump not on a just account,—
As in these cases, where the aim reports,
'Tis oft with difference—yet do they all confirm
A Turkish fleet, and bearing up to Cyprus.

DUKE: Nay, it is possible enough to judgement:
I do not so secure me in the error,
But the main articles I do approve
In fearful sense.

SAILOR: [*Within*] What, ho! what, ho! what, ho!

FIRST OFFICER: A messenger from the galleys.

Enter a Sailor.

DUKE: Now, what 's the business?

SAILOR: The Turkish preparation makes for Rhodes;
So was I bid report here to the state
By Signior Angelo.

DUKE: How say you by this change?

FIRST SENATOR: This cannot be,
By no assay of reason: 'tis a pageant,
To keep us in false gaze. When we consider
The importancy of Cyprus to the Turk,
And let ourselves again but understand,
That as it more concerns the Turk than Rhodes,
So may he with more facile question bear it,
For that it stands not in such warlike brace,
But altogether lacks the abilities

That Rhodes is dress'd in: if we make thought of this,
We must not think the Turk is so unskilful
To leave that latest which concerns him first,
Neglecting an attempt of ease and gain,
To wake and wage a danger profitless.

DUKE: Nay, in all confidence, he 's not for Rhodes.

FIRST OFFICER: Here is more news.

Enter a Messenger.

MESSENGER: The Ottomites, reverend and gracious,
Steering with due course towards the isle of Rhodes,
Have there injointed them with an after fleet.

FIRST SENATOR: Ay, so I thought. How many, as you guess?

MESSENGER: Of thirty sail: and now they do re-stem
Their backward course, bearing with frank appearance
Their purposes toward Cyprus. Signior Montano,
Your trusty and most valiant servitor,
With his free duty recommends you thus,
And prays you to believe him.

DUKE: 'Tis certain, then, for Cyprus.
Marcus Luccicos, is not he in town?

FIRST SENATOR: He 's now in Florence.

DUKE: Write from us to him; post-post-haste dispatch.

FIRST SENATOR: Here comes Brabantio and the valiant Moor.

Enter Brabantio, Othello, Iago, Roderigo, and Officers.

DUKE: Valiant Othello, we must straight employ you
Against the general enemy Ottoman.
[*To Brabantio*] I did not see you; welcome, gentle signior;
We lack'd your counsel and your help to-night.

BRABANTIO: So did I yours. Good your grace, pardon me;
Neither my place nor aught I heard of business
Hath raised me from my bed, nor doth the general care
Take hold on me, for my particular grief
Is of so flood-gate and o'erbearing nature

That it engluts and swallows other sorrows
And it is still itself.

    DUKE: Why, what 's the matter?

    BRABANTIO: My daughter! O, my daughter!

    DUKE AND SENATOR: Dead?

    BRABANTIO: Ay, to me;

She is abused, stol'n from me, and corrupted
By spells and medicines bought of mountebanks;
For nature so preposterously to err,
Being not deficient, blind, or lame of sense,
Sans witchcraft could not.

    DUKE: Whoe'er he be that in this foul proceeding
Hath thus beguiled your daughter of herself
And you of her, the bloody book of law
You shall yourself read in the bitter letter
After your own sense, yea, though our proper son
Stood in your action.

    BRABANTIO: Humbly I thank your grace.
Here is the man, this Moor, whom now, it seems,
Your special mandate for the state-affairs
Hath hither brought.

    DUKE AND SENATOR: We are very sorry for 't.

    DUKE: [*To Othello*] What, in your own part, can you say to this?

    BRABANTIO: Nothing, but this is so.

    OTHELLO: Most potent, grave, and reverend signiors,
My very noble and approved good masters,
That I have ta'en away this old man's daughter,
It is most true; true, I have married her:
The very head and front of my offending
Hath this extent, no more. Rude am I in my speech,
And little bless'd with the soft phrase of peace;
For since these arms of mine had seven years' pith.
Till now some nine moons wasted, they have used
Their dearest action in the tented field,
And little of this great world can I speak,

More than pertains to feats of broil and battle,
And therefore little shall I grace my cause
In speaking for myself. Yet, by your gracious patience,
I will a round unvarnish'd tale deliver
Of my whole course of love; what drugs, what charms,
What conjuration and what mighty magic,
For such proceeding I am charged withal,
I won his daughter.
    BRABANTIO: A maiden never bold;
Of spirit so still and quiet, that her motion
Blush'd at herself; and she, in spite of nature,
Of years, of country, credit, every thing,
To fall in love with what she fear'd to look on!
It is a judgement maim'd and most imperfect
That will confess perfection so could err
Against all rules of nature, and must be driven
To find out practices of cunning hell,
Why this should be. I therefore vouch again
That with some mixtures powerful o'er the blood,
Or with some dram conjured to this effect,
He wrought upon her.
    DUKE: To vouch this, is no proof,
Without more wider and more overt test
Than these thin habits and poor likelihoods
Of modern seeming do prefer against him.
    FIRST SENATOR: But, Othello, speak:
Did you by indirect and forced courses
Subdue and poison this young maid's affections?
Or came it by request and such fair question
As soul to soul affordeth?
    OTHELLO: I do beseech you,
Send for the lady to the Sagittary,
And let her speak of me before her father:
If you do find me foul in her report,
The trust, the office I do hold of you,

Not only take away, but let your sentence
Even fall upon my life.

    DUKE: Fetch Desdemona hither.

    OTHELLO: Ancient, conduct them; you best know the place.

                         [*Exeunt Iago and Attendants.*

And, till she come, as truly as to heaven
I do confess the vices of my blood,
So justly to your grave ears I' ll present
How I did thrive in this fair lady's love,
And she in mine.

    DUKE: Say it, Othello.

    OTHELLO: Her father loved me; oft invited me;
Still question'd me the story of my life,
From year to year, the battles, sieges, fortunes,
That I have pass'd.
I ran it through, even from my boyish days,
To the very moment that he bade me tell it;
Wherein I spake of most disastrous chances,
Of moving accidents by flood and field,
Of hair-breadth scapes i' the imminent deadly breach.
Of being taken by the insolent foe
And sold to slavery, of my redemption thence
And portance in my travels' history:
Wherein of antres vast and deserts idle,
Rough quarries, rocks and hills whose heads touch heaven,
It was my hint to speak,—such was the process;
And of the Cannibals that each other eat,
The Anthropophagi and men whose heads
Do grow beneath their shoulders. This to hear
Would Desdemona seriously incline:
But still the house-affairs would draw her thence:
Which ever as she could with haste dispatch,
She 'ld come again, and with a greedy ear
Devour up my discourse: which I observing,
Took once a pliant hour, and found good means

To draw from her a prayer of earnest heart
That I would all my pilgrimage dilate,
Whereof by parcels she had something heard,
But not intentively: I did consent,
And often did beguile her of her tears,
When I did speak of some distressful stroke
That my youth suffer'd. My story being done,
She gave me for my pains a world of sighs:
She swore, in faith, 'twas strange, 'twas passing strange,
'Twas pitiful, 'twas wondrous pitiful:
She wish'd she had not heard it, yet she wish'd
That heaven had made her such a man: she thank'd me,
And bade me, if I had a friend that loved her,
I should but teach him how to tell my story,
And that would woo her. Upon this hint I spake:
She loved me for the dangers I had pass'd,
And I loved her that she did pity them.
This only is the witchcraft I have used:
Here comes the lady; let her witness it.

Enter Desdemona, Iago, and Attendants.

DUKE: I think this tale would win my daughter too.
Good Brabantio,
Take up this mangled matter at the best:
Men do their broken weapons rather use
Than their bare hands.
BRABANTIO: I pray you, hear her speak:
If she confess that she was half the wooer,
Destruction on my head, if my bad blame
Light on the man! Come hither, gentle mistress:
Do you perceive in all this noble company
Where most you owe obedience?
DESDEMONA: My noble father,
I do perceive here a divided duty:
To you I am bound for life and education;

My life and education both do learn me
How to respect you; you are the lord of duty;
I am hitherto your daughter: but here 's my husband,
And so much duty as my mother show'd
To you, preferring you before her father,
So much I challenge that I may profess
Due to the Moor my lord.

    BRABANTIO: God be wi' you! I have done.
Please it your grace, on to the state-affairs:
I had rather to adopt a child than get it.
Come hither, Moor:
I here do give thee that with all my heart
Which, but thou hast already, with all my heart
I would keep from thee. For your sake, jewel,
I am glad at soul I have no other child;
For thy escape would teach me tyranny,
To hang clogs on them. I have done, my lord.

    DUKE: Let me speak like yourself, and lay a sentence,
Which, as a grise or step, may help these lovers
Into your favour.
When remedies are past, the griefs are ended
By seeing the worst, which late on hopes depended.
To mourn a mischief that is past and gone
Is the next way to draw new mischief on.
What cannot be preserved when fortune takes
Patience her injury a mockery makes.
The robb'd that smiles steals something from the thief;
He robs himself that spends a bootless grief.

    BRABANTIO: So let the Turk of Cyprus us beguile:
We lose it not, so long as we can smile.
He bears the sentence well that nothing bears
But the free comfort which from thence he hears,
But he bears both the sentence and the sorrow
That, to pay grief, must of poor patience borrow.
These sentences, to sugar, or to gall,

Being strong on both sides, are equivocal:
But words are words; I never yet did hear
That the bruised heart was pierced through the ear.
I humbly beseech you, proceed to the affairs of state.

DUKE: The Turk with a most mighty preparation makes for
Cyprus. Othello, the fortitude of the place is best known to you;
and though we have there a substitute of most allowed sufficiency, yet opinion, a sovereign mistress of effects, throws a more
safer voice on you: you must therefore be content to slubber the
gloss of your new fortunes with this more stubborn and boisterous expedition.

OTHELLO: The tyrant custom, most grave senators,
Hath made the flinty and steel couch of war
My thrice-driven bed of down: I do agnize
A natural and prompt alacrity
I find in hardness, and do undertake
These present wars against the Ottomites.
Most humbly therefore bending to your state,
I crave fit disposition for my wife,
Due reference of place and exhibition,
With such accommodation and besort
As levels with her breeding.

DUKE: If you please,
Be 't at her father's.

BRABANTIO: I 'll not have it so.

OTHELLO: Nor I.

DESDEMONA: Nor I; I would not there reside,
To put my father in impatient thoughts
By being in his eye. Most gracious duke,
To my unfolding lend your prosperous ear;
And let me find a charter in your voice,
To assist my simpleness.

DUKE: What would you, Desdemona?

DESDEMONA: That I did love the Moor to live with him,
My downright violence and storm of fortunes

May trumpet to the world: my heart's subdued
Even to the very quality of my lord:
I saw Othello's visage in his mind,
And to his honours and his valiant parts
Did I my soul and fortunes consecrate.
So that, dear lords, if I be left behind,
A moth of peace, and he go to the war,
The rites for which I love him are bereft me,
And I a heavy interim shall support
By his dear absence. Let me go with him.
    OTHELLO: Let her have your voices.
Vouch with me, heaven, I therefore beg it not,
To please the palate of my appetite,
Nor to comply with heat—the young affects
In me defunct—and proper satisfaction,
But to be free and bounteous to her mind:
And heaven defend your good souls, that you think
I will your serious and great business scant
For she is with me: no, when light-wing'd toys
Of feather'd Cupid seel with wanton dullness
My speculative and officed instruments,
That my disports corrupt and taint my business,
Let housewives make a skillet of my helm,
And all indign and base adversities
Make head against my estimation!
    DUKE: Be it as you shall privately determine,
Either for her stay or going: the affair cries haste,
And speed must answer it.
    FIRST SENATOR: You must away to-night.
    OTHELLO: With all my heart.
    DUKE: At nine i' the morning here we 'll meet again.
Othello, leave some officer behind,
And he shall our commission bring to you;
With such things else of quality and respect
As doth import you.

OTHELLO: So please your grace, my ancient;
A man he is of honesty and trust:
To his conveyance I assign my wife,
With what else needful your good grace shall think
To be sent after me.
    DUKE: Let it be so.
Good night to every one. [*To Brabantio*] And, noble signior,
If virtue no delighted beauty lack,
Your son-in-law is far more fair than black.
    FIRST SENATOR: Adieu, brave Moor; use Desdemona well.
    BRABANTIO: Look to her, Moor, if thou hast eyes to see:
She has deceived her father, and may thee.
                        [*Exeunt Duke, Senators, Officers, &c.*
    OTHELLO: My life upon her faith! Honest Iago,
My Desdemona must I leave to thee:
I prithee, let thy wife attend on her;
And bring them after in the best advantage.
Come Desdemona; I have but an hour
Of love, of worldly matters and direction,
To spend with thee: we must obey the time.
                        [*Exeunt Othello and Desdemona.*
    RODERIGO: Iago,—
    IAGO: What say'st thou, noble heart?
    RODERIGO: What will I do, thinkest thou?
    IAGO: Why, go to bed, and sleep.
    RODERIGO: I will incontinently drown myself.
    IAGO: If thou dost, I shall never love thee after. Why, thou silly
gentleman!
    RODERIGO: It is silliness to live when to live is torment; and
then have we a prescription to die when death is our physician.
    IAGO: O villainous! I have looked upon the world for four
times seven years; and since I could distinguish betwixt a benefit
and an injury, I never found man that knew how to love himself.
Ere I would say, I would drown myself for the love of a guinea-
hen, I would change my humanity with a baboon.

RODERIGO: What should I do? I confess it is my shame to be so fond; but it is not in my virtue to amend it.

IAGO: Virtue! a fig! 'tis in ourselves that we are thus or thus. Our bodies are our gardens, to the which our wills are gardeners; so that if we will plant nettles, or sow lettuce, set hyssop and weed up thyme, supply it with one gender of herbs, or district it with many, either to have it sterile with idleness, or manured with industry, why, the power and corrigible authority of this lies in our wills. If the balance of our lives had not one scale of reason to poise another of sensuality, the blood and baseness of our natures would conduct us to most preposterous conclusions: but we have reason to cool our raging motions, our carnal stings, our unbitted lusts, whereof I take this that you call love to be a sect or scion.

RODERIGO: It cannot be.

IAGO: It is merely a lust of the blood and a permission of the will. Come, be a man. Drown thyself! drown cats and blind puppies. I have professed me thy friend and I confess me knit to thy deserving with cables of perdurable toughness; I could never better stead thee than now. Put money in thy purse; follow thou the wars; defeat thy favour with an unsurped beard; I say, put money in thy purse. It cannot be that Desdemona should long continue her love to the Moor,—put money in thy purse,—nor he his to her; it was a violent commencement, and thou shalt see an answerable sequestration:—put but money in thy purse. These Moors are changeable in their wills:—fill thy purse with money: —the food that to him now is as luscious as locusts, shall be to him shortly as bitter as coloquintida. She must change for youth: when she is sated with his body, she will find the error of her choice: she must have change, she must: therefore put money in thy purse. If thou wilt needs damn thyself, do it a more delicate way than drowning. Make all the money thou canst: if sanctimony and a frail vow betwixt an erring barbarian and a supersubtle Venetian be not too hard for my wits and all the tribe of hell, thou shalt enjoy her; therefore make money. A pox of drowning thyself! it is clean out of the way: seek thou rather to be hanged in compassing thy joy than to be drowned and go without her.

RODERIGO: Wilt thou be fast to my hopes, if I depend on the issue?

IAGO: Thou art sure of me:—go, make money:—I have told thee often, and I re-tell thee again and again, I hate the Moor: my cause is hearted; thine hath no less reason. Let us be conjunctive in our revenge against him; if thou canst cuckold him, thou dost thyself a pleasure, me a sport. There are many events in the womb of time which will be delivered. Traverse! go, provide thy money. We will have more of this to-morrow. Adieu.

RODERIGO: Where shall we meet i' the morning?

IAGO: At my lodging.

RODERIGO: I 'll be with thee betimes.

IAGO: Go to; farewell. Do you hear, Roderigo?

RODERIGO: What say you?

IAGO: No more of drowning, do you hear?

RODERIGO: I am changed: I 'll go sell all my land.   [Exit.

IAGO: Thus do I ever make my fool my purse;
For I mine own gain'd knowledge should profane,
If I would time expend with such a snipe,
But for my sport and profit. I hate the Moor;
And it is thought abroad, that 'twixt my sheets
He hath done my office: I know not if 't be true;
But I, for mere suspicion in that kind,
Will do as if for surety. He holds me well;
The better shall my purpose work on him.
Cassio 's a proper man: let me see now:
To get his place and to plume up my will
In double knavery—How, how?—Let 's see:—
After some time, to abuse Othello's ear
That he is too familiar with his wife.
He hath a person and a smooth dispose
To be suspected, framed to make women false.
The Moor is of a free and open nature,

That thinks men honest that but seem to be so,
And will as tenderly be led by the nose
As asses are.
I have 't. It is engender'd. Hell and night
Must bring this monstrous birth to the world's light.   [*Exit.*

ACT II.

SCENE I. *A Sea-port in Cyprus. An open place near the quay.*
Enter Montano and two Gentlemen.

MONTANO: What from the cape can you discern at sea?
FIRST GENTLEMAN: Nothing at all: it is a high-wrought flood;
I cannot, 'twixt the heaven and the main,
Descry a sail.
MONTANO: Methinks the wind hath spoke aloud at land;
A fuller blast ne'er shook our battlements:
If it hath ruffian'd so upon the sea,
What ribs of oak, when mountains melt on them,
Can hold the mortise? What shall we hear of this?
SECOND GENTLEMAN: A segregation of the Turkish fleet:
For do but stand upon the foaming shore,
The chidden billow seems to pelt the clouds;
The wind-shaked surge, with high and monstrous mane,
Seems to cast water on the burning bear,
And quench the guards of the ever-fixed pole:
I never did like molestation view
On the enchafed flood.
MONTANO: If that the Turkish fleet
Be not enshelter'd and embay'd, they are drown'd;
It is impossible they bear it out.

Enter a third Gentleman.

THIRD GENTLEMAN: News, lads! our wars are done.

This desperate tempest hath so bang'd the Turks,
That their designment halts: a noble ship of Venice
Hath seen a grievous wreck and sufferance
On most part of their fleet.

    MONTANO: How! is this true?

    THIRD GENTLEMAN: The ship is here put in,
A Veronesa; Michael Cassio,
Lieutenant to the warlike Moor Othello,
Is come on shore: the Moor himself at sea,
And is in full commission here for Cyprus.

    MONTANO: I am glad on 't; 'tis a worthy governor.

    THIRD GENTLEMAN: But this same Cassio, though he speak of
        comfort
Touching the Turkish loss, yet he looks sadly,
And prays the Moor be safe; for they were parted
With foul and violent tempest.

    MONTANO: Pray heavens he be;
For I have served him, and the man commands
Like a full soldier. Let 's to the seaside, ho!
As well to see the vessel that 's come in
As to throw out our eyes for brave Othello,
Even till we make the main and the aerial blue
An indistinct regard.

    THIRD GENTLEMAN: Come, let 's do so;
For every minute is expectancy
Of more arrivance.

Enter Cassio.

    CASSIO: Thanks, you the valiant of this warlike isle,
That so approve the Moor! O, let the heavens
Give him defence against the elements,
For I have lost him on a dangerous sea.

    MONTANO: Is he well shipp'd?

    CASSIO: His bark is stoutly timber'd, and his pilot
Of very expert and approved allowance;

Therefore my hopes, not surfeited to death,
Stand in bold cure.   [*A cry within* 'A sail, a sail, a sail!'

Enter a fourth Gentleman.

  CASSIO: What noise?
  FOURTH GENTLEMAN: The town is empty; on the brow o' the sea
Stand ranks of people, and they cry 'A sail!'
  CASSIO: My hopes do shape him for the governor. [*Guns heard.*
  SECOND GENTLEMAN: They do discharge their shot of courtesy:
Our friends at least.
  CASSIO: I pray you, sir, go forth,
And give us truth who 'tis that is arrived.
  SECOND GENTLEMAN: I shall.   [*Exit.*
  MONTANO: But, good lieutenant, is your general wived?
  CASSIO: Most fortunately: he hath achieved a maid
That paragons description and wild fame;
One that excels the quirks of blazoning pens,
And in the essential vesture of creation
Does tire the ingener.

Re-enter second Gentleman.

                          How now! who has put in?
  SECOND GENTLEMAN: 'Tis one Iago, ancient to the general.
  CASSIO: Has had most favourable and happy speed:
Tempests themselves, high seas and howling winds,
The gutter'd rocks and congregated sands,—
Traitors ensleep'd to clog the guiltless keel,—
As having sense of beauty, do omit
Their mortal natures, letting so safely by
The divine Desdemona.
  MONTANO: What is she?
  CASSIO: She that I spake of, our great captain's captain,
Left in the conduct of the bold Iago,
Whose footing here anticipates our thoughts
A se'nnight's speed. Great Jove, Othello guard,

And swell his sail with thine own powerful breath,
That he may bless this bay with his tall ship,
Make love's quick pants in Desdemona's arms,
Give renew'd fire to our extinced spirits,
And bring all Cyprus comfort!

Enter Desdemona, Emilia, Iago, Roderigo, and Attendants.

                    O, behold,
The riches of the ship is come on shore!
Ye men of Cyprus, let her have your knees.
Hail to thee, lady! and the grace of heaven,
Before, behind thee and on every hand,
Enwheel thee round!

    DESDEMONA: I thank you, valiant Cassio.
What tidings can you tell me of my lord?

    CASSIO: He is not yet arrived: nor know I aught
But that he 's well and will be shortly here.

    DESDEMONA: O, but I fear—How lost you company?

    CASSIO: The great contention of the sea and skies
Parted our fellowship—But, hark! a sail.

                   [*Within* 'A sail, a sail!' *Guns heard.*

    SECOND GENTLEMAN: They give their greeting to the citadel:
This likewise is a friend.

    CASSIO: See for the news.   [*Exit Gentleman.*
Good ancient, you are welcome. [*To Emilia*] Welcome, mistress:
Let it not gall your patience, good Iago,
That I extend my manners; 'tis my breeding
That gives me this bold show of courtesy.   [*Kissing her.*

    IAGO: Sir, would she give you so much of her lips
As of her tongue she oft bestows on me,
You 'ld have enough.

    DESDEMONA: Alas, she has no speech.

    IAGO: In faith, too much;
I find it still, when I have list to sleep:
Marry, before your ladyship, I grant,

She puts her tongue a little in her heart,
And chides with thinking.

    EMILIA: You have little cause to say so.

    IAGO: Come on, come on; you are pictures out of doors,
Bells in your parlours, wild-cats in your kitchens,
Saints in your injuries, devils being offended,
Players in your housewifery, and housewives in your beds.

    DESDEMONA: O, fie upon thee, slanderer!

    IAGO: Nay, it is true, or else I am a Turk:
You rise to play and go to bed to work.

    EMILIA: You shall not write my praise.

    IAGO: No, let me not.

    DESDEMONA: What wouldst thou write of me, if thou shouldst
    praise me?

    IAGO: O gentle lady, do not put me to 't;
For I am nothing, if not critical.

    DESDEMONA: Come on, assay. There 's one gone to the harbour?

    IAGO: Ay, madam.

    DESDEMONA: I am not merry; but I do beguile
The thing I am, by seeming otherwise.
Come, how wouldst thou praise me?

    IAGO: I am about it; but indeed my invention
Comes from my pate as birdlime does from frize;
It plucks out brains and all: but my Muse labours,
And thus she is deliver'd.
If she be fair and wise, fairness and wit,
The one 's for use, the other useth it.

    DESDEMONA: Well praised! How if she be black and witty?

    IAGO: If she be black, and thereto have a wit,
She 'll find a white that shall her blackness fit.

    DESDEMONA: Worse and worse.

    EMILIA: How if fair and foolish?

    IAGO: She never yet was foolish that was fair;
For ever her folly help'd her to an heir.

    DESDEMONA: These are old fond paradoxes to make fools laugh

i' the alehouse. What miserable praise hast thou for her that's foul and foolish?

IAGO: There's none so foul and foolish thereunto,
But does foul pranks which fair and wise ones do.

DESDEMONA: O heavy ignorance! thou praisest the worst best. But what praise couldst thou bestow on a deserving woman indeed, one that, in the authority of her merit, did justly put on the vouch of very malice itself?

IAGO: She that was ever fair and never proud,
Had tongue at will and yet was never loud,
Never lack'd gold and yet went never gay,
Fled from her wish and yet said 'Now I may,'
She that being anger'd, her revenge being nigh,
Bade her wrong stay and her displeasure fly,
She that in wisdom never was so frail
To change the cod's head for the salmon's tail,
She that could think and ne'er disclose her mind,
See suitors following and not look behind,
She was a wight, if ever such a wight were,—

DESDEMONA: To do what?

IAGO: To suckle fools and chronicle small beer.

DESDEMONA: O most lame and impotent conclusion! Do not learn of him, Emilia, though he be thy husband. How say you, Cassio? is he not a most profane and liberal counsellor?

CASSIO: He speaks home, madam: you may relish him more in the soldier than in the scholar.

IAGO: [Aside] He takes her by the palm: ay, well said, whisper: with as little a web as this will I ensnare as great a fly as Cassio. Ay, smile upon her, do; I will gyve thee in thine own courtship. You say true; 'tis so, indeed: if such tricks as these strip you out of your lieutenantry, it had been better you had not kissed your three fingers so oft, which now again you are most apt to play the sir in. Very good; well kissed! an excellent courtesy! 'tis so, indeed. Yet again your fingers to your lips? would they were clyster-pipes for your sake! [Trumpet within.] The Moor! I know his trumpet.

CASSIO: 'Tis truly so.

DESDEMONA: Let 's meet him and receive him.

CASSIO: Lo, where he comes!

Enter Othello and Attendants.

OTHELLO: O my fair warrior!

DESDEMONA: My dear Othello!

OTHELLO: It gives me wonder great as my content
To see you here before me. O my soul's joy!
If after every tempest come such calms,
May the winds blow till they have waken'd death!
And let the labouring bark climb hills of seas
Olympus-high and duck again as low
As hell 's from heaven! If it were now to die,
'Twere now to be most happy; for, I fear,
My soul hath her content so absolute
That not another comfort like to this
Succeeds in unknown fate.

DESDEMONA: The heavens forbid
But that our loves and comforts should increase,
Even as our days do grow!

OTHELLO: Amen to that, sweet powers!
I cannot speak enough of this content;
It stops me here; it is too much of joy:
And this, and this, the greatest discords be   [*Kissing her.*
That e'er our hearts shall make!

IAGO: [*Aside*] O, you are well tuned now!
But I 'll set down the pegs that make this music,
As honest as I am.

OTHELLO: Come, let us to the castle.
News, friends; our wars are done, the Turks are drown'd.
How does my old acquaintance of this isle?
Honey, you shall be well desired in Cyprus;
I have found great love amongst them. O my sweet,
I prattle out of fashion, and I dote

In mine own comforts. I prithee, good Iago,
Go to the bay and disembark my coffers:
Bring thou the master to the citadel;
He is a good one, and his worthiness
Does challenge much respect. Come, Desdemona,
Once more, well met at Cyprus.

> [*Exeunt Othello, Desdemona, and Attendants.*

IAGO: Do thou meet me presently at the harbour. Come hither. If thou be'st valiant,—as, they say, base men being in love have then a nobility in their natures more than is native to them,—list me. The lieutenant to-night watches on the court of guard:—first, I must tell thee this—Desdemona is directly in love with him.

RODERIGO: With him! why, 'tis not possible.

IAGO: Lay thy finger thus, and let thy soul be instructed. Mark me with what violence she first loved the Moor, but for bragging and telling her fantastical lies: and will she love him still for prating? let not thy discreet heart think it. Her eye must be fed; and what delight shall she have to look on the devil? When the blood is made dull with the act of sport, there should be, again to inflame it and to give satiety a fresh appetite, loveliness in favour, sympathy in years, manners and beauties; all which the Moor is defective in: now, for want of these required conveniences, her delicate tenderness will find itself abused, begin to heave the gorge, disrelish and abhor the Moor; very nature will instruct her in it and compel her to some second choice. Now, sir, this granted,—as it is a most pregnant and unforced position—who stands so eminent in the degree of this fortune as Cassio does? a knave very voluble; no further conscionable than in putting on the mere form of civil and humane seeming, for the better compassing of his salt and most hidden loose affection? why, none; why, none: a slipper and subtle knave, a finder of occasions, that has an eye can stamp and counterfeit advantages, though true advantage never present itself; a devilish knave. Besides, the knave is handsome, young, and hath all those requisites in him that folly and green minds look after: a pestilent complete knave; and the woman hath found him already.

RODERIGO: I cannot believe that in her; she 's full of most blessed condition.

IAGO: Blessed fig's-end! the wine she drinks is made of grapes: if she had been blessed, she would never have loved the Moor. Blessed pudding! Didst thou not see her paddle with the palm of his hand? didst not mark that?

RODERIGO: Yes, that I did; but that was but courtesy.

IAGO: Lechery, by this hand; an index and obscure prologue to the history of lust and foul thoughts. They met so near with their lips that their breaths embraced together. Villanous thoughts, Roderigo! when these mutualities so marshal the way, hard at hand comes the master and main exercise, the incorporate conclusion, Pish! But, sir, be you ruled by me: I have brought you from Venice. Watch you to-night; for the command, I 'll lay 't upon you. Cassio knows you not. I' ll not be far from you: do you find some occasion to anger Cassio, either by speaking too loud, or tainting his discipline; or from what other course you please, which the time shall more favourably minister.

RODERIGO: Well.

IAGO: Sir, he is rash and very sudden in choler, and haply may strike at you: provoke him, that he may; for even out of that will I cause thee of Cyprus to mutiny; whose qualification shall come into no true taste again but by the displanting of Cassio. So shall you have a shorter journey to your desires by the means I shall then have to prefer them; and the impediment most profitably removed, without the which there were no expectation of our prosperity.

RODERIGO: I will do this, if I can bring it to any opportunity.

IAGO: I warrant thee. Meet me by and by at the citadel: I must fetch his necessaries ashore. Farewell.

RODERIGO: Adieu.   [Exit.

IAGO: That Cassio loves her, I do well believe it;
That she loves him, 'tis apt and of great credit:

The Moor, howbeit that I endure him not,
Is of a constant, loving, noble nature,
And I dare think he 'll prove to Desdemona
A most dear husband. Now, I do love her too;
Not out of absolute lust, though peradventure
I stand accountant for as great a sin,
But partly led to diet my revenge,
For that I do suspect the lusty Moor
Hath leap'd into my seat; the thought whereof
Doth, like a poisonous mineral, gnaw my inwards;
And nothing can or shall content my soul
Till I am even'd with him, wife for wife,
Or failing so, yet that I put the Moor
At least into a jealousy so strong
That judgement cannot cure. Which thing to do,
If this poor trash of Venice, whom I trash
For his quick hunting, stand the putting on,
I 'll have our Michael Cassio on the hip,
Abuse him to the Moor in the rank garb—
For I fear Cassio with my night-cap too—
Make the Moor thank me, love me and reward me,
For making him egregiously an ass
And practising upon his peace and quiet
Even to madness. 'Tis here, but yet confused:
Knavery's plain face is never seen till used.   [*Exit.*

SCENE II. *A street.*
Enter a Herald with a proclamation; People following.

HERALD: It is Othello's pleasure, our noble and valiant general,
that, upon certain tidings now arrived, importing the mere perdition of the Turkish fleet, every man put himself into triumph;
some to dance, some to make bonfires, each man to what sport
and revels his addiction leads him: for, besides these bene-
ficial news, it is the celebration of his nuptial. So much was his

pleasure should be proclaimed. All offices are open, and there is full liberty of feasting from this present hour of five till the bell have told eleven. Heaven bless the isle of Cyprus and our noble general Othello!   [*Exeunt.*

SCENE III. *A hall in the castle.*
Enter Othello, Desdemona, Cassio, and Attendants.

OTHELLO: Good Michael, look you to the guard to-night:
Let 's teach ourselves that honourable stop,
Not to outsport discretion.
    CASSIO: Iago hath direction what to do;
But, notwithstanding, with my personal eye
Will I look to 't.
    OTHELLO: Iago is most honest.
Michael, good night: to-morrow with your earliest
Let me have speech with you. [*To Desdemona*] Come, my dear love,
The purchase made, the fruits are to ensue;
That profit 's yet to come 'tween me and you.
Good night.   [*Exeunt Othello, Desdemona, and Attendants.*

Enter Iago.

    CASSIO: Welcome, Iago; we must to the watch.
    IAGO: Not this hour, lieutenant; 'tis not yet ten o' the clock. Our general casts us thus early for the love of his Desdemona; who let us not therefore blame: he hath not yet made wanton the night with her; and she is sport for Jove.
    CASSIO: She 's a most exquisite lady.
    IAGO: And, I 'll warrant her, full of game.
    CASSIO: Indeed, she 's a most fresh and delicate creature.
    IAGO: What an eye she has! methinks it sounds a parley of provocation.
    CASSIO: An inviting eye; and yet methinks right modest.
    IAGO: And when she speaks, is it not an alarum to love?
    CASSIO: She is indeed perfection.

IAGO: Well, happiness to their sheets! Come, lieutenant, I have a stoup of wine; and here without are a brace of Cyprus gallants that would fain have a measure to the health of black Othello.

CASSIO: Not to-night, good Iago: I have very poor and unhappy brains for drinking: I could well wish courtesy would invent some other custom of entertainment.

IAGO: O, they are our friends; but one cup: I 'll drink for you.

CASSIO: I have drunk but one cup to-night, and that was craftily qualified too, and, behold, what innovation it makes here: I am unfortunate in the infirmity, and dare not task my weakness with any more.

IAGO: What, man! 'tis a night of revels; the gallants desire it.

CASSIO: Where are they?

IAGO: Here at the door; I pray you, call them in.

CASSIO: I 'll do 't; but it dislikes me.   [*Exit.*

IAGO: If I can fasten but one cup upon him,
With that which he hath drunk to-night already,
He 'll be as full of quarrel and offence
As my young mistress' dog. Now, my sick fool Roderigo,
Whom love hath turn'd almost the wrong side out,
To Desdemona hath to-night caroused
Potations pottle-deep; and he 's to watch:
Three lads of Cyprus, noble swelling spirits,
That hold their honours in a wary distance,
The very elements of this warlike isle,
Have I to-night fluster'd with flowing cups,
And they watch too. Now, 'mongst this flock of drunkards,
Am I to put our Cassio in some action
That may offend the isle,—But here they come:
If consequence do but approve my dream,
My boat sails freely, both with wind and stream.

Re-enter Cassio; with him Montano and Gentlemen;
Servants following with wine.

CASSIO: 'Fore God, they have given me a rouse already.

MONTANO: Good faith, a little one; not past a pint, as I am a soldier.

IAGO: Some wine, ho!

[*Sings*] And let me the canaki clink, clink;
   And let me the canakin clink:
    A soldier 's but a man;
    A life 's but a span;
   Why, then, let a soldier drink.

Some wine, boys!

CASSIO: 'Fore God, an excellent song.

IAGO: I learned it in England, where, indeed, they are most potent in potting: your Dane, your German, and your swag-bellied Hollander—Drink, ho!—are nothing to your English.

CASSIO: Is your Englishman so expert in his drinking?

IAGO: Why, he drinks you, with facility, your Dane dead drunk; he sweats not to overthrow your Almain; he gives your Hollander a vomit, ere the next pottle can be filled.

CASSIO: To the health of our general!

MONTANO: I am for it, lieutenant; and I 'll do you justice.

IAGO: O sweet England!

King Stephen was a worthy peer,
  His breeches cost him but a crown;
He held them sixpence all too dear,
  With that he call'd the tailor lown.
He was a wight of high renown,
  And thou art but of low degree:
'Tis pride that pulls the country down;
  Then take thine auld cloak about thee.

Some wine, ho!

CASSIO: Why, this is a more exquisite song than the other.

IAGO: Will you hear 't again?

CASSIO: No; for I hold him to be unworthy of his place that does those things. Well, God 's above all; and there be souls must be saved, and there be souls must not be saved.

IAGO: It 's true, good lieutenant.

CASSIO: For mine own part,—no offence to the general, nor any man of quality,—I hope to be saved.

IAGO: And so do I too, lieutenant.

CASSIO: Ay, but, by your leave, not before me; the lieutenant is to be saved before the ancient. Let 's have no more of this; let 's to our affairs.—Forgive us our sins!—Gentlemen, let 's look to our business. Do not think, gentlemen, I am drunk: this is my ancient: this is my right hand, and this is my left: I am not drunk now; I can stand well enough, and speak well enough.

ALL: Excellent well.

CASSIO: Why, very well then; you must not think then that I am drunk.

MONTANO: To the platform, masters; come, let 's set the watch.

IAGO: You see this fellow that is gone before;
He is a soldier fit to stand by Cæsar
And give direction: and do but see his vice;
'Tis to his virtue a just equinox,
The one as long as the other: 'tis pity of him.
I fear the trust Othello puts him in,
On some odd time of his infirmity,
Will shake this island.

MONTANO: But is he often thus?

IAGO: 'Tis evermore the prologue to his sleep:
He 'll watch the horologe a double set,
If drink rock not his cradle.

MONTANO: It were well
The general were put in mind of it.
Perhaps he sees it not; or his good nature
Prizes the virtue that appears in Cassio,
And looks not on his evils: is not this true?

Enter Roderigo.

IAGO: [*Aside to him*] How now, Roderigo!
I pray you, after the lieutenant; go.   [*Exit Roderigo.*

MONTANO: And 'tis great pity that the noble Moor

Should hazard such a place as his own second
With one of an ingraft infirmity:
It were an honest action to say
So to the Moor.

IAGO: Not I, for this fair island:
I do love Cassio well; and would do much
To cure him of this evil—But, hark! what noise?

                        [*Cry within:* 'Help! help!']

Re-enter Cassio, driving in Roderigo.

CASSIO: You rogue! you rascal!
MONTANO: What 's the matter, lieutenant?
CASSIO: A knave teach me my duty!
I 'll beat the knave into a twiggen bottle.
RODERIGO: Beat me!
CASSIO: Dost thou prate, rogue?   [*Striking Roderigo.*
MONTANO: Nay, good lieutenant;   [*Staying him.*
I pray you, sir, hold your hand.
CASSIO: Let me go, sir,
Or I 'll knock you o'er the mazzard.
MONTANO: Come, come, you' re drunk.
CASSIO: Drunk!   [*They fight.*
IAGO: [*Aside to Roderigo*] Away, I say; go out, and cry a mutiny.

                           [*Exit Roderigo.*

Nay, good lieutenant,—alas, gentlemen;—
Help, ho!—Lieutenant,—sir,—Montano,—sir;—
Help, masters!—Here 's a goodly watch indeed!   [*Bell rings.*
Who 's that which rings the bell?—Diablo, ho!
The town will rise: God's will, lieutenant, hold!
You will be shamed for ever.

Re-enter Othello and Attendants.

OTHELLO: What is the matter here?
MONTANO: 'Zounds, I bleed still; I am hurt to the death.

                                  [*Faints.*

OTHELLO: Hold, for your lives!

IAGO: Hold, ho! Lieutenant,—sir,—Montano,—gentlemen,—
Have you forgot all sense of place and duty?
Hold! the general speaks to you; hold, hold, for shame!

OTHELLO: Why, how now, ho! from whence ariseth this?
Are we turn'd Turks, and to ourselves do that
Which heaven hath forbid the Ottomites?
For Christian shame, put by this barbarous brawl:
He that stirs next to carve for his own rage
Holds his soul light; he dies upon his motion.
Silence that dreadful bell: it frights the isle
From her propriety. What is the matter, masters?
Honest Iago, that look'st dead with grieving,
Speak, who began this? on thy love, I charge thee.

IAGO: I do not know: friends all but now, even now,
In quarter, and in terms like bride and groom
Devesting them for bed; and then, but now—
As if some planet had unwitted men—
Swords out, and tilting one at other's breast,
In opposition bloody. I cannot speak
Any beginning to this peevish odds;
And would in action glorious I had lost
Those legs that brought me to a part of it!

OTHELLO: How comes it, Michael, you are thus forgot?

CASSIO: I pray you, pardon me; I cannot speak.

OTHELLO: Worthy Montano, you were wont be civil;
The gravity and stillness of your youth
The world hath noted, and your name is great
In mouths of wisest censure: what 's the matter,
That you unlace your reputation thus
And spend your rich opinion for the name
Of a night-brawler? give me answer to it.

MONTANO: Worthy Othello, I am hurt to danger:
Your officer, Iago, can inform you,—
While I spare speech, which something now offends me,—

Of all that I do know: nor know I aught
By me that 's said or done amiss this night;
Unless self-charity be sometimes a vice,
And to defend ourselves it be a sin
When violence assails us.

OTHELLO: Now, by heaven,
My blood begins my safer guides to rule;
And passion, having my best judgement collied,
Assays to lead the way: if I once stir,
Or do but lift this arm, the best of you
Shall sink in my rebuke. Give me to know
How this foul rant began, who set it on;
And he that is approved in this offence,
Though he had twinn'd with me, both at a birth,
Shall lose me. What! in a town of war,
Yet wild, the people's hearts brimful of fear,
To manage private and domestic quarrel,
In night, and on the court and guard of safety!
'Tis monstrous. Iago, who began 't?

MONTANO: If partially affined, or leagued in office,
Thou dost deliver more or less than truth,
Thou art no soldier.

IAGO: Touch me not so near:
I had rather have this tongue cut from my mouth
Than it should do offence to Michael Cassio;
Yet, I persuade myself, to speak the truth
Shall nothing wrong him. Thus it is, general.
Montano and myself being in speech,
There comes a fellow crying out for help;
And Cassio following him with determined sword,
To execute upon him. Sir, this gentleman
Steps in to Cassio, and entreats his pause:
Myself the crying fellow did pursue,
Lest by his clamour—as it so fell out—
The town might fall in fright: he, swift of foot,

Outran my purpose; and I return'd the rather
For that I heard the clink and fall of swords,
And Cassio high in oath; which till to-night
I ne'er might say before. When I came back—
For this was brief—I found them close together,
At blow and thrust; even as again they were
When you yourself did part them.
More of this matter cannot I report:
But men are men; the best sometimes forget:
Though Cassio did some little wrong to him,
As men in rage strike those that wish them best,
Yet surely Cassio, I believe, received
From him that fled some strange indignity,
Which patience, could not pass.

OTHELLO: I know, Iago,
Thy honesty and love doth mince this matter,
Making it light to Cassio. Cassio, I love thee;
But never more be officer of mine.

Re-enter Desdemona, attended.

Look, if my gentle love be not raised up!
I 'll make thee an example.

DESDEMONA: What 's the matter?

OTHELLO: All 's well now, sweeting; come away to bed.
Sir, for your hurts, myself will be your surgeon:
Lead him off.   [*To Montano, who is led off.*
Iago, look with care about the town.
And silence those whom this vile brawl distracted.
Come, Desdemona: 'tis the soldiers' life
To have their balmy slumbers waked with strife.
                              [*Exeunt all but Iago and Cassio.*

IAGO: What, are you hurt, lieutenant?

CASSIO: Ay, past all surgery.

IAGO: Marry, heaven forbid!

CASSIO: Reputation, reputation, reputation! O, I have lost my reputation! I have lost the immortal part of myself, and what remains is bestial. My reputation, Iago, my reputation!

IAGO: As I am an honest man, I thought you had received some bodily wound; there is more sense in that than in reputation. Reputation is an idle and most false imposition; oft got without merit, and lost without deserving: you have lost no reputation at all, unless you repute yourself such a loser. What, man! there are ways to recover the general again: you are but now cast in his mood, a punishment more in policy than in malice; even so as one would beat his offenceless dog to affright an imperious lion: sue to him again, and he 's yours.

CASSIO: I will rather sue to be despised than to deceive so good a commander with so slight, so drunken, and so indiscreet an officer. Drunk? and speak parrot? and squabble? swagger? swear? and discourse fustian with one's own shadow? O thou invisible spirit of wine, if thou hast no name to be known by, let us call thee devil!

IAGO: What was he that you followed with your sword? What had he done to you?

CASSIO: I know not.

IAGO: Is 't possible?

CASSIO: I remember a mass of things, but nothing distinctly; a quarrel, but nothing wherefore. O God, that men should put an enemy in their mouths to steal away their brains! that we should, with joy, pleasance, revel and applause transform ourselves into beasts!

IAGO: Why, but you are now well enough: how came you thus recovered?

CASSIO: It hath pleased the devil drunkenness to give place to the devil wrath: one unperfectness shows me another, to make me frankly despise myself.

IAGO: Come, you are too severe a moraler: as the time, the place, and the condition of this country stands, I could heartily wish this had not befallen; but, since it is as it is, mend it for your own good.

CASSIO: I will ask him for my place again; he shall tell me I am a drunkard! Had I as many mouths as Hydra, such an answer would stop them all. To be now a sensible man, by and by a fool, and presently a beast! O strange! Every inordinate cup is unblessed and the ingredient is a devil.

IAGO: Come, come, good wine is a good familiar creature, if it be well used: exclaim no more against it. And, good lieutenant, I think you think I love you.

CASSIO: I have well approved it, sir. I drunk!

IAGO: You or any man living may be drunk at a time, man. I 'll tell you what you shall do. Our general's wife is now the general: I may say so in this respect, for that he hath devoted and given up himself to the contemplation, mark, and denotement of her parts and graces: confess yourself freely to her; importune her help to put you in your place again: she is of so free, so kind, so apt, so blessed a disposition, she holds it a vice in her goodness not to do more than she is requested: this broken joint between you and her husband entreat her to splinter; and, my fortunes against any lay worth naming, this crack of your love shall grow stronger than it was before.

CASSIO: You advise me well.

IAGO: I protest, in the sincerity of love and honest kindness.

CASSIO: I think it freely; and betimes in the morning I will beseech the virtuous Desdemona to undertake for me: I am desperate of my fortunes if they check me here.

IAGO: You are in the right. Good night, lieutenant; I must to the watch.

CASSIO: Good night, honest Iago. [*Exit.*

IAGO: And what 's he then that says I play the villain?
When this advice is free I give and honest,
Probal to thinking and indeed the course
To win the Moor again? For 'tis most easy
The inclining Desdemona to subdue
In any honest suit: she 's framed as fruitful
As the free elements. And then for her

To win the Moor—were 't to renounce his baptism,
All seals and symbols of redeemed sin,
His soul is so enfetter'd to her love,
That she may make, unmake, do what she list,
Even as her appetite shall play the god
With his weak function. How am I then a villain
To counsel Cassio to this parallel course,
Directly to his good? Divinity of hell!
When devils will the blackest sins put on,
They do suggest at first with heavenly shows,
As I do now: for whiles this honest fool
Plies Desdemona to repair his fortunes
And she for him pleads strongly to the Moor,
I 'll pour this pestilence into his ear,
That she repeals him for her body's lust;
And by how much she strives to do him good,
She shall undo her credit with the Moor.
So will I turn her virtue into pitch,
And out of her own goodness make the net
That shall enmesh them all.

Re-enter Roderigo.

How now, Roderigo!

RODERIGO: I do follow here in the chase, not like a hound that
hunts, but one that fills up the cry. My money is almost spent;
I have been to-night exceedingly well cudgelled; and I think
the issue will be, I shall have so much experience for my pains,
and so, with no money at all and a little more wit, return again
to Venice.

IAGO: How poor are they that have not patience!
What wound did ever heal but by degrees?
Thou know'st we work by wit, and not by witchcraft;
And wit depends on dilatory time.
Does 't not go well? Cassio hath beaten thee,
And thou, by that small hurt, hast cashier'd Cassio:

Though other things grow fair against the sun,
Yet fruits that blossom first will first be ripe:
Content thyself awhile. By the mass, 'tis morning;
Pleasure and action make the hours seem short.
Retire thee; go where thou art billeted:
Away, I say; thou shalt know more hereafter:
Nay, get thee gone. [*Exit Roderigo.*] Two things are to be done:
My wife must move for Cassio to her mistress;
I 'll set her on;
Myself the while to draw the Moor apart,
And bring him jump when he may Cassio find
Soliciting his wife: ay, that 's the way:
Dull not device by coldness and delay.   [*Exit.*

ACT III.

SCENE I. *Before the castle.*
Enter Cassio and some Musicians.

CASSIO: Masters, play here; I will content your pains;
Something that 's brief; and bid 'Good morrow, general.'   [*Music.*

Enter Clown.

CLOWN: Why, masters, have your instruments been in Naples, that they speak i' the nose thus?

FIRST MUSICIAN: How, sir, how!

CLOWN: Are these, I pray you, wind-instruments?

FIRST MUSICIAN: Ay, marry, are they, sir.

CLOWN: O, thereby hangs a tail.

FIRST MUSICIAN: Whereby hangs a tale, sir?

CLOWN: Marry, sir, by many a wind-instrument that I know. But, masters, here 's money for you: and the general so likes your music, that he desires you, for love's sake, to make no more noise with it.

FIRST MUSICIAN: Well, sir, we will not.

CLOWN: If you have any music that may not be heard, to 't again: but, as they say, to hear music the general does not greatly care.

FIRST MUSICIAN: We have none such, sir.

CLOWN: Then put up your pipes in your bag, for I 'll away: go; vanish into air; away! [*Exeunt Musicians.*

CASSIO: Dost thou hear, my honest friend?

CLOWN: No, I hear not your honest friend; I hear you.

CASSIO: Prithee, keep up thy quillets. There 's a poor piece of gold for thee: if the gentlewoman that attends the general's wife be stirring, tell her there 's one Cassio entreats her a little favour of speech: wilt thou do this?

CLOWN: She is stirring, sir: if she will stir hither, I shall seem to notify unto her.

CASSIO: Do, good my friend. [*Exit Clown.*

Enter Iago.

In happy time, Iago.

IAGO: You have not been a-bed, then?

CASSIO: Why, no; the day had broke
Before we parted. I have made bold, Iago,
To send in to your wife: my suit to her
Is, that she will to virtuous Desdemona
Procure me some access.

IAGO: I 'll send her to you presently;
And I 'll devise a mean to draw the Moor
Out of the way, that your converse and business
May be more free.

CASSIO: I humbly thank you for 't. [*Exit Iago.*] I never knew
A Florentine more kind and honest.

Enter Emilia.

EMILIA: Good morrow, good lieutenant: I am sorry
For your displeasure; but all will sure be well.
The general and his wife are talking of it;

And she speaks for you stoutly: the Moor replies,
That he you hurt is of great fame in Cyprus
And great affinity and that in wholesome wisdom
He might not but refuse you, but he protests he loves you
And needs no other suitor but his likings
To take the safest occasion by the front
To bring you in again.

CASSIO:　　　　　　　Yet, I beseech you,
If you think fit, or that it may be done,
Give me advantage of some brief discourse
With Desdemona alone.

EMILIA:　　　　　　Pray you, come in:
I will bestow you where you shall have time
To speak your bosom freely.

CASSIO:　　　　　　　　I am much bound to you.　　[Exeunt.

SCENE II. *A room in the castle.*
Enter Othello, Iago, and Gentlemen.

OTHELLO: These letters give, Iago, to the pilot;
And by him do my duties to the senate:
That done, I will be walking on the works;
Repair there to me.

IAGO:　　　　　Well, my good lord, I'll do 't.

OTHELLO: This fortification, gentlemen, shall we see 't?

GENTLEMEN: We 'll wait upon your lordship.　　[*Exeunt.*

SCENE III. *The garden of the castle.*
Enter Desdemona, Cassio, and Emilia.

DESDEMONA: Be thou assured, good Cassio, I will do
All my abilities in thy behalf.

EMILIA: Good madam, do: I warrant it grieves my husband,
As if the case were his.

DESDEMONA: O, that 's an honest fellow. Do not doubt, Cassio,

But I will have my lord and you again
As friendly as you were.

CASSIO: Bounteous madam,
Whatever shall become of Michael Cassio,
He 's never any thing but your true servant.

DESDEMONA: I know 't; I thank you. You do love my lord:
You have known him long; and be you well assured
He shall in strangeness stand no further off
Than in a politic distance.

CASSIO: Ay, but, lady,
That policy may either last so long,
Or feed upon such nice and waterish diet,
Or breed itself so out of circumstance,
That, I being absent and my place supplied,
My general will forget my love and service.

DESDEMONA: Do not doubt that; before Emilia here
I give thee warrant of thy place: assure thee,
If I do vow a friendship, I 'll perform it
To the last article: my lord shall never rest;
I 'll watch him tame and talk him out of patience:
His bed shall seem a school, his board a shrift;
I 'll intermingle every thing he does
With Cassio's suit: therefore be merry, Cassio;
For thy solicitor shall rather die
Than give thy cause away.

EMILIA: Madam, here comes my lord.

CASSIO: Madam, I 'll take my leave.

DESDEMONA: Why, stay, and hear me speak.

CASSIO: Madam, not now: I am very ill at ease,
Unfit for mine own purposes.

DESDEMONA: Well, do your discretion.   [*Exit Cassio.*

Enter Othello and Iago.

IAGO: Ha! I like not that.

OTHELLO: What dost thou say?

IAGO: Nothing, my lord: or if—I know not what.

OTHELLO: Was not that Cassio parted from my wife?

IAGO: Cassio, my lord! No, sure, I cannot think it,
That he would steal away so guilty-like,
Seeing you coming.

OTHELLO: I do believe 'twas he.

DESDEMONA: How now, my lord!
I have been talking with a suitor here,
A man that languishes in your displeasure.

OTHELLO: Who is 't you mean?

DESDEMONA: Why, your lieutenant, Cassio. Good my lord,
If I have any grace or power to move you,
His present reconciliation take;
For if he be not one that truly loves you,
That errs in ignorance and not in cunning,
I have no judgement in an honest face:
I prithee, call him back.

OTHELLO: Went he hence now?

DESDEMONA: Ay, sooth; so humbled
That he hath left part of his grief with me,
To suffer with him. Good love, call him back.

OTHELLO: Not now, sweet Desdemona; some other time.

DESDEMONA: But shall 't be shortly?

OTHELLO: The sooner, sweet, for you.

DESDEMONA: Shall 't be to-night at supper?

OTHELLO: No, not to-night.

DESDEMONA: To-morrow dinner, then?

OTHELLO: I shall not dine at home;
I meet the captains at the citadel.

DESDEMONA: Why, then, to-morrow night; or Tuesday morn;
On Tuesday noon, or night; on Wednesday morn:
I prithee, name the time, but let it not
Exceed three days: in faith, he 's penitent;
And yet his trespass, in our common reason—
Save that, they say, the wars must make examples

Out of their best—is not almost a fault
To incur a private check. When shall he come?
Tell me, Othello: I wonder in my soul,
What you would ask me, that I should deny,
Or stand so mammering on. What! Michael Cassio,
That came a-wooing with you, and so many a time,
When I have spoke of you dispraisingly,
Hath ta'en your part; to have so much to do
To bring him in! Trust me, I could do much,—

OTHELLO: Prithee, no more: let him come when he will;
I will deny thee nothing.

DESDEMONA:　　　　　Why, this is not a boon;
'Tis as I should entreat you wear your gloves,
Or feed on nourishing dishes, or keep you warm,
Or sue to you to do a peculiar profit
To your own person: nay, when I have a suit
Wherein I mean to touch your love indeed,
It shall be full of poise and difficult weight
And fearful to be granted.

OTHELLO:　　　　　I will deny thee nothing:
Whereon, I do beseech thee, grant me this,
To leave me but a little to myself.

DESDEMONA: Shall I deny you? no: farewell, my lord.

OTHELLO: Farewell, my Desdemona: I 'll come to thee straight.

DESDEMONA: Emilia, come. Be as your fancies teach you;
Whate'er you be, I am obedient.　　[Exeunt Desdemona and Emilia.

OTHELLO: Excellent wretch! Perdition catch my soul,
But I do love thee! and when I love thee not,
Chaos is come again.

IAGO: My noble lord,—

OTHELLO:　　　　　What dost thou say, Iago?

IAGO: Did Michael Cassio, when you woo'd my lady,
Know of your love?

OTHELLO: He did, from first to last: why dost thou ask?

IAGO: But for a satisfaction of my thought;

No further harm.

OTHELLO: Why of thy thought, Iago?

IAGO: I did not think he had been acquainted with her.

OTHELLO: O, yes; and went between us very oft.

IAGO: Indeed!

OTHELLO: Indeed! ay, indeed: discern'st thou aught in that?
Is he not honest?

IAGO: Honest, my lord!

OTHELLO: Honest! ay, honest.

IAGO: My lord, for aught I know.

OTHELLO: What dost thou think?

IAGO: Think, my lord!

OTHELLO: Think my lord!
By heaven, he echoes me,
As if there were some monster in his thought
Too hideous to be shown. Thou dost mean something:
I heard thee say even now, thou likedst not that,
When Cassio left my wife: what didst not like?
And when I told thee he was of my counsel
In my whole course of wooing, thou criedst 'Indeed!'
And didst contract and purse thy brow together,
As if thou then hadst shut up in thy brain
Some horrible conceit: if thou dost love me,
Show me thy thought.

IAGO: My lord, you know I love you.

OTHELLO: I think thou dost;
And, for I know thou 'rt full of love and honesty,
And weigh'st thy words before thou givest them breath,
Therefore these stops of thine fright me the more:
For such things in a false disloyal knave
Are tricks of custom, but in a man that 's just
They are close delations, working from the heart
That passion cannot rule.

IAGO: For Michael Cassio
I dare be sworn I think that he is honest.

OTHELLO: I think so too.

IAGO: Men should be what they seem;
Or those that be not, would they might seem none!

OTHELLO: Certain, men should be what they seem.

IAGO: Why, then, I think Cassio's an honest man.

OTHELLO: Nay, yet there 's more in this:
I prithee, speak to me as to thy thinkings,
As thou dost ruminate, and give thy worst of thoughts
The worst of words.

IAGO: Good my lord, pardon me:
Though I am bound to every act of duty,
I am not bound to that all slaves are free to.
Utter my thoughts? Why, say they are vile and false;
As where 's that palace whereinto foul things
Sometimes intrude not? who has a breast so pure,
But some uncleanly apprehensions
Keep leets and law-days and in session sit
With meditations lawful?

OTHELLO: Thou dost conspire against thy friend, Iago,
If thou but think'st him wrong'd and makest his ear
A stranger to thy thoughts.

IAGO: I do beseech you—
Though I perchance am vicious in my guess,
As, I confess, it is my nature's plague
To spy into abuses, and oft my jealousy
Shapes faults that are not—that your wisdom yet,
From one that so imperfectly conceits,
Would take no notice, nor build yourself a trouble
Out of his scattering and unsure observance.
It were not for your quiet nor your good,
Nor for my manhood, honesty, or wisdom
To let you know my thoughts.

OTHELLO: What dost thou mean?

IAGO: Good name in man and woman, dear my lord,
Is the immediate jewel of their souls:

Who steals my purse steals trash; 'tis something, nothing;
'Twas mine, 'tis his, and has been slave to thousands;
But he that filches from me my good name
Robs me of that which not enriches him
And makes me poor indeed.

   OTHELLO: By heaven, I 'll know thy thoughts.

   IAGO: You cannot, if my heart were in your hand;
Nor shall not, whilst 'tis in my custody.

   OTHELLO: Ha!

   IAGO: O, beware, my lord, of jealousy;
It is the green-eyed monster which doth mock
The meat it feeds on: that cuckold lives in bliss
Who, certain of his fate, loves not his wronger;
But, O, what damned minutes tells he o'er
Who dotes, yet doubts, suspects, yet strongly loves!

   OTHELLO: O misery!

   IAGO: Poor and content is rich and rich enough,
But riches fineless is as poor as winter
To him that ever fears he shall be poor.
Good heaven, the souls of all my tribe defend
From jealousy!

   OTHELLO: Why, why is this?
Think'st thou I 'ld make a life of jealousy,
To follow still the changes of the moon
With fresh suspicions? No; to be once in doubt
Is once to be resolved: exchange me for a goat,
When I shall turn the business of my soul
To such exsufflicate and blown surmises,
Matching thy inference. 'Tis not to make me jealous
To say my wife is fair, feeds well, loves company,
Is freed of speech, sings, plays and dances well;
Where virtue is, these are more virtuous:
Nor from mine own weak merits will I draw
The smallest fear or doubt of her revolt;
For she had eyes, and chose me. No, Iago;

I 'll see before I doubt; when I doubt, prove;
And on the proof, there is no more but this,—
Away at once with love or jealousy!
 IAGO: I am glad of it; for now I shall have reason
To show the love and duty that I bear you
With franker spirit: therefore, as I am bound,
Receive it from me. I speak not yet of proof.
Look to your wife; observe her well with Cassio;
Wear your eye thus, not jealous nor secure:
I would not have your free and noble nature,
Out of self-bounty, be abused; look to 't:
I know our country disposition well;
In Venice they do let heaven see the pranks
They dare not show their husbands; their best conscience
Is not to leave 't undone, but keep 't unknown.
 OTHELLO: Dost thou say so?
 IAGO: She did deceive her father, marrying you;
And when she seem'd to shake and fear your looks,
She loved them most.
 OTHELLO: And so she did.
 IAGO: Why, go to then;
She that, so young, could give out such a seeming,
To seel her father's eyes up close as oak—
He thought 'twas witchcraft—but I am much to blame;
I humbly do beseech you of your pardon
For too much loving you.
 OTHELLO: I am bound to thee for ever.
 IAGO: I see this hath a little dash'd your spirits.
 OTHELLO: Not a jot, not a jot.
 IAGO: I' faith, I fear it has.
I hope you will consider what is spoke
Come from my love. But I do see you 're moved:
I am to pray you not to strain my speech
To grosser issues nor to larger reach
Than to suspicion.

OTHELLO: I will not.

IAGO: Should you do so, my lord,
My speech should fall into such vile success
As my thoughts aim not at. Cassio 's my worthy friend—
My lord, I see you 're moved.

OTHELLO: No, not much moved:
I do not think but Desdemona's honest.

IAGO: Long live she so! and long live you to think so!

OTHELLO: And yet, how nature erring from itself,—

IAGO: Ay, there 's the point: as—to be bold with you—
Not to affect many proposed matches
Of her own clime, complexion, and degree,
Whereto we see in all things nature tends—
Foh! one may smell in such a will most rank,
Foul disproportion, thoughts unnatural.
But pardon me; I do not in position
Distinctly speak of her; though I may fear
Her will, recoiling to her better judgement,
May fall to match you with her country forms
And happily repent.

OTHELLO: Farewell, farewell:
If more thou dost perceive, let me know more;
Set on thy wife to observe: leave me, Iago.

IAGO: [Going] My lord, I take my leave.

OTHELLO: Why did I marry? This honest creature doubtless
Sees and knows more, much more, than he unfolds.

IAGO: [Returning] My lord, I would I might entreat your honour
To scan this thing no further; leave it to time:
Though it be fit that Cassio have his place,
For, sure, he fills it up with great ability,
Yet, if you please to hold him off awhile,
You shall by that perceive him and his means:
Note, if your lady strain his entertainment
With any strong or vehement importunity;
Much will be seen in that. In the mean time,

Let me be thought too busy in my fears—
As worthy cause I have to fear I am—
And hold her free, I do beseech your honour.

    OTHELLO: Fear not my government.

    IAGO: I once more take my leave.   [*Exit.*

    OTHELLO: This fellow 's of exceeding honesty,
And knows all qualities, with a learned spirit,
Of human dealings. If I do prove her haggard,
Though that her jesses were my dear heartstrings,
I 'ld whistle her off and let her down the wind,
To prey at fortune. Haply, for I am black
And have not those soft parts of conversation
That chamberers have, or for I am declined
Into the vale of years,—yet that 's not much—
She 's gone. I am abused; and my relief
Must be to loathe her. O curse of marriage,
That we can call these delicate creatures ours,
And not their appetites! I had rather be a toad,
And live upon the vapour of a dungeon,
Than keep a corner in the thing I love
For others' uses. Yet, 'tis the plague of great ones;
Prerogatived are they less than the base;
'Tis destiny unshunnable, like death:
Even then this forked plague is fated to us
When we do quicken. Desdemona comes:

Re-enter Desdemona and Emilia.

If she be false, O, then heaven mocks itself!
I 'll not believe 't.

    DESDEMONA: How now, my dear Othello!
Your dinner, and the generous islanders
By you invited, do attend your presence.

    OTHELLO: I am to blame.

    DESDEMONA: Why do you speak so faintly?
Are you not well?

OTHELLO: I have a pain upon my forehead here.

DESDEMONA: 'Faith, that 's with watching; 'twill away again:
Let me but bind it hard, within this hour
It will be well.

OTHELLO: Your napkin is too little:

     [*He puts the handkerchief from him; and it drops.*
Let it alone. Come, I 'll go in with you.

DESDEMONA: I am very sorry that you are not well.

       [*Exeunt Othello and Desdemona.*

EMILIA: I am glad I have found this napkin:
This was her first remembrance from the Moor:
My wayward husband hath a hundred times
Woo'd me to steal it; but she so loves the token,
For he conjured her she should ever keep it,
That she reserves it evermore about her
To kiss and talk to. I 'll have the work ta'en out,
And give 't Iago: what he will do with it
Heaven knows, not I;
I nothing but to please his fantasy.

Re-enter Iago.

IAGO: How now! what do you here alone?

EMILIA: Do not you chide; I have a thing for you.

IAGO: A thing for me? it is a common thing—

EMILIA: Ha!

IAGO: To have a foolish wife.

EMILIA: O, is that all? What will you give me now
For that same handkerchief?

IAGO: What handkerchief?

EMILIA: What handkerchief!
Why, that the Moor first gave to Desdemona;
That which so often you did bid me steal.

IAGO: Hast stol'n it from her?

EMILIA: No, 'faith; she let it drop by negligence,
And, to the advantage, I, being here, took 't up.

Look, here it is.

IAGO: A good wench; give it me.

EMILIA: What will you do with 't, that you have been so earnest
To have me filch it?

IAGO: [*Snatching it*] Why, what 's that to you?

EMILIA: If it be not for some purpose of import,
Give 't me again: poor lady, she 'll run mad
When she shall lack it.

IAGO: Be not acknown on 't; I have use for it.
Go, leave me.   [*Exit Emilia.*
I will in Cassio's lodging lose this napkin,
And let him find it. Trifles light as air
Are to the jealous confirmations strong
As proofs of holy writ: this may do something.
The Moor already changes with my poison:
Dangerous conceits are, in their natures, poisons,
Which at the first are scarce found to distaste,
But with a little act upon the blood,
Burn like the mines of sulphur. I did say so:
Look, where he comes!

Re-enter Othello.

Not poppy, nor mandragora,
Nor all the drowsy syrups of the world,
Shall ever medicine thee to that sweet sleep
Which thou owedst yesterday.

OTHELLO: Ha! ha! false to me?

IAGO: Why, how now, general! no more of that.

OTHELLO: Avaunt! be gone! thou hast set me on the rack:
I swear 'tis better to be much abused
Than but to know 't a little.

IAGO: How now, my lord!

OTHELLO: What sense had I of her stol'n hours of lust?
I saw 't not, thought it not, it harm'd not me:
I slept the next night well, was free and merry;

I found not Cassio's kisses on her lips:
He that is robb'd, not wanting what is stol'n,
Let him not know 't, and he 's not robb'd at all.

    IAGO: I am sorry to hear this.

    OTHELLO: I had been happy, if the general camp,
Pioners and all, had tasted her sweet body,
So I had nothing known. O, now, for ever
Farewell the tranquil mind! farewell content!
Farewell the plumed troop, and the big wars,
That make ambition virtue! O, farewell!
Farewell the neighing steed, and the shrill trump,
The spirit-stirring drum, the ear-piercing fife,
The royal banner, and all quality,
Pride, pomp and circumstance of glorious war!
And, O you mortal engines, whose rude throats
The immortal Jove's dread clamours counterfeit,
Farewell! Othello's occupation 's gone!

    IAGO: Is 't possible, my lord?

    OTHELLO: Villain, be sure thou prove my love a whore,
Be sure of it; give me the ocular proof;
Or, by the worth of man's eternal soul,
Thou hadst been better have been born a dog
Than answer my waked wrath!

    IAGO: Is 't come to this?

    OTHELLO: Make me to see 't; or, at the least, so prove it,
That the probation bear no hinge nor loop
To hang a doubt on; or woe upon thy life!

    IAGO: My noble lord,—

    OTHELLO: If thou dost slander her and torture me,
Never pray more; abandon all remorse;
On horror's head horrors accumulate;
Do deeds to make heaven weep, all earth amazed;
For nothing canst thou to damnation add
Greater than that.

    IAGO: O grace! O heaven forgive me!

Are you a man? have you a soul or sense?
God be wi' you; take mine office. O wretched fool,
That livest to make thine honesty a vice!
O monstrous world! Take note, take note, O world,
To be direct and honest is not safe.
I thank you for this profit; and from hence
I'll love no friend, sith love breeds such offence.

OTHELLO: Nay, stay: thou shouldst be honest.

IAGO: I should be wise, for honesty's a fool
And loses that it works for.

OTHELLO: By the world,
I think my wife be honest and think she is not;
I think that thou art just and think thou art not.
I'll have some proof. Her name, that was as fresh
As Dian's visage, is now begrimed and black
As mine own face. If there be cords, or knives,
Poison, or fire, or suffocating streams,
I'll not endure it. Would I were satisfied!

IAGO: I see, sir, you are eaten up with passion:
I do repent me that I put it to you.
You would be satisfied?

OTHELLO: Would! nay, I will.

IAGO: And may: but, how? how satisfied, my lord?
Would you, the supervisor, grossly gape on—
Behold her topp'd?

OTHELLO: Death and damnation! O!

IAGO: It were a tedious difficulty, I think,
To bring them to that prospect: damn them then,
If ever mortal eyes do see them bolster
More than their own! What then? how then?
What shall I say? Where's satisfaction?
It is impossible you should see this,
Were they as prime as goats, as hot as monkeys,
As salt as wolves in pride, and fools as gross
As ignorance made drunk. But yet, I say,

If imputation and strong circumstances,
Which lead directly to the door of truth,
Will give you satisfaction, you may have 't.

    OTHELLO: Give me a living reason she 's disloyal.

    IAGO: I do not like the office:
But, sith, I am enter'd in this cause so far,
Prick'd to 't by foolish honesty and love,
I will go on. I lay with Cassio lately;
And, being troubled with a raging tooth,
I could not sleep.
There are a kind of men so loose of soul,
That in their sleeps will mutter their affairs:
One of this kind is Cassio:
In sleep I heard him say, 'Sweet Desdemona,
Let us be wary, let us hide our loves;'
And then, sir, would he gripe and wring my hand,
Cry 'O sweet creature!' and then kiss me hard,
As if he pluck'd up kisses by the roots
That grew upon my lips; then laid his leg
Over my thigh, and sigh'd, and kiss'd; and then
Cried 'Cursed fate that gave thee to the Moor!'

    OTHELLO: O monstrous! monstrous!

    IAGO: Nay, this was but his dream.

    OTHELLO: But this denoted a foregone conclusion:
'Tis a shrewd doubt, though it be but a dream.

    IAGO: And this may help to thicken other proofs
That do demonstrate thinly.

    OTHELLO: I 'll tear her all to pieces.

    IAGO: Nay, but be wise: yet we see nothing done;
She may be honest yet. Tell me but this,
Have you not sometimes seen a handkerchief
Spotted with strawberries in your wife's hand?

    OTHELLO: I gave her such a one; 'twas my first gift.

    IAGO: I know not that: but such a handkerchief—
I am sure it was your wife's—did I to-day

See Cassio wipe his beard with.

OTHELLO: If it be that,—

IAGO: If it be that, or any that was hers,
It speaks against her with the other proofs.

OTHELLO: O, that the slave had forty thousand lives!
One is too poor, too weak for my revenge.
Now do I see 'tis true. Look here, Iago;
All my fond love thus do I blow to heaven.
'Tis gone.
Arise, black vengeance, from thy hollow cell!
Yield up, O love, thy crown and hearted throne
To tyrannous hate! Swell, bosom, with thy fraught,
For 'tis of aspics' tongues!

IAGO: Yet be content.

OTHELLO: O, blood, blood, blood!

IAGO: Patience, I say, your mind perhaps may change.

OTHELLO: Never, Iago. Like to the Pontic sea,
Whose icy current and compulsive course
Ne'er feels retiring ebb, but keeps due on
To the Propontic and the Hellespont,
Even so my bloody thoughts, with violent pace,
Shall ne'er look back, ne'er ebb to humble love,
Till that a capable and wide revenge
Swallow them up. Now, by yond marble heaven,
[*Kneels*] In the due reverence of a sacred vow
I here engage my words.

IAGO: Do not rise yet.
[*Kneels*] Witness, you ever-burning lights above,
You elements that clip us round about,
Witness that here Iago doth give up
The execution of his wit, hands, heart,
To wrong'd Othello's service! Let him command,
And to obey shall be in me remorse,
What bloody business ever.   [*They rise.*

OTHELLO: I greet thy love,

Not with vain thanks, but with acceptance bounteous,
And will upon the instant put thee to 't:
Within these three days let me hear thee say
That Cassio 's not alive.

IAGO: My friend is dead; 'tis done at your request:
But let her live.

OTHELLO: Damn her, lewd minx! O, damn her!
Come, go with me apart; I will withdraw,
To furnish me with some swift means of death
For the fair devil. Now art thou my lieutenant.

IAGO: I am your own for ever.   [*Exeunt.*

SCENE IV. *Before the castle.*
Enter Desdemona, Emilia, and Clown.

DESDEMONA: Do you know sirrah, where Lieutenant Cassio lies?

CLOWN: I dare not say he lies any where.

DESDEMONA: Why, man?

CLOWN: He 's a soldier, and for one to say a soldier lies, is stabbing.

DESDEMONA: Go to: where lodges he?

CLOWN: To tell you where he lodges, is to tell you where I lie.

DESDEMONA: Can any thing be made of this?

CLOWN: I know not where he lodges, and for me to devise a lodging and say he lies here or he lies there, were to lie in mine own throat.

DESDEMONA: Can you inquire him out, and be edified by report?

CLOWN: I will catechize the world for him; that is, make questions, and by them answer.

DESDEMONA: Seek him, bid him come hither: tell him I have moved my lord on his behalf, and hope all will be well.

CLOWN: To do this is within the compass of man's wit; and therefore I will attempt the doing it.   [*Exit.*

DESDEMONA: Where should I lose that handkerchief, Emilia?

EMILIA: I know not, madam.

DESDEMONA: Believe me, I had rather have lost my purse
Full of crusadoes: and, but my noble Moor
Is true of mind and made of no such baseness
As jealous creatures are, it were enough
To put him to ill thinking.
EMILIA: Is he not jealous?
DESDEMONA: Who, he? I think the sun where he was born
Drew all such humours from him.
EMILIA: Look, where he comes.
DESDEMONA: I will not leave him now till Cassio
Be call'd to him.

Enter Othello.

                              How is 't with you, my lord?
OTHELLO: Well, my good lady. [*Aside*] O, hardness to dissem-
    ble!—
How do you, Desdemona?
DESDEMONA: Well, my good lord.
OTHELLO: Give me your hand: this hand is moist, my lady.
DESDEMONA: It yet hath felt no age nor known no sorrow.
OTHELLO: This argues fruitfulness and liberal heart:
Hot, hot, and moist: this hand of yours requires
A sequester from liberty, fasting and prayer,
Much castigation, exercise devout;
For here 's a young and sweating devil here,
That commonly rebels. 'Tis a good hand,
A frank one.
DESDEMONA: You may, indeed, say so;
For 'twas that hand that gave away my heart.
OTHELLO: A liberal hand: the hearts of old gave hands;
But our new heraldry is hands, not hearts.
DESDEMONA: I cannot speak of this. Come now, your promise.
OTHELLO: What promise, chuck?
DESDEMONA: I have sent to bid Cassio come speak with you.
OTHELLO: I have a salt and sorry rheum offends me;

Lend me thy handkerchief.

DESDEMONA: Here, my lord.

OTHELLO: That which I gave you.

DESDEMONA: I have it not about me.

OTHELLO: Not?

DESDEMONA: No, indeed, my lord.

OTHELLO: That is a fault.

That handkerchief
Did an Egyptian to my mother give;
She was a charmer, and could almost read
The thoughts of people: she told her, while she kept it,
'Twould make her amiable and subdue my father
Entirely to her love, but if she lost it
Or made a gift of it, my father's eye
Should hold her loathed and his spirits should hunt
After new fancies: she, dying, gave it me;
And bid me, when my fate would have me wive,
To give it her. I did so: and take heed on 't;
Make it a darling like your precious eye;
To lose 't or give 't away were such perdition
As nothing else could match.

DESDEMONA: Is 't possible?

OTHELLO: 'Tis true: there 's magic in the web of it:
A sibyl, that had number'd in the world
The sun to course two hundred compasses,
In her prophetic fury sew'd the work;
The worms were hallow'd that did breed the silk;
And it was dyed in mummy which the skilful
Conserved of maidens' hearts.

DESDEMONA: Indeed! is 't true?

OTHELLO: Most veritable; therefore look to 't well.

DESDEMONA: Then would to God that I had never seen 't!

OTHELLO: Ha! wherefore?

DESDEMONA: Why do you speak so startingly and rash?

OTHELLO: Is 't lost? is 't gone? speak, is it out o' the way?

DESDEMONA: Heaven bless us!

OTHELLO: Say you?

DESDEMONA: It is not lost; but what an if it were?

OTHELLO: How!

DESDEMONA: I say, it is not lost.

OTHELLO: Fetch 't, let me see 't.

DESDEMONA: Why, so I can, sir, but I will not now.
This is a trick to put me from my suit:
Pray you, let Cassio be received again.

OTHELLO: Fetch me the handkerchief: my mind misgives.

DESDEMONA: Come, come;
You 'll never meet a more sufficient man.

OTHELLO: The handkerchief!

DESDEMONA: I pray, talk me of Cassio.

OTHELLO: The handkerchief!

DESDEMONA: A man that all this time
Hath founded his good fortunes on your love,
Shared dangers with you,—

OTHELLO: The handkerchief!

DESDEMONA: In sooth, you are to blame.

OTHELLO: Away!   [Exit.

EMILIA: Is not this man jealous?

DESDEMONA: I ne'er saw this before.
Sure, there 's some wonder in this handkerchief:
I am most unhappy in the loss of it.

EMILIA: 'Tis not a year or two shows us a man:
They are all but stomachs, and we all but food;
They eat us hungerly, and when they are full,
They belch us. Look you, Cassio and my husband!

Enter Cassio and Iago.

IAGO: There is no other way; 'tis she must do 't:
And, lo, the happiness! go, and importune her.

DESDEMONA: How now, good Cassio! what 's the news with you?

CASSIO: Madam, my former suit: I do beseech you

That by your virtuous means I may again
Exist, and be a member of his love
Whom I with all the office of my heart
Entirely honour: I would not be delay'd.
If my offence be of such mortal kind
That nor my service past, nor present sorrows,
Nor purposed merit in futurity,
Can ransom me into his love again,
But to know so must be my benefit;
So shall I clothe me in a forced content,
And shut myself up in some other course,
To fortune's alms.

    DESDEMONA: Alas, thrice-gentle Cassio!
My advocation is not now in tune;
My lord is not my lord; nor should I know him,
Were he in favour as in humour alter'd.
So help me every spirit sanctified,
As I have spoken for you all my best
And stood within the blank of his displeasure
For my free speech! you must awhile be patient:
What I can do I will; and more I will
Than for myself I dare: let that suffice you.

    IAGO: Is my lord angry?

    EMILIA: He went hence but now,
And certainly in strange unquietness.

    IAGO: Can he be angry? I have seen the cannon,
When it hath blown his ranks into the air,
And, like the devil, from his very arm
Puff'd his own brother:—and can he be angry?
Something of moment then: I will go meet him:
There 's matter in 't indeed, if he be angry.

    DESDEMONA: I prithee, do so.   [Exit Iago.
                            Something, sure, of state,
Either from Venice, or some unhatch'd practice
Made demonstrable here in Cyprus to him,

Hath puddled his clear spirit; and in such cases
Men's natures wrangle with inferior things,
Though great ones are their object. 'Tis even so;
For let our finger ache, and it indues
Our other healthful members even to that sense
Of pain: nay, we must think men are not gods,
Nor of them look for such observances
As fit the bridal. Beshrew me much. Emilia,
I was, unhandsome warrior as I am,
Arraigning his unkindness with my soul;
But now I find I had suborn'd the witness,
And he 's indicted falsely.

    EMILIA: Pray heaven it be state-matters, as you think,
And no conception nor no jealous toy
Concerning you.

    DESDEMONA: Alas the day! I never gave him cause.

    EMILIA: But jealous souls will not be answer'd so;
They are not ever jealous for the cause,
But jealous for they are jealous: 'tis a monster
Begot upon itself, born on itself.

    DESDEMONA: Heaven keep that monster from Othello's mind!

    EMILIA: Lady, amen.

    DESDEMONA: I will go seek him. Cassio, walk here about:
If I do find him fit, I 'll move your suit
And seek to effect it to my uttermost.

    CASSIO: I humbly thank your ladyship.

                        [Exeunt Desdemona and Emilia.

Enter Bianca.

    BIANCA: Save you, friend Cassio!

    CASSIO: What make you from home?
How is it with you, my most fair Bianca?
I' faith, sweet love, I was coming to your house.

    BIANCA: And I was going to your lodging, Cassio.
What, keep a week away? seven days and nights?

Eight score eight hours? And lovers' absent hours,
More tedious than the dial eight score times?
O weary reckoning!

CASSIO: Pardon me, Bianca:
I have this while with leaden thoughts been press'd;
But I shall, in a more continuate time,
Strike off this score of absence. Sweet Bianca,

                    [*Giving her Desdemona's handkerchief.*
Take me this work out.

BIANCA: O Cassio, whence came this?
This is some token from a newer friend:
To the felt absence now I feel a cause:
Is 't come to this? Well, well.

CASSIO: Go to, woman!
Throw your vile guesses in the devil's teeth,
From whence you have them. You are jealous now
That this is from some mistress, some remembrance:
No, in good troth, Bianca.

BIANCA: Why, whose is it?

CASSIO: I know not, sweet: I found it in my chamber.
I like the work well: ere it be demanded—
As like enough it will—I 'ld have it copied:
Take it, and do 't; and leave me for this time.

BIANCA: Leave you! wherefore?

CASSIO: I do attend here on the general;
And think it no addition, nor my wish,
To have him see me woman 'd.

BIANCA: Why, I pray you?

CASSIO: Not that I love you not.

BIANCA: But that you do not love me.
I pray you, bring me on the way a little,
And say if I shall see you soon at night.

CASSIO: 'Tis but a little way that I can bring you;
For I attend here: but I 'll see you soon.

BIANCA: 'Tis very good; I must be circumstanced.   [*Exeunt.*

ACT IV.

SCENE I. *Cyprus. Before the castle.*
Enter Othello and Iago.

IAGO: Will you think so?

OTHELLO: Think so, Iago!

IAGO: What,
To kiss in private?

OTHELLO: An unauthorized kiss.

IAGO: Or to be naked with her friend in bed
An hour or more, not meaning any harm?

OTHELLO: Naked in bed, Iago, and not mean harm!
It is hypocrisy against the devil:
They that mean virtuously, and yet do so,
The devil their virtue tempts, and they tempt heaven.

IAGO: So they do nothing, 'tis a venial slip:
But if I give my wife a handkerchief,—

OTHELLO: What then?

IAGO: Why, then, 'tis hers, my lord; and, being hers,
She may, I think, bestow 't on any man.

OTHELLO: She is protectress of her honour too:
May she give that?

IAGO: Her honour is an essence that 's not seen;
They have it very oft that have it not:
But, for the handkerchief,—

OTHELLO: By heaven, I would most gladly have forgot it.
Thou said'st—O, it comes o'er my memory,
As doth the raven o'er the infected house,
Boding to all—he had my handkerchief.

IAGO: Ay, what of that?

OTHELLO: That 's not so good now.

IAGO: What,
If I had said I had seen him do you wrong?
Or heard him say,—as knaves be such abroad,

Who having, by their own importunate suit,
Or voluntary dotage of some mistress,
Convinced or supplied them, cannot choose
But they must blab—

OTHELLO: Hath he said any thing?

IAGO: He hath, my lord; but be you well assured,
No more than he 'll unswear.

OTHELLO: What hath he said?

IAGO: 'Faith, that he did—I know not what he did.

OTHELLO: What? what?

IAGO: Lie—

OTHELLO: With her?

IAGO: With her, on her; what you will.

OTHELLO: Lie with her! lie on her! We say lie on her, when
they belie her. Lie with her! that 's fulsome.—Handkerchief—con-
fessions—handkerchief!—To confess, and be hanged for his
labour;—first, to be hanged, and then to confess.—I tremble at it.
Nature would not invest herself in such shadowing passion without some instruction. It is not words that shake me thus. Pish!
Noses, ears, and lips—Is 't possible?—Confess—handkerchief!—
O devil!   [Falls in a trance.

IAGO: Work on,
My medicine, work! Thus credulous fools are caught;
And many worthy and chaste dames even thus,
All guiltless, meet reproach. What, ho! my lord!
My lord, I say! Othello!

Enter Cassio.

                    How now, Cassio!

CASSIO: What 's the matter?

IAGO: My lord is fall'n into an epilepsy:
This is his second fit; he had one yesterday.

CASSIO: Rub him about the temples.

IAGO: No, forbear;
The lethargy must have his quiet course:

If not, he foams at mouth and by and by
Breaks out to savage madness. Look, he stirs:
Do you withdraw yourself a little while,
He will recover straight: when he is gone,
I would on great occasion speak with you.   [*Exit Cassio.*

How is it, general? have you not hurt your head?

    OTHELLO: Dost thou mock me?

    IAGO: I mock you! no, by heaven.
Would you would bear your fortune like a man!

    OTHELLO: A horned man 's a monster and a beast.

    IAGO: There 's many a beast then in a populous city,
And many a civil monster.

    OTHELLO: Did he confess it?

    IAGO: Good sir, be a man;
Think every bearded fellow that 's but yoked
May draw with you: there 's millions now alive
That nightly lie in those unproper beds
Which they dare swear peculiar: your case is better.
O, 'tis the spite of hell, the fiend's arch-mock,
To lip a wanton in a secure couch,
And to suppose her chaste! No, let me know;
And knowing what I am, I know what she shall be.

    OTHELLO: O, thou art wise; 'tis certain.

    IAGO: Stand you awhile apart;
Confine yourself but in a patient list.
Whilst you were here o'erwhelmed with your grief—
A passion most unsuiting such a man—
Cassio came hither: I shifted him away,
And laid good 'scuse upon your ecstasy,
Bade him anon return and here speak with me;
The which he promised. Do but encave yourself,
And mark the fleers, the gibes, and notable scorns,
That dwell in every region of his face;
For I will make him tell the tale anew,
Where, how, how oft, how long ago, and when

He hath, and is again to cope your wife:
I say, but mark his gesture. Marry, patience;
Or I shall say you are all in all in spleen,
And nothing of a man.

OTHELLO: Dost thou hear, Iago?
I will be found most cunning in my patience;
But—dost thou hear?—most bloody.

IAGO: That 's not amiss;
But yet keep time in all. Will you withdraw?   [*Othello retires.*
Now will I question Cassio of Bianca,
A housewife that by selling her desires
Buys herself bread and clothes: it is a creature
That dotes on Cassio; as 'tis the strumpet's plague
To beguile many and be beguiled by one:
He, when he hears of her, cannot refrain
From the excess of laughter. Here he comes:

Re-enter Cassio.

As he shall smile, Othello shall go mad;
And his unbookish jealousy must construe
Poor Cassio's smiles, gestures and light behaviour,
Quite in the wrong. How do you now, lieutenant?

CASSIO: The worser that you give me the addition
Whose want even kills me.

IAGO: Ply Desdemona well, and you are sure on 't.
[*Speaking lower*] Now, if this suit lay in Bianca's power,
How quickly should you speed!

CASSIO: Alas, poor caitiff!

OTHELLO: Look, how he laughs already!

IAGO: I never knew woman love man so.

CASSIO: Alas, poor rogue! I think, i' faith, she loves me.

OTHELLO: Now he denies it faintly, and laughs it out.

IAGO: Do you hear, Cassio?

OTHELLO: Now he importunes him
To tell it o'er: go to; well said, well said.

IAGO: She gives it out that you shall marry her:
Do you intend it?

CASSIO: Ha, ha, ha!

OTHELLO: Do you triumph, Roman? do you triumph?

CASSIO: I marry her! what? a customer! Prithee, bear some charity to my wit; do not think it so unwholesome. Ha, ha, ha!

OTHELLO: So, so, so, so: they laugh that win.

IAGO: 'Faith, the cry goes that you shall marry her:

CASSIO: Prithee, say true.

IAGO: I am a very villain else.

OTHELLO: Have you scored me? Well.

CASSIO: This is the monkey's own giving out: she is persuaded I will marry her, out of her own love and flattery, not out of my promise.

OTHELLO: Iago beckons me; now he begins the story.

CASSIO: She was here even now; she haunts me in every place. I was the other day talking on the sea-bank with certain Venetians; and thither comes the bauble, and, by this hand, she falls me thus about my neck—

OTHELLO: Crying 'O dear Cassio!' as it were: his gesture imports it.

CASSIO: So hangs, and lolls, and weeps upon me; so hales, and pulls me: ha, ha, ha!

OTHELLO: Now he tells how she plucked him to my chamber. O, I see that nose of yours, but not that dog I shall throw it to.

CASSIO: Well, I must leave her company.

IAGO: Before me! look, where she comes.

CASSIO: 'Tis such another fitchew! marry, a perfumed one.

Enter Bianca.

What do you mean by this haunting of me?

BIANCA: Let the devil and his dam haunt you! What did you mean by that same handkerchief you gave me even now? I was a fine fool to take it. I must take out the work?—A likely piece of work, that you should find it in your chamber, and not know who left it there? This is some minx's token, and I must take out the work? There: give it your hobby-horse: wheresoever you had it, I 'll take out no work on 't.

CASSIO: How now, my sweet Bianca! how now! how now!

OTHELLO: By heaven, that should be my handkerchief!

BIANCA: An you 'll come to supper to-night, you may; and you will not, come when you are next prepared for.   [*Exit.*

IAGO: After her, after her.

CASSIO: 'Faith, I must; she 'll rail in the street else.

IAGO: Will you sup there?

CASSIO: 'Faith, I intend so.

IAGO: Well, I may chance to see you; for I would very fain speak with you.

CASSIO: Prithee, come; will you?

IAGO: Go to; say no more.   [*Exit Cassio.*

OTHELLO: [*Advancing*] How shall I murder him, Iago?

IAGO: Did you perceive how he laughed at his vice?

OTHELLO: O Iago!

IAGO: And did you see the handkerchief?

OTHELLO: Was that mine?

IAGO: Yours, by this hand: and to see how he prizes the foolish woman your wife! she gave it him, and he hath given it his whore.

OTHELLO: I would have him nine years a-killing. A fine woman! a fair woman! a sweet woman!

IAGO: Nay, you must forget that.

OTHELLO: Ay, let her rot, and perish, and be damned to-night; for she shall not live: no, my heart is turned to stone; I strike it, and it hurts my hand. O, the world hath not a sweeter creature: she might lie by an emperor's side and command him tasks.

IAGO: Nay, that 's not your way.

OTHELLO: Hang her! I do but say what she is: so delicate with her needle: an admirable musician: O! she will sing the savageness out of a bear: of so high and plenteous wit and invention:—

IAGO: She's the worse for all this.

OTHELLO: O, a thousand thousand times: and then, of so gentle a condition!

IAGO: Ay, too gentle.

OTHELLO: Nay, that 's certain: but yet the pity of it, Iago! O Iago, the pity of it, Iago!

IAGO: If you are so fond over her inquity, give her patent to offend; for, if it touch not you, it comes near nobody.

OTHELLO: I will chop her into messes: cuckold me!

IAGO: O, 'tis foul in her.

OTHELLO: With mine officer!

IAGO: That 's fouler.

OTHELLO: Get me some poison, Iago: this night: I 'll not expostulate with her, lest her body and beauty unprovide my mind again: this night, Iago.

IAGO: Do it not with poison, strangle her in her bed, even the bed she hath contaminated.

OTHELLO: Good, good: the justice of it pleases: very good.

IAGO: And for Cassio, let me be his undertaker: you shall hear more by midnight.

OTHELLO: Excellent good. [*A trumpet within.*] What trumpet is that same?

IAGO: Something from Venice, sure. 'Tis Lodovico
Come from the duke: and, see, your wife is with him.

Enter Lodovico, Desdemona, and Attendants.

LODOVICO: Save you, worthy general!

OTHELLO: With all my heart, sir.

LODOVICO: The duke and senators of Venice greet you.
                                    [*Gives him a letter.*

OTHELLO: I kiss the instrument of their pleasures.
                                    [*Opens letter, and reads.*

DESDEMONA: And what 's the news, good cousin Lodovico?

IAGO: I am very glad to see you, signior; Welcome to Cyprus.

LODOVICO: I thank you. How does Lieutenant Cassio?

IAGO: Lives, sir.

DESDEMONA: Cousin, there 's fall'n between him and my lord
An unkind breach: but you shall make all well.

OTHELLO: Are you sure of that?

DESDEMONA: My lord?

OTHELLO: [*Reads*] 'This fail you not to do, as you will—'

LODOVICO: He did not call; he 's busy in the paper.
Is there division 'twixt my lord and Cassio?

DESDEMONA: A most unhappy one: I would do much
To atone them, for the love I bear Cassio.

OTHELLO: Fire and brimstone!

DESDEMONA: My lord?

OTHELLO: Are you wise?

DESDEMONA: What, is he angry?

LODOVICO: May be the letter moved him;
For, as I think, they do command him home,
Deputing Cassio in his government.

DESDEMONA: Trust me, I am glad on 't.

OTHELLO: Indeed!

DESDEMONA: My lord?

OTHELLO: I am glad to see you mad.

DESDEMONA: Why, sweet Othello,—

OTHELLO: [*Striking her*] Devil!

DESDEMONA: I have not deserved this.

LODOVICO: My lord, this would not be believed in Venice,
Though I should swear I saw 't: 'tis very much:
Make her amends; she weeps.

OTHELLO: O devil, devil!
If that the earth could teem with woman's tears,
Each drop she falls would prove a crocodile.
Out of my sight!

DESDEMONA: I will not stay to offend you.   [*Going.*

LODOVICO: Truly, an obedient lady:
I do beseech your lordship, call her back.

OTHELLO: Mistress!

DESDEMONA: My lord?

OTHELLO: What would you with her, sir?

LODOVICO: Who, I, my lord?

OTHELLO: Ay; you did wish that I would make her turn:
Sir, she can turn, and turn, and yet go on,
And turn again; and she can weep, sir, weep;
And she 's obedient, as you say, obedient,
Very obedient. Proceed you in your tears.
Concerning this, sir,—O well-painted passion!—
I am commanded home. Get you away:
I 'll send for you anon. Sir, I obey the mandate,
And will return to Venice. Hence, avaunt!   [Exit Desdemona.
Cassio shall have my place. And, sir, to-night,
I do entreat that we may sup together:
You are welcome, sir, to Cyprus.—Goats and monkeys!   [Exit.

LODOVICO: Is this the noble Moor whom our full senate
Call all in all sufficient? Is this the nature
Whom passion could not shake? whose solid virtue
The shot of accident, nor dart of chance,
Could neither graze nor pierce?

IAGO: He is much changed.

LODOVICO: Are his wits safe? is he not light of brain?

IAGO: He 's that he is: I may not breathe my censure
What he might be: if what he might he is not,
I would to heaven he were!

LODOVICO: What, strike his wife!

IAGO: 'Faith, that was not so well; yet would I knew
That stroke would prove the worst!

LODOVICO: Is it his use?
Or did the letters work upon his blood,
And new-create this fault?

IAGO: Alas, alas!
It is not honesty in me to speak
What I have seen and known. You shall observe him,
And his own courses will denote him so

That I may save my speech: do but go after,
And mark how he continues.

    LODOVICO: I am sorry that I am deceived in him.   [*Exeunt.*

SCENE II. *A room in the castle.*
Enter Othello and Emilia.

    OTHELLO: You have seen nothing then?
    EMILIA: Nor ever heard, nor ever did suspect.
    OTHELLO: Yes, you have seen Cassio and she together.
    EMILIA: But then I saw no harm, and then I heard
Each syllable that breath made up between them.
    OTHELLO: What, did they never whisper?
    EMILIA: Never, my lord.
    OTHELLO: Nor send you out o' the way?
    EMILIA: Never.
    OTHELLO: To fetch her fan, her gloves, her mask, nor nothing?
    EMILIA: Never, my lord.
    OTHELLO: That 's strange.
    EMILIA: I durst, my lord, to wager she is honest,
Lay down my soul at stake: if you think other,
Remove your thought; it doth abuse your bosom.
If any wretch have put this in your head,
Let heaven requite it with the serpent's curse!
For, if she be not honest, chaste, and true.
There 's no man happy; the purest of their wives
Is foul as slander.
    OTHELLO: Bid her come hither: go.   [*Exit Emilia.*
She says enough; yet she 's a simple bawd
That cannot say as much. This is a subtle whore,
A closet lock and key of villanous secrets:
And yet she 'll kneel and pray; I have seen her do 't.

Enter Desdemona with Emilia.

    DESDEMONA: My lord, what is your will?

OTHELLO: Pray, chuck, come hither.
DESDEMONA: What is your pleasure?
OTHELLO: Let me see your eyes;
Look in my face.
DESDEMONA: What horrible fancy 's this?
OTHELLO: [*To Emilia*] Some of your function, mistress;
Leave procreants alone and shut the door;
Cough, or cry 'hem,' if any body come:
Your mystery, your mystery: nay, dispatch.   [*Exit Emilia.*
DESDEMONA: Upon my knees, what doth your speech import?
I understand a fury in your words,
But not the words.
OTHELLO: Why, what art thou?
DESDEMONA: Your wife, my lord: your true
And loyal wife.
OTHELLO: Come, swear it, damn thyself;
Lest, being like one of heaven, the devils themselves
Should fear to seize thee: therefore be double damn'd:
Swear thou art honest.
DESDEMONA: Heaven doth truly know it.
OTHELLO: Heaven truly knows that thou art false as hell.
DESDEMONA: To whom, my lord? with whom? how am I false?
OTHELLO: O Desdemona! away! away! away!
DESDEMONA: Alas the heavy day! Why do you weep?
Am I the motive of these tears, my lord?
If haply you my father do suspect
An instrument of this your calling back,
Lay not your blame on me: if you have lost him,
Why, I have lost him too.
OTHELLO: Had it pleased heaven
To try me with affliction; had they rain'd
All kinds of sores and shames on my bare head,
Steep'd me in poverty to the very lips,
Given to captivity me and my utmost hopes,
I should have found in some place of my soul

A drop of patience: but, alas, to make me
A fixed figure for the time of scorn
To point his slow unmoving finger at!
Yet could I bear that too; well, very well:
But there, where I have garner'd up my heart,
Where either I must live, or bear no life;
The fountain from the which my current runs,
Or else dries up; to be discarded thence!
Or keep it as a cistern for foul toads
To knot and gender in! Turn thy complexion there,
Patience, thou young and rose-lipp'd cherubin,—
Ay, there, look grim as hell!
    DESDEMONA: I hope my noble lord esteems me honest.
    OTHELLO: O, ay; as summer flies are in the shambles,
That quicken even with blowing. O thou weed,
Who art so lovely fair and smell'st so sweet
That the sense aches at thee, would thou hadst ne'er been born!
    DESDEMONA: Alas, what ignorant sin have I committed?
    OTHELLO: Was this fair paper, this most goodly book,
Made to write 'whore' upon? What committed!
Committed! O thou public commoner!
I should make very forges of my cheeks,
That would to cinders burn up modesty,
Did I but speak thy deeds. What committed!
Heaven stops the nose at it and the moon winks,
The bawdy wind that kisses all it meets
Is hush'd within the hollow mine of earth.
And will not hear it. What committed!
Impudent strumpet!
    DESDEMONA: By heaven, you do me wrong.
    OTHELLO: Are not you a strumpet?
    DESDEMONA: No, as I am a Christian:
If to preserve this vessel for my lord
From any other foul unlawful touch
Be not to be a strumpet, I am none.

OTHELLO: What, not a whore?

DESDEMONA: No, as I shall be saved.

OTHELLO: Is 't possible?

DESDEMONA: O, heaven forgive us!

OTHELLO: I cry you mercy, then:
I took you for that cunning whore of Venice
That married with Othello. [*Raising his voice*] You, mistress,
That have the office opposite to Saint Peter,
And keep the gate of hell!

Re-enter Emilia.

                              You, you, ay, you!
We have done our course; there 's money for your pains:
I pray you, turn the key and keep our counsel.   [*Exit.*

    EMILIA: Alas, what does this gentleman conceive?
How do you, madam? how do you, my good lady?

    DESDEMONA: 'Faith, half asleep.

    EMILIA: Good madam, what 's the matter with my lord?

    DESDEMONA: With who?

    EMILIA: Why, with my lord, madam.

    DESDEMONA: Who is thy lord?

    EMILIA: He that is yours, sweet lady.

    DESDEMONA: I have none: do not talk to me, Emilia;
I cannot weep; nor answer have I none,
But what should go by water. Prithee, to-night
Lay on my bed my wedding sheets: remember;
And call thy husband hither.

    EMILIA: Here 's a change indeed!   [*Exit.*

    DESDEMONA: 'Tis meet I should be used so, very meet.
How have I been behaved, that he might stick
The small'st opinion on my least misuse?

Re-enter Emilia with Iago.

    IAGO: What is your pleasure, madam? How is 't with you?

    DESDEMONA: I cannot tell. Those that do teach young babes

Do it with gentle means and easy tasks:
He might have chid me so; for, in good faith,
I am a child to chiding.

IAGO: What 's the matter, lady?

EMILIA: Alas, Iago, my lord hath so bewhored her,
Thrown such despite and heavy terms upon her,
As true hearts cannot bear.

DESDEMONA: Am I that name, Iago?

IAGO: What name, fair lady?

DESDEMONA: Such as she says my lord did say I was.

EMILIA: He call'd her whore: a beggar in his drink
Could not have laid such terms upon his callet.

IAGO: Why did he so?

DESDEMONA: I do not know; I am sure I am none such.

IAGO: Do not weep, do not weep. Alas the day!

EMILIA: Hath she forsook so many noble matches,
Her father, and her country and her friends,
To be call'd whore? would it not make one weep?

DESDEMONA: It is my wretched fortune.

IAGO: Beshrew him for 't!
How comes this trick upon him?

DESDEMONA: Nay, heaven doth know.

EMILIA: I will be hang'd, if some eternal villain,
Some busy and insinuating rogue,
Some cogging, cozening slave, to get some office,
Have not devised this slander; I 'll be hang'd else.

IAGO: Fie, there is no such man; it is impossible.

DESDEMONA: If any such there be, heaven pardon him!

EMILIA: A halter pardon him! and hell gnaw his bones!
Why should he call her whore? who keeps her company?
What place? what time? what form? what likelihood?
The Moor 's abused by some most villanous knave,
Some base notorious knave, some scurvy fellow.
O heaven, that such companions thou 'ldst unfold,
And put in every honest hand a whip

To lash the rascals naked through the world
Even from the east to the west!

IAGO: Speak within door.

EMILIA: O, fie upon them! Some such squire he was
That turn'd your wit the seamy side without,
And made you to suspect me with the Moor.

IAGO: You are a fool; go to.

DESDEMONA: O good Iago,
What shall I do to win my lord again?
Good friend, go to him; for, by this light of heaven,
I know not how I lost him. Here I kneel:
If e'er my will did trespass 'gainst his love,
Either in discourse of thought or actual deed,
Or that mine eyes, mine ears, or any sense,
Delighted them in any other form;
Or that I do not yet, and ever did,
And ever will—though he do shake me off
To beggarly divorcement—love him dearly,
Comfort forswear me! Unkindness may do much;
And his unkindness may defeat my life,
But never taint my love. I cannot say 'whore:'
It doth abhor me now I speak the word;
To do the act that might the addition earn
Not the world's mass of vanity could make me.

IAGO: I pray you, be content; 'tis but his humour:
The business of the state does him offence,
And he does chide with you.

DESDEMONA: If 'twere no other,—

IAGO: 'Tis but so, I warrant.

                                        [*Trumpets within.*

Hark, how these instruments summon to supper!
The messengers of Venice stay the meat:
Go in, and weep not; all things shall be well.

                          [*Exeunt Desdemona and Emilia.*

Enter Roderigo.

How now, Roderigo!

RODERIGO: I do not find that thou dealest justly with me.

IAGO: What in the contrary?

RODERIGO: Every day thou daffest me with some device, Iago; and rather, as it seems to me now, keepest from me all conveniency than suppliest me with the least advantage of hope. I will indeed no longer endure it, nor am I yet persuaded to put up in peace what already I have foolishly suffered.

IAGO: Will you hear me, Roderigo?

RODERIGO: 'Faith, I have heard too much, for your words and performances are no kin together.

IAGO: You charge me most unjustly.

RODERIGO: With nought but truth. I have wasted myself out of my means. The jewels you have had from me to deliver to Desdemona would half have corrupted a votarist: you have told me she hath received them and returned me expectations and comforts of sudden respect and acquaintance, but I find none.

IAGO: Well; go to; very well.

RODERIGO: Very well! go to! I cannot go to man; nor 'tis not very well: nay, I think it is scurvy, and begin to find myself fopped in it.

IAGO: Very well.

RODERIGO: I tell you 'tis not very well. I will make myself known to Desdemona: if she will return me my jewels, I will give over my suit and repent my unlawful solicitation; if not, assure yourself I will seek satisfaction of you.

IAGO: You have said now.

RODERIGO: Ay, and said nothing but what I protest intendment of doing.

IAGO: Why, now I see there 's mettle in thee, and even from this instant do build on thee a better opinion than ever before. Give me thy hand, Roderigo: thou hast taken against me a most just exception; but yet, I protest, I have dealt most directly in thy affair.

RODERIGO: It hath not appeared.

IAGO: I grant indeed it hath not appeared, and your suspicion is not without wit and judgement. But, Roderigo, if thou hast that in thee indeed, which I have greater reason to believe now than ever, I mean purpose, courage and valour, this night show it: if thou the next night following enjoy not Desdemona, take me from this world with treachery and devise engines for my life.

RODERIGO: Well, what is it? is it within reason and compass?

IAGO: Sir, there is especial commission come from Venice to depute Cassio in Othello's place.

RODERIGO: Is that true? why, then Othello and Desdemona return again to Venice.

IAGO: O, no; he goes into Mauritania and takes away with him the fair Desdemona; unless his abode be lingered here by some accident: wherein none can be so determinate as the removing of Cassio.

RODERIGO: How do you mean, removing of him?

IAGO: Why, by making him uncapable of Othello's place; knocking out his brains.

RODERIGO: And that you would have me to do?

IAGO: Ay, if you dare do yourself a profit and a right. He sups to-night with a harlotry, and thither will I go to him: he knows not yet of his honourable fortune. If you will watch his going thence, which I will fashion to fall out between twelve and one, you may take him at your pleasure: I will be near to second your attempt, and he shall fall between us. Come, stand not amazed at it, but go along with me; I will show you such a necessity in his death that you shall think yourself bound to put it on him. It is now high supper-time, and the night grows to waste: about it.

RODERIGO: I will hear further reason for this.

IAGO: And you shall be satisfied.   [*Exeunt.*

SCENE III. *Another room in the castle.*
Enter Othello, Lodovico, Desdemona, Emilia, and Attendants.

LODOVICO: I do beseech you, sir, trouble yourself no further.
OTHELLO: O, pardon me; 'twill do me good to walk.
LODOVICO: Madam, good night; I humbly thank your ladyship.
DESDEMONA: Your honour is most welcome.
OTHELLO: Will you walk, sir?
O,—Desdemona,—
DESDEMONA: My lord?
OTHELLO: Get you to bed on the instant; I will be returned
forthwith: dismiss your attendant there: look it be done.
DESDEMONA: I will, my lord.
                          [*Exeunt Othello, Lodovico, and Attendants.*
EMILIA: How goes it now? he looks gentler than he did.
DESDEMONA: He says he will return incontinent:
He hath commanded me to go to bed,
And bade me to dismiss you.
EMILIA: Dismiss me!
DESDEMONA: It was his bidding; therefore, good Emilia,
Give me my nightly wearing, and adieu:
We must not now displease him.
EMILIA: I would you had never seen him!
DESDEMONA: So would not I: my love doth so approve him,
That even his stubbornness, his checks, his frowns,—
Prithee, unpin me,—have grace and favour in them.
EMILIA: I have laid those sheets you bade me on the bed.
DESDEMONA: All 's one. Good faith, how foolish are our minds!
If I do die before thee, prithee, shroud me
In one of those same sheets.
EMILIA: Come, come, you talk.
DESDEMONA: My mother had a maid call'd Barbara:
She was in love, and he she loved proved mad
And did forsake her: she had a song of 'willow:'
An old thing 'twas, but it express'd her fortune,

And she died singing it: that song to-night
Will not go from my mind; I have much to do,
But to go hang my head all at one side,
And sing it like poor Barbara. Prithee, dispatch.

EMILIA: Shall I go fetch your night-gown?

DESDEMONA: No, unpin me here.
This Lodovico is a proper man.

EMILIA: A very handsome man.

DESDEMONA: He speaks well.

EMILIA: I know a lady in Venice would have walked barefoot to
Palestine for a touch of his nether lip.

DESDEMONA: [*Singing*] The poor soul sat sighing by a sycamore
    tree,
    Sing all a green willow;
Her hand on her bosom, her head on her knee,
    Sing willow, willow, willow:
The fresh streams ran by her, and murmur'd her moans;
    Sing willow, willow, willow;
Her salt tears fell from her, and soften'd the stones;—
Lay by these:—
[*Singing*] Sing willow, willow, willow;
Prithee, hie thee; he 'll come anon:—
[*Singing*] Sing all a green willow must be my garland.
    Let nobody blame him; his scorn I approve,—
Nay, that 's not next.—Hark! who is 't that knocks?

EMILIA: It 's the wind.

DESDEMONA: [*Singing*] I call'd my love false love; but what said
    he then?
    Sing willow, willow, willow:
If I court moe women, you 'll couch with moe men.—
So, get thee gone; good night. Mine eyes do itch;
Doth that bode weeping?

EMILIA: 'Tis neither here nor there.

DESDEMONA: I have heard it said so. O, these men, these men!
Dost thou in conscience think,—tell me, Emilia,—

That there be women do abuse their husbands
In such gross kind?

EMILIA: There be some such, no question.

DESDEMONA: Wouldst thou do such a deed for all the world?

EMILIA: Why, would not you?

DESDEMONA: No, by this heavenly light!

EMILIA: Nor I neither by this heavenly light;
I might do 't as well i' the dark.

DESDEMONA: Wouldst thou do such a deed for all the world?

EMILIA: The world 's a huge thing: it is a great price
For a small vice.

DESDEMONA: In troth, I think thou wouldst not.

EMILIA: In troth, I think I should; and undo 't when I had done. Marry, I would not do such a thing for a joint-ring, nor for measures of lawn, nor for gowns, petticoats, nor caps, nor any petty exhibition; but, for the whole world,—why, who would not make her husband a cuckold to make him a monarch? I should venture purgatory for 't.

DESDEMONA: Beshrew me, if I would do such a wrong
For the whole world.

EMILIA: Why, the wrong is but a wrong i' the world; and having the world for your labour, 'tis a wrong in your own world, and you might quickly make it right.

DESDEMONA: I do not think there is any such woman.

EMILIA: Yes, a dozen; and as many to the vantage as would store the world they played for.
But I do think it is their husbands' faults
If wives do fall: say that they slack their duties,
And pour our treasures into foreign laps,
Or else break out in peevish jealousies,
Throwing restraint upon us; or say they strike us,
Or scant our former having in despite;
Why, we have galls, and though we have some grace,
Yet have we some revenge. Let husbands know
Their wives have sense like them: they see and smell

And have their palates both for sweet and sour,
As husbands have. What is it that they do
When they change us for others? Is it sport?
I think it is: and doth affection breed it?
I think it doth: is 't frailty that thus errs?
It is so too: and have not we affections,
Desires for sport, and frailty, as men have?
Then let them use us well: else let them know,
The ills we do, their ills instruct us so.

   DESDEMONA: Good night, good night: heaven me such uses
     send,
Not to pick bad from bad, but by bad mend!   [*Exeunt.*

ACT V.

SCENE I. *Cyprus. A street.*
Enter Iago and Roderigo.

   IAGO: Here, stand behind this bulk; straight will he come:
Wear thy good rapier bare, and put it home:
Quick, quick; fear nothing; I 'll be at thy elbow:
It makes us, or it mars us; think on that,
And fix most firm thy resolution.

   RODERIGO: Be near at hand; I may miscarry in 't.

   IAGO: Here, at thy hand: be bold, and take thy stand.   [*Retires.*

   RODERIGO: I have no great devotion to the deed;
And yet he hath given me satisfying reasons:
'Tis but a man gone. Forth, my sword: he dies.

   IAGO: I have rubb'd this young quat almost to the sense,
And he grows angry. Now, whether he kill Cassio,
Or Cassio him, or each do kill the other,
Every way makes my gain: live Roderigo,
He calls me to a restitution large
Of gold and jewels that I bobb'd from him,

As gifts to Desdemona;
It must not be: if Cassio do remain,
He hath a daily beauty in his life
That makes me ugly; and, besides, the Moor
May unfold me to him; there stand I in much peril;
No, he must die. But so: I hear him coming.

Enter Cassio.

RODERIGO: I know his gait, 'tis he.—Villain, thou diest!
                        [Makes a pass at Cassio.
CASSIO: That thrust had been mine enemy indeed,
But that my coat is better than thou know'st:
I will make proof of thine.   *[Draws, and wounds Roderigo.*
RODERIGO: O, I am slain!
       [Iago from behind wounds Cassio in the leg, and exit.
CASSIO: I am maim'd for ever. Help, ho! murder! murder!
                             [Falls.

Enter Othello.

OTHELLO: The voice of Cassio: Iago keeps his word.
RODERIGO: O, villain that I am!
OTHELLO: It is even so.
CASSIO: O, help, ho! light! a surgeon!
OTHELLO: 'Tis he:—O brave Iago, honest and just,
That hast such noble sense of thy friend's wrong!
Thou teachest me. Minion, your dear lies dead,
And your unblest fate hies: strumpet, I come.
Forth of my heart those charms, thine eyes, are blotted;
Thy bed, lust-stain'd, shall with lust's blood be spotted.   *[Exit.*

Enter Lodovico and Gratiano.

CASSIO: What, ho! no watch? no passage? murder! murder!
GRATIANO: 'Tis some mischance; the cry is very direful.
CASSIO: O, help!
LODOVICO: Hark!

RODERIGO: O wretched villain!

LODOVICO: Two or three groan: it is a heavy night:
These may be counterfeits: let 's think 't unsafe
To come in to the cry without more help.

RODERIGO: Nobody come? then shall I bleed to death.

LODOVICO: Hark!

Re-enter Iago, with a light.

GRATIANO: Here 's one comes in his shirt, with light and
    weapons.

IAGO: Who 's there? whose noise is this that cries on murder?

LODOVICO: We do not know.

IAGO: Did not you hear a cry?

CASSIO: Here, here! for heaven's sake, help me!

IAGO: What 's the matter?

GRATIANO: This is Othello's ancient, as I take it.

LODOVICO: The same indeed; a very valiant fellow.

IAGO: What are you here that cry so grievously?

CASSIO: Iago? O, I am spoil'd, undone by villains!
Give me some help.

IAGO: O me, lieutenant! what villains have done this?

CASSIO: I think that one of them is hereabout,
And cannot make away.

IAGO: O treacherous villains!
What are you there? come in, and give some help.
                          [*To Lodovico and Gratiano.*

RODERIGO: O, help me here!

CASSIO: That 's one of them.

IAGO: O murderous slave! O villain!
                                [*Stabs Roderigo.*

RODERIGO: O damn'd Iago! O inhuman dog!

IAGO: Kill men i' the dark!—Where be these bloody thieves?—
How silent is this town!—Ho! murder! murder!—
What may you be? are you of good or evil?

LODOVICO: As you shall prove us, praise us.

IAGO: Signior Lodovico?

LODOVICO: He, sir.

IAGO: I cry you mercy. Here 's Cassio hurt by villains.

GRATIANO: Cassio!

IAGO: How is 't, brother!

CASSIO: My leg is cut in two.

IAGO: Marry, heaven forbid!
Light, gentleman: I 'll bind it with my shirt.

Enter Bianca.

BIANCA: What is the matter, ho! who is 't that cried?

IAGO: Who is 't that cried!

BIANCA: O my dear Cassio! my sweet Cassio!
O Cassio, Cassio, Cassio!

IAGO: O notable strumpet! Cassio, may you suspect
Who they should be that have thus mangled you?

CASSIO: No.

GRATIANO: I am sorry to find you thus: I have been to seek you.

IAGO: Lend me a garter. So. O, for a chair,
To bear him easily hence!

BIANCA: Alas, he faints! O Cassio, Cassio, Cassio!

IAGO: Gentlemen all, I do suspect this trash
To be a party in this injury.
Patience awhile, good Cassio. Come, come:
Lend me a light. Know we this face or no?
Alas, my friend and my dear countryman
Roderigo! no:—yes, sure:—O heaven! Roderigo.

GRATIANO: What, of Venice?

IAGO: Even he, sir: did you know him?

GRATIANO: Know him! ay.

IAGO: Signior Gratiano? I cry you gentle pardon;
These bloody accidents must excuse my manners,
That so neglected you.

GRATIANO: I am glad to see you.

IAGO: How do you, Cassio? O, a chair, a chair!

GRATIANO: Roderigo!

IAGO: He, he, 'tis he. [*A chair brought in.*] O, that's well said; the
    chair.
Some good man bear him carefully from hence;
I 'll fetch the general's surgeon. [*To Bianca*] For you, mistress,
Save you your labour. He that lies slain here, Cassio,
Was my dear friend: what malice was between you?

CASSIO: None in the world; nor do I know the man.

IAGO: [*To Bianca*] What, look you pale?
O, bear him out o' the air.   [*Cassio and Roderigo are borne off.*
Stay you, good gentlemen. Look you pale, mistress?
Do you perceive the gastness of her eye?
Nay, if you stare, we shall hear more anon.
Behold her well; I pray you, look upon her:
Do you see, gentlemen? nay, guiltiness will speak,
Though tongues were out of use.

Enter Emilia.

EMILIA: 'Las, what 's the matter? what 's the matter, husband?

IAGO: Cassio hath here been set on in the dark
By Roderigo and fellows that are scaped:
He 's almost slain, and Roderigo dead.

EMILIA: Alas, good gentlemen! alas, good Cassio!

IAGO: This is the fruit of whoring. Prithee, Emilia,
Go know of Cassio where he supp'd to-night.
[*To Bianca*] What, do you shake at that?

BIANCA: He supp'd at my house; but I therefore shake not.

IAGO: O, did he so? I charge you, go with me.

EMILIA: Fie, fie upon thee, strumpet!

BIANCA: I am no strumpet; but of life as honest
As you that thus abuse me.

EMILIA: As I! foh! fie upon thee!

IAGO: Kind gentlemen, let 's go see poor Cassio dress'd.
Come, mistress, you must tell 's another tale.
Emilia, run you to the citadel.

And tell my lord and lady what hath happ'd.
Will you go on? I pray. [*Aside*] This is the night
That either makes me or fordoes me quite.   [*Exeunt.*

SCENE II. *A bedchamber in the castle:*
Desdemona in bed asleep; a light burning.
Enter Othello.

OTHELLO: It is the cause, it is the cause, my soul,—
Let me not name it to you, you chaste stars!—
It is the cause. Yet I 'll not shed her blood:
Nor scar that whiter skin of her than snow,
And smooth as monumental alabaster.
Yet she must die, else she 'll betray more men.
Put out the light, and then put out the light:
If I quench thee, thou flaming minister,
I can again thy former light restore,
Should I repent me: but once put out thy light,
Thou cunning'st pattern of excelling nature,
I know not where is that Promethean heat
That can thy light relume. When I have pluck'd the rose,
I cannot give it vital growth again,
It must needs wither: I 'll smell it on the tree.   [*Kissing her.*
Ah, balmy breath, that doth almost persuade
Justice to break her sword! One more, one more.
Be thus when thou art dead, and I will kill thee,
And love thee after. One more, and this the last:
So sweet was ne'er so fatal. I must weep,
But they are cruel tears: this sorrow 's heavenly;
It strikes where it doth love. She wakes.
DESDEMONA: Who 's there? Othello?
OTHELLO: Ay, Desdemona.
DESDEMONA: Will you come to bed, my lord?
OTHELLO: Have you pray'd to-night, Desdemona?
DESDEMONA: Ay, my lord.

OTHELLO: If you bethink yourself of any crime
Unreconciled as yet to heaven and grace,
Solicit for it straight.

DESDEMONA: Alas, my lord, what do you mean by that?

OTHELLO: Well, do it, and be brief; I will walk by:
I would not kill thy unprepared spirit;
No; heaven forfend! I would not kill thy soul.

DESDEMONA: Talk you of killing?

OTHELLO: Ay, I do.

DESDEMONA: Then heaven
Have mercy on me!

OTHELLO: Amen, with all my heart!

DESDEMONA: If you say so, I hope you will not kill me.

OTHELLO: Hum!

DESDEMONA: And yet I fear you; for you are fatal then
When your eyes roll so: why I should fear I know not,
Since guiltiness I know not; but yet I feel I fear.

OTHELLO: Think on thy sins.

DESDEMONA: They are loves I bear to you.

OTHELLO: Ay, and for that thou diest.

DESDEMONA: That death's unnatural that kills for loving.
Alas, why gnaw you so your nether lip?
Some bloody passion shakes your very frame:
These are portents: but yet I hope, I hope,
They do not point on me.

OTHELLO: Peace, and be still!

DESDEMONA: I will so. What's the matter?

OTHELLO: That handkerchief which I so loved and gave thee
Thou gavest to Cassio.

DESDEMONA: No, by my life and soul!
Send for the man, and ask him.

OTHELLO: Sweet soul, take heed,
Take heed of perjury; thou art on thy deathbed.

DESDEMONA: Ay, but not yet to die.

OTHELLO: Yes, presently:

Therefore confess thee freely of thy sin;
For to deny each article with oath
Cannot remove nor choke the strong conception
That I do groan withal. Thou art to die.

DESDEMONA: Then Lord have mercy on me!

OTHELLO: I say, amen.

DESDEMONA: And have you mercy too! I never did
Offend you in my life; never loved Cassio
But with such general warranty of heaven
As I might love; I never gave him token.

OTHELLO: By heaven, I saw my handkerchief in 's hand.
O perjured woman! thou dost stone my heart,
And makest me call what I intended to do
A murder, which I thought a sacrifice:
I saw the handkerchief.

DESDEMONA: He found it then;
I never gave it him: send for him hither;
Let him confess a truth.

OTHELLO: He hath confess'd.

DESDEMONA: What, my lord?

OTHELLO: That he hath used thee.

DESDEMONA: How? unlawfully?

OTHELLO: Ay.

DESDEMONA: He will not say so.

OTHELLO: No, his mouth is stopp'd;
Honest Iago hath ta'en order for 't.

DESDEMONA: O! my fear interprets: what, is he dead?

OTHELLO: Had all his hairs been lives, my great revenge
Had stomach for them all.

DESDEMONA: Alas! he is betray'd and I undone.

OTHELLO: Out, strumpet! weep'st thou for him to my face?

DESDEMONA: O, banish me, my lord, but kill me not!

OTHELLO: Down, strumpet!

DESDEMONA: Kill me to-morrow: let me live to-night!

OTHELLO: Nay, if you strive,—

DESDEMONA: But half an hour!

OTHELLO: Being done, there is no pause.

DESDEMONA: But while I say one prayer!

OTHELLO: It is too late.

                                    [*He stifles her.*

EMILIA: [*Within*] My lord, my lord! what, ho! my lord, my
    lord!

OTHELLO: What noise is this? Not dead? not yet quite dead?
I that am cruel am yet merciful;
I would not have thee linger in thy pain:
So, so.

EMILIA: [*Within*] What, ho! my lord, my lord!

OTHELLO: Who 's there?

EMILIA: [*Within*] O, good my lord, I would speak a word with
    you!

OTHELLO: Yes: 'tis Emilia. By and by. She 's dead.
'Tis like she comes to speak of Cassio's death.—
The noise was here. Ha! no more moving?
Still as the grave. Shall she come in? were 't good?—
I think she stirs again:—no. What 's best to do?
If she come in, she 'll sure speak to my wife:
My wife! my wife! what wife? I have no wife.
O, insupportable! O heavy hour!
Methinks it should be now a huge eclipse
Of sun and moon, and that the affrighted globe
Should yawn at alteration.

EMILIA: [*Within*] I do beseech you
That I may speak with you, O, good my lord!

OTHELLO: I had forgot thee: O, come in, Emilia:
Soft; by and by. Let me the curtains draw.
Where art thou?   [*Unlocks the door.*

Enter Emilia.

                What 's the matter with thee now?

EMILIA: O, my good lord, yonder 's foul murders done!

OTHELLO: What, now?

EMILIA: But now, my lord.

OTHELLO: It is the very error of the moon;
She comes more nearer earth than she was wont,
And makes men mad.

EMILIA: Cassio, my lord, hath kill'd a young Venetian
Call'd Roderigo.

OTHELLO: Roderigo kill'd!
And Cassio kill'd!

EMILIA: No, Cassio is not kill'd.

OTHELLO: Not Cassio kill'd! then murder 's out of tune,
And sweet revenge grows harsh.

DESDEMONA: O, falsely, falsely murder'd!

EMILIA: Alas, what cry is that?

OTHELLO: That! what?

EMILIA: Out, and alas! that was my lady's voice.
Help! help, ho! help! O lady, speak again!
Sweet Desdemona! O sweet mistress, speak!

DESDEMONA: A guiltless death I die.

EMILIA: O, who hath done this deed?

DESDEMONA: Nobody; I myself. Farewell:
Commend me to my kind lord: O, farewell!   [*Dies.*

OTHELLO: Why, how should she be murder'd?

EMILIA: Alas, who knows?

OTHELLO: You heard her say herself, it was not I.

EMILIA: She said so: I must needs report the truth.

OTHELLO: She 's, like a liar, gone to burning hell:
'Twas I that kill'd her.

EMILIA: O, the more angel she,
And you the blacker devil!

OTHELLO: She turn'd to folly, and she was a whore.

EMILIA: Thou dost belie her, and thou art a devil.

OTHELLO: She was false as water.

EMILIA: Thou art rash as fire, to say
That she was false: O, she was heavenly true!

OTHELLO: Cassio did top her; ask thy husband else.
O, I were damn'd beneath all depth in hell,
But that I did proceed upon just grounds
To this extremity. Thy husband knew it all.

EMILIA: My husband!

OTHELLO: Thy husband.

EMILIA: That she was false to wedlock?

OTHELLO: Ay, with Cassio. Nay, had she been true,
If heaven would make me such another world
Of one entire and perfect chrysolite,
I 'ld not have sold her for it.

EMILIA: My husband!

OTHELLO: Ay, 'twas he that told me first:
An honest man he is, and hates the slime
That sticks on filthy deeds.

EMILIA: My husband!

OTHELLO: What needs this iteration, woman? I say thy husband.

EMILIA: O mistress, villany hath made mocks with love!
My husband say that she was false!

OTHELLO: He, woman;
I say thy husband: dost understand the word?
My friend, thy husband, honest, honest Iago.

EMILIA: If he say so, may his pernicious soul
Rot half a grain a day! he lies to the heart:
She was too fond of her most filthy bargain.

OTHELLO: Ha!

EMILIA: Do thy worst:
This deed of thine is no more worthy heaven
Than thou wast worthy her.

OTHELLO: Peace, you were best.

EMILIA: Thou hast not half that power to do me harm
As I have to be hurt. O gull! O dolt!
As ignorant as dirt! thou hast done a deed—
I care not for thy sword: I 'll make thee known,
Though I lost twenty lives.—Help! help, ho! help!

The Moor hath kill'd my mistress! Murder! murder!

Enter Montano, Gratiano, Iago, and others.

MONTANO: What is the matter? How now, general!

EMILIA: O, are you come, Iago? you have done well,
That men must lay their murders on your neck.

GRATIANO: What is the matter?

EMILIA: Disprove this villain, if thou be'st a man:
He says thou told'st him that his wife was false:
I know thou didst not, thou 'rt not such a villain:
Speak, for my heart is full.

IAGO: I told him what I thought, and told no more
Than what he found himself was apt and true.

EMILIA: But did you ever tell him she was false?

IAGO: I did.

EMILIA: You told a lie; an odious, damned lie;
Upon my soul, a lie, a wicked lie.
She false with Cassio!—did you say with Cassio?

IAGO: With Cassio, mistress. Go to, charm your tongue.

EMILIA: I will not charm my tongue; I am bound to speak:
My mistress here lies murder'd in her bed,—

ALL: O heavens forfend!

EMILIA: And your reports have set the murder on.

OTHELLO: Nay, stare not, masters: it is true, indeed.

GRATIANO: 'Tis a strange truth.

MONTANO: O monstrous act!

EMILIA: Villany, villany, villany!
I think upon 't, I think: I smell 't: O villany!—
I thought so then:—I 'll kill myself for grief:—
O villany, villany!

IAGO: What, are you mad? I charge you, get you home.

EMILIA: Good gentlemen, let me have leave to speak:
'Tis proper I obey him, but not now.
Perchance, Iago, I will ne'er go home.

OTHELLO: O! O! O!   [*He falls on the bed.*

EMILIA: Nay, lay thee down and roar;
For thou hast kill'd the sweetest innocent
That e'er did lift up eye.

OTHELLO: [*Rising*] O, she was foul!
I scarce did know you, uncle: there lies your niece,
Whose breath, indeed, these hands have newly stopp'd:
I know this act shows horrible and grim.

GRATIANO: Poor Desdemona! I am glad thy father 's dead:
Thy match was mortal to him, and pure grief
Shore his old thread in twain: did he live now,
This sight would make him do a desperate turn,
Yea, curse his better angel from his side,
And fall to reprobation.

OTHELLO: 'Tis pitiful; but yet Iago knows
That she with Cassio hath the act of shame
A thousand times committed; Cassio confess'd it:
And she did gratify his amorous works
With that recognizance and pledge of love
Which I first gave her; I saw it in his hand:
It was a handkerchief, an antique token
My father gave my mother.

EMILIA: O heaven! O heavenly powers!

IAGO: Come, hold your peace.

EMILIA: 'Twill out, 'twill out: I peace!
No, I will speak as liberal as the north:
Let heaven and men and devils, let them all,
All, all, cry shame against me, yet I 'll speak.

IAGO: Be wise, and get you home.

EMILIA: I will not.

                              [*Iago offers to stab Emilia.*

GRATIANO: Fie!
Your sword upon a woman?

EMILIA: O thou dull Moor! that handkerchief thou speak'st of
I found by fortune and did give my husband;
For often, with a solemn earnestness,

More than indeed belong'd to such a trifle,
He begg'd of me to steal it.

IAGO: Villanous whore!

EMILIA: She give it Cassio! no, alas! I found it,
And I did give 't my husband.

IAGO: Filth, thou liest!

EMILIA: By heaven, I do not, I do not, gentlemen.
O murderous coxcomb! what should such a fool
Do with so good a woman?

OTHELLO: Are there no stones in heaven
But what serve for the thunder?—Precious villain!

      [*He runs at Iago: Iago, from behind, stabs Emilia, and exit.*

GRATIANO: The woman falls; sure, he hath kill'd his wife.

EMILIA: Ay, ay: O, lay me by my mistress' side.

GRATIANO: He 's gone, but his wife 's kill'd.

MONTANO: 'Tis a notorious villain. Take you this weapon,
Which I have here recover'd from the Moor:
Come, guard the door without; let him not pass,
But kill him rather. I 'll after that same villain,
For 'tis a damned slave.   [*Exeunt Montano and Gratiano.*

OTHELLO: I am not valiant neither,
But every puny whipster gets my sword:
But why should honour outlive honesty?
Let it go all.

EMILIA: What did thy song bode, lady?
Hark, canst thou hear me? I will play the swan,
And die in music. [*Singing*] Willow, willow, willow.—
Moor, she was chaste; she loved thee, cruel Moor;
So come my soul to bliss, as I speak true;
So speaking as I think, I die, I die.   [*Dies.*

OTHELLO: I have another weapon in this chamber;
It is a sword of Spain, the ice-brook's temper:—
O, here it is. Uncle, I must come forth.

GRATIANO: [*Within*] If thou attempt it, it will cost thee dear:
Thou hast no weapon, and perforce must suffer.

OTHELLO: Look in upon me then and speak with me,
Or, naked as I am, I will assault thee.

Re-enter Gratiano.

GRATIANO: What is the matter?
OTHELLO: Behold, I have a weapon:
A better never did itself sustain
Upon a soldier's thigh: I have seen the day
That, with this little arm and this good sword,
I have made my way through more impediments
Than twenty times your stop: but, O vain boast!
Who can control his fate? 'tis not so now.
Be not afraid, though you do see me weapon'd;
Here is my journey's end, here is my butt,
And very sea-mark of my utmost sail.
Do you go back dismay'd? 'tis a lost fear;
Man but a rush against Othello's breast,
And he retires. Where should Othello go?
Now, how dost thou look now? O ill-starr'd wench!
Pale as thy smock! when we shall meet at compt,
This look of thine will hurl my soul from heaven,
And fiends will snatch at it. Cold, cold, my girl!
Even like thy charity. O cursed slave!
Whip me, ye devils,
From the possession of this heavenly sight!
Blow me about in winds! roast me in sulphur!
Wash me in steep-down gulfs of liquid fire!
O Desdemona! Desdemona! dead!
Oh! Oh! Oh!

Enter Lodovico, Montano, Cassio carried in a chair,
and Officers with Iago, prisoner.

LODOVICO: Where is this rash and most unfortunate man?
OTHELLO: That 's he that was Othello: here I am.
LODOVICO: Where is that viper? bring the villain forth.

OTHELLO: I look down towards his feet; but that's a fable.
If that thou be'st a devil, I cannot kill thee.   [*Wounds Iago.*

LODOVICO: Wrench his sword from him.

IAGO: I bleed, sir; but not kill'd.

OTHELLO: I am not sorry neither: I 'ld have thee live;
For, in my sense, 'tis happiness to die.

LODOVICO: O thou Othello, that wert once so good,
Fall'n in the practice of a damned slave
What shall be said to thee?

OTHELLO: Why, any thing:
An honourable murderer, if you will;
For nought I did in hate, but all in honour.

LODOVICO: This wretch hath part confess'd his villany:
Did you and he consent in Cassio's death?

OTHELLO: Ay.

CASSIO: Dear general, I never gave you cause.

OTHELLO: I do believe it, and I ask you pardon.
Will you, I pray, demand that demi-devil
Why he hath thus ensnared my soul and body?

IAGO: Demand me nothing: what you know, you know:
From this time forth I never will speak word.

LODOVICO: What, not to pray?

GRATIANO: Torments will ope your lips.

OTHELLO: Well, thou dost best.

LODOVICO: Sir, you shall understand what hath befall'n,
Which, as I think, you know not. Here is a letter
Found in the pocket of the slain Roderigo;
And here another: the one of them imports
The death of Cassio to be undertook
By Roderigo.

OTHELLO: O villain!

CASSIO: Most heathenish and most gross!

LODOVICO: Now here 's another discontented paper,
Found in his pocket too; and this, it seems,
Roderigo meant to have sent this damned villain;

But that belike Iago in the interim
Came in and satisfied him.

    OTHELLO: O the pernicious caitiff!
How came you, Cassio, by that handkerchief
That was my wife's?

    CASSIO: I found it in my chamber:
And he himself confess'd but even now
That there he dropp'd it for a special purpose
Which wrought to his desire.

    OTHELLO: O fool! fool! fool!

    CASSIO: There is besides in Roderigo's letter,
How he upbraids Iago, that he made him
Brave me upon the watch; whereon it came
That I was cast: and even but now he spake,
After long seeming dead, Iago hurt him,
Iago set him on.

    LODOVICO: You must forsake this room, and go with us:
Your power and your command is taken off,
And Cassio rules in Cyprus. For this slave,
If there be any cunning cruelty
That can torment him much and hold him long,
It shall be his. You shall close prisoner rest,
Till that the nature of your fault be known
To the Venetian state. Come, bring him away.

    OTHELLO: Soft you; a word or two before you go.
I have done the state some service, and they know 't.
No more of that. I pray you, in your letters,
When you shall these unlucky deeds relate,
Speak of me as I am; nothing extenuate,
Nor set down aught in malice: then must you speak
Of one that loved not wisely but too well;
Of one not easily jealous, but being wrought
Perplex'd in the extreme; of one whose hand,
Like the base Indian, threw a pearl away
Richer than all his tribe; of one whose subdued eyes,

Albeit unused to the melting mood,
Drop tears as fast as the Arabian trees
Their medicinal gum. Set you down this;
And say besides, that in Aleppo once,
Where a malignant and a turban'd Turk
Beat a Venetian and traduced the state,
I took by the throat the circumcised dog,
And smote him, thus.   [*Stabs himself.*

    LODOVICO: O bloody period!

    GRATIANO: All that 's spoke is marr'd.

    OTHELLO: I kiss'd thee ere I kill'd thee: no way but this;
Killing myself, to die upon a kiss.   [*Falls on the bed, and dies.*

    CASSIO: This did I fear, but thought he had no weapon;
For he was great of heart.

    LODOVICO: [*To Iago*] O Spartan dog,
More fell than anguish, hunger, or the sea!
Look on the tragic loading of this bed;
This is thy work: the object poisons sight;
Let it be hid. Gratiano, keep the house,
And seize upon the fortunes of the Moor,
For they succeed on you. To you, lord governor,
Remains the censure of this hellish villain;
The time, the place, the torture: O, enforce it!
Myself will straight aboard; and to the state
This heavy act with heavy heart relate.   [*Exeunt.*

HAMLET
PRINCE OF DENMARK

DRAMATIS PERSONÆ

CLAUDIUS, king of Denmark.
HAMLET, son to the late, and
    nephew to the present king.
POLONIUS, lord chamberlain.
HORATIO, friend to Hamlet.
LAERTES, son to Polonius.
VOLTIMAND,
CORNELIUS,
ROSENCRANTZ, } courtiers.
GUILDENSTERN,
OSRIC,
A Gentleman,
A Priest.
MARCELLUS, } officers.
BERNARDO,
FRANCISCO, a soldier.

REYNALDO, servant to Polonius.
Players.
Two Clowns, grave-diggers.
FORTINBRAS, prince of Norway.
A Captain.
English Ambassadors.
GERTRUDE, queen of Denmark,
    and mother to Hamlet.
OPHELIA, daughter to Polonius.
Lords, Ladies, Officers,
    Soldiers, Sailors, Messen-
    gers, and other Attendants.
Ghost of Hamlet's Father.

SCENE:
Denmark.

ACT I.

SCENE I. *Elsinore. A platform before the castle.*
Francisco at his post. Enter to him Bernardo.

BERNARDO: Who 's there?

FRANCISCO: Nay, answer me: stand, and unfold yourself.

BERNARDO: Long live the king!

FRANCISCO: Bernardo?

BERNARDO: He.

FRANCISCO: You come most carefully upon your hour.

BERNARDO: 'Tis now struck twelve; get thee to bed, Francisco.

FRANCISCO: For this relief much thanks: 'tis bitter cold,
And I am sick at heart.

BERNARDO: Have you had quiet guard?

FRANCISCO: Not a mouse stirring.
BERNARDO: Well, good night.
If you do meet Horatio and Marcellus,
The rivals of my watch, bid them make haste.
FRANCISCO: I think I hear them. Stand, ho! Who 's there?

Enter Horatio and Marcellus.

HORATIO: Friends to this ground.
MARCELLUS: And liegemen to the Dane.
FRANCISCO: Give you good night.
MARCELLUS: O, farewell, honest soldier:
Who hath relieved you:
FRANCISCO: Bernardo has my place.
Give you good night.   [*Exit.*
MARCELLUS: Holla! Bernardo!
BERNARDO: Say,
What, is Horatio there?
HORATIO: A piece of him.
BERNARDO: Welcome, Horatio: welcome, good Marcellus.
MARCELLUS: What, has this thing appear'd again to-night?
BERNARDO: I have seen nothing.
MARCELLUS: Horatio says 'tis but our fantasy,
And will not let belief take hold of him
Touching this dreaded sight, twice seen of us:
Therefore I have entreated him along
With us to watch the minutes of this night;
That if again this apparition come,
He may approve our eyes and speak to it.
HORATIO: Tush, tush, 'twill not appear.
BERNARDO: Sit down awhile;
And let us once again assail your ears,
That are so fortified against our story
What we have two nights seen.
HORATIO: Well, sit we down,
And let us hear Bernardo speak of this.

BERNARDO: Last night of all,
When yond same star that 's westward from the pole
Had made his course to illume that part of heaven
Where now it-burns, Marcellus and myself,
The bell then beating one,—

Enter Ghost.

MARCELLUS: Peace, break thee off; look, where it comes again!
BERNARDO: In the same figure, like the king that's dead.
MARCELLUS: Thou art a scholar; speak to it, Horatio.
BERNARDO: Looks it not like the king? mark it, Horatio.
HORATIO: Most like: it harrows me with fear and wonder.
BERNARDO: It would be spoke to.
MARCELLUS: Question it, Horatio.
HORATIO: What art thou that usurp'st this time of night,
Together with that fair and warlike form
In which the majesty of buried Denmark
Did sometimes march? by heaven I charge thee, speak!
MARCELLUS: It is offended.
BERNARDO: See, it stalks away!
HORATIO: Stay! speak, speak! I charge thee, speak!   [*Exit Ghost.*
MARCELLUS: 'Tis gone, and will not answer.
BERNARDO: How now, Horatio! you tremble and look pale:
Is not this something more than fantasy?
What think you on 't?
HORATIO: Before my God, I might not this believe
Without the sensible and true avouch
Of mine own eyes.
MARCELLUS: Is it not like the king?
HORATIO: As thou art to thyself:
Such was the very armour he had on
When he the ambitious Norway combated;
So frown'd he once, when, in an angry parle,
He smote the sledded Polacks on the ice.
'Tis strange.

MARCELLUS: Thus twice before, and jump at this dead hour,
With martial stalk hath he gone by our watch.

HORATIO: In what particular thought to work I know not:
But in the gross and scope of my opinion,
This bodes some strange eruption to our state.

MARCELLUS: Good now, sit down, and tell me, he that knows,
Why this same strict and most observant watch
So nightly toils the subject of the land,
And why such daily cast of brazen cannon,
And foreign mart for implements of war;
Why such impress of shipwrights, whose sore task
Does not divide the Sunday from the week;
What might be toward, that this sweaty haste
Doth make the night joint-labourer with the day:
Who is 't that can inform me?

HORATIO: That can I;
At least, the whisper goes so. Our last king,
Whose image even but now appear'd to us,
Was, as you know, by Fortinbras of Norway,
Thereto prick'd on by a most emulate pride,
Dared to the combat; in which our valiant Hamlet—
For so this side of our known world esteem'd him—
Did slay this Fortinbras; who, by a seal'd compact,
Well ratified by law and heraldry,
Did forfeit, with his life, all those his lands
Which he stood seized of, to the conqueror:
Against the which, a moiety competent
Was gaged by our king; which had return'd
To the inheritance of Fortinbras,
Had he been vanquisher; as, by the same covenant,
And carriage of the article design'd,
His fell to Hamlet. Now, sir, young Fortinbras,
Of unimproved mettle hot and full,
Hath in the skirts of Norway here and there
Shark'd up a list of lawless resolutes,

For food and diet, to some enterprise
That hath a stomach in 't; which is no other—
As it doth well appear unto our state—
But to recover of us, by strong hand
And terms compulsatory, those foresaid lands
So by his father lost: and this, I take it,
Is the main motive of our preparations,
The source of this our watch and the chief head
Of this post-haste and romage in the land.

BERNARDO: I think it be no other but e'en so:
Well may it sort that this portentous figure
Comes armed through our watch; so like the king
That was and is the question of these wars.

HORATIO: A mote it is to trouble the mind's eye.
In the most high and palmy state of Rome,
A little ere the mightiest Julius fell,
The graves stood tenantless and the sheeted dead
Did squeak and gibber in the Roman streets:
As stars with trains of fire and dews of blood,
Disasters in the sun; and the moist star
Upon whose influence Neptune's empire stands
Was sick almost to doomsday with eclipse:
And even the like precurse of fierce events,
As harbingers preceding still the fates
And prologue to the omen coming on.
Have heaven and earth together demonstrated
Unto our climatures and countrymen.—
But soft, behold! lo, where it comes again!

Re-enter Ghost.

I 'll cross it, though it blast me. Stay, illusion!
If thou hast any sound, or use of voice,
Speak to me:
If there be any good thing to be done,
That may to thee do ease and grace to me,

Speak to me: [*Cock crows.*
If thou art privy to thy country's fate,
Which, happily, foreknowing may avoid,
O, speak!
Or if thou hast uphoarded in thy life
Extorted treasure in the womb of earth,
For which they say, you spirits oft walk in death,
Speak of it: stay, and speak! Stop it, Marcellus.
   MARCELLUS: Shall I strike at it with my partisan?
   HORATIO: Do, if it will not stand.
   BERNARDO: 'Tis here!
   HORATIO: 'Tis here!
   MARCELLUS: 'Tis gone!   [*Exit Ghost.*
We do it wrong, being so majestical,
To offer it the show of violence;
For it is, as the air, invulnerable,
And our vain blows malicious mockery.
   BERNARDO: It was about to speak, when the cock crew.
   HORATIO: And then it started like a guilty thing
Upon a fearful summons. I have heard,
The cock, that is the trumpet to the morn,
Doth with his lofty and shrill-sounding throat
Awake the god of day; and, at his warning,
Whether in sea or fire, in earth or air,
The extravagant and erring spirit hies
To his confine: and of the truth herein
This present object made probation.
   MARCELLUS: It faded on the crowing of the cock.
Some say that ever 'gainst that season comes
Wherein our Saviour's birth is celebrated,
The bird of dawning singeth all night long:
And then, they say, no spirit dare stir abroad;
The nights are wholesome; then no planets strike,
No fairy takes, nor witch hath power to charm,
So hallow'd and so gracious is the time.

HORATIO: So have I heard and do in part believe it.
But, look, the morn, in russet mantle clad,
Walks o'er the dew of yon high eastward hill:
Break we our watch up; and by my advice,
Let us impart what we have seen to-night
Unto young Hamlet; for, upon my life,
This spirit, dumb to us, will speak to him.
Do you consent we shall acquaint him with it,
As needful in our loves, fitting our duty?

MARCELLUS: Let 's do 't, I pray; and I this morning know
Where we shall find him most conveniently.   [*Exeunt.*

SCENE II. *A room of state in the castle.*
Enter the King, Queen, Hamlet, Polonius, Laertes,
Voltimand, Cornelius, Lords, and Attendants.

KING: Though yet of Hamlet our dear brother's death
The memory be green, and that it us befitted
To bear our hearts in grief and our whole kingdom
To be contracted in one brow of woe,
Yet so far hath discretion fought with nature
That we with wisest sorrow think on him,
Together with remembrance of ourselves.
Therefore our sometime sister, now our queen,
The imperial jointress to this warlike state,
Have we, as 'twere with a defeated joy,—
With an auspicious and a dropping eye,
With mirth in funeral and with dirge in marriage,
In equal scale weighing delight and dole,—
Taken to wife: nor have we herein barr'd
Your better wisdoms, which have freely gone
With this affair along. For all, our thanks.
Now follows, that you know, young Fortinbras,
Holding a weak supposal of our worth,
Or thinking by our late dear brother's death

Our state to be disjoint and out of frame,
Colleagued with the dream of his advantage,
He hath not fail'd to pester us with message,
Importing the surrender of those lands
Lost by his father, with all bonds of law,
To our most valiant brother. So much for him.
Now for ourself and for this time of meeting:
Thus much the business is: we have here writ
To Norway, uncle of young Fortinbras,—
Who, impotent and bed-rid, scarcely hears
Of this his nephew's purpose,—to suppress
His further gait herein; in that the levies,
The lists and full proportions, are all made
Out of his subject: and we here dispatch
You, good Cornelius, and you, Voltimand,
For bearers of this greeting to old Norway;
Giving to you no further personal power
To business with the king, more than the scope
Of these delated articles allow.
Farewell, and let your haste commend your duty.

CORNELIUS: ⎫
VOLTIMAND: ⎬ In that and all things will we show our duty.

KING: We doubt it nothing: heartily farewell.

                                        [*Exeunt Voltimand and Cornelius.*

And now, Laertes, what 's the news with you?
You told us of some suit; what is 't, Laertes?
You cannot speak of reason to the Dane,
And lose your voice: what wouldst thou beg, Laertes,
That shall not be my offer, not thy asking?
The head is not more native to the heart,
The hand more instrumental to the mouth,
Than is the throne of Denmark to thy father.
What wouldst thou have, Laertes?

LAERTES: My dread Lord,
Your leave and favour to return to France;

From whence though willingly I came to Denmark,
To show my duty in your coronation,
Yet now, I must confess, that duty done,
My thoughts and wishes bend again toward France
And bow them to your gracious leave and pardon.

    KING: Have you your father's leave? What says Polonius?

    POLONIUS: He hath, my lord, wrung from me my slow leave
By laboursome petition, and at last
Upon his will I seal'd my hard consent:
I do beseech you, give him leave to go.

    KING: Take thy fair hour, Laertes; time be thine,
And thy best graces spend it at thy will!
But now, my cousin Hamlet, and my son,—

    HAMLET: [*Aside*] A little more than kin, and less than kind.

    KING: How is it that the clouds still hang on you?

    HAMLET: Not so, my lord; I am too much i' the sun.

    QUEEN: Good Hamlet, cast thy nighted colour off,
And let thine eye look like a friend on Denmark.
Do not for ever with thy vailed lids
Seek for thy noble father in the dust:
Thou know'st 'tis common; all that lives must die,
Passing through nature to eternity.

    HAMLET: Ay, madam, it is common.

    QUEEN: If it be,
Why seems it so particular with thee?

    HAMLET: Seems, madam! nay, it is; I know not 'seems.'
'Tis not alone my inky cloak, good mother,
Nor customary suits of solemn black;
Nor windy suspiration of forced breath,
No, nor the fruitful river in the eye,
Nor the dejected 'haviour of the visage,
Together with all forms, moods, shapes of grief,
That can denote me truly: these indeed seem,
For they are actions that a man might play:
But I have that within which passeth show;

These but the trappings and the suits of woe.

KING: 'Tis sweet and commendable in your nature, Hamlet,
To give these mourning duties to your father:
But, you must know, your father lost a father;
That father lost, lost his, and the survivor bound
In filial obligation for some term
To do obsequious sorrow: but to persever
In obstinate condolement is a course
Of impious stubbornness; 'tis unmanly grief;
It shows a will most incorrect to heaven,
A heart unfortified, a mind impatient,
An understanding simple and unschool'd:
For what we know must be and is as common
As any the most vulgar thing to sense,
Why should we in our peevish opposition
Take it to heart? Fie! 'tis a fault to heaven,
A fault against the dead, a fault to nature,
To reason most absurd; whose common theme
Is death of fathers, and who still hath cried,
From the first corse till he that died to-day,
'This must be so.' We pray you, throw to earth
This unprevailing woe, and think of us
As of a father: for let the world take note,
You are the most immediate to our throne;
And with no less nobility of love
Than that which dearest father bears his son,
Do I impart toward you. For your intent
In going back to school in Wittenberg,
Is it most retrograde to our desire:
And we beseech you, bend you to remain
Here, in the cheer and comfort of our eye,
Our chiefest courtier, cousin, and our son.

QUEEN: Let not thy mother lose her prayers, Hamlet:
I pray thee, stay with us: go not to Wittenberg.

HAMLET: I shall in all my best obey you, madam.

KING: Why, 'tis a loving and a fair reply:
Be as ourself in Denmark. Madam, come;
This gentle and unforced accord of Hamlet
Sits smiling to my heart: in grace whereof,
No jocund health that Denmark drinks to-day,
But the great cannon to the clouds shall tell,
And the king's rouse the heavens shall bruit again,
Re-speaking earthly thunder. Come away.   [*Exeunt all but Hamlet.*
   HAMLET: O, that this is too too solid flesh would melt,
Thaw and resolve itself into a dew!
Or that the Everlasting had not fix'd
His canon 'gainst self-slaughter! O God! God!
How weary, stale, flat and unprofitable,
Seem to me all the uses of this world!
Fie on 't! ah fie! 'tis an unweeded garden,
That grows to seed; things rank and gross in nature
Possess it merely. That it should come to this!
But two months dead: nay, not so much, not two:
So excellent a king; that was, to this,
Hyperion to a satyr; so loving to my mother
That he might not beteem the winds of heaven
Visit her face too roughly. Heaven and earth!
Must I remember? why, she would hang on him,
As if increase of appetite had grown
By what it fed on: and yet, within a month—
Let me not think on 't—Frailty, thy name is woman!—
A little month, or ere those shoes were old
With which she follow'd my poor father's body,
Like Niobe, all tears:—why she, even she—
O God! a beast, that wants discourse of reason,
Would have mourn'd longer—married with my uncle,
My father's brother, but no more like my father
Than I to Hercules: within a month:
Ere yet the salt of most unrighteous tears
Had left the flushing in her galled eyes,

She married. O, most wicked speed, to post
With such dexterity to incestuous sheets!
It is not nor it cannot come to good:
But break, my heart; for I must hold my tongue.

Enter Horatio, Marcellus, and Bernardo.

HORATIO: Hail to your lordship!

HAMLET: I am glad to see you well:
Horatio,—or I do forget myself.

HORATIO: The same, my lordship, and your poor servant ever.

HAMLET: Sir, my good friend; I 'll change that name with you:
And what make you from Wittenberg, Horatio?
Marcellus?

MARCELLUS: My good lord—

HAMLET: I am very glad to see you. Good even, sir.
But what, in faith, make you from Wittenberg?

HORATIO: A truant disposition, good my lord.

HAMLET: I would not hear your enemy say so,
Nor shall you do mine ear that violence,
To make it truster of your own report
Against yourself: I know you are no truant.
But what is your affair in Elsinore?
We 'll teach you to drink deep ere you depart.

HORATIO: My lord, I came to see your father's funeral.

HAMLET: I pray thee, do not mock me, fellow-student;
I think it was to see my mother's wedding.

HORATIO: Indeed, my lord, it follow'd hard upon.

HAMLET: Thrift, thrift, Horatio! the funeral baked meats
Did coldly furnish forth the marriage tables.
Would I had met my dearest foe in heaven
Or ever I had seen that day, Horatio!
My father!—methinks I see my father.

HORATIO: Where, my lord?

HAMLET: In my mind's eye, Horatio.

HORATIO: I saw him once; he was a goodly king.

HAMLET: He was a man, take him for all in all,
I shall not look upon his like again.
    HORATIO: My lord, I think I saw him yesterday night.
    HAMLET: Saw? who?
    HORATIO: My lord, the king your father.
    HAMLET: The king my father!
    HORATIO: Season your admiration for a while
With an attent ear, till I may deliver,
Upon the witness of these gentlemen,
This marvel to you.
    HAMLET: For God's love, let me hear.
    HORATIO: Two nights together had these gentlemen,
Marcellus and Bernardo, on their watch,
In the dead vast and middle of the night,
Been thus encounter'd. A figure like your father,
Armed at point exactly, cap-a-pe,
Appears before them, and with solemn march
Goes slow and stately by them: thrice he walk'd
By their oppress'd and fear surprised eyes,
Within his truncheon's length; whilst they, distill'd
Almost to jelly with the act of fear,
Stand dumb and speak not to him. This to me
In dreadful secrecy impart they did;
And I with them the third night kept the watch:
Where, as they had deliver'd, both in time,
Form of the thing, each word made true and good,
The apparition comes: I knew your father;
These hands are not more like.
    HAMLET: But where was this?
    MARCELLUS: My lord, upon the platform where we watch'd.
    HAMLET: Did you not speak to it?
    HORATIO: My lord, I did;
But answer made it none: yet once methought
It lifted up its head and did address
Itself to motion, like as it would speak;

But even then the morning cock crew loud,
And at the sound it shrunk in haste away,
And vanish'd from our sight.

HAMLET: 'Tis very strange.

HORATIO: As I do live, my honour'd lord, 'tis true;
And we did think it writ down in our duty
To let you know of it.

HAMLET: Indeed, indeed, sirs, but this troubles me.
Hold you the watch to-night?

MARCELLUS:⎫
BERNARDO: ⎭   We do, my lord.

HAMLET: Arm'd say you?

MARCELLUS:⎫
BERNARDO: ⎬ Arm'd my lord.

HAMLET: From top to toe?

MARCELLUS:⎫
BERNARDO: ⎬ My lord, from head to foot.

HAMLET: Then saw you not his face?

HORATIO: O, yes, my lord; he wore his beaver up.

HAMLET: What, look'd he frowningly?

HORATIO: A countenance more in sorrow than in anger.

HAMLET: Pale or red?

HORATIO: Nay, very pale.

HAMLET: And fix'd his eyes upon you?

HORATIO: Most constantly.

HAMLET: I would I had been there.

HORATIO: It would have much amazed you.

HAMLET: Very like, very like. Stay'd it long?

HORATIO: While one with moderate haste might tell a hundred.

MARCELLUS:⎫
BERNARDO: ⎬ Longer, longer.

HORATIO: Not when I saw 't.

HAMLET: His beard was grizzled,—no?

HORATIO: It was, as I have seen it in his life,
A sable silver'd.

HAMLET: I will watch to-night;
Perchance 'twill walk again.
HORATIO: I warrant it will.
HAMLET: If it assume my noble father's person,
I 'll speak to it, though hell itself should gape
And bid me hold my peace. I pray you all,
If you have hitherto conceal'd this sight,
Let it be tenable in your silence still;
And whatsoever else shall hap to-night,
Give it an understanding, but no tongue:
I will requite your loves. So, fare you well:
Upon the platform, 'twixt eleven and twelve,
I 'll visit you.
ALL: Our duty to your honour.
HAMLET: Your loves, as mine to you: farewell.
                                        [*Exeunt all but Hamlet.*
My father's spirit in arms! all is not well;
I doubt some foul play: would the night were come!
Till then sit still, my soul: foul deeds will rise,
Though all the earth o'erwhelm them, to men's eyes.   [*Exit.*

SCENE III. *A room in Polonius' house.*
Enter Laertes and Ophelia.

LAERTES: My necessaries are embark'd: farewell:
And, sister, as the winds give benefit
And convoy is assistant, do not sleep,
But let me hear from you.
OPHELIA: Do you doubt that?
LAERTES: For Hamlet and the trifling of his favour,
Hold it a fashion and a toy in blood,
A violet in the youth of primy nature,
Forward, not permanent, sweet, not lasting,
The perfume and suppliance of a minute;
No more.

OPHELIA: No more but so?

LAERTES: Think it no more:
For nature, crescent, does not grow alone
In thews and bulk, but, as this temple waxes,
The inward service of the mind and soul
Grows wide withal. Perhaps he loves you now,
And now no soil nor cautel doth besmirch
The virtue of his will: but you must fear,
His greatness weigh'd, his will is not his own;
For he himself is subject to his birth:
He may not, as unvalued persons do,
Carve for himself; for on his choice depends
The safety and health of this whole state;
And therefore must his choice be circumscribed
Unto the voice and yielding of that body
Whereof he is the head. Then if he says he loves you,
It fits your wisdom so far to believe it
As he in his particular act and place
May give his saying deed; which is no further
Than the main voice of Denmark goes withal.
Then weigh what loss your honour may sustain,
If with too credent ear you list his songs,
Or lose your heart, or your chaste treasure open
To his unmaster'd importunity.
Fear it, Ophelia, fear it, my dear sister,
And keep you in the rear of your affection,
Out of the shot and danger of desire.
The chariest maid is prodigal enough,
If she unmask her beauty to the moon:
Virtue itself 'scapes not calumnious strokes:
The canker galls the infants of the spring,
Too oft before their buttons be disclosed,
And in the morn and liquid dew of youth
Contagious blastments are most imminent,
Be wary then; best safety lies in fear:

Youth to itself rebels, though none else near.

    OPHELIA: I shall the effect of this good lesson keep,
As watchman to my heart. But, good my brother,
Do not, as some ungracious pastors do,
Show me the steep and thorny way to heaven;
Whiles, like a puff'd and reckless libertine,
Himself the primrose path of dalliance treads,
And recks not his own rede.

    LAERTES: O, fear me not.
I stay too long: but here my father comes.

Enter Polonius.

A double blessing is a double grace;
Occasion smiles upon a second leave.

    POLONIUS: Yet here, Laertes! aboard, aboard, for shame!
The wind sits in the shoulder of your sail,
And you are stay'd for. There; my blessing with thee!
And these few precepts in thy memory
See thou character. Give thy thoughts no tongue,
Nor any unproportion'd thought his act.
Be thou familiar, but by no means vulgar.
Those friends thou hast, and their adoption tried,
Grapple them to thy soul with hoops of steel;
But do not dull thy palm with entertainment
Of each new-hatch'd, unfledged comrade. Beware
Of entrance to a quarrel, but being in,
Bear 't that the opposed may beware of thee.
Give every man thy ear, but few thy voice;
Take each man's censure, but reserve thy judgement.
Costly thy habit as thy purse can buy,
But not express'd in fancy; rich, not gaudy;
For the apparel oft proclaims the man,
And they in France of the best rank and station
Are of a most select and generous chief in that.
Neither a borrower nor a lender be;

For loan oft loses both itself and friend,
And borrowing dulls the edge of husbandry.
This above all: to thine own self be true,
And it must follow, as the night the day,
Thou canst not then be false to any man.
Farewell: my blessing season this in thee!

    LAERTES: Most humbly do I take my leave, my lord.

    POLONIUS: The time invites you; go; your servants tend.

    LAERTES: Farewell, Ophelia; and remember well
What I have said to you.

    OPHELIA: 'Tis in my memory lock'd,
And you yourself shall keep the key of it.

    LAERTES: Farewell.   [*Exit.*

    POLONIUS: What is 't, Ophelia, he hath said to you?

    OPHELIA: So please you, something touching the Lord Hamlet.

    POLONIUS: Marry, well bethought:
'Tis told me, he hath very oft of late
Given private time to you; and you yourself
Have of your audience been most free and bounteous:
If it be so, as so 'tis put on me,
And that in way of caution, I must tell you,
You do not understand yourself so clearly
As it behoves my daughter and your honour.
What is between you? give me up the truth.

    OPHELIA: He hath, my lord, of late made many tenders
Of his affection to me.

    POLONIUS: Affection! pooh! you speak like a green girl,
Unsifted in such perilous circumstance.
Do you believe his tenders, as you call them?

    OPHELIA: I do not know, my lord, what I should think.

    POLONIUS: Marry, I 'll teach you: think yourself a baby;
That you have ta'en these tenders for true pay,
Which are not sterling. Tender yourself more dearly;
Or—not to crack the wind of the poor phrase,
Running it thus—you 'll tender me a fool.

OPHELIA: My lord, he hath importuned me with love
In honourable fashion.
POLONIUS: Ah, fashion you may call it; go to, go to.
OPHELIA: And hath given countenance to his speech, my lord,
With almost all the holy vows of heaven.
POLONIUS: Ay, springes to catch woodcocks. I do know,
When the blood burns, how prodigal the soul
Lends the tongue vows: these blazes, daughter,
Giving more light than heat, extinct in both,
Even in their promise, as it is a-making,
You must not take for fire. From this time
Be somewhat scanter of your maiden presence;
Set your entreatments at a higher rate
Than a command to parley. For Lord Hamlet,
Believe so much in him, that he is young,
And with a larger tether may he walk
Than may be given you: in few, Ophelia,
Do not believe his vows; for they are brokers,
Not of that dye which their investments show,
But mere implorators of unholy suits,
Breathing like sanctified and pious bawds,
The better to beguile. This is for all:
I would not, in plain terms, from this time forth,
Have you so slander any moment leisure,
As to give words to talk with the Lord Hamlet.
Look to 't, I charge you: come your ways.
OPHELIA: I shall obey, my lord.   [*Exeunt.*

SCENE IV. *The platform.*
Enter Hamlet, Horatio, and Marcellus.

HAMLET: The air bites shrewdly; it is very cold.
HORATIO: It is a nipping and an eager air.
HAMLET: What hour now?
HORATIO: I think it lacks of twelve.

MARCELLUS: No, it is struck.

HORATIO: Indeed? I heard it not: then it draws near the season
Wherein the spirit held his wont to walk.

> [*A flourish of trumpets, and ordnance shot off, within.*

What does this mean my lord?

HAMLET: The king doth wake to-night and takes his rouse,
Keeps wassail, and the swaggering up-spring reels;
And, as he drains his draughts of Rhenish down,
The kettle-drum and trumpet thus bray out
The triumph of his pledge.

HORATIO: Is it a custom?

HAMLET: Ay, marry, is 't:
But to my mind, though I am native here
And to the manner born, it is a custom
More honour'd in the breach than the observance.
This heavy-headed revel east and west
Makes us traduced and tax'd of other nations:
They clepe us drunkards, and with swinish phrase
Soil our addition; and indeed it takes
From our achievements, though perform'd at height,
The pith and marrow of our attribute.
So, oft it chances in particular men,
That for some vicious mole of nature in them,
As, in their birth—wherein they are not guilty,
Since nature cannot choose his origin—
By the o'ergrowth of some complexion,
Oft breaking down the pales and forts of reason,
Or by some habit that too much o'er-leavens
The form of plausive manners, that these men,
Carrying, I say, the stamp of one defect,
Being nature's livery, or fortune's star,—
Their virtues else—be they as pure as grace,
As infinite as man may undergo—
Shall in the general censure take corruption
From that particular fault: the dram of evil

Doth all the noble substance of a doubt
To his own scandal.

    HORATIO: Look, my lord, it comes!

Enter Ghost.

    HAMLET: Angels and ministers of grace defend us!
Be thou a spirit of health or goblin damn'd,
Bring with thee airs from heaven or blasts from hell,
Be thy intents wicked or charitable,
Thou comest in such a questionable shape
That I will speak to thee: I 'll call thee Hamlet,
King, father, royal Dane: O, answer me!
Let me not burst in ignorance; but tell
Why thy canonized bones, hearsed in death,
Have burst their cerements; why the sepulchre,
Wherein we saw thee quietly inurn'd,
Hath oped his ponderous and marble jaws,
To cast thee up again. What may this mean,
That thou, dead corse, again in complete steel
Revisit'st thus the glimpses of the moon,
Making night hideous; and we fools of nature
So horridly to shake our disposition
With thoughts beyond the reaches of our souls?
Say, why is this? wherefore? what should we do?

                    [*Ghost beckons Hamlet.*

    HORATIO: It beckons you to go away with it,
As if it some impartment did desire
To you alone.

    MARCELLUS: Look, with what courteous action
It waves you to a more removed ground:
But do not go with it.

    HORATIO: No, by no means.

    HAMLET: It will not speak; then I will follow it.

    HORATIO: Do not, my lord.

    HAMLET: Why, what should be the fear?

I do not set my life at a pin's fee;
And for my soul, what can it do to that,
Being a thing immortal as itself?
It waves me forth again: I 'll follow it.

HORATIO: What if it tempt you toward the flood, my lord,
Or to the dreadful summit of the cliff
That beetles o'er his base into the sea,
And there assume some other horrible form,
Which might deprive your sovereignty of reason
And draw you into madness? think of it:
The very place puts toys of desperation,
Without more motive, into every brain
That looks so many fathoms to the sea
And hears it roar beneath.

HAMLET: It waves me still.
Go on; I 'll follow thee.

MARCELLUS: You shall not go, my lord.

HAMLET: Hold off your hands.

HORATIO: Be ruled; you shall not go.

HAMLET: My fate cries out,
And makes each petty artery in this body
As hardy as the Nemean lion's nerve.
Still am I call'd. Unhand me, gentlemen.
By heaven, I 'll make a ghost of him that lets me!
I say, away! Go on; I 'll follow thee.   [Exeunt Ghost and Hamlet.

HORATIO: He waxes desperate with imagination.

MARCELLUS: Let 's follow; 'tis not fit thus to obey him.

HORATIO: Have after. To what issue will this come?

MARCELLUS: Something is rotten in the state of Denmark.

HORATIO: Heaven will direct it.

MARCELLUS: Nay, let 's follow him.   [Exeunt.

SCENE V. *Another part of the platform.*
Enter Ghost and Hamlet.

HAMLET: Where wilt thou lead me? speak; I 'll go no further.
GHOST: Mark me.
HAMLET: I will.
GHOST: My hour is almost come,
When I to sulphurous and tormenting flames
Must render up myself.
    HAMLET: Alas, poor ghost!
    GHOST: Pity me not, but lend thy serious hearing
To what I shall unfold.
    HAMLET: Speak; I am bound to hear.
    GHOST: So art thou to revenge, when thou shalt hear.
    HAMLET: What?
    GHOST: I am thy father's spirit,
Doom'd for a certain term to walk the night,
And for the day confined to fast in fires,
Till the foul crimes done in my days of nature
Are burnt and purged away. But that I am forbid
To tell the secrets of my prison-house,
I could a tale unfold whose lightest word
Would harrow up thy soul, freeze thy young blood,
Make thy two eyes, like stars, start from their spheres,
Thy knotted and combined locks to part
And each particular hair to stand on end,
Like quills upon the fretful porpentine:
But this eternal blazon must not be
To ears of flesh and blood. List, list, O, list:
If thou didst ever thy dear father love—
    HAMLET: O God!
    GHOST: Revenge his foul and most unnatural murder.
    HAMLET: Murder!
    GHOST: Murder most foul, as in the best it is;
But this most foul, strange and unnatural.

HAMLET: Haste me to know 't, that I, with wings as swift
As meditation or the thoughts of love,
May sweep to my revenge.
    GHOST: I find thee apt;
And duller shouldst thou be than the fat weed
That roots itself in ease on Lethe wharf,
Wouldst thou not stir in this. Now, Hamlet, hear:
'Tis given out that, sleeping in my orchard,
A serpent stung me; so the whole ear of Denmark
Is by a forged process of my death
Rankly abused; but know, thou noble youth,
The serpent that did sting thy father's life
Now wears his crown.
    HAMLET: O my prophetic soul!
My uncle!
    GHOST: Ay, that incestuous, that adulterate beast,
With witchcraft of his wit, with traitorous gifts,—
O wicked wit and gifts, that have the power
So to seduce!—won to his shameful lust
The will of my most seeming-virtuous queen:
O Hamlet, what a falling-off was there!
From me, whose love was of that dignity
That it went hand in hand even with the vow
I made to her in marriage, and to decline
Upon a wretch whose natural gifts were poor
To those of mine!
But virtue, as it never will be moved,
Though lewdness court it in a shape of heaven,
So lust, though to a radiant angel link'd,
With sate itself in a celestial bed,
And prey on garbage.
But, soft! methinks I scent the morning air;
Brief let me be. Sleeping within my orchard,
My custom always of the afternoon,
Upon my secure hour thy uncle stole,

With juice of cursed hebenon in a vial,
And in the porches of my ears did pour
The leperous distilment; whose effect
Holds such an enmity with blood of man
That swift as quicksilver it courses through
The natural gates and alleys of the body,
And with a sudden vigour it doth posset
And curd, like eager droppings into milk,
The thin and wholesome blood: so did it mine;
And a most instant tetter bark'd about,
Most lazar-like, with vile and loathsome crust,
All my smooth body.
Thus was I, sleeping, by a brother's hand
Of life, of crown, of queen, at once dispatch'd:
Cut off even in the blossoms of my sin,
Unhousel'd, disappointed, unaneled,
No reckoning made, but sent to my account
With all my imperfections on my head:
O, horrible! O horrible! most horrible!
If thou hast nature in thee, bear it not;
Let not the royal bed of Denmark be
A couch for luxury and damned incest.
But, howsoever thou pursuest this act,
Taint not thy mind, nor let thy soul contrive
Against thy mother aught: leave her to heaven
And to those thorns that in her bosom lodge,
To prick and sting her. Fare thee well at once!
The glow-worm shows the matin to be near,
And 'gins to pale his uneffectual fire:
Adieu! adieu! Hamlet, remember me.   [*Exit.*

     HAMLET: O all you host of heaven! O earth! what else?
And shall I couple hell? O, fie! Hold, hold, my heart;
And you, my sinews, grow not instant old,
But bear me stiffly up. Remember thee!
Ay, thou poor ghost, while memory holds a seat

In this distracted globe. Remember thee!
Yea, from the table of my memory
I 'll wipe away all trivial fond records,
All saws of books, all forms, all pressures past,
That youth and observation copied there;
And thy commandment all alone shall live
Within the book and volume of my brain,
Unmix'd with baser matter: yes, by heaven!
O most pernicious woman!
O villain, villain, smiling, damned villain!
My tables,—meet it is I set it down,
That one may smile, and smile, and be a villain;
At least I 'm sure it may be so in Denmark: [*Writing.*
So uncle, there you are. Now to my word;
It is 'Adieu, adieu! remember me.'
I have sworn 't.

> MARCELLUS: } [*Within*] My lord, my lord,—
> HORATIO:

> MARCELLUS: [*Within*] Lord Hamlet.—
> HORATIO: [*Within*] Heaven secure him!
> HAMLET: So be it!
> HORATIO: [*Within*] Hillo, ho, ho, my lord!
> HAMLET: Hillo, ho, ho, boy! come, bird, come.

Enter Horatio and Marcellus.

> MARCELLUS: How is 't, my noble lord?
> HORATIO: What news, my lord?
> HAMLET: O wonderful!
> HORATIO: Good my lord, tell it.
> HAMLET: No; you 'll reveal it.
> HORATIO: Not I, my lord, by heaven.
> MARCELLUS: Nor I, my lord.
> HAMLET: How say you, then; would heart of man once think
>   it?

But you 'll be secret?

HORATIO:⎫
MARCELLUS:⎭ Ay, by heaven, my lord.

HAMLET: There 's ne'er a villain dwelling in all Denmark
But he 's an arrant knave.

HORATIO: There needs no ghost, my lord, come from the grave
To tell us this.

HAMLET: Why, right; you are i' the right;
And so, without more circumstance at all,
I hold it fit that we shake hands and part:
You, as your business and desire shall point you;
For every man has business and desire,
Such as it is; and for mine own poor part,
Look you, I 'll go pray.

HORATIO: These are but wild and whirling words, my lord.

HAMLET: I am sorry they offend you, heartily;
Yes, 'faith, heartily.

HORATIO: There 's no offence, my lord.

HAMLET: Yes, by Saint Patrick, but there is, Horatio,
And much offence too. Touching this vision here,
It is an honest ghost, that let tell you:
For your desire to know what is between us,
O'ermaster 't as you may. And now, good friends,
As you are friends, scholars and soldiers,
Give me one poor request.

HORATIO: What is 't, my lord? we will.

HAMLET: Never make known what you have seen to-night.

HORATIO:⎫
MARCELLUS:⎭ My lord, we will not.

HAMLET: Nay, but swear 't.

HORATIO: In faith,
My lord, not I.

MARCELLUS: Nor I, my lord, in faith.

HAMLET: Upon my sword.

MARCELLUS: We have sworn, my lord, already.

HAMLET: Indeed, upon my sword, indeed.

GHOST: [*Beneath*] Swear.

HAMLET: Ah, ha, boy! say'st thou so? art thou there, truepenny?
Come on—you hear this fellow in the cellarage—
Consent to swear.

HORATIO: Propose the oath, my lord.

HAMLET: Never to speak of this that you have seen,
Swear by my sword.

GHOST: [*Beneath*] Swear.

HAMLET: Hic et ubique? then we 'll shift our ground.
Come hither, gentlemen,
And lay your hands again upon my sword:
Never to speak of this that you have heard,
Swear by my sword.

GHOST: [*Beneath*] Swear.

HAMLET: Well said, old mole! canst work i' the earth so fast?
A worthy pioner! Once more remove, good friends.

HORATIO: O day and night, but this is wondrous strange!

HAMLET: And therefore as a stranger give it welcome.
There are more things in heaven and earth, Horatio,
Than are dreamt of in your philosophy.
But come;
Here, as before, never, so help you mercy,
How strange or odd soe'er I bear myself,
As I perchance hereafter shall think meet
To put an antic disposition on,
That you, at such times seeing me, never shall,
With arms encumber'd this, or this headshake,
Or by pronouncing of some doubtful phrase,
As 'Well, well, we know,' or 'We could, an if we would,'
Or 'If we list to speak,' or 'There be, an if they might,'
Or such ambiguous giving out, to note
That you know aught of me: this not to do,
So grace and mercy at your most need help you,
Swear.

GHOST: [*Beneath*] Swear.

HAMLET: Rest, rest, perturbed spirit! [*They swear.*] So, gentle-
    men,
With all my love I do commend me to you:
And what so poor a man as Hamlet is
May do, to express his love and friending to you,
God willing, shall not lack. Let us go in together;
And still your fingers on your lips, I pray.
The time is out of joint: O cursed spite,
That ever I was born to set it right!
Nay, come, let's go together.   [*Exeunt.*

ACT II.

SCENE I. *A room in Polonius' house.*
Enter Polonius and Reynaldo.

POLONIUS: Give him this money and these notes, Reynaldo.
REYNALDO: I will, my lord.
POLONIUS: You shall do marvellous wisely, good Reynaldo,
Before you visit him, to make inquire
Of his behaviour.
REYNALDO: My lord, I did intend it.
POLONIUS: Marry, well said; very well said. Look you, sir,
Inquire me first what Danskers are in Paris;
And how, and who, what means, and where they keep,
What company, at what expense; and finding
By this encompassment and drift of question
That they do know my son, come you more nearer
Than your particular demands will touch it:
Take you, as 'twere, some distant knowledge of him;
As thus, 'I know his father and his friends,
And in part him:' do you mark this, Reynaldo?
REYNALDO: Ay, very well, my lord.
POLONIUS: 'And in part him; but' you may say 'not well:

But, if 't be he I mean, he 's very wild;
Addicted so and so:' and there put on him
What forgeries you please; marry, none so rank
As may dishonour him; take heed of that;
But, sir, such wanton, wild and usual slips
As are companions noted and most known
To youth and liberty.

REYNALDO: As gaming, my lord.

POLONIUS: Ay, or drinking, fencing, swearing, quarrelling,
Drabbing: you may go so far.

REYNALDO: My lord, that would dishonour him.

POLONIUS: 'Faith, no; as you may season it in the charge.
You must not put another scandal on him,
That he is open to incontinency;
That 's not my meaning; but breathe his faults so quaintly
That they may seem the taints of liberty,
The flash and outbreak of a fiery mind,
A savageness in unreclaimed blood,
Of general assault.

REYNALDO: But, my good lord,—

POLONIUS: Wherefore should you do this?

REYNALDO: Ay, my lord.
I would know that.

POLONIUS: Marry sir, here 's my drift;
And, I believe, it is a fetch of wit:
You laying these slight sullies on my son,
As 'twere a thing a little soil'd i' the working,
Mark you,
Your party in converse, him you would sound,
Having ever seen in the prenominate crimes
The youth you breathe of guilty, be assured
He closes with you in this consequence;
'Good sir,' or so, or 'friend,' or 'gentleman,'
According to the phrase or the addition
Of man and country.

REYNALDO: Very good, my lord.

POLONIUS: And then, sir, does he this—he does—what was I
about to say? By the mass, I was about to say something: where
did I leave?

REYNALDO: At 'closes in the consequence,' at 'friend or so,' and
'gentleman.'

POLONIUS: At 'closes in the consequence,' ay, marry;
He closes thus: 'I know the gentleman;
I saw him yesterday, or t' other day,
Or then, or then; with such, or such; and, as you say,
There was a' gaming; there o'ertook in 's rouse;
There falling out at tennis:' or perchance,
'I saw him enter such a house of sale,'
Videlicet, a brothel, or so forth.
See you now;
Your bait of falsehood takes this carp of truth:
And thus do we of wisdom and of reach,
With windlasses and with assays of bias,
By indirections find directions out:
So by my former lecture and advice,
Shall you my son. You have me, have you not?

REYNALDO: My lord, I have.

POLONIUS: God be wi' you; fare you well.

REYNALDO: Good my lord!

POLONIUS: Observe his inclination in yourself.

REYNALDO: I shall, my lord.

POLONIUS: And let him ply his music.

REYNALDO: Well, my lord.

POLONIUS: Farewell!   [Exit Reynaldo.

Enter Ophelia.

How now, Ophelia! what 's the matter?

OPHELIA: O, my lord, my lord, I have been so affrighted!

POLONIUS: With what, i' the name of God?

OPHELIA: My lord, as I was sewing in my closet,

Lord Hamlet, with his doublet all unbraced;
No hat upon his head; his stockings foul'd,
Ungarter'd and down-gyved to his ancle;
Pale as his shirt; his knees knocking each other;
And with a look so piteous in purport
As if he had been loosed out of hell
To speak of horrors,—he comes before me.
  POLONIUS: Mad for thy love?
  OPHELIA: My lord, I do not know;
But truly, I do fear it.
  POLONIUS: What said he?
  OPHELIA: He took me by the wrist and held me hard;
Then goes he to the length of all his arm;
And, with his other hand thus o'er his brow,
He falls to such perusal of my face
As he would draw it. Long stay'd he so;
At last, a little shaking of mine arm
And thrice his head thus waving up and down,
He raised a sigh so piteous and profound
As it did seem to shatter all his bulk
And end his being: that done, he lets me go:
And, with his head over his shoulder turn'd,
He seem'd to find his way without his eyes;
For out o' doors he went without their helps,
And, to the last, bended their light on me.
  POLONIUS: Come, go with me: I will go seek the king.
This is the very ecstasy of love,
Whose violent property fordoes itself
And leads the will to desperate undertakings
As oft as any passion under heaven
That does afflict our natures. I am sorry.
What, have you given him any hard words of late?
  OPHELIA: No, my good lord, but, as you did command,
I did repel his letters and denied
His access to me.

POLONIUS: That hath made him mad.
I am sorry that with better heed and judgement
I had not quoted him: I fear'd he did but trifle,
And meant to wreck thee; but, beshrew my jealousy!
By heaven, it is as proper to our age
To cast beyond ourselves in our opinions
As it is common for the younger sort
To lack discretion. Come, go we to the king:
This must be known; which, being kept close, might move
More grief to hide than hate to utter love.   [*Exeunt.*

SCENE II. *A room in the castle.*
Enter King, Queen, Rosencrantz, Guildenstern, and Attendants.

KING: Welcome, dear Rosencrantz and Guildenstern!
Moreover that we much did long to see you,
The need we have to use you did provoke
Our hasty sending. Something have you heard
Of Hamlet's transformation; so call it,
Sith nor the exterior nor the inward man
Resembles that it was. What it should be,
More than his father's death, that thus hath put him
So much from the understanding of himself,
I cannot dream of: I entreat you both,
That, being of so young days brought up with him,
And sith so neighbour'd to his youth and haviour,
That you vouchsafe your rest here in our court
Some little time: so by your companies
To draw him on to pleasures, and to gather,
So much as from occasion you may glean,
Whether aught, to us unknown, afflicts him thus,
That, open 'd lies within our remedy.
QUEEN: Good gentlemen, he hath much talk'd of you;
And sure I am two men there are not living
To whom he more adheres. If it will please you

To show us so much gentry and good will
As to expend your time with us awhile,
For the supply and profit of our hope,
Your visitation shall receive such thanks
As fits a king's remembrance.

ROSENCRANTZ: Both your majesties
Might, by the sovereign power you have of us,
Put your dread pleasures more into command
Than to entreaty.

GUILDENSTERN: But we both obey,
And here give up ourselves, in the full bent
To lay our service freely at your feet,
To be commanded.

KING: Thanks, Rosencrantz and gentle Guildenstern.

QUEEN: Thanks, Guildenstern and gentle Rosencrantz:
And I beseech you instantly to visit
My too much changed son. Go, some of you,
And bring these gentlemen where Hamlet is.

GUILDENSTERN: Heavens make our presence and our practices
Pleasant and helpful to him!

QUEEN: Ay, amen!
        [*Exeunt Rosencrantz, Guildenstern, and some Attendants.*

Enter Polonius.

POLONIUS: The ambassadors from Norway, my good lord,
Are joyfully return'd.

KING: Thou still hast been the father of good news.

POLONIUS: Have I, my lord? I assure my good liege,
I hold my duty, as I hold my soul,
Both to my God and to my gracious king:
And I do think, or else this brain of mine
Hunts not the trail of policy so sure
As it hath used to do, that I have found
The very cause of Hamlet's lunacy.

KING: O, speak of that; that do I long to hear.

POLONIUS: Give first admittance to the ambassadors;
My news shall be the fruit to that great feast.
    KING: Thyself do grace to them, and bring them in.

                                            [*Exit Polonius.*

He tells me, my dear Gertrude, he hath found
The head and source of all your son's distemper.
    QUEEN: I doubt it is no other but the main;
His father's death, and our o'erhasty marriage.
    KING: Well, we shall sift him.

Re-enter Polonius, with Voltimand and Cornelius.

                              Welcome, my good friends!
Say, Voltimand, what from our brother Norway?
    VOLTIMAND: Most fair return of greetings and desires.
Upon our first, he sent out to suppress
His nephew's levies; which to him appear'd
To be a preparation 'gainst the Polack;
But, better look'd into, he truly found
It was against your highness: whereat grieved,
That so his sickness, age and impotence
Was falsely borne in hand, sends out arrests
On Fortinbras; which he, in brief, obeys;
Receives rebuke from Norway, and in fine
Makes vow before his uncle never more
To give the assay of arms against your majesty.
Whereon old Norway, overcome with joy,
Gives him three thousand crowns in annual fee,
And his commission to employ those soldiers,
So levied as before, against the Polack:
With an entreaty, herein further shown,   [*Giving a paper.*
That it might please you to give quiet pass
Through your dominions for this enterprise,
On such regards of safety and allowance
As therein are set down.
    KING: It likes us well;

And at our more consider'd time we 'll read,
Answer, and think upon this business.
Meantime we thank you for your well-took labour:
Go to your rest; at night we 'll feast together:
Most welcome home!   [*Exeunt Voltimand and Cornelius.*

  POLONIUS: This business is well ended.
My liege, and madam, to expostulate
What majesty should be, what duty is,
Why day is day, night night, and time is time,
Were nothing but to waste night, day and time.
Therefore, since brevity is the soul of wit,
And tediousness the limbs and outward flourishes,
I will be brief: your noble son is mad:
Mad call I it; for, to define true madness,
What is 't but to be nothing else but mad?
But let that go.

  QUEEN: More matter, with less art.

  POLONIUS: Madam, I swear I use no art at all.
That he is mad, 'tis true: 'tis true 'tis pity;
And pity 'tis 'tis true: a foolish figure;
But farewell it, for I will use no art.
Mad let us grant him, then: and now remains
That we find out the cause of this effect,
Or rather say, the cause of this defect,
For this effect defective comes by cause:
Thus it remains, and the remainder thus.
Perpend.
I have a daughter—have while she is mine—
Who, in her duty and obedience, mark,
Hath given me this: now gather, and surmise.   [*Reads.*
'To the celestial and my soul's idol, the most beautified Ophelia,'—
That 's an ill phrase, a vile phrase; 'beautified' is a vile phrase: but
  you shall hear.
Thus: [*Reads.*
'In her excellent white bosom, these, &c.'

QUEEN: Came this from Hamlet to her?

POLONIUS: Good madam, stay awhile; I will be faithful.   [*Reads*.
'Doubt thou the stars are fire;
    Doubt that the sun doth move;
Doubt truth to be a liar;
    But never doubt I love.
'O dear Ophelia, I am ill at these numbers; I have not art to
reckon my groans: but that I love thee best, O most best, believe
it. Adieu.
        'Thine evermore, most dear lady, whilst
          this machine is to him, HAMLET.'
This, in obedience, hath my daughter shown me.
And more above, hath his solicitings,
As they fell out by time, by means and place,
All given to mine ear.

KING: But how hath she
Received his love?

POLONIUS: What do you think of me?

KING: As of a man faithful and honourable.

POLONIUS: I would fain prove so. But what might you think,
When I had seen this hot love on the wing—
As I perceived it, I must tell you that,
Before my daughter told me—what might you,
Or my dear majesty your queen here, think,
If I had play'd the deck or table-book,
Or given my heart a winking, mute and dumb,
Or look'd upon this love with idle sight;
What might you think? No, I went round to work,
And my young mistress thus I did bespeak:
'Lord Hamlet is a prince, out of thy star;
This must not be:' and then I prescripts gave her,
That she should lock herself from his resort,
Admit no messengers, receive no tokens.
Which done, she took the fruits of my advice;
And he, repulsed—a short tale to make—

Fell into a sadness, then into a fast,
Thence to a watch, thence into a weakness,
Thence to a lightness, and, by this declension,
Into the madness wherein now he raves,
And all we mourn for.

KING: Do you think 'tis this?

QUEEN: It may be, very likely.

POLONIUS: Hath there been such a time—I 'd fain know that—
That I have positive said ''Tis so,'
When it proved otherwise?

KING: Not that I know.

POLONIUS: [*Pointing to his head and shoulders*] Take this from
    this, if this be otherwise:
If circumstances lead me, I will find
Where truth is hid, though it were hid indeed
Within the centre.

KING: How may we try it further?

POLONIUS: You know, sometimes he walks four hours together
Here in the lobby.

QUEEN: So he does indeed.

POLONIUS: At such a time I 'll loose my daughter to him:
Be you and I behind an arras then;
Mark the encounter: if he love her not
And be not from his reason fall'n thereon,
Let me be no assistant for a state,
But keep a farm and carters.

KING: We will try it.

QUEEN: But, look, where sadly the poor wretch comes reading.

POLONIUS: Away, I do beseech you, both away:
I 'll board him presently.   [*Exeunt King, Queen, and Attendants.*

Enter Hamlet, reading.

               O, give me leave:
How does my good Lord Hamlet?

HAMLET: Well, God-a-mercy.

POLONIUS: Do you know me, my lord?

HAMLET: Excellent well; you are a fishmonger.

POLONIUS: Not I, my lord.

HAMLET: Then I would you were so honest a man.

POLONIUS: Honest, my lord!

HAMLET: Ay, sir; to be honest, as this world goes, is to be one man picked out of ten thousand.

POLONIUS: That 's very true, my lord.

HAMLET: For if the sun breed maggots in a dead dog, being a god kissing carrion,—Have you a daughter?

POLONIUS: I have, my lord.

HAMLET: Let her not walk i' the sun: conception is a blessing: but not as your daughter may conceive. Friend, look to 't.

POLONIUS: [Aside] How say you by that? Still harping on my daughter: yet he knew me not at first; he said I was a fishmonger: he is far gone, far gone; and truly in my youth I suffered much extremity for love; very near this. I 'll speak to him again. What do you read, my lord?

HAMLET: Words, words, words.

POLONIUS: What is the matter, my lord?

HAMLET: Between who?

POLONIUS: I mean, the matter that you read, my lord.

HAMLET: Slanders, sir: for the satirical rogue says here that old men have grey beards, that their faces are wrinkled, their eyes purging thick amber and plum-tree gum and that they have a plentiful lack of wit, together with most weak hams: all which, sir, though I most powerfully and potently believe, yet I hold it not honesty to have it thus set down for yourself, sir, should be old as I am, if like a crab you could go backward.

POLONIUS: [Aside] Though this be madness, yet there is method in 't. Will you walk out of the air, my lord?

HAMLET: Into my grave.

POLONIUS: Indeed, that is out o' the air. [Aside] How pregnant sometimes his replies are! a happiness that often madness hits on, which reason and sanity could not so prosperously be delivered of. I will leave him, and suddenly contrive the means of meeting between him and my daughter.—My honourable lord, I will most humbly take my leave of you.

HAMLET: You cannot, sir, take from me any thing that I will more willingly part withal: except my life, except my life, except my life.

POLONIUS: Fare you well, my lord.

HAMLET: These tedious old fools!

Enter Rosencrantz and Guildenstern.

POLONIUS: You go to seek the Lord Hamlet; there he is.

ROSENCRANTZ: [*To Polonius*] God save you, sir!   [*Exit Polonius.*

GUILDENSTERN: My honoured lord!

ROSENCRANTZ: My most dear lord!

HAMLET: My excellent good friends! How dost thou, Guilden- stern? Ah, Rosencrantz! Good lads, how do ye both?

ROSENCRANTZ: As the indifferent children of the earth.

GUILDENSTERN: Happy, in that we are not over-happy;
On fortune's cap we are not the very button.

HAMLET: Nor the soles of her shoe?

ROSENCRANTZ: Neither, my lord.

HAMLET: Then you live about her waist, or in the middle of her favours?

GUILDENSTERN: 'Faith, her privates we.

HAMLET: In the secret parts of fortune? O, most true; she is a strumpet. What 's the news?

ROSENCRANTZ: None, my lord, but that the world 's grown honest.

HAMLET: Then is doomsday near: but your news is not true. Let me question more in particular: what have you, my good friends, deserved at the hands of fortune, that she sends you to prison thither?

GUILDENSTERN: Prison, my lord!

HAMLET: Denmark 's a prison.

ROSENCRANTZ: Then is the world one.

HAMLET: A goodly one; in which there are many confines, wards and dungeons, Denmark being one o' the worst.

ROSENCRANTZ: We think not so, my lord.

HAMLET: Why, then, 'tis none to you; for there is nothing either good or bad, but thinking makes it so: to me it is a prison.

ROSENCRANTZ: Why then, your ambition makes it one; 'tis too narrow for your mind.

HAMLET: O God, I could be bounded in a nutshell and count myself a king of infinite space, were it not that I have bad dreams.

GUILDENSTERN: Which dreams indeed are ambition, for the very substance of the ambition is merely the shadow of a dream.

HAMLET: A dream itself is but a shadow.

ROSENCRANTZ: Truly, and I hold ambition of so airy and light a quality that it is but a shadow's shadow.

HAMLET: Then are our beggars bodies, and our monarchs and outstretched heroes the beggars' shadows. Shall we to the court? for, by my fay, I cannot reason.

ROSENCRANTZ: ⎫
GUILDENSTERN: ⎭ We'll wait upon you.

HAMLET: No such matter: I will not sort you with the rest of my servants, for, to speak to you like an honest man, I am most dreadfully attended. But, in the beaten way of friendship, what make you at Elsinore?

ROSENCRANTZ: To visit you, my lord; no other occasion.

HAMLET: Beggar that I am, I am even poor in thanks; but I thank you: and sure, dear friends, my thanks are too dear a half-penny. Were you not sent for? Is it your own inclining? Is it a free visitation? Come, deal justly with me: come, come; nay, speak.

GUILDENSTERN: What should we say, my lord?

HAMLET: Why, any thing, but to the purpose. You were sent for; and there is a kind of confession in your looks which your modesties have not craft enough to colour: I know the good king and queen have sent for you.

ROSENCRANTZ: To what end, my lord?

HAMLET: That you must teach me. But let me conjure you, by the rights of our fellowship by the consonancy of our youth, by the obligation of our ever-preserved love, and by what more dear a better proposer could charge you withal, be even and direct with me, whether you were sent for, or not?

ROSENCRANTZ: [*Aside to Guildenstern*] What say you?

HAMLET: [*Aside*] Nay, then, I have an eye of you.—If you love me, hold not off.

GUILDENSTERN: My lord, we were sent for.

HAMLET: I will tell you why; so shall my anticipation prevent your discovery, and your secrecy to the king and queen moult no feather. I have of late—but wherefore I know not—lost all my mirth, forgone all custom of exercises; and indeed it goes so heavily with my disposition that this goodly frame, the earth, seems to me a sterile promontory, this most excellent canopy, the air, look you, this brave o'erhanging firmament, this majestical roof fretted with golden fire, why, it appears no other thing to me than a foul and pestilent congregation of vapours. What a piece of work is a man! how noble in reason! how infinite in faculty! in form and moving how express and admirable! in action how like an angel! in apprehension how like a god! the beauty of the world! the paragon of animals! And yet, to me, what is this quintessence of dust? man delights not me: no, nor woman neither, though by your smiling you seem to say so.

ROSENCRANTZ: My lord, there was no such stuff in my thoughts.

HAMLET: Why did you laugh then, when I said 'man delights not me'?

ROSENCRANTZ: To think, my lord, if you delight not in man, what lenten entertainment the players shall receive from you: we coted them on the way; and hither are they coming, to offer you service.

HAMLET: He that plays the king shall be welcome; his majesty shall have tribute of me; the adventurous knight shall use his foil and target; the lover shall not sigh gratis; the humourous man shall end his part in peace; the clown shall make those laugh whose lungs are tickle o' the sere; and the lady shall say her mind freely, or the blank verse shall halt for 't. What players are they?

ROSENCRANTZ: Even those you were wont to take delight in, the tragedians of the city.

HAMLET: How chances it they travel? their residence, both in reputation and profit, was better both ways.

ROSENCRANTZ: I think their inhibition comes by the means of the late innovation.

HAMLET: Do they hold the same estimation they did when I was in the city? are they so followed?

ROSENCRANTZ: No, indeed, are they not.

HAMLET: How comes it? do they grow rusty?

ROSENCRANTZ: Nay, their endeavour keeps in the wonted pace: but there is, sir, an aery of children, little eyases, that cry out on the top of question, and are most tyrannically clapped for 't: these are now the fashion, and so berattle the common stages—so they call them—that many wearing rapiers are afraid of goose-quills and dare scarce come thither.

HAMLET: What, are they children? who maintains 'em? how are they escoted? Will they pursue the quality no longer than they can sing? will they not say afterwards, if they should grow themselves to common players—as it is most like, if their means are no better—their writers do them wrong, to make them exclaim against their own succession?

ROSENCRANTZ: 'Faith, there has been much to do on both sides; and the nation holds it no sin to tarre them to controversy: there was, for a while, no money bid for argument, unless the poet and the player went to cuffs in the question.

HAMLET: Is 't possible?

GUILDENSTERN: O, there has been much throwing about of brains.

HAMLET: Do the boys carry it away?

ROSENCRANTZ: Ay, that they do, my lord; Hercules and his load too.

HAMLET: It is not very strange; for mine uncle is king of Denmark, and those that would make mows at him while my father lived, give twenty, forty, fifty, an hundred ducats a-piece for his picture in little. 'Sblood, there is something in this more than natural, if philosophy could find it out.   [*Flourish of trumpets within.*

GUILDENSTERN: There are the players.

HAMLET: Gentlemen, you are welcome to Elsinore. Your hands, come then: the appurtenance of welcome is fashion and ceremony: let me comply with you in this garb, lest my extent to the players, which, I tell you, must show fairly outward, should more appear like entertainment than yours. You are welcome: but my uncle-father and aunt-mother are deceived.

GUILDENSTERN: In what, my dear lord?

HAMLET: I am but mad north-north-west: when the wind is southerly I know a hawk from a handsaw.

Re-enter Polonius.

POLONIUS: Well be with you, gentlemen!

HAMLET: Hark you, Guildenstern; and you too: at each ear a hearer: that great baby you see there is not yet out of his swaddling-clouts.

ROSENCRANTZ: Happily he 's the second time come to them; for they say an old man is twice a child.

HAMLET: I will prophesy he comes to tell me of the players; mark it. You say right, sir: o' Monday morning; 'twas so indeed.

POLONIUS: My lord, I have news to tell you.

HAMLET: My lord, I have news to tell you. When Roscius was an actor in Rome,—

POLONIUS: The actors are come hither, my lord.

HAMLET: Buz, buz!

POLONIUS: Upon mine honour,—

HAMLET: Then came each actor on his ass,—

POLONIUS: The best actors in the world, either for tragedy, comedy, history, pastoral, pastoral-comical, historical-pastoral, tragical-historical, tragical-comical-historical-pastoral, scene individable, or poem unlimited: Seneca cannot be too heavy, nor Plautus too light. For the law of writ and the liberty, these are the only men.

HAMLET: O Jephthah, judge of Israel, what a treasure hadst thou!

POLONIUS: What a treasure had he, my lord?

HAMLET: Why,

'One fair daughter, and no more,
    The which he loved passing well.'
POLONIUS: [*Aside*] Still on my daughter.
HAMLET: Am I not i' the right, old Jephthah?
POLONIUS: If you call me Jephthah, my lord, I have a daughter
that I love passing well.
HAMLET: Nay, that follows not.
POLONIUS: What follows, then, my lord?
HAMLET: Why,
    'As by lot, God wot,'
and then, you know,
'It came to pass, as most like it was,'—the first row of the pious
chanson will show you more; for look, where my abridgement
comes.

Enter four or five Players.

You are welcome, masters; welcome all. I am glad to see thee well.
Welcome, good friends. O, my old friend! thy face is valanced
since I saw thee last: comest thou to beard me in Denmark?
What, my young lady and mistress! By 'r lady, your ladyship is
nearer to heaven than when I saw you last, by the altitude of a
chopine. Pray God, your voice, like a piece of uncurrent gold, be
not cracked within the ring. Masters, you are all welcome. We 'll
e'en to 't like French falconers, fly at any thing we see: we 'll have
a speech straight: come, give us a taste of your quality; come, a
passionate speech.
FIRST PLAYER: What speech, my lord?
HAMLET: I heard thee speak me a speech once, but it was never
acted; or, if it was, not above once; for the play, I remember,
pleased not the million; 'twas caviare to the general: but it was—
as I received it, and others, whose judgements in such matters
cried in the top of mine—an excellent play, well digested in the
scenes, set down with as much modesty as cunning. I remember,
one said there were no sallets in the lines to make the matter
savoury, nor no matter in the phrase that might indict the author

of affectation; but called it an honest method, as wholesome as
sweet, and by very much more handsome than fine. One speech
in it I chiefly loved: 'twas Æneas' tale to Dido; and thereabout of it
especially, where he speaks of Priam's slaughter: if it live in your
memory, begin at this line: let me see, let me see—

'The rugged Pyrrhus, like the Hyrcanian beast,'—
it is not so:—it begins with Pyrrhus:—

'The rugged Pyrrhus, he whose sable arms,
Black as his purpose, did the night resemble
When he lay couched in the ominous horse,
Hath now this dread and black complexion smear'd
With heraldry more dismal; head to foot
Now is he total gules; horridly trick'd
With blood of fathers, mothers, daughters, sons,
Baked and impasted with the parching streets,
That lend a tyrannous and damned light
To their lord's murder: roasted in wrath and fire,
And thus o'er-sized with coagulate gore,
With eyes like carbuncles, the hellish Pyrrhus
Old grandsire Priam seeks.'

So, proceed you.

POLONIUS: 'Fore God, my lord, well spoken, with good accent
and good discretion.

FIRST PLAYER: 'Anon he finds him
Striking too short at Greeks; his antique sword,
Rebellious to his arm, lies where it falls,
Repugnant to command: unequal match'd,
Pyrrhus at Priam drives; in rage strikes wide;
But with the whiff and wind of his fell sword
The unnerved father falls. Then senseless Ilium,
Seeming to feel this blow, with flaming top
Stoops to his base, and with a hideous crash
Takes prisoner Pyrrhus' ear: for, lo! his sword,
Which was declining on the milky head
Of reverend Priam, seem'd i' the air to stick:

So, as a painted tyrant, Pyrrhus stood,
And like a neutral to his will and matter,
Did nothing.
But, as we often see, against some storm,
A silence in the heavens, the rack stand still,
The bold winds speechless and the orb below
As hush as death, anon the dreadful thunder
Doth rend the region, so, after Pyrrhus' pause,
Aroused vengeance sets him new a-work;
And never did the Cyclops' hammers fall
On Mars's armour forged for proof eterne
With less remorse than Pyrrhus' bleeding sword
Now falls on Priam.
Out, out, thou strumpet, Fortune! All you gods,
In general synod, take away her power;
Break all the spokes and fellies from her wheel,
And bowl the round nave down the hill of heaven,
As low as to the fiends!'

POLONIUS: This is too long.

HAMLET: It shall to the barber's, with your beard. Prithee, say on: he 's for a jig or a tale of bawdry, or he sleeps: say on: come to Hecuba.

FIRST PLAYER: 'But who, O, who had seen the mobled queen—'

HAMLET: 'The mobled queen?'

POLONIUS: That 's good; 'mobled queen' is good.

FIRST PLAYER: 'Run barefoot up and down threatening the flames
With bisson rheum; a clout upon that head
Where late the diadem stood, and for a robe,
About her lank and all o'er-teemed loins,
A blanket, in the alarm of fear caught up;
Who this had seen, with tongue in venom steep'd,
'Gainst Fortune's state would treason have pronounced:
But if the gods themselves did see her then
When she saw Pyrrhus make malicious sport
In mincing with his sword her husband's limbs,

The instant burst of clamour that she made,
Unless things mortal move them not at all,
Would have made milch the burning eyes of heaven,
And passion in the gods.'

POLONIUS: Look, whether he has not turned his colour and has tears in 's eyes. Pray you, no more.

HAMLET: 'Tis well; I 'll have thee speak out the rest soon. Good my lord, will you see the players well bestowed? Do you hear, let them be well used; for they are the abstract and brief chronicles of the time: after your death you were better have a bad epitaph than their ill report while you live.

POLONIUS: My lord, I will use them according to their desert.

HAMLET: God's bodykins, man, much better: use every man after his desert, and who should 'scape whipping? Use them after your own honour and dignity: the less they deserve, the more merit is in your bounty. Take them in.

POLONIUS: Come, sirs.

HAMLET: Follow him, friends: we 'll hear a play to-morrow. [*Exit Polonius with all the Players but the First.*] Dost thou hear me, old friend; can you play the Murder of Gonzago?

FIRST PLAYER: Ay, my lord.

HAMLET: We 'll ha 't to-morrow night. You could, for a need, study a speech of some dozen or sixteen lines, which I would set down and insert in 't, could you not?

FIRST PLAYER: Ay, my lord.

HAMLET: Very well. Follow that lord; and look you mock him not. [*Exit First Player.*] My good friends, I 'll leave you till night: you are welcome to Elsinore.

ROSENCRANTZ: Good my lord!

HAMLET: Ay, so, God be wi' ye; [*Exeunt Rosencrantz and Guildenstern.*] Now I am alone.
O, what a rogue and peasant slave am I!
Is it not monstrous that this player here,
But in a fiction, in a dream of passion,
Could force so his soul to his own conceit

That from her working all his visage wann'd,
Tears in his eyes, distraction in 's aspect,
A broken voice, and his whole function suiting
With forms to his conceit? and all for nothing!
For Hecuba!
What 's Hecuba to him, or he to Hecuba,
That he should weep for her? What would he do,
Had he the motive and the cue for passion
That I have? He would drown the stage with tears
And cleave the general ear with horrid speech,
Make mad the guilty and appal the free,
Confound the ignorant, and amaze indeed
The very faculties of eyes and ears.
Yet I,
A dull and muddy-mettled rascal, peak,
Like John-a-dreams, unpregnant of my cause,
And can say nothing; no, not for a king,
Upon whose property and most dear life
A damn'd defeat was made. Am I a coward?
Who calls me villain? breaks my pate across?
Plucks off my beard, and blows it in my face?
Tweaks me by the nose? gives me the lie i' the throat,
As deep as to the lungs? who does me this?
Ha!
'Swounds, I should take it: for it cannot be
But I am pigeon-liver'd and lack gall
To make oppression bitter, or ere this
I should have fatted all the region kites
With this slave's offal: bloody, bawdy villain!
Remorseless, treacherous, lecherous, kindless villain!
O, vengeance!
Why, what an ass am I! This is most brave,
That I, the son of a dear father murder'd,
Prompted to my revenge by heaven and hell,
Must, like a whore, unpack my heart with words,

And fall a-cursing, like a very drab,
A scullion!
Fie upon 't! foh! About, my brain! I have heard
That guilty creatures sitting at a play
Have by the very cunning of the scene
Been struck so to the soul that presently
They have proclaim'd their malefactions;
For murder, though it have no tongue, will speak
With most miraculous organ. I 'll have these players
Play something like the murder of my father
Before mine uncle: I 'll observe his looks;
I 'll tent him to the quick: if he but blench,
I know my course. The spirit that I have seen
May be the devil: and the devil hath power
To assume a pleasing shape; yea, and perhaps
Out of my weakness and my melancholy,
As he is very potent with such spirits,
Abuses me to damn me: I 'll have grounds
More relative than this: the play 's the thing
Wherein I 'll catch the conscience of the king.   [*Exit.*

ACT III.

SCENE I. *A room in the castle.*
Enter King, Queen, Polonius, Ophelia,
Rosencrantz, and Guildenstern.

KING: And can you, by no drift of circumstance,
Get from him why he puts on this confusion,
Grating so harshly all his days of quiet
With turbulent and dangerous lunacy?
ROSENCRANTZ: He does confess he feels himself distracted;
But from what cause he will by no means speak.
GUILDENSTERN: Nor do we find him forward to be sounded,

But, with a crafty madness, keeps aloof,
When we would bring him on to some confession
Of his true state.
    QUEEN: Did he receive you well?
    ROSENCRANTZ: Most like a gentleman.
    GUILDENSTERN: But with much forcing of his disposition.
    ROSENCRANTZ: Niggard of question; but, of our demands,
Most free in his reply.
    QUEEN: Did you assay him
To any pastime?
    ROSENCRANTZ: Madam, it so fell out, that certain players
We o'er-raught on the way: of these we told him;
And there did seem in him a kind of joy
To hear of it: they are about the court,
And, as I think, they have already order
This night to play before him.
    POLONIUS: 'Tis most true:
And he beseech'd me to entreat your majesties
To hear and see the matter.
    KING: With all my heart; and it doth much content me
To hear him so inclined.
Good gentlemen, give him a further edge,
And drive his purpose on to these delights.
    ROSENCRANTZ: We shall, my lord.
                  [*Exeunt Rosencrantz and Guildenstern.*
    KING: Sweet Gertrude, leave us too;
For we have closely sent for Hamlet hither,
That he, as 'twere by accident, may here
Affront Ophelia:
Her father and myself, lawful espials,
Will so bestow ourselves that, seeing, unseen,
We may of their encounter frankly judge,
And gather by him, as he is behaved,
If 't be the affliction of his love or no
That thus he suffers for.

QUEEN: I shall obey you.
And for your part, Ophelia, I do wish
That your good beauties be the happy cause
Of Hamlet's wildness: so shall I hope your virtues
Will bring him to his wonted way again,
To both your honours.

    OPHELIA: Madam, I wish it may.   [*Exit Queen.*

    POLONIUS: Ophelia, walk you here. Gracious, so please you,
We will bestow ourselves. [*To Ophelia*] Read on this book;
That show of such an exercise may colour
Your loneliness. We are oft to blame in this,—
'Tis too much proved—that with devotion's visage
And pious action we do sugar o'er
The devil himself.

    KING: [*Aside*] O, 'tis too true!
How smart a lash that speech doth give my conscience!
The harlot's cheek, beautied with plastering art,
Is not more ugly to the thing that helps it
Than is my deed to my most painted word:
O heavy burthen!

    POLONIUS: I hear him coming: let 's withdraw, my lord.

                           [*Exeunt King and Polonius.*

Enter Hamlet.

    HAMLET: To be, or not to be: that is the question:
Whether 'tis nobler in the mind to suffer
The slings and arrows of outrageous fortune,
Or to take arms against a sea of troubles,
And by opposing end them?   To die: to sleep;
No more; and by a sleep to say we end
The heart-ache and the thousand natural shocks
That flesh is heir to, 'tis a consummation
Devoutly to be wish'd. To die, to sleep;
To sleep: perchance to dream: ay, there 's the rub;
For in that sleep of death what dreams may come

When we have shuffled off this mortal coil,
Must give us pause: there 's the respect
That makes calamity of so long life;
For who would bear the whips and scorns of time,
The oppressor's wrong, the proud man's contumely,
The pangs of despised love, the law's delay,
The insolence of office and the spurns
That patient merit of the unworthy takes,
When he himself might his quietus make
With a bare bodkin? who would fardels bear,
To grunt and sweat under a weary life,
But that the dread of something after death,
The undiscover'd country from whose bourn
No traveller returns, puzzles the will
And makes us rather bear those ills we have
Than fly to others that we know not of?
Thus conscience does make cowards of us all;
And thus the native hue of resolution
Is sicklied o'er with the pale cast of thought,
And enterprises of great pitch and moment
With this regard their currents turn awry,
And lose the name of action.—Soft you now!
The fair Ophelia! Nymph, in thy orisons
Be all my sins remember'd.

OPHELIA: Good my lord,
How does your honour for this many a day?

HAMLET: I humbly thank you; well, well, well.

OPHELIA: My lord, I have remembrances of yours,
That I have longed long to re-deliver;
I pray you, now receive them.

HAMLET: No, not I;
I never gave you aught.

OPHELIA: My honour'd lord, you know right well you did;
And, with them, words of so sweet breath composed
As made the things more rich: their perfume lost,

Take these again; for to the noble mind
Rich gifts wax poor when givers prove unkind.
There, my lord.

HAMLET: Ha, ha! are you honest?

OPHELIA: My lord?

HAMLET: Are you fair?

OPHELIA: What means your lordship?

HAMLET: That if you be honest and fair, your honesty should admit no discourse to your beauty.

OPHELIA: Could beauty, my lord, have better commerce than with honesty?

HAMLET: Ay, truly; for the power of beauty will sooner transform honesty from what it is to a bawd than the force of honesty can translate beauty into his likeness: this was sometime a paradox, but now the time gives it proof. I did love you once.

OPHELIA: Indeed, my lord, you made me believe so.

HAMLET: You should not have believed me; for virtue cannot so inoculate our old stock but we shall relish of it: I loved you not.

OPHELIA: I was the more deceived.

HAMLET: Get thee to a nunnery: why wouldst thou be a breeder of sinners? I am myself indifferent honest; but yet I could accuse me of such things that it were better my mother had not borne me: I am very proud, revengeful, ambitious, with more offences at my beck than I have thoughts to put them in, imagination to give them shape, or time to act them in. What should such fellows as I do crawling between earth and heaven? We are arrant knaves, all; believe none of us. Go thy ways to a nunnery. Where's your father?

OPHELIA: At home, my lord.

HAMLET: Let the doors be shut upon him, that he may play the fool no where but in 's own house. Farewell.

OPHELIA: O, help him, you sweet heavens!

HAMLET: If thou dost marry, I 'll give thee this plague for thy dowry: be thou as chaste as ice, as pure as snow, thou shalt not escape calumny. Get thee to a nunnery, go: farewell. Or, if thou wilt needs marry, marry a fool; for wise men know well enough

what monsters you make of them. To a nunnery, go, and quickly
too. Farewell.

OPHELIA: O heavenly powers, restore him!

HAMLET: I have heard of your paintings too, well enough; God
has given you one face, and you make yourselves another: you
jig, you amble, and you lisp, and nick-name God's creatures, and
make your wantonness your ignorance. Go to, I 'll no more on 't;
it hath made me mad. I say, we will have no more marriages:
those that are married already, all but one, shall live; the rest shall
keep as they are. To a nunnery, go.   [*Exit.*

OPHELIA: O, what a noble mind is here o'erthrown!
The courtier's, soldier's, scholar's, eye, tongue, sword;
The expectancy and rose of the fair state,
The glass of fashion and the mould of form,
The observed of all observers, quite, quite down!
And I, of ladies most deject and wretched,
That suck'd the honey of his music vows,
Now see that noble and most sovereign reason,
Like sweet bells jangled, out of tune and harsh;
That unmatch'd form and feature of blown youth
Blasted with ecstasy: O, woe is me,
To have seen what I have seen, see what I see!

Re-enter King and Polonius.

KING: Love! his affections do not that way tend;
Nor what he spake, though it lack'd form a little,
Was not like madness. There 's something in his soul,
O'er which his melancholy sits on brood;
And I do doubt the hatch and the disclose
Will be some danger: which for to prevent,
I have in quick determination
Thus set it down: he shall with speed to England,
For the demand of our neglected tribute:
Haply the seas and country different
With variable objects shall expel

This something-settled matter in his heart,
Whereon his brains still beating puts him thus
From fashion of himself. What think you on 't?
   POLONIUS: It shall do well: but yet do I believe
The origin and commencement of his grief
Sprung from neglected love. How now, Ophelia!
You need not tell us what Lord Hamlet said:
We heard it all. My lord, do as you please;
But, if you hold it fit, after the play
Let his queen mother all alone entreat him
To show his grief: let her be round with him;
And I 'll be placed, so please you, in the ear
Of all their conference. If she find him not,
To England send him, or confine him where
Your wisdom best shall think.
   KING: It shall be so:
Madness in great ones must not unwatch'd go.   [*Exeunt.*

SCENE II. *A hall in the castle.*
Enter Hamlet and Players.

HAMLET: Speak the speech, I pray you, as I pronounced it to
you, trippingly on the tongue: but if you mouth it, as many of
your players do, I had as lief the town-crier spoke my lines. Nor
do not saw the air too much with your hand, thus, but use all
gently; for in the very torrent, tempest, and, as I may say, the
whirlwind of passion, you must acquire and beget a temperance
that may give it smoothness. O, it offends me to the soul to hear a
robustious periwig-pated fellow tear a passion to tatters, to very
rags, to split the ears of the groundlings, who for the most part are
capable of nothing but inexplicable dumb-shows and noise: I
would have such a fellow whipped for o'erdoing Termagant: it
out-herods Herod: pray you, avoid it.
   FIRST PLAYER: I warrant your honour.
   HAMLET: Be not too tame neither, but let your own discretion

be your tutor: suit the action to the word, the word to the action; with this special observance, that you o'erstep not the modesty of nature: for any thing so overdone is from the purpose of playing, whose end, both at the first and now, was and is, to hold as 'twere, the mirror up to nature; to show virtue her own feature, scorn her own image, and the very age and body of the time his form and pressure. Now this overdone, or come tardy off, though it make the unskilful laugh, cannot but make the judicious grieve; the censure of the which one must in your allowance o'erweigh a whole theatre of others. O, there be players that I have seen play, and heard others praise, and that highly, not to speak it profanely, that, neither having the accent of Christians nor the gait of Christian, pagan, nor man, have so strutted and bellowed that I have thought some of nature's journeymen had made men and made them well, they imitated humanity so abominably.

FIRST PLAYER: I hope we have reformed that indifferently with us, sir.

HAMLET: O, reform it altogether. And let those that play your clowns speak no more than is set down for them; for there be of them that will themselves laugh, to set on some quantity of barren spectators to laugh too; though, in the mean time, some necessary question of the play be then to be considered: that's villanous, and shows a most pitiful ambition in the fool that uses it. Go, make you ready.   [*Exeunt Players.*

Enter Polonius, Rosencrantz, and Guildenstern.

How now, my lord! will the king hear this piece of work?

POLONIUS: And the queen too, and that presently.

HAMLET: Bid the players make haste. [*Exit Polonius.*] Will you two help to hasten them?

ROSENCRANTZ: } We will, my lord.
GUILDENSTERN:

                                   [*Exeunt Rosencrantz and Guildenstern.*

HAMLET: What ho! Horatio!

Enter Horatio.

HORATIO: Here, sweet lord, at your service.

HAMLET: Horatio, thou art e'en as just a man
As e'er my conversation coped withal.

HORATIO: O, my dear lord,—

HAMLET: Nay, do not think I flatter;
For what advancement may I hope from thee
That no revenue hast but thy good spirits,
To feed and clothe thee? Why should the poor be flatter'd?
No, let the candied tongue lick absurd pomp,
And crook the pregnant hinges of the knee
Where thrift may follow fawning. Dost thou hear?
Since my dear soul was mistress of her choice
And could of men distinguish, her election
Hath seal'd thee for herself; for thou hast been
As one, in suffering all, that suffers nothing,
A man that fortune's buffets and rewards
Hast ta'en with equal thanks: and blest are those
Whose blood and judgement are so well commingled,
That they are not a pipe for fortune's finger
To sound what stop she please. Give me that man
That is not passion's slave, and I will wear him
In my heart's core, ay, in my heart of heart,
As I do thee.—Something too much of this.—
There is a play to-night before the king;
One scene of it comes near the circumstance
Which I have told thee of my father's death:
I prithee, when thou seest that act afoot,
Even with the very comment of thy soul
Observe mine uncle: if his occulted guilt
Do not itself unkennel in one speech,
It is a damned ghost that we have seen,
And my imaginations are as foul
As Vulcan's stithy. Give him heedful note;
For I mine eyes will rivet to his face,
And after we will both our judgements join

In censure of his seeming.

HORATIO: Well, my lord:
If he steal aught the whilst this play is playing,
And 'scape detecting, I will pay the theft.

HAMLET: They are coming to the play: I must be idle:
Get you a place.

Danish march. A flourish. Enter King, Queen, Polonius,
Ophelia, Rosencrantz, Guildenstern, and others.

KING: How fares our cousin Hamlet?

HAMLET: Excellent, i' faith; of the chameleon's dish: I eat the
air, promise-crammed: you cannot feed capons so.

KING: I have nothing with this answer,
Hamlet; these words are not mine.

HAMLET: No, nor mine now. [*To Polonius*] My lord, you played
once i' the university, you say?

POLONIUS: That did I, my lord; and was accounted a good actor.

HAMLET: What did you enact?

POLONIUS: I did enact Julius Caesar: I was killed i' the Capitol;
Brutus killed me.

HAMLET: It was a brute part of him to kill so capital a calf there.
Be the players ready?

ROSENCRANTZ: Ay, my lord; they stay upon your patience.

QUEEN: Come hither, my dear Hamlet, sit by me.

HAMLET: No, good mother, here 's metal more attractive.

POLONIUS: [*To the King*] O, ho! do you mark that?

HAMLET: Lady, shall I lie in your lap?

[*Lying down at Ophelia's feet.*

OPHELIA: No, my lord.

HAMLET: I mean, my head upon your lap?

OPHELIA: Ay, my lord.

HAMLET: Do you think I meant country matters?

OPHELIA: I think nothing, my lord.

HAMLET: That 's a fair thought to lie between maids' legs.

OPHELIA: What is, my lord?

HAMLET: Nothing.

OPHELIA: You are merry, my lord.

HAMLET: Who, I?

OPHELIA: Ay, my lord.

HAMLET: O God, your only jig-maker. What should a man do but be merry? for, look you, how cheerfully my mother looks, and my father died within these two hours.

OPHELIA: Nay, 'tis twice two month, my lord.

HAMLET: So long? Nay then, let the devil wear black, for I 'll have a suit of sables. O heavens! die two months ago, and not forgotten yet! Then there 's hope a great man's memory may outlive his life half a year: but, by 'r lady, he must build churches, then; or else shall he suffer not thinking on, with the hobby-horse, whose epitaph is 'For, O, for O, the hobby-horse is forgot.'

Hautboys play. The dumb-show enters.

Enter a King and a Queen very lovingly: the Queen embracing him, and he her. She kneels, and makes show of protestation unto him. He takes her up, and declines his head upon her neck: lays him down upon a bank of flowers: she, seeing him asleep, leaves him. Anon comes in a fellow, takes off his crown, kisses it, and pours poison in the King's ears, and exit. The Queen returns; finds the King dead, and makes passionate action. The Poisoner, with some two or three Mutes, comes in again, seeming to lament with her. The dead body is carried away. The Poisoner wooes the Queen with gifts: she seems loath and unwilling awhile, but in the end accepts his love.   [Exeunt.

OPHELIA: What means this, my lord?

HAMLET: Marry, this is miching mallecho; it means mischief.

OPHELIA: Belike this show imports the argument of the play.

Enter Prologue.

HAMLET: We shall know by this fellow: the players cannot keep counsel; they 'll tell all.

OPHELIA: Will he tell us what this show meant?

HAMLET: Ay, or any show that you 'll show him: be not you
    ashamed to show, he 'll not shame to tell you what it means.
OPHELIA: You are naught, you are naught: I 'll make the play.
PROLOGUE: For us, and for our tragedy,
                Here stoping to your clemency,
                We beg your hearing patiently.   [*Exit.*
HAMLET: Is this a prologue, or the posy of a ring?
OPHELIA: 'Tis brief, my lord.
HAMLET: As woman's love.

Enter two Players, King and Queen.

PLAYER KING: Full thirty times hath Phoebus' cart gone round
Neptune's salt wash and Tellus' orbed ground,
And thirty dozen moons with borrow'd sheen
About the world have times twelve thirties been,
Since love our hearts and Hymen did our hands
Unite commutual in most sacred bands.
    PLAYER QUEEN: So many journeys may the sun and moon
Make again count o'er ere love be done!
But, woe is me, you are so sick of late,
So far from cheer and from your former state,
That I distrust you. Yet, though I distrust,
Discomfort you, my lord, it nothing must:
For women's fear and love holds quantity:
In either aught, or in extremity.
Now, what my love is, proof hath made you know;
And as my love is sized, my fear is so:
Where love is great, the littlest doubts are fear;
Where little fears grow great, great love grows there.
    PLAYER KING: 'Faith, I must leave thee, love, and shortly too;
My operant powers their functions leave to do:
And thou shalt live in this fair world behind,
Honour'd, beloved; and haply one as kind
For husband shalt thou—
    PLAYER QUEEN: O, confound the rest!

Such love must needs be treason in my breast:
In second husband let me be accurst!
None wed the second but who kill'd the first.

    HAMLET: [*Aside*] Wormwood, wormwood.

    PLAYER QUEEN: The instances that second marriage move
Are base respects of thrift, but none of love:
A second time I kill my husband dead,
When second husband kisses me in bed.

    PLAYER KING: I do believe you think what now you speak;
But what we do determine oft we break.
Purpose is but the slave to memory,
Of violent birth, but poor validity:
Which now, like fruit unripe, sticks on the tree;
But fall, unshaken, when they mellow be.
Most necessary 'tis that we forget
To pay ourselves what to ourselves is debt:
What to ourselves in passion we propose,
The passion ending, doth the purpose lose.
The violence of either grief or joy
Their own enactures with themselves destroy:
Where joy most revels, grief doth most lament;
Grief joys, joy grieves, on slender accident.
This world is not for aye, nor 'tis not strange
That even our loves should with our fortunes change;
For 'tis a question left us yet to prove,
Whether love lead fortune, or else fortune love.
The great man down, you mark his favourite flies;
The poor advanced makes friends of enemies,
And hitherto doth love on fortune tend;
For who not needs shall never lack a friend,
And who in want a hollow friend doth try,
Directly seasons him his enemy.
But, orderly to end where I begun,
Our wills and fates do so contrary run
That our devices still are overthrown;

Our thoughts are ours, their ends none of our own:
So think thou wilt no second husband wed;
But die thy thoughts when thy first lord is dead.
　　　PLAYER QUEEN: Nor earth to me give food, nor heaven light!
Sport and repose lock from me day and night!
To desperation turn my trust and hope!
An anchor's cheer in prison be my scope!
Each opposite that blanks the face of joy
Meet what I would have well and it destroy!
Both here and hence pursue me lasting strife,
If, once a widow, ever I be wife!
　　　HAMLET: If she should break it now!
　　　PLAYER KING: 'Tis deeply sworn. Sweet, leave me here awhile;
My spirits grow dull, and fain I would beguile
The tedious day with sleep.   [*Sleeps.*
　　　PLAYER QUEEN:　　　　　Sleep rock thy brain;
And never come mischance between us twain!   [*Exit.*
　　　HAMLET: Madam, how like you this play?
　　　QUEEN: The lady doth protest too much, methinks.
　　　HAMLET: O, but she 'll keep her word.
　　　KING: Have you heard the argument? Is there no offence in 't?
　　　HAMLET: No, no, they do but jest, poison in jest; no offence i'
the world.
　　　KING: What do you call the play?
　　　HAMLET: The Mouse-trap. Marry, how? Tropically. This play is
the image of a murder done in Vienna: Gonzago is the duke's
name; his wife, Baptista; you shall see anon; 'tis a knavish piece of
work: but what o' that? your majesty and we that have free souls, it
touches us not: let the galled jade wince, our withers are unwrung.

Enter Lucianus.

This is one Lucianus, nephew to the king.
　　　OPHELIA: You are as good as a chorus, my lord.
　　　HAMLET: I could interpret between you and your love, if I
could see the puppets dallying.

OPHELIA: You are keen, my lord, you are keen.

HAMLET: It would cost you a groaning to take off my edge.

OPHELIA: Still better, and worse.

HAMLET: So you must take your husbands. Begin, murderer; pox, leave thy damnable faces, and begin. Come: 'the croaking raven doth bellow for revenge.'

LUCIANUS: Thoughts black, hands apt, drugs fit and time agree-
    ing;
Confederate season, else no creature seeing;
Thou mixture rank, of midnight weeds collected,
With Hecate's ban thrice blasted, thrice infected,
Thy natural magic and dire property,
On wholesome life usurp immediately.
                    [*Pours the poison into the sleeper's ears.*

HAMLET: He poisons him i' the garden for 's estate. His name 's Gonzago: the story is extant, and writ in choice Italian: you shall see anon how the murderer gets the love of Gonzago's wife.

OPHELIA: The king rises.

HAMLET: What, frighted with false fire!

QUEEN: How fares my lord?

POLONIUS: Give o'er the play.

KING: Give some light: away!

ALL: Lights, lights, lights!   [*Exeunt all but Hamlet and Horatio.*

HAMLET: Why, let the stricken deer go weep,
    The heart ungalled play;
For some must watch, while some must sleep:
    So runs the world away.
Would not this, sir, and a forest of feathers—if the rest of my fortunes turn Turk with me—with two Provincial roses on my razed
shoes, get me a fellowship in a cry of players, sir?

HORATIO: Half a share.

HAMLET: A whole one, I.
    For thou dost know, O Damon dear,
    This realm dismantled was
Of Jove himself; and now reigns here

    A very, very—pajock.

HORATIO: You might have rhymed.

HAMLET: O good Horatio, I 'll take the ghost's word for a thousand pound. Didst perceive?

HORATIO: Very well, my lord.

HAMLET: Upon the talk of the poisoning?

HORATIO: I did very well note him.

HAMLET: Ah, ha! come, some music! come, the recorders!
    For if the king like not the comedy,
    Why, then, belike, he likes it not, perdy.
Come, some music!

Re-enter Rosencrantz and Guildenstern.

GUILDENSTERN: Good my lord, vouchsafe me a word with you.

HAMLET: Sir, a whole history.

GUILDENSTERN: The king, sir,—

HAMLET: Ay, sir, what of him?

GUILDENSTERN: Is in his retirement marvellous distempered.

HAMLET: With drink, sir?

GUILDENSTERN: No, my lord, rather with choler.

HAMLET: Your wisdom should show itself more richer to signify this to his doctor; for, for me to put him to his purgation would perhaps plunge him into far more choler.

GUILDENSTERN: Good my lord, put your discourse into some frame and start not so wildly from my affair.

HAMLET: I am tame, sir: pronounce.

GUILDENSTERN: The queen, your mother, in most great affliction of spirit, hath sent me to you.

HAMLET: You are welcome.

GUILDENSTERN: Nay, good my lord, this courtesy is not of the right breed. If it shall please you to make me a wholesome answer, I will do your mother's commandment: if not, your pardon and my return shall be the end of my business.

HAMLET: Sir, I cannot.

GUILDENSTERN: What, my lord?

HAMLET: Make you a wholesome answer; my wit 's diseased; but, sir, such answer as I can make, you shall command; or, rather, as you say, my mother: therefore no more, but to the matter: my mother, you say,—

ROSENCRANTZ: Then thus she says; your behaviour hath struck her into amazement and admiration.

HAMLET: O wonderful son, that can so astonish a mother! But is there no sequel at the heels of this mother's admiration? Impart.

ROSENCRANTZ: She desires to speak with you in her closet, ere you go to bed.

HAMLET: We shall obey, were she ten times our mother. Have you any further trade with us?

ROSENCRANTZ: My lord, you once did love me.

HAMLET: So I do still, by these pickers and stealers.

ROSENCRANTZ: Good my lord, what is your cause of distemper? you do, surely, bar the door upon your own liberty, if you deny your griefs to your friend.

HAMLET: Sir, I lack advancement.

ROSENCRANTZ: How can that be, when you have the voice of the king himself for your succession in Denmark?

HAMLET: Ay, sir, but 'While the grass grows,'—the proverb is something musty.

Re-enter Players with recorders.

O, the recorders! let me see one. To withdraw with you:—why do you go about to recover the wind of me, as if you would drive me into a toil?

GUILDENSTERN: O, my lord, if my duty be too bold, my love is too unmannerly.

HAMLET: I do not well understand that. Will you play upon this pipe?

GUILDENSTERN: My lord, I cannot.

HAMLET: I pray you.

GUILDENSTERN: Believe me, I cannot.

HAMLET: I do beseech you.

GUILDENSTERN: I know no touch of it, my lord.

HAMLET: 'Tis as easy as lying: govern these ventages with your fingers and thumb, give it breath with your mouth, and it will discourse most eloquent music. Look you, these are the stops.

GUILDENSTERN: But these cannot I command to any utterance of harmony; I have not the skill.

HAMLET: Why, look you now, how unworthy a thing you make of me! You would play upon me; you would seem to know my stops; you would pluck out the heart of my mystery; you would sound me from my lowest note to the top of my compass: and there is much music, excellent voice, in this little organ; yet cannot you make it speak. 'S blood, do you think I am easier to be played on than a pipe? Call me what instrument you will, though you can fret me, yet you cannot play upon me.

Enter Polonius.

God bless you, sir!

POLONIUS: My lord, the queen would speak with you, and presently.

HAMLET: Do you see yonder cloud that 's almost in shape of a camel?

POLONIUS: By the mass, and 'tis like a camel, indeed.

HAMLET: Methinks it is like a weasel.

POLONIUS: It is backed like a weasel.

HAMLET: Or like a whale?

POLONIUS: Very like a whale.

HAMLET: Then I will come to my mother by and by. They fool me to the top of my bent. I will come by and by.

POLONIUS: I will say so.

HAMLET: By and by is easily said. [*Exit Polonius.*] Leave me, friends.   [*Exeunt all but Hamlet.*

'Tis now the very witching time of night,
When churchyards yawn and hell itself breathes out
Contagion to this world: now could I drink hot blood,
And do such bitter business as the day

Would quake to look on. Soft! now to my mother.
O heart, lose not thy nature; let not ever
The soul of Nero enter this firm bosom:
Let me be cruel, not unnatural:
I will speak daggers to her, but use none;
My tongue and soul in this be hypocrites;
How in my words soever she be shent,
To give them seals never, my soul, consent!   [*Exit.*

SCENE III. *A room in the castle.*
Enter King, Rosencrantz, and Guildenstern.

KING: I like him not, nor stands it safe with us
To let his madness range. Therefore prepare you;
I your commission will forthwith dispatch,
And he to England shall along with you:
The terms of our estate may not endure
Hazard so near us as doth hourly grow
Out of his lunacies.

GUILDENSTERN: We will ourselves provide:
Most holy and religious fear it is
To keep those many many bodies safe
That live and feed upon your majesty.

ROSENCRANTZ: The single and peculiar life is bound,
With all the strength and armour of the mind,
To keep itself from noyance; but much more
That spirit upon whose weal depend and rest
The lives of many. The cease of majesty
Dies not alone; but, like a gulf, doth draw
What 's near it with it: it is a massy wheel,
Fix'd on the summit of the highest mount,
To whose huge spokes ten thousand lesser things
Are mortised and adjoin'd; which, when it falls,
Each small annexment, petty consequence,
Attends the boisterous ruin. Never alone

Did the king sigh, but with a general groan.

KING: Arm you, I pray you, to this speedy voyage;
For we will fetters put upon this fear,
Which now goes too free-footed.

ROSENCRANTZ: }
GUILDENSTERN: } We will haste us.

[*Exeunt Rosencrantz and Guildenstern.*

Enter Polonius.

POLONIUS: My lord, he 's going to his mother's closet:
Behind the arras I 'll convey myself,
To hear the process; I 'll warrant she 'll tax him home:
And, as you said, and wisely was it said,
'Tis meet that some more audience than a mother,
Since nature makes them partial, should o'erhear
The speech, of vantage. Fare you well, my liege:
I 'll call upon you ere you go to bed,
And tell you what I know.

KING: Thanks, dear my lord.   [*Exit Polonius.*
O, my offence is rank, it smells to heaven;
It hath the primal eldest curse upon 't,
A brother's murder. Pray can I not,
Though inclination be as sharp as will:
My stronger guilt defeats my strong intent;
And, like a man to double business bound,
I stand in pause where I shall first begin,
And both neglect. What if this cursed hand
Were thicker than itself with brother's blood,
Is there not rain enough in the sweet heavens
To wash it white as snow? Whereto serves mercy
But to confront the visage of offence?
And what 's in prayer but this two-fold force,
To be forestalled ere we come to fall,
Or pardon'd being down? Then I 'll look up;
My fault is past. But, O, what form of prayer

Can serve my term? 'Forgive me my foul murder'?
That cannot be; since I am still possess'd
Of those effects for which I did the murder,
My crown, mine own ambition and my queen.
May one be pardon'd and retain the offence?
In the corrupted currents of this world
Offence's gilded hand may shove by justice,
And oft 'tis seen the wicked prize itself
Buys out the law: but 'tis not so above;
There is no shuffling, there the action lies
In his true nature; and we ourselves compell'd,
Even to the teeth and forehead of our faults,
To give in evidence. What then? what rests?
Try what repentance can: what can it not?
Yet what can it when one can not repent?
O wretched state! O bosom black as death!
O limed soul, that, struggling to be free,
Art more engaged! Help, angels! Make assay!
Bow, stubborn knees; and, heart with strings of steel,
Be soft as sinews of the new-born babe!
All may be well.   [*Retires and kneels.*

Enter Hamlet.

HAMLET: Now might I do it pat, now he is praying;
And now I 'll do 't. And so he goes to heaven;
And so am I revenged. That would be scann'd:
A villain kills my father; and for that,
I, his sole son, do this same villain send
To heaven.
O, this is hire and salary, not revenge.
He took my father grossly, full of bread;
With all his crimes broad blown, as flush as May;
And how his audit stands who knows save heaven?
But in our circumstance and course of thought,
'Tis heavy with him: and am I then revenged,

To take him in the purging of his soul,
When he is fit and season'd for his passage?
No!
Up, sword; and know thou a more horrid hent:
When he is drunk asleep, or in his rage,
Or in the incestuous pleasure of his bed;
At gaming, swearing, or about some act
That has no relish of salvation in 't;
Then trip him, that his heels may kick at heaven,
And that his soul may be as damn'd and black
As hell, whereto it goes. My mother stays:
This physic but prolongs thy sickly days.   [*Exit.*

    KING: [*Rising*] My words fly up, my thoughts remain below:
Words without thoughts never to heaven go.   [*Exit.*

SCENE IV. *The Queen's closet.*
Enter Queen and Polonius.

    POLONIUS: He will come straight. Look you lay home to him:
Tell him his pranks have been too broad to bear with,
And that your grace hath screen'd and stood between
Much heat and him. I 'll sconce me even here.
Pray you, be round with him.
    HAMLET: [*Within*] Mother, mother, mother!
    QUEEN: I 'll warrant you,
Fear me not: withdraw, I hear him coming.
                    [*Polonius hides behind the arras.*

Enter Hamlet.

    HAMLET: Now, mother, what 's the matter?
    QUEEN: Hamlet, thou hast thy father much offended.
    HAMLET: Mother, you have my father much offended.
    QUEEN: Come, come, you answer with an idle tongue.
    HAMLET: Go, go, you question with a wicked tongue.
    QUEEN: Why, how now, Hamlet!

HAMLET: What 's the matter now?

QUEEN: Have you forgot me?

HAMLET: No, by the rood, not so:
You are the queen, your husband's brother's wife;
And—would it were not so!—you are my mother.

QUEEN: Nay, then, I 'll set those to you that can speak.

HAMLET: Come, come, and sit you down; you shall not budge;
You go not till I set you up a glass
Where you may see the inmost part of you.

QUEEN: What wilt thou do? thou wilt not murder me?
Help, help, ho!

POLONIUS: [Behind] What, ho! help, help, help!

HAMLET: [Drawing] How now! a rat? Dead, for a ducat, dead!
                              [Makes a pass through the arras.

POLONIUS: [Behind] O, I am slain!   [Falls and dies.

QUEEN: O me, what hast thou done?

HAMLET: Nay, I know not:
Is it the king?

QUEEN: O, what a rash and bloody deed is this!

HAMLET: A bloody deed! almost as bad, good mother,
As kill a king, and marry with his brother.

QUEEN: As kill a king!

HAMLET: Ay, lady, 'twas my word.
                    [Lifts up the arras and discovers Polonius.
Thou wretched, rash, intruding fool, farewell!
I took thee for thy better: take thy fortune;
Thou find'st to be too busy is some danger.
Leave wringing of your hands: peace! sit you down,
And let me wring your heart; for so I shall,
If it be made of penetrable stuff,
If damned custom have not brass'd it so
That it be proof and bulwark against sense.

QUEEN: What have I done, that thou darest wag thy tongue
In noise so rude against me?

HAMLET: Such an act

That blurs the grace and blush of modesty,
Calls virtue hypocrite, takes off the rose
From the fair forehead of an innocent love
And sets a blister there, makes marriage-vows
As false as dicers' oaths: O, such a deed
As from the body of contraction plucks
The very soul, and sweet religion makes
A rhapsody of words: heaven's face doth glow;
Yea, this solidity and compound mass,
With tristful visage, as against the doom,
Is thought-sick at the act.
    QUEEN: Ay me, what act,
That roars so loud, and thunders in the index?
    HAMLET: Look here, upon this picture, and on this,
The counterfeit presentment of two brothers.
See, what a grace was seated on this brow;
Hyperion's curls; the front of Jove himself;
An eye like Mars, to threaten and command;
A station like the herald Mercury
New-lighted on a heaven-kissing hill;
A combination and a form indeed,
Where every god did seem to set his seal,
To give the world assurance of a man:
This was your husband. Look you now, what follows:
Here is your husband; like a mildew'd ear,
Blasting his wholesome brother. Have you eyes?
Could you on this fair mountain leave to feed,
And batten on this moor? Ha! have you eyes?
You cannot call it love; for at your age
The hey-day in the blood is tame, it 's humble,
And waits upon the judgement: and what judgement
Would step from this to this? Sense, sure, you have,
Else could you not have motion; but sure, that sense
Is apoplex'd; for madness would not err,
Nor sense to ecstasy was ne'er so thrall'd

But it reserved some quantity of choice,
To serve in such a difference. What devil was 't
That thus hath cozen'd you at hoodman-blind?
Eyes without feeling, feeling without sight,
Ears without hands or eyes, smelling sans all,
Or but a sickly part of one true sense
Could not so mope.
O shame! where is thy blush? Rebellious hell,
If thou canst mutine in a matron's bones,
To flaming youth let virtue be as wax,
And melt in her own fire: proclaim no shame
When the compulsive ardour gives the charge,
Since frost itself as actively doth burn
And reason pandars will.

QUEEN: O Hamlet, speak no more:
Thou turn'st mine eyes into my very soul;
And there I see such black and grained spots
As will not leave their tinct.

HAMLET: Nay, but to live
In the rank sweat of an enseamed bed,
Stew'd in corruption, honeying and making love
Over the nasty sty,—

QUEEN: O, speak to me no more;
These words, like daggers, enter in mine ears;
No more, sweet Hamlet!

HAMLET: A murderer and a villain;
A slave that is not twentieth part the tithe
Of your precedent lord; a vice of kings;
A cutpurse of the empire and the rule,
That from a shelf the precious diadem stole,
And put it in his pocket!

QUEEN: No more!

HAMLET: A king of shreds and patches,—

Enter Ghost.

Save me, and hover o'er me with your wings,
You heavenly guards! What would your gracious figure?
    QUEEN: Alas, he 's mad!
    HAMLET: Do you not come your tardy son to chide,
That, lapsed in time and passion, lets go by
The important acting of your dread command?
O, say!
    GHOST: Do not forget: this visitation
Is but to whet thy almost blunted purpose.
But, look, amazement on thy mother sits:
O, step between her and her fighting soul:
Conceit in weakest bodies strongest works:
Speak to her, Hamlet.
    HAMLET: How is it with you, lady?
    QUEEN: Alas, how is 't with you,
That you do bend your eye on vacancy
And with the incorporal air do hold discourse?
Forth at your eyes your spirits wildly peep;
And, as the sleeping soldiers in the alarm,
Your bedded hair, like life in excrements,
Start up, and stand an end. O gently son,
Upon the heat and flame of thy distemper
Sprinkle cool patience. Whereon do you look?
    HAMLET: On him, on him! Look you, how pale he glares!
His form and cause conjoin'd, preaching to stones,
Would make them capable. Do not look upon me;
Lest with this piteous action you convert
My stern effects: then what I have to do
Will want true colour; tears perchance for blood.
    QUEEN: To whom do you speak this?
    HAMLET: Do you see nothing there?
    QUEEN: Nothing at all; yet all that is I see.
    HAMLET: Nor did you nothing hear?
    QUEEN: No, nothing but ourselves.
    HAMLET: Why, look you there! look, how it steals away!

My father, in his habit as he lived!
Look, where he goes, even now, out at the portal! [*Exit Ghost.*

  QUEEN: This is the very coinage of your brain:
This bodiless creation ecstasy
Is very cunning in.

  HAMLET: Ecstasy!
My pulse, as yours, doth temperately keep time,
And makes as healthful music: it is not madness
That I have utter'd: bring me to the test,
And I the matter will re-word; which madness
Would gambol from. Mother, for love of grace,
Lay not that flattering unction to your soul,
That not your trespass, but my madness speaks:
It will but skin and film the ulcerous place,
Whiles rank corruption, mining all within,
Infects unseen. Confess yourself to heaven;
Repent what 's past; avoid what is to come;
And do not spread the compost on the weeds,
To make them ranker. Forgive me this my virtue;
For in the fatness of these pursy times
Virtue itself of vice must pardon beg,
Yea, curb and woo for leave to do him good.

  QUEEN: O Hamlet, thou hast cleft my heart in twain.

  HAMLET: O, throw away the worser part of it,
And live the purer with the other half.
Good night: but go not to mine uncle's bed;
Assume a virtue, if you have it not.
That monster, custom, who all sense doth eat,
Of habits devil, is angel yet in this,
That to the use of actions fair and good
He likewise gives a frock or livery,
That aptly is put on. Refrain to-night,
And that shall lend a kind of easiness
To the next abstinence: the next more easy;
For use almost can change the stamp of nature,

And either . . . . the devil, or throw him out
With wondrous potency. Once more, good night:
And when you are desirous to be bless'd,
I 'll blessing beg of you. For this same lord,   [*Pointing to Polonius.*
I do repent: but heaven hath pleased it so,
To punish me with this and this with me,
That I must be their scourge and minister.
I will bestow him, and will answer well
The death I gave him. So, again, good night.
I must be cruel, only to be kind:
Thus bad begins and worse remains behind.
One word more, good lady.

    QUEEN: What shall I do?

    HAMLET: Not this, by no means, that I bid you do:
Let the bloat king tempt you again to bed;
Pinch wanton on your cheek; call you his mouse;
And let him, for a pair of reechy kisses,
Or paddling in your neck with his damn'd fingers,
Make you to ravel all this matter out,
That I essentially am not in madness,
But mad in craft. 'Twere good you let him know;
For who, that 's but a queen, fair, sober, wise,
Would from a paddock, from a bat, a gib,
Such dear concernings hide? who would do so?
No, in despite of sense and secrecy,
Unpeg the basket on the house's top,
Let the birds fly, and, like the famous ape,
To try conclusions, in the basket creep,
And break your own neck down.

    QUEEN: Be thou assured, if words be made of breath,
And breath of life, I have no life to breathe
What thou hast said to me.

    HAMLET: I must to England; you know that?

    QUEEN: Alack,
I had forgot: 'tis so concluded on.

HAMLET: There 's letters seal'd: and my two schoolfellows,
Whom I will trust as I will adders fang'd,
They bear the mandate; they must sweep my way,
And marshal me to knavery. Let it work;
For 'tis the sport to have the enginer
Hoist with his own petar: and 't shall go hard
But I will delve one yard below their mines,
And blow them at the moon: O, 'tis most sweet,
When in one line two crafts directly meet.
This man shall set me packing:
I 'll lug the guts into the neighbour room.
Mother, good night. Indeed this counsellor
Is now most still, most secret and most grave,
Who was in life a foolish prating knave.
Come, sir, to draw toward an end with you.
Good night, mother.

                    [*Exeunt severally; Hamlet dragging in Polonius.*

ACT IV.

SCENE I. *A room in the castle.*
Enter King, Queen, Rosencrantz, and Guildenstern.

KING: There 's matter in these sighs, these profound heaves:
You must translate: 'tis fit we understand them
Where is your son?
    QUEEN: Bestow this place on us a little while.

                    [*Exeunt Rosencrantz and Guildenstern.*
Ah, mine own lord, what have I seen tonight!
    KING: What, Gertrude? How does Hamlet?
    QUEEN: Mad as the sea and wind, when both contend
Which is the mightier: in his lawless fit,
Behind the arras hearing something stir,
Whips out his rapier, cries, 'A rat, a rat!'

And, in this brainish apprehension, kills
The unseen good old man.
    KING: O heavy deed!
It had been so with us, had we been there:
His liberty is full of threats to all;
To you yourself, to us, to every one.
Alas, how shall this bloody deed be answer'd?
It will be laid to us, whose providence
Should have kept short, restrain'd and out of haunt,
This mad young man: but so much was our love,
We would not understand what was most fit;
But, like the owner of a foul disease,
To keep it from divulging, let it feed
Even on the pith of life. Where is he gone?
    QUEEN: To draw apart the body he hath kill'd:
O'er whom his very madness, like some ore
Among a mineral of metals base,
Shows itself pure; he weeps for what is done.
    KING: O Gertrude, come away!
The sun no sooner shall the mountains touch,
But we will ship him hence: and this vile deed
We must, with all our majesty and skill,
Both countenance and excuse. Ho, Guildenstern!

Re-enter Rosencrantz and Guildenstern.

Friends both, go join you with some further aid:
Hamlet in madness hath Polonius slain,
And from his mother's closet hath he dragg'd him:
Go seek him out; speak fair, and bring the body
Into the chapel. I pray you, haste in this.
                      [Exeunt Rosencrantz and Guildenstern.
Come, Gertrude, we 'll call up our wisest friends;
And let them know, both what we mean to do,
And what 's untimely done . . . .
Whose whisper o'er the world's diameter,

As level as the cannon to his blank,
Transports his poison'd shot, may miss our name,
And hit the woundless air. O, come away!
My soul is full of discord and dismay.   [*Exeunt*.

SCENE II. *Another room in the castle.*
Enter Hamlet.

HAMLET: Safely stowed.
ROSENCRANTZ: } [*Within*] Hamlet! Lord Hamlet!
GUILDENSTERN:
HAMLET: But soft, what noise? who calls on Hamlet? O, here
they come.

Enter Rosencrantz and Guildenstern.

ROSENCRANTZ: What have you done, my lord, with the dead
body?
HAMLET: Compounded it with dust, whereto 'tis kin.
ROSENCRANTZ: Tell us where 'tis, that we may take it thence
And bear it to the chapel.
HAMLET: Do not believe it.
ROSENCRANTZ: Believe what?
HAMLET: That I can keep your counsel and not mine own. Be-
sides, to be demanded of a sponge! what replication should be
made by the son of a king?
ROSENCRANTZ: Take you me for a sponge, my lord?
HAMLET: Ay, sir, that soaks up the king's countenance, his
rewards, his authorities. But such officers do the king best service in
the end: he keeps them, like an ape, in the corner of his jaw; first
mouthed, to be last swallowed: when he needs what you have
gleaned, it is but squeezing you, and, sponge, you shall be dry again.
ROSENCRANTZ: I understand you not, my lord.
HAMLET: I am glad of it: a knavish speech sleeps in a foolish ear.
ROSENCRANTZ: My lord, you must tell us where the body is, and
go with us to the king.

HAMLET: The body is with the king, but the king is not with the body. The king is a thing—

GUILDENSTERN: A thing, my lord!

HAMLET: Of nothing: bring me to him. Hide fox, and all after.

[*Exeunt.*

SCENE III. *Another room in the castle.*
Enter King attended.

KING: I have sent to seek him, and to find the body.
How dangerous is it that this man goes loose!
Yet must not we put the strong law on him:
He 's loved of the distracted multitude,
Who like not in their judgement, but their eyes;
And where 'tis so, the offender's scourge is weigh'd,
But never the offence. To bear all smooth and even,
This sudden sending him away must seem
Deliberate pause: diseases desperate grown
By desperate appliance are relieved,
Or not at all.

Enter Rosencrantz.

        How now! what hath befall'n?

ROSENCRANTZ: Where the dead body is bestow'd, my lord,
We cannot get from him.

KING: But where is he?

ROSENCRANTZ: Without, my lord; guarded, to know your pleasure.

KING: Bring him before us.

ROSENCRANTZ: Ho, Guildenstern! bring in my lord.

Enter Hamlet and Guildenstern.

KING: Now, Hamlet, where 's Polonius?

HAMLET: At supper.

KING: At supper! where?

HAMLET: Not where he eats, but where he is eaten: a certain

convocation of politic worms are e'en at him. Your worm is your only emperor for diet: we fat all creatures else to fat us, and we fat ourselves for maggots: your fat king and your lean beggar is but variable service, two dishes, but to one table: that 's the end.

KING: Alas, alas!

HAMLET: A man may fish with the worm that hath eat of a king, and eat of the fish that hath fed of that worm.

KING: What dost thou mean by this?

HAMLET: Nothing but to show you how a king may go a progress through the guts of a beggar.

KING: Where is Polonius?

HAMLET: In heaven; send thither to see: if your messenger find him not there, see him i' the other place yourself. But indeed, if you find him not within this month, you shall nose him as you go up the stairs into the lobby.

KING: Go seek him there.   [*To some Attendants.*

HAMLET: He will stay till you come.   [*Exeunt Attendants.*

KING: Hamlet, this deed, for thine especial safety,—
Which we do tender, as we dearly grieve
For that which thou hast done, —must send thee hence
With fiery quickness; therefore prepare thyself;
The bark is ready, and the wind at help,
The associates tend, and every thing is bent
For England.

HAMLET: For England!

KING: Ay, Hamlet.

HAMLET: Good.

KING: So is it, if thou knew'st our purposes.

HAMLET: I see a cherub that sees them. But, come; for England! Farewell, dear mother.

KING: Thy loving father, Hamlet.

HAMLET: My mother: father and mother is man and wife; man and wife is one flesh; and so, my mother. Come, for England!

                                              [*Exit.*

KING: Follow him at foot; tempt him with speed aboard;

Delay it not; I 'll have him hence to-night:
Away! for every thing is seal'd and done
That else leans on the affair: pray you, make haste.

[*Exeunt Rosencrantz and Guildenstern.*

And, England, if my love thou hold'st at aught—
As my great power thereof may give thee sense,
Since yet thy cicatrice looks raw and red
After the Danish sword, and thy free awe
Pays homage to us—thou mayst not coldly set
Our sovereign process; which imports at full,
By letters conjuring to that effect,
The present death of Hamlet. Do it, England;
For like the hectic in my blood he rages,
And thou must cure me: till I know 'tis done,
Howe'er my haps, my joys were ne'er begun.   [*Exit.*

SCENE IV. *A plain in Denmark.*
Enter Fortinbras, a Captain, and Soldiers, marching.

FORTINBRAS: Go, captain, from me greet the Danish king;
Tell him that, by his license, Fortinbras
Craves the conveyance of a promised march
Over his kingdom. You know the rendezvous.
If that his majesty would aught with us,
We shall express our duty in his eye;
And let him know so.

CAPTAIN: I will do 't, my lord.

FORTINBRAS: Go softly on.   [*Exeunt Fortinbras and Soldiers.*

Enter Hamlet, Rosencrantz, Guildenstern, and others.

HAMLET: Good sir, whose powers are these?
CAPTAIN: They are of Norway, sir.
HAMLET: How purposed, sir, I pray you?
CAPTAIN: Against some part of Poland.
HAMLET: Who commands them, sir?

CAPTAIN: The nephew to old Norway, Fortinbras.

HAMLET: Goes it against the main of Poland, sir,
Or some frontier?

CAPTAIN: Truly to speak, and with no addition,
We go to gain a little patch of ground
That hath in it no profit but the name.
To pay five ducats, five, I would not farm it;
Nor will it yield to Norway or the Pole
A ranker rate, should it be sold in fee.

HAMLET: Why, then the Polack never will defend it.

CAPTAIN: Yes, it is already garrison'd.

HAMLET: Two thousand souls and twenty thousand ducats
Will not debate the question of this straw:
This is the imposthume of much wealth and peace,
That inward breaks, and shows no cause without
Why the man dies. I humbly thank you, sir.

CAPTAIN: God be wi' you, sir.   [Exit.

ROSENCRANTZ: Will 't please you go, my lord?

HAMLET: I 'll be with you straight. Go a little before.
                                        [Exeunt all except Hamlet.
How all occasions do inform against me,
And spur my dull revenge! What is a man,
If his chief good and market of his time
Be but to sleep and feed? a beast, no more.
Sure, he that made us with such large discourse,
Looking before and after, gave us not
That capability and god-like reason
To fust in us unused. Now, whether it be
Bestial oblivion, or some craven scruple
Of thinking too precisely on the event,
A thought which, quarter'd, hath but one part wisdom
And ever three parts coward, I do not know
Why yet I live to say 'This thing 's to do;'
Sith I have cause and will and strength and means
To do 't. Examples gross as earth exhort me:

Witness this army of such mass and charge
Led by a delicate and tender prince,
Whose spirit with divine ambition puff'd
Makes mouths at the invisible event,
Exposing what is mortal and unsure
To all that fortune, death and danger dare,
Even for an egg-shell. Rightly to be great
Is not to stir without great argument,
But greatly to find quarrel in a straw
When honour 's at the stake. How stand I then.
That have a father kill'd, a mother stain'd,
Excitements of my reason and my blood,
And let all sleep? while, to my shame, I see
The imminent death of twenty thousand men,
That, for a fantasy and trick of fame,
Go to their graves like beds, fight for a plot
Whereon the numbers cannot try the cause,
Which is not tomb enough and continent
To hide the slain? O, from this time forth,
My thoughts be bloody, or be nothing worth!   [*Exit.*

SCENE V. *Elsinore. A room in the castle.*
Enter Queen , Horatio, and a Gentleman.

QUEEN: I will not speak with her.
GENTLEMAN: She is importunate, indeed distract:
Her mood will needs be pitied.
QUEEN: What would she have?
GENTLEMAN: She speaks much of her father; says she hears
There 's tricks i' the world; and hems, and beats her heart;
Spurns enviously at straws; speaks things in doubt,
That carry but half sense: her speech is nothing,
Yet the unshaped use of it doth move
The hearers to collection; they aim at it,
And botch the words up fit to their own thoughts;

Which, as her winks, and nods, and gestures yield them,
Indeed would make one think there might be thought,
Though nothing sure, yet much unhappily.

    HORATIO: 'Twere good she were spoken with: for she may strew
Dangerous conjectures in ill-breeding minds.

    QUEEN: Let her come in.   [*Exit Horatio.*
To my sick soul, as sin 's true nature is,
Each toy seems prologue to some great amiss:
So full of artless jealousy is guilt,
It spills itself in fearing to be spilt.

Re-enter Horatio, with Ophelia.

    OPHELIA: Where is the beauteous majesty of Denmark?

    QUEEN: How now, Ophelia!

    OPHELIA: [*Sings*] How should I your true love know
                    From another one?
              By his cockle hat and staff,
              And his sandal shoon.

    QUEEN: Alas, sweet lady, what imports this song?

    OPHELIA: Say you? nay, pray you, mark.
           [*Sings*] He is dead and gone, lady,
                He is dead and gone;
            At his head a grass-green turf,
              At his heels a stone.

    QUEEN: Nay, but, Ophelia,—

    OPHELIA: Pray you, mark.
           [*Sings*] White his shroud as the mountain snow,—

Enter King.

    QUEEN: Alas, look here, my lord.

    OPHELIA: [*Sings*] Larded with sweet flowers;
Which bewept to the grave did go
    With true-love showers.

    KING: How do you, pretty lady?

    OPHELIA: Well, God 'ild you! They say the owl was a baker's

daughter. Lord, we know what we are, but know not what we may be. God be at your table!

KING: Conceit upon her father.

OPHELIA: Pray you, let 's have no words of this; but when they ask you what it means, say you this:

> [*Sings*] To-morrow is Saint Valentine's day,
>   All in the morning betime,
>   And I a maid at your window,
>   To be your Valentine.
>   Then up he rose, and donn'd his clothes,
>   And dupp'd the chamber door;
>   Let in the maid, that out a maid
>   Never departed more.

KING: Pretty Ophelia!

OPHELIA: Indeed, la, without an oath, I 'll make an end on 't:

> [*Sings*] By Gis and by Saint Charity,
>   Alack, and fie for shame!
>   Young men will do 't, if they come to 't;
>   By cock, they are to blame.
>   Quoth she, before you tumbled me,
>   You promised me to wed.
>   So would I ha' done, by yonder sun,
>   An thou hadst not come to my bed.

KING: How long hath she been thus?

OPHELIA: I hope all will be well. We must be patient: but I cannot choose but weep, to think they should lay him i' the cold ground. My brother shall know of it: and so I thank you for your good counsel. Come, my coach! Good night, ladies; good night, sweet ladies; good night, good night.   [*Exit.*

KING: Follow her close; give her good watch, I pray you.

[*Exit Horatio.*

O, this is the poison of deep grief; it springs
All from her father's death. O Gertrude, Gertrude,
When sorrows come, they come not single spies,
But in battalions. First, her father slain:

Next, your son gone; and he most violent author
Of his own just remove: the people muddied,
Thick and unwholesome in their thoughts and whispers,
For good Polonius' death; and we have done but greenly,
In hugger-mugger to inter him: poor Ophelia
Divided from herself and her fair judgement,
Without the which we are pictures, or mere beasts:
Last, and as much containing as all these,
Her brother is in secret come from France;
Feeds on his wonder, keeps himself in clouds,
And wants not buzzers to infect his ear
With pestilent speeches of his father's death;
Wherein necessity, of matter beggar'd,
Will nothing stick our person to arraign
In ear and ear. O my dear Gertrude, this,
Like to a murdering-piece, in many places
Gives me superfluous death.   [*A noise within.*

    QUEEN: Alack, what noise is this?
    KING: Where are my Switzers? Let them guard the door.

Enter another Gentleman.

What is the matter?
    GENTLEMAN: Save yourself, my lord:
The ocean, overpeering of his list,
Eats not the flats with more impetuous haste
Than young Laertes, in a riotous head,
O'erbears your officers. The rabble call him lord;
And, as the world were now but to begin,
Antiquity forgot, custom not known,
The ratifiers and props of every word,
They cry, 'Choose we: Laertes shall be king:'
Caps, hands, and tongues, applaud it to the clouds:
'Laertes shall be king. Laertes king!'
    QUEEN: How cheerfully on the false trail they cry!
O, this is counter, you false Danish dogs!

KING: The doors are broke.   [*Noise within.*

Enter Laertes, armed; Danes following.

LAERTES: Where is this king? Sirs, stand you all without.
DANES: No, let 's come in.
LAERTES: I pray you, give me leave.
DANES: We will, we will.   [*They retire without the door.*
LAERTES: I thank you; keep the door. O thou vile king,
Give me my father!
QUEEN: Calmly, good Laertes.
LAERTES: That drop of blood that 's calm proclaims me bas-
           tard,
Cries cuckold to my father, brands the harlot
Even here, between the chaste unsmirched brow
Of my true mother.
KING: What is the cause, Laertes,
That thy rebellion looks so giant-like?
Let him go, Gertrude; do not fear our person:
There 's such divinity doth hedge a king,
That treason can but peep to what it would,
Acts little of his will. Tell us, Laertes,
Why thou art thus incensed. Let him go, Gertrude.
Speak, man.
LAERTES: Where is my father?
KING: Dead.
QUEEN: But not by him.
KING: Let him demand his fill.
LAERTES: How came he dead? I 'll not be juggled with:
To hell, allegiance! vows, to the blackest devil!
Conscience and grace, to the profoundest pit!
I dare damnation. To this point I stand,
That both the worlds I give to negligence,
Let come what comes; only I 'll be revenged
Most thoroughly for my father.
KING: Who shall stay you?

LAERTES: My will, not all the world:
And for my means, I 'll husband them so well,
They shall go far with little.
    KING: Good Laertes,
If you desire to know the certainty
Of your dear father's death, is 't writ in your revenge,
That, swoopstake, you will draw both friend and foe,
Winner and loser?
    LAERTES: None but his enemies.
    KING: Will you know them then?
    LAERTES: To his good friends thus wide I 'll ope my arms;
And like the kind life-rendering pelican,
Repast them with my blood.
    KING: Why, now you speak
Like a good child and a true gentleman,
That I am guiltless of your father's death,
And am most sensibly in grief for it,
It shall as level to your judgement pierce
As day does to your eye.
    DANES: [*Within*]   Let her come in.
    LAERTES: How now! what noise is that?

Re-enter Ophelia.

O heat, dry up my brains! tears seven times salt,
Burn out the sense and virtue of mine eye!
By heaven, thy madness shall be paid with weight,
Till our scale turn the beam. O rose of May!
Dear maid, kind sister, sweet Ophelia!
O heavens! is 't possible, a young maid's wits
Should be as mortal as an old man's life?
Nature is fine in love, and where 'tis fine,
It sends some precious instance of itself
After the thing it loves.
    OPHELIA: [*Sings*]
        They bore him barefaced on the bier;

Hey non nonny, nonny, hey nonny;

And in his grave rain'd many a tear:—
Fare you well, my dove!

LAERTES: Hadst thou thy wits, and didst persuade revenge,
It could not move thus.

OPHELIA: [*Sings*] You must sing a-down a-down,

An you call him a-down-a.
O, how the wheel becomes it! It is the false steward, that stole his
master's daughter.

LAERTES: This nothing 's more than matter.

OPHELIA: There 's rosemary, that 's for remembrance; pray, love,
remember: and there is pansies, that 's for thoughts.

LAERTES: A document in madness, thoughts and remembrance
fitted.

OPHELIA: There 's fennel for you, and columbines: there 's rue
for you; and here 's some for me: we may call it herb-grace o' Sundays: O, you must wear your rue with a difference. There 's a
daisy: I would give you some violets, but they withered all when
my father died: they say he made a good end,—

[*Sings*] For bonny sweet Robin is all my joy.

LAERTES: Thought and affliction, passion, hell itself,
She turns to favour and to prettiness.

OPHELIA: [*Sings*] And will he not come again?

And will he not come again?

No, no, he is dead:

Go to thy death-bed:

He never will come again.

His beard was as white as snow,

All flaxen was his poll:

He is gone, he is gone,

And we cast away moan:

God ha' mercy on his soul!
And of all Christian souls, I pray God. God be wi' ye.   [*Exit.*

LAERTES: Do you see this, O God?

KING: Laertes, I must commune with your grief,

Or you deny me right. Go but apart,
Make choice of whom your wisest friends you will,
And they shall hear and judge 'twixt you and me:
If by direct or by collateral hand
They find us touch'd, we will our kingdom give,
Our crown, our life, and all that we call ours,
To you in satisfaction; but if not,
Be you content to lend your patience to us,
And we shall jointly labour with your soul
To give it due content.

LAERTES: Let this be so;
His means of death, his obscure funeral—
No trophy, sword, nor hatchment o'er his bones,
No noble rite nor formal ostentation—
Cry to be heard, as 'twere from heaven to earth,
That I must call 't in question.

KING: So you shall;
And where the offence is let the great axe fall.
I pray you, go with me.   [*Exeunt.*

SCENE VI. *Another room in the castle.*
Enter Horatio and a Servant.

HORATIO: What are they that would speak with me?
SERVANT: Sailors, sir: they say they have letters for you.
HORATIO: Let them come in.   [*Exit Servant.*
I do not know from what part of the world I should be greeted, if
not from Lord Hamlet.

Enter Sailors

FIRST SAILOR: God bless you, sir.
HORATIO: Let him bless thee too.
FIRST SAILOR: He shall, sir, an 't please him. There 's a letter for
you, sir; it comes from the ambassador that was bound for England; if your name be Horatio, as I am let to know it is.

HORATIO: [*Reads*] 'Horatio, when thou shalt have overlooked this, give these fellows some means to the king: they have letters for him. Ere we were two days old at sea, a pirate of very warlike appointment gave us chase. Finding ourselves too slow of sail, we put on a compelled valour, and in the grapple I boarded them: on the instant they got clear of our ship; so I alone became their prisoner. They have dealt with me like thieves of mercy: but they knew what they did; I am to do a good turn for them. Let the king have the letters I have sent: and repair thou to me with as much speed as thou wouldst fly death. I have words to speak in thine ear will make thee dumb; yet are they much too light for the bore of the matter. These good fellows will bring thee where I am. Rosencrantz and Guildenstern hold their course for England: of them I have much to tell thee. Farewell.

'He that thou knowest thine, HAMLET.'
Come, I will make you way for these your letters;
And do 't the speedier, that you may direct me
To him from whom you brought them.   [*Exeunt.*

SCENE VII. *Another room in the castle.*
Enter King and Laertes.

KING: Now must your conscience my acquittance seal,
And you must put me in your heart for friend,
Sith you have heard, and with a knowing ear,
That he which hath your noble father slain
Pursued my life.
LAERTES: It well appears: but tell me
Why you proceeded not against these feats,
So crimeful and so capital in nature,
As by your safety, wisdom, all things else,
You mainly were stirr'd up.
KING: O, for two special reasons;
Which may to you, perhaps, seem much unsinew'd,
But yet to me they are strong. The queen his mother

Lives almost by his looks; and for myself—
My virtue or my plague, be it either which—
She's so conjunctive to my life and soul,
That, as the star moves not but in his sphere,
I could not but by her. The other motive,
Why to a public count I might not go,
Is the great love the general gender bear him;
Who, dipping all his faults in their affection,
Would, like the spring that turneth wood to stone,
Convert his gyves to graces; so that my arrows,
Too slightly timber'd for so loud a wind,
Would have reverted to my bow again,
And not where I had aimed them.

    LAERTES: And so have I a noble father lost;
A sister driven into desperate terms,
Whose worth, if praises may go back again,
Stood challenger on mount of all the age
For her perfections: but my revenge will come.

    KING: Break not your sleeps for that: you must not think
That we are made of stuff so flat and dull
That we can let our beard be shook with danger
And think it pastime. You shortly shall hear more:
I loved your father, and we love ourself;
And that, I hope, will teach you to imagine—

Enter a Messenger.

How now! what news?
    MESSENGER: Letters, my lord, from Hamlet:
This to your majesty; this to the queen.
    KING: From Hamlet! who brought them?
    MESSENGER: Sailors, my lord, they say; I saw them not:
They were given me by Claudio; he received them
Of him that brought them.
    KING: Laertes, you shall hear them.
Leave us.   *[Exit Messenger.*

[*Reads*] 'High and mighty, You shall know I am set naked on your
kingdom. To-morrow shall I beg leave to see your kingly eyes:
when I shall, first asking your pardon thereunto, recount the occasion of my sudden and more strange return.

'HAMLET.'

What should this mean? Are all the rest come back?
Or is it some abuse and no such thing?
    LAERTES: Know you the hand?
    KING: 'Tis Hamlet's character. 'Naked!'
And in a postscript here, he says 'alone.'
Can you advise me?
    LAERTES: I 'm lost in it, my lord. But let him come;
It warms the very sickness in my heart,
That I shall live and tell him to his teeth,
'Thus didest thou.'
    KING: If it be so, Laertes—
As how should it be so? how otherwise?—
Will you be ruled by me?
    LAERTES: Ay, my lord;
So you will not o'errule me to a peace.
    KING: To thine own peace. If he be now return'd,
As checking at his voyage, and that he means
No more to undertake it, I will work him
To an exploit, now ripe in my device,
Under the which he shall not choose but fall:
And for his death no wind of blame shall breathe,
But even his mother shall uncharge the practice
And call it accident.
    LAERTES: My lord, I will be ruled;
The rather, if you could devise it so
That I might be the organ.
    KING: It falls right.
You have been talk'd of since your travel much,
And that in Hamlet's hearing, for a quality
Wherein, they say, you shine: your sum of parts

Did not together pluck such envy from him
As did that one, and that, in my regard,
Of the unworthiest siege.
    LAERTES: What part is that, my lord?
    KING: A very riband in the cap of youth,
Yet needful too; for youth no less becomes
The light and careless livery that it wears
Than settled age his sables and his weeds,
Importing health and graveness. Two months since,
Here was a gentleman of Normandy:—
I 've seen myself, and served against, the French,
And they can well on horseback: but this gallant
Had witchcraft in 't; he grew unto his seat;
And to such wondrous doing brought his horse,
As had he been incorpsed and demi-natured
With the brave beast: so far he topp'd my thought,
That I, in forgery of shapes and tricks,
Come short of what he did.
    LAERTES: A Norman was 't?
    KING: A Norman.
    LAERTES: Upon my life, Lamond.
    KING: The very same.
    LAERTES: I know him well: he is the brooch indeed
And gem of all the nation.
    KING: He made confession of you,
And gave you such a masterly report
For art and exercise in your defence
And for your rapier most especial,
That he cried out, 'twould be a sight indeed,
If one could match you: the scrimers of their nation,
He swore, had neither motion, guard, nor eye,
If you opposed them. Sir, this report of his
Did Hamlet so envenom with his envy
That he could nothing do but wish and beg
Your sudden coming o'er, to play with him.

Now, out of this,—

LAERTES: What out of this, my lord?

KING: Laertes, was your father dear to you?
Or are you like the painting of a sorrow,
A face without a heart?

LAERTES: Why ask you this?

KING: Not that I think you did not love your father;
But that I know love is begun by time;
And that I see, in passages of proof,
Time qualifies the spark and fire of it.
There lives within the very flame of love
A kind of wick or snuff that will abate it;
And nothing is at a like goodness still;
For goodness, growing to a plurisy,
Dies in his own too much: that we would do,
We should do when we would; for this 'would' changes
And hath abatements and delays as many
As there are tongues, are hands, are accidents;
And then this 'should' is like a spendthrift sigh,
That hurts by easing. But, to the quick o' the ulcer:—
Hamlet comes back: what would you undertake,
To show yourself your father's son in deed
More than in words?

LAERTES: To cut his throat i' the church.

KING: No place, indeed, should murder sanctuarize;
Revenge should have no bounds. But, good Laertes,
Will you do this, keep close within your chamber.
Hamlet return'd shall know you are come home:
We 'll put on those shall praise your excellence
And set a double varnish on the fame
The Frenchman gave you, bring you in fine together
And wager on your heads: he, being remiss,
Most generous and free from all contriving,
Will not peruse the foils; so that, with ease,
Or with a little shuffling, you may choose

A sword unbated, and in a pass of practice
Requite him for your father.
    LAERTES: I will do 't:
And, for that purpose, I 'll anoint my sword.
I bought an unction of a mountebank,
So mortal that, but dip a knife in it,
Where it draws blood no cataplasm so rare,
Collected from all simples that have virtue
Under the moon, can save the thing from death
That is but scratch'd withal: I 'll touch my point
With this contagion, that, if I gall him slightly,
It may be death.
    KING: Let 's further think of this;
Weigh what convenience both of time and means
May fit us to our shape: if this should fail,
And that our drift look through our bad performance,
'Twere better not assay'd: therefore this project
Should have a back or second, that might hold,
If this should blast in proof. Soft! let me see:
We 'll make a solemn wager on your cunnings:
I ha 't:
When in your motion you are hot and dry—
And make your bouts more violent to that end—
And that he calls for drink, I 'll have prepared him
A chalice for the nonce, whereon but sipping,
If he by chance escape your venom'd stuck,
Our purpose may hold there.

Enter Queen.

                      How now, sweet queen!
    QUEEN: One woe doth tread upon another's heel,
So fast they follow: your sister 's drown'd, Laertes.
    LAERTES: Drown'd! O, where?
    QUEEN: There is a willow grows aslant a brook,
That shows his hoar leaves in the glassy stream;

There with fantastic garlands did she come
Of crow-flowers, nettles, daisies, and long purples
That liberal shepherds give a grosser name,
But our cold maids do dead men's fingers call them:
There, on the pendent boughs her coronet weeds
Clambering to hang, an envious sliver broke:
When down her weedy trophies and herself
Fell in the weeping brook. Her clothes spread wide;
And, mermaid-like, awhile they bore her up:
Which time she chanted snatches of old tunes;
As one incapable of her own distress,
Or like a creature native and indued
Unto that element: but long it could not be
Till that her garments, heavy with their drink,
Pull'd the poor wretch from her melodious lay
To muddy death.

    LAERTES: Alas, then, she is drown'd?

    QUEEN: Drown'd, drown'd.

    LAERTES: Too much of water hast thou, poor Ophelia,
And therefore I forbid my tears: but yet
It is our trick; nature her custom holds,
Let shame say what it will: when these are gone,
The women will be out. Adieu, my lord:
I have a speech of fire, that fain would blaze,
But that this folly douts it.   [*Exit.*

    KING: Let 's follow, Gertrude:
How much I had to do to calm his rage!
Now fear I this will give it start again;
Therefore let 's follow.   [*Exeunt.*

ACT V.

SCENE I. *A churchyard.*
Enter two Clowns, with spades, &c.

FIRST CLOWN: Is she to be buried in Christian burial that wilfully seeks her own salvation?

SECOND CLOWN: I tell thee she is; and therefore make her grave straight: the crowner hath sat on her, and finds it Christian burial.

FIRST CLOWN: How can that be, unless she drowned herself in her own defence?

SECOND CLOWN: Why, 'tis found so.

FIRST CLOWN: It must be 'se offendendo;' it cannot be else. For here lies the point: if I drown myself wittingly, it argues an act: and an act hath three branches; it is, to act, to do, and to perform: argal, she drowned herself wittingly.

SECOND CLOWN: Nay, but here you, goodman delver,—

FIRST CLOWN: Give me leave. Here lies the water; good: here stands the man; good: if the man go to this water, and drown himself, it is, will he, nill he, he goes,—mark you that; but if the water come to him and drown him, he drowns not himself: argal, he that is not guilty of his own death shortens not his own life.

SECOND CLOWN: But is this law?

FIRST CLOWN: Ay, marry, is 't; crowner's quest law.

SECOND CLOWN: Will you ha' the truth on 't? If this had not been a gentlewoman, she should have been buried out o' Christian burial.

FIRST CLOWN: Why, there thou say'st: and the more pity that great folk should have countenance in this world to drown or hang themselves, more than their even Christian. Come, my spade. There is no ancient gentlemen but gardeners, ditchers, and grave-makers: they hold up Adam's profession.

SECOND CLOWN: Was he a gentleman?

FIRST CLOWN: A' was the first that ever bore arms.

SECOND CLOWN: Why, he had none.

FIRST CLOWN: What, art a heathen? How dost thou understand the Scripture? The Scripture says 'Adam digged:' could he dig without arms? I 'll put another question to thee: if thou answerest me not to the purpose, confess thyself—

SECOND CLOWN: Go to.

FIRST CLOWN: What is he that builds stronger than either the mason, the shipwright, or the carpenter?

SECOND CLOWN: The gallows-maker; for that frame outlives a thousand tenants.

FIRST CLOWN: I like thy wit well, in good faith: the gallows does well; but how does it well? it does well to those that do ill: now thou dost ill to say the gallows is built stronger than the church: argal, the gallows may do well to thee. To 't again, come.

SECOND CLOWN: 'Who builds stronger than a mason, a ship-wright, or a carpenter?'

FIRST CLOWN: Ay, tell me that, and unyoke.

SECOND CLOWN: Marry, now I can tell.

FIRST CLOWN: To 't.

SECOND CLOWN: Mass, I cannot tell.

Enter Hamlet and Horatio, at a distance.

FIRST CLOWN: Cudgel thy brains no more about it, for your dull ass will not mend his pace with beating; and, when you are asked this question next, say 'a grave-maker:' the houses that he makes last till doomsday. Go, get thee to Yaughan: fetch me a stoup of liquor.   [*Exit Second Clown.*

                                        [*He digs, and sings.*

    In youth, when I did love, did love,
        Methought it was very sweet,
  To contract, O, the time, for, ah, my behove,
        O, methought, there was nothing meet.

HAMLET: Has this fellow no feeling of his business, that he sings at grave-making?

HORATIO: Custom hath made it in him a property of easiness.

HAMLET: 'Tis e'en so: the hand of little employment hath the daintier sense.

FIRST CLOWN: [Sings]

But age, with his stealing steps,
   Hath claw'd me in his clutch,
And hath shipped me intil the land,
   As if I had never been such.   [Throws up a skull.

HAMLET: That skull had a tongue in it, and could sing once: how the knave jowls it to the ground, as if it were Cain's jaw-bone, that did the first murder! It might be the pate of a politician, which this ass now o'er-reaches: one that would circumvent God, might it not?

HORATIO: It might, my lord.

HAMLET: Or of a courtier; which could say 'Good morrow, sweet lord! How dost thou, good lord?' This might be my lord such-a-one, that praised my lord such-a-one's horse, when he meant to beg it; might it not?

HORATIO: Ay, my lord.

HAMLET: Why, e'en so: and now my Lady Worm's; chapless, and knocked about the mazzard with a sexton's spade: here 's fine revolution, an we had the trick to see 't. Did these bones cost no more the breeding, but to play at loggats with 'em? mine ache to think on 't.

FIRST CLOWN: [Sings]

A pick-axe, and a spade, a spade,
   For and a shrouding sheet:
O, a pit of clay for to be made
   For such a guest is meet.   [Throws up another skull.

HAMLET: There 's another: why may not that be the skull of a lawyer? Where be his quiddities now, his quillets, his cases, his tenures, and his tricks? why does he suffer this rude knave now to knock him about the sconce with a dirty shovel, and will not tell him of his action of battery? Hum! This fellow might be in 's time a great buyer of land, with his statutes, his recognizances, his fines, his double vouchers, his recoveries: is this the fine of his fines, and the recovery of his recoveries, to have his fine pate full of fine dirt? will his vouchers vouch him no more of his purchases, and double ones too, than the length and breadth of a pair of indentures? The very conveyances of his lands will hardly lie in this box; and must the inheritor himself have no more, ha?

HORATIO: Not a jot more, my lord.

HAMLET: Is not parchment made of sheepskins?

HORATIO: Ay, my lord, and of calf-skins too.

HAMLET: They are sheep and calves which seek out assurance in that. I will speak to this fellow. Whose grave 's this, sirrah?

FIRST CLOWN: Mine, sir.

[*Sings*] O, a pit of clay for to be made
           For such a guest is meet.

HAMLET: I think it be thine, indeed; for thou liest in 't.

FIRST CLOWN: You lie on 't, sir, and therefore it is not yours: for my part, I do not lie in 't, and yet it is mine.

HAMLET: Thou dost lie in 't, to be in 't and say it is thine: 'tis for the dead, not for the quick; therefore thou liest.

FIRST CLOWN: 'Tis a quick lie, sir; 'twill away again, from me to you.

HAMLET: What man dost thou dig it for?

FIRST CLOWN: For no man, sir.

HAMLET: What woman, then?

FIRST CLOWN: For none, neither.

HAMLET: Who is to be buried in 't?

FIRST CLOWN: One that was a woman, sir; but, rest her soul, she 's dead.

HAMLET: How absolute the knave is! we must speak by the card, or equivocation will undo us. By the Lord, Horatio, these three years I have taken note of it; the age is grown so picked that the toe of the peasant comes so near the heel of the courtier, he galls his kibe. How long hast thou been a grave-digger?

FIRST CLOWN: All the days i' the year, I came to 't that day that our last king Hamlet overcame Fortinbras.

HAMLET: How long is that since?

FIRST CLOWN: Cannot you tell that? every fool can tell that: it was the very day that young Hamlet was born; he that is mad, and sent into England.

HAMLET: Ay, marry, why was he sent into England?

FIRST CLOWN: Why, because he was mad: he shall recover his wits there; or, if he do not, it's no great matter there.

HAMLET: Why?

FIRST CLOWN: 'Twill not be seen in him there; there the men are as mad as he.

HAMLET: How came he mad?

FIRST CLOWN: Very strangely, they say.

HAMLET: How strangely?

FIRST CLOWN: Faith, e'en with losing his wits.

HAMLET: Upon what ground?

FIRST CLOWN: Why, here in Denmark: I have been sexton here, man and boy, thirty years.

HAMLET: How long will a man lie i' the earth ere he rot!

FIRST CLOWN: I' faith, if he be not rotten before he die—as we have many pocky corses now-a-days, that will scarce hold the laying in—he will last you some eight year or nine year: a tanner will last you nine year.

HAMLET: Why he more than another?

FIRST CLOWN: Why, sir, his hide is so tanned with his trade, that he will keep out water a great while; and your water is a sore decayer of your whoreson dead body. Here's a skull now; this skull has lain in the earth three and twenty years.

HAMLET: Whose was it?

FIRST CLOWN: A whoreson mad fellow's it was: whose do you think it was?

HAMLET: Nay, I know not.

FIRST CLOWN: A pestilence on him for a mad rogue! a' poured a flagon of Rhenish on my head once. This same skull, sir, was Yorick's skull, the king's jester.

HAMLET: This?

FIRST CLOWN: E'en that.

HAMLET: Let me see. [*Takes the skull.*] Alas, poor Yorick! I knew him, Horatio: a fellow of infinite jest, of most excellent fancy: he hath borne me on his back a thousand times; and now, how abhorred in my imagination it is! my gorge rises at it. Here hung those lips that I have kissed I know not how oft. Where be your gibes now? your gambols? your songs? your flashes of merriment, that were wont to set the table on a roar? Not one now, to mock your own grinning? quite chapfallen? Now get you to my lady's chamber, and tell her, let her paint an inch thick, to this favour she must come; make her laugh at that. Prithee, Horatio, tell me one thing.

HORATIO: What 's that, my lord?

HAMLET: Dost thou think Alexander looked o' this fashion i' the earth?

HORATIO: E'en so.

HAMLET: And smelt so? pah! [*Puts down the skull.*

HORATIO: E'en so, my lord.

HAMLET: To what base uses we may return, Horatio! Why may not imagination trace the noble dust of Alexander, till he find it stopping a bung-hole?

HORATIO: 'Twere to consider too curiously, to consider so.

HAMLET: No, faith, not a jot; but to follow him thither with modesty enough, and likelihood to lead it: as thus: Alexander died, Alexander was buried, Alexander returneth into dust; the dust is earth; of earth we make loam; and why of that loam, whereto he was converted, might they not stop a beer-barrel?

Imperious Caesar, dead and turn'd to clay,
Might stop a hole to keep the wind away:
O, that that earth, which kept the world in awe,
Should patch a wall to expel the winter's flaw!

But soft! but soft! aside: here comes the king,

Enter Priests, &c in procession; the Corpse of Ophelia,
Laertes and Mourners following; King, Queen, their trains, &c.

The queen, the courtiers: who is this they follow?

And with such maimed rites? This doth betoken
The corse they follow did with desperate hand
Fordo its own life: 'twas of some estate.
A very noble youth: mark.   [*Retiring with Horatio.*

    LAERTES: What ceremony else?
    HAMLET: That is Laertes,
A noble youth, mark.
    LAERTES: What ceremony else?
    FIRST PRIEST: Her obsequies have been as far enlarged
As we have warranty: her death was doubtful;
And, but that great command o'ersways the order,
She should in ground unsanctified have lodged
Till the last trumpet; for charitable prayers,
Shards, flints and pebbles should be thrown on her:
Yet here she is allow'd her virgin crants,
Her maiden strewments and the bringing home
Of bell and burial.
    LAERTES: Must there no more be done?
    FIRST PRIEST: No more be done:
We should profane the service of the dead
To sing a requiem and such rest to her
As to peace-parted souls.
    LAERTES: Lay her i' the earth:
And from her fair and unpolluted flesh
May violets spring! I tell thee, churlish priest,
A ministering angel shall my sister be,
When thou liest howling.
    HAMLET: What, the fair Ophelia!
    QUEEN: Sweets to the sweet: farewell!   [*Scattering flowers.*
I hoped thou shouldst have been my Hamlet's wife;
I thought thy bride-bed to have deck'd, sweet maid,
And not have strew'd thy grave.
    LAERTES: O, treble woe
Fall ten times treble on that cursed head,
Whose wicked deed thy most ingenious sense

Deprived thee of! Hold off the earth awhile,
Till I have caught her once more in mine arms:

          [Leaps into the grave.

Now pile your dust upon the quick and dead,
Till of this flat a mountain you have made,
To o'ertop olf Pelion, or the skyish head
Of blue Olympus.

 HAMLET: [*Advancing*] What is he whose grief
Bears such an emphasis? whose phrase of sorrow
Conjures the wandering stars, and makes them stand
Like wonder-wounded hearers? This is I,
Hamlet the Dane.   *[Leaps into the grave.*

 LAERTES: The devil take thy soul! *[Grappling with him.*

 HAMLET: Thou pray'st not well.
I prithee, take thy fingers from my throat;
For, though I am not splenitive and rash,
Yet have I something in me dangerous,
Which let thy wiseness fear: hold off thy hand.

 KING: Pluck them asunder.

 QUEEN: Hamlet, Hamlet!

 ALL: Gentlemen,—

 HORATIO: Good my lord, be quiet.

   [The Attendants part them, and they come out of the grave.

 HAMLET: Why, I will fight with him upon this theme
Until my eyelids will no longer wag.

 QUEEN: O my son, what theme?

 HAMLET: I loved Ophelia: forty thousand brothers
Could not, with all their quantity of love,
Make up my sum. What wilt thou do for her?

 KING: O, he is mad, Laertes.

 QUEEN: For love of God, forbear him.

 HAMLET: 'Swounds, show me what thou 'lt do:
Woo 't weep? woo 't fight? woo 't fast? woo 't tear thyself?
Woo 't drink up eisel? eat a crocodile
I 'll do 't. Dost thou come here to whine?

To outface me with leaping in her grave?
Be buried quick with her, and so will I:
And, if thou prate of mountains, let them throw
Millions of acres on us, till our ground,
Singeing his pate against the burning zone,
Make Ossa like a wart! Nay, an thou 'lt mouth,
I 'll rant as well as thou.

QUEEN: This is mere madness:
And thus awhile the fit will work on him;
Anon, as patient as the female dove,
When that her golden couplets are disclosed,
His silence will sit drooping.

HAMLET: Hear you, sir;
What is the reason that you use me thus?
I loved you ever: but it is no matter;
Let Hercules himself do what he may,
The cat will mew and dog will have his day.   [*Exit.*

KING: I pray you, good Horatio, wait upon him. [*Exit Horatio.*
[*To Laertes*] Strengthen your patience in our last night's speech;
We 'll put the matter to the present push.
Good Gertrude, set some watch over your son.
This grave shall have a living monument:
An hour of quiet shortly shall we see;
Till then, in patience our proceeding be.   [*Exeunt.*

SCENE II. *A hall in the castle.*
Enter Hamlet and Horatio.

HAMLET: So much for this, sir: now shall you see the other;
You do remember all the circumstance?
HORATIO: Remember it, my lord!
HAMLET: Sir, in my heart there was a kind of fighting,
That would not let me sleep: methought I lay
Worse than the mutines in the bilboes. Rashly,
And praised be rashness for it, let us know,

Our indiscretion sometimes serves us well,
When our deep plots do pall: and that should teach us
There 's a divinity that shapes our ends,
Rough-hew them how we will,—
   HORATIO: That is most certain.
   HAMLET: Up from my cabin,
My sea-gown scarf'd about me, in the dark
Groped I to find out them; had my desire,
Finger'd their packet, and in fine withdrew
To mine own room again; making so bold,
My fears forgetting manners, to unseal
Their grand commission; where I found,
   Horatio,—
O royal knavery!—an exact command,
Larded with many several sorts of reasons
Importing Denmark's health and England's too,
With ho! such bugs and goblins in my life,
That, on the supervise, no leisure bated,
No, not to stay the grinding of the axe,
My head should be struck off.
   HORATIO: Is 't possible?
   HAMLET: Here 's the commission: read it at more leisure.
But wilt thou hear me how I did proceed?
   HORATIO: I beseech you.
   HAMLET: Being thus be-netted round with villanies,—
Ere I could make a prologue to my brains,
They had begun the play—I sat me down,
Devised a new commission, wrote it fair:
I once did hold it, as our statists do,
A baseness to write fair and labour'd much
How to forget that learning, but, sir, now
It did me yeoman's service: wilt thou know
The effect of what I wrote?
   HORATIO: Ay, good my lord.
   HAMLET: An earnest conjuration from the king,

As England was his faithful tributary,
As love between them like the palm might flourish,
As peace should still her wheaten garland wear
And stand a comma 'tween their amities,
And many such-like 'As 'es of great charge,
That, on the view and knowing of these contents.
Without debatement further, more or less,
He should the bearers put to sudden death,
Not shriving-time allow'd.

    HORATIO: How was this seal'd?

    HAMLET: Why, even in that was heaven ordinant.
I had my father's signet in my purse,
Which was the model of that Danish seal;
Folded the writ up in form of the other,
Subscribed it, gave 't the impression, placed it safely,
The changeling never known. Now, the next day
Was our sea-fight; and what to this was sequent
Thou know'st already.

    HORATIO: So Guildenstern and Rosencrantz go to 't.

    HAMLET: Why, man, they did make love to this employment;
They are not near my conscience; their defeat
Does by their own insinuation grow:
'Tis dangerous when the baser nature comes
Between the pass and fell incensed points
Of mighty opposites.

    HORATIO: Why, what a king is this!

    HAMLET: Does it not, think'st thee, stand me, now upon—
He that hath kill'd my king and whored my mother,
Popp'd in between the election and my hopes,
Thrown out his angle for my proper life,
And with such cozenage—is 't not perfect conscience,
To quit him with this arm? and is 't not to be damn'd,
To let this canker of our nature come
In further evil?

    HORATIO: It must be shortly known to him from England

What is the issue of the business there.

HAMLET: It will be short: the interim is mine;
And a man's life 's no more than to say 'One.'
But I am very sorry, good Horatio,
That to Laertes I forgot myself;
For, by the image of my cause, I see
The portraiture of his: I 'll court his favours:
But, sure, the bravery of his grief did put me
Into a towering passion.

HORATIO: Peace! who comes here?

Enter Osric.

OSRIC: Your lordship is right welcome back to Denmark.

HAMLET: I humbly thank you, sir. Dost know this water-fly?

HORATIO: No, my good lord.

HAMLET: Thy state is the more gracious; for 'tis a vice to know
him. He hath much land, and fertile: let a beast be lord of beasts,
and his crib shall stand at the king's mess: 'tis a chough; but, as I
say, spacious in the possession of dirt.

OSRIC: Sweet lord, if your lordship were at leisure, I should
impart a thing to you from his majesty.

HAMLET: I will receive it, sir, with all diligence of spirit. Put
your bonnet to his right use; 'tis for the head.

OSRIC: I thank your lordship, it is very hot.

HAMLET: No, believe me, 'tis very cold; the wind is northerly.

OSRIC: It is indifferent cold, my lord, indeed.

HAMLET: But yet methinks it is very sultry and hot for my complexion.

OSRIC: Exceedingly, my lord; it is very sultry,—as 'twere,—I cannot tell how. But, my lord, his majesty bade me signify to you that
he has laid a great wager on your head: sir, this is the matter,—

HAMLET: I beseech you, remember—

                    [*Hamlet moves him to put on his hat.*
OSRIC: Nay, good my lord; for mine ease, in good faith. Sir, here
is newly come to court Laertes; believe me, an absolute gentleman,

full of most excellent differences, of very soft society and great showing: indeed, to speak feelingly of him, he is the card or calendar of gentry, for you shall find in him the continent of what part a gentleman would see.

HAMLET: Sir, his definement suffers no perdition in you; though, I know, to divide him inventorially would dizzy the arithmetic of memory, and yet but yaw neither, in respect of his quick sail. But, in the verity of extolment, I take him to be a soul of great article; and his infusion of such dearth and rareness, as, to make true direction of him, his semblable is his mirror; and who else would trace him, his umbrage, nothing more.

OSRIC: Your lordship speaks most infallibly of him.

HAMLET: The concernancy, sir? why do we wrap the gentleman in our more rawer breath?

OSRIC: Sir?

HORATIO: Is 't not possible to understand in another tongue? You will do 't, sir, really.

HAMLET: What imports the nomination of this gentleman?

OSRIC: Of Laertes?

HORATIO: His purse is empty already; all 's golden words are spent.

HAMLET: Of him, sir.

OSRIC: I know you are not ignorant—

HAMLET: I would you did, sir; yet, in faith, if you did, it would not much approve me. Well, sir?

OSRIC: You are not ignorant of what excellence Laertes is—

HAMLET: I dare not confess that, lest I should compare with him in excellence; but, to know a man well, were to know himself.

OSRIC: I mean, sir, for his weapon; but in the imputation laid on him by them, in his meed he 's unfellowed.

HAMLET: What 's his weapon?

OSRIC: Rapier and dagger.

HAMLET: That 's two of his weapons: but, well.

OSRIC: The king, sir, hath wagered with him six Barbary horses: against the which he has imponed, as I take it, six French rapiers

and poniards, with their assigns, as girdle, hangers, and so: three
of the carriages, in faith, are very dear to fancy, very responsive to
the hilts, most delicate carriages, and of very liberal conceit.

HAMLET: What call you the carriages?

HORATIO: I knew you must be edified by the margent ere you
had done.

OSRIC: The carriages, sir, are the hangers.

HAMLET: The phrase would be more german to the matter, if we
could carry cannon by our sides: I would it might be hangers till
then. But, on: six Barbary horses against six French swords, their
assigns, and three liberal-conceited carriages; that 's the French bet
against the Danish. Why is this 'imponed,' as you call it?

OSRIC: The king, sir, hath laid, that in a dozen passes between
yourself and him, he shall not exceed you three hits: he hath laid
on twelve for nine; and it would come to immediate trial, if your
lordship would vouchsafe the answer.

HAMLET: How if I answer 'no'?

OSRIC: I mean, my lord, the opposition of your person in trial.

HAMLET: Sir, I will walk here in the hall: if it please his majesty,
'tis the breathing time of day with me; let the foils be brought, the
gentleman willing, and the king hold his purpose. I will win for
him an I can; if not, I will gain nothing but my shame and the
odd hits.

OSRIC: Shall I re-deliver you e'en so?

HAMLET: To this effect, sir; after what flourish your nature will.

OSRIC: I commend my duty to your lordship.

HAMLET: Yours, yours. [*Exit Osric.*] He does well to commend
it himself; there are no tongues else for 's turn.

HORATIO: This lapwing runs away with the shell on his head.

HAMLET: He did comply with his dug, before he sucked it.
Thus has he—and many more of the same breed that I know the
drossy age dotes on—only got the tune of the time and outward
habit of encounter; a kind of yesty collection, which carries them
through and through the most fond and winnowed opinions; and
do but blow them to their trial, the bubbles are out.

Enter a Lord.

LORD: My lord, his majesty commended him to you by young Osric, who brings back to him, that you attend him in the hall: he sends to know if your pleasure hold to play with Laertes, or that you will take longer time.

HAMLET: I am constant to my purposes; they follow the king's pleasure: if his fitness speaks, mine is ready; now or whensoever, provided I be so able as now.

LORD: The king and queen and all are coming down.

HAMLET: In happy time.

LORD: The queen desires you to use some gentle entertainment to Laertes before you fall to play.

HAMLET: She well instructs me.   [*Exit Lord.*

HORATIO: You will lose this wager, my lord.

HAMLET: I do not think so; since he went into France, I have been in continual practice; I shall win at the odds. But thou wouldst not think how ill all 's here about my heart: but it is no matter.

HORATIO: Nay, good my lord,—

HAMLET: It is but foolery; but it is such a kind of gain-giving, as would perhaps trouble a woman.

HORATIO: If your mind dislike any thing, obey it: I will forestall their repair hither, and say you are not fit.

HAMLET: Not a whit, we defy augury: there 's a special providence in the fall of a sparrow. If it be now, 'tis not to come; if it be not to come, it will be now; if it be not now, yet it will come: the readiness is all: since no man has aught of what he leaves, what is 't to leave betimes? Let be.

Enter King, Queen, Laertes, Lords, Osric,
and Attendants with foils, &c.

KING: Come, Hamlet, come, and take this hand from me.
                    [*The King puts Laertes' hand into Hamlet's.*
HAMLET: Give me your pardon, sir: I 've done you wrong;
But pardon 't, as you are a gentleman.

This presence knows,
And you must needs have heard, how I am punish'd
With sore distraction. What I have done,
That might your nature, honour and exception
Roughly awake, I here proclaim was madness.
Was 't Hamlet wrong'd Laertes? Never Hamlet:
If Hamlet from himself be ta'en away,
And when he 's not himself does wrong Laertes,
Then Hamlet does it not, Hamlet denies it.
Who does it, then? His madness: if 't be so,
Hamlet is of the faction that is wrong'd;
His madness is poor Hamlet's enemy.
Sir, in this audience,
Let my disclaiming from a purposed evil
Free me so far in your most generous thoughts,
That I have shot mine arrow o'er the house,
And hurt my brother.

LAERTES: I am satisfied in nature,
Whose motive, in this case, should stir me most
To my revenge: but in my terms of honour,
I stand aloof; and will no reconcilement,
Till by some elder masters, of known honour,
I have a voice and precedent of peace,
To keep my name ungored. But till that time,
I do receive your offer'd love like love,
And will not wrong it.

HAMLET: I embrace it freely;
And will this brother's wager frankly play.
Give us the foils. Come on.

LAERTES: Come, one for me.

HAMLET: I 'll be your foil, Laertes: in mine ignorance
Your skill shall, like a star i' the darkest night,
Stick fiery off indeed.

LAERTES: You mock me, sir.

HAMLET: No, by this hand.

KING: Give them the foils, young Osric.
Cousin Hamlet,
You know the wager?
HAMLET: Very well, my lord;
Your grace hath laid the odds o' the weaker side.
KING: I do not fear it; I have seen you both:
But since he is better'd, we have therefore odds.
LAERTES: This is too heavy, let me see another.
HAMLET: This likes me well. These foils have all a length?
                                        [*They prepare to play.*
OSRIC: Ay, my good lord.
KING: Set me the stoups of wine upon that table.
If Hamlet give the first or second hit,
Or quit in answer of the third exchange,
Let all the battlements their ordnance fire;
The king shall drink to Hamlet's better breath;
And in the cup an union shall he throw,
Richer than that which four successive kings
In Denmark's crown have worn. Give me the cups;
And let the kettle to the trumpet speak,
The trumpet to the cannoneer without,
The cannons to the heavens, the heavens to earth,
'Now the king drinks to Hamlet.' Come, begin:
And you, the judges, bear a wary eye.
HAMLET: Come on, sir.
LAERTES: Come, my lord.   [*They play.*
HAMLET: One.
LAERTES: No.
HAMLET: Judgement.
OSRIC: A hit, a very palpable hit.
LAERTES: Well; again.
KING: Stay; give me drink. Hamlet, this pearl is thine;
Here 's to thy health.   [*Trumpets sound, and cannon shot off within.*
                    Give him the cup.
HAMLET: I 'll play this bout first; set it by awhile.

Come. [*They play.*] Another hit; what say you?

LAERTES: A touch, a touch, I do confess.

KING: Our son shall win.

QUEEN: He 's fat, and scant of breath.
Here, Hamlet, take my napkin, rub thy brows:
The queen carouses to thy fortune, Hamlet.

HAMLET: Good madam!

KING: Gertrude, do not drink!

QUEEN: I will, my lord; I pray you, pardon me.

KING: [*Aside*] It is the poison'd cup: it is too late.

HAMLET: I dare not drink yet, madam; by and by.

QUEEN: Come, let me wipe thy face.

LAERTES: My lord, I 'll hit him now.

KING: I do not think 't.

LAERTES: [*Aside*] And yet 'tis almost 'gainst my conscience.

HAMLET: Come, for the third, Laertes: you but dally;
I pray you, pass with our best violence;
I am afeard you make a wanton of me.

LAERTES: Say you so? come on.   [*They play.*

OSRIC: Nothing, neither way.

LAERTES: Have at you now!   [*Laertes wounds Hamlet; then, in
          scuffling, they change rapiers, and Hamlet wounds Laertes.*

KING: Part them: they are incensed.

HAMLET: Nay, come, again.   [*The Queen falls.*

OSRIC: Look to the queen there, ho!

HORATIO: They bleed on both sides. How is it, my lord?

OSRIC: How is 't, Laertes?

LAERTES: Why, as a woodcock to mine own spring, Osric;
I am justly kill'd with mine own treachery.

HAMLET: How does the queen?

KING: She swounds to see them bleed.

QUEEN: No, no, the drink, the drink,—O my dear Hamlet,—
The drink, the drink! I am poison'd.   [*Dies.*

HAMLET: O villany! Ho! let the door be lock'd:
Treachery! Seek it out.

LAERTES: It is here, Hamlet: Hamlet, thou art slain;
No medicine in the world can do thee good;
In thee there is not half an hour of life;
The treacherous instrument is in thy hand,
Unbated and envenom'd: the foul practice
Hath turn'd itself on me; lo, here I lie,
Never to rise again: thy mother 's poison'd:
I can no more: the king, the king 's to blame.
HAMLET: The point envenom'd too!
Then, venom, to thy work.   [*Stabs the King.*
ALL: Treason! treason!
KING: O, yet defend me, friends; I am but hurt.
HAMLET: Here, thou incestuous, murderous, damned Dane,
Drink off this potion. Is thy union here?
Follow my mother.   [*King dies.*
LAERTES: He is justly served;
It is a poison temper'd by himself.
Exchange forgiveness with me, noble Hamlet:
Mine and my father's death come not upon thee,
Nor thine on me!   [*Dies.*
HAMLET: Heaven make thee free of it! I follow thee.
I am dead, Horatio. Wretched queen, adieu!
You that look pale and tremble at this chance,
That are but mutes or audience to this act,
Had I but time—as this fell sergeant, death,
Is strict in his arrest—O, I could tell you—
But let it be. Horatio, I am dead;
Thou livest; report me and my cause aright
To the unsatisfied.
HORATIO: Never believe it:
I am more an antique Roman than a Dane:
Here 's yet some liquor left.
HAMLET: As thou 'rt a man,
Give me the cup: let go; by heaven, I 'll have 't.
O good Horatio, what a wounded name,

Things standing thus unknown, shall live behind me!
If thou didst ever hold me in thy heart,
Absent thee from felicity awhile,
And in this harsh world draw thy breath in pain,
To tell my story.   [*March afar off, and shot within.*
            What warlike noise is this?
    OSRIC: Young Fortinbras, with conquest come from Poland,
To the ambassadors of England gives
This warlike volley.
    HAMLET: O, I die, Horatio;
The potent poison quite o'er-crows my spirit:
I cannot live to hear the news from England;
But I do prophesy the election lights
On Fortinbras: he has my dying voice;
So tell him, with the occurrents, more and less,
Which have solicited. The rest is silence.   [*Dies.*
    HORATIO: Now cracks a noble heart. Good night, sweet prince;
And flights of angels sing thee to thy rest!
Why does the drum come hither?   [*March within.*

Enter Fortinbras, the English Ambassadors, and others.

    FORTINBRAS: Where is this sight?
    HORATIO: What is it ye would see?
If aught of woe or wonder, cease your search.
    FORTINBRAS: This quarry cries on havoc. O proud death,
What feast is toward in thine eternal cell,
That thou so many princes at a shot
So bloodily hast struck?
    FIRST AMBASSADOR: The sight is dismal;
And our affairs from England come too late:
The ears are senseless that should give us hearing,
To tell him his commandment is fulfill'd.
That Rosencrantz and Guildenstern are dead:
Where should we have our thanks?
    HORATIO: Not from his mouth,

Had it the ability of life to thank you:
He never gave commandment for their death.
But since, so jump upon this bloody question,
You from the Polack wars, and you from England,
Are here arrived, give order that these bodies
High on a stage be placed to the view;
And let me speak to the yet unknowing world
How these things came about: so shall you hear
Of carnal, bloody, and unnatural acts,
Of accidental judgements, casual slaughters,
Of deaths put on by cunning and forced cause,
And, in this upshot, purposes mistook
Fall'n on the inventor's heads: all this can I
Truly deliver.
    FORTINBRAS: Let us haste to hear it,
And call the noblest to the audience.
For me, with sorrow I embrace my fortune:
I have some rights of memory in this kingdom,
Which now to claim my vantage doth invite me.
    HORATIO: Of that I shall have also cause to speak,
And from his mouth whose voice will draw on more:
But let this same be presently perform'd,
Even while men's minds are wild; lest more mischance,
On plots and errors, happen.
    FORTINBRAS: Let four captains
Bear Hamlet, like a soldier, to the stage;
For he was likely, had he been put on,
To have proved most royally: and, for his passage,
The soldiers' music and the rites of war as this
Speak loudly for him.
Take up the bodies: such a sight
Becomes the field, but here shows much amiss.
Go, bid the soldiers shoot.
                  [*A dead march. Exeunt, bearing off the dead bodies;*
                        after which a peal of ordnance is shot off.

. . .

Essay

From *Shakespeare and the Popular Dramatic Tradition*
by S. L. Bethell

INTRODUCTION BY

T. S. ELIOT

As the volume of Shakespeare criticism increases, year by year, the common reader must be inclined to wonder, what has all this to do with him? and to reiterate the objection, that what really matters is the plays themselves, and not what an endless succession of critics say about them. . . . We all know that Shakespeare has presented a different appearance to every age. In the work of any Shakespeare critic of the past we can see, when we have made the deduction of individual genius and individual limitations, the outlines of the consciousness of the critic's age. It is possible that one age may miss what a previous age had grasped. There are variations also, under the influence of a passing philosophy. One age may see Shakespeare more in the study, another more in the theater. . . . But on the whole, we must assume (as posterity will assume after us) that we are in a better position to understand Shakespeare than any of our predecessors. This is not merely an assumption of the Shakespeare critic, or of the literary critic in general, but the assumption implicit in all historical study: that we understand the past better than previous generations did, simply because there is more of it. We assume, and must assume, a progressive development of consciousness.

The constant reader of Shakespeare should be also, to the best of his opportunities, the constant theatergoer: for any play of Shakespeare requires to be seen and heard, as well as read, many times; and seen and heard in as many different productions as possible. But however much he frequents the theater, he probably does not realize the extent to which stage production has been influenced by criticism. . . . This influence is not necessarily quite direct; but it is possible that some future producer . . . will present a *Hamlet* rather different, in consequence, from previous *Hamlets*. Meanwhile, however, the reader may ask himself, why need I be conscious of all these things in Shakespeare's plays, of which Shakespeare himself was perhaps not quite conscious? Why can I not enjoy the play simply, as a contemporary would have done? The answer is, of course, that we cannot escape from the criticism of the past except through the criticism of the present.

The extent to which the past weighs upon us, and forces upon our attention problems which for the contemporary did not exist, has been brought home to me in attempting to cope with the difficulties of writing verse drama today. It is only a humble statement of fact, to say that the verse dramatist today has to be much more conscious of what he is doing than Shakespeare was, and, even to produce a result comparatively trifling, has to surmount obstacles which to Shakespeare were unknown. For instance, a poet, trying to write something for the theater, discovers first of all that it is not only a question of laboring to acquire the technique of the theater: it is a question of a different kind of poetry, a different kind of verse, than the kind for which his previous experience has qualified him. How, he must ask himself, would people today speak if they could speak in poetry? They cannot be translated to a fairyland where they may talk appropriately in verse; they must on your stage be able to perform the same actions, and lead the same lives, as in the real world. But they must somehow disclose (not necessarily be aware of) a deeper reality than that of the plane of most of our conscious living; and what they disclose must be, not the psychologist's intellectualization of this reality, but the reality itself. And the poetry must express, in a way in which natural speech cannot, not only the reality of the individual, but the reality of a situation composed of a fusion, in sympathy or antipathy, of two or more individuals. A verse play is not a play done into verse, but a different kind of play: in a way more realistic than "naturalistic drama," because, instead of clothing nature in poetry, it should remove the surface of things, expose the underneath, or the inside, of the natural surface appearance. It may allow the characters to behave inconsistently, but only with respect to a deeper consistency. It may use any device to show their real feelings and volitions, instead of just what, in actual life, they would normally profess or be conscious of; it must reveal, underneath the vacillating or infirm character, the indomitable unconscious will; and underneath the resolute purpose of the planning animal, the victim of circumstance and the doomed or sanctified being. So the poet with ambitions of the theater, must discover the laws, both of another kind of verse and of another kind of drama. The difficulty of the author is also the difficulty of the audience. Both have to be trained; both need to be conscious of many things which neither an Elizabethan dramatist, nor an Elizabethan audience, had any need to know; and if a book . . . is helpful to the writer of verse plays, I am sure that it should be to those who hear and read them also.

February 19, 1944.

T. S. Eliot (1888–1965) was born in St. Louis, Missouri. A poet, playwright, and critic, Eliot received the Nobel Prize for literature in 1948 and is best known for his poems "The Love Song of J. Alfred Prufrock" and *The Waste Land.*